Beginning C++ Programming

This is the start of your journey into the most powerful
language available to the programming public

Richard Grimes

BIRMINGHAM - MUMBAI

Beginning C++ Programming

First published: April 2017

Production reference: 1180417

Published by Packt Publishing Ltd.
Livery Place
35 Livery Street
Birmingham
B3 2PB, UK.
ISBN 978-1-78712-494-3

www.packtpub.com

Credits

Author	**Copy Editor**
Richard Grimes	Safis Editing
Reviewer	**Project Coordinator**
Angel Hernandez	Vaidehi Sawant
Commissioning Editor	**Proofreader**
Aaron Lazar	Safis Editing
Acquisition Editor	**Indexer**
Nitin Dasan	Tejal Daruwale Soni
Content Development Editor	**Graphics**
Zeeyan Pinheiro	Abhinash Sahu
Technical Editor	**Production Coordinator**
Pavan Ramchandani	Shraddha Falebhai

About the Author

Richard Grimes has been programming in C++ for 25 years, working on projects as diverse as scientific control and analysis and finance analysis to remote objects for the automotive manufacturing industry. He has spoken at 70 international conferences on Microsoft technologies (including C++ and C#) and has written 8 books, 150 articles for programming journals, and 5 training courses for Microsoft. Richard was awarded Microsoft MVP for 10 years (1998-2007). He has a reputation for his deep understanding of the .NET framework and C++ and the frank way in which he assesses new technology.

For my wife Ellinor: it is only with your love and support that I am able to do anything at all

About the Reviewer

Angel Hernandez is a highly regarded senior solutions, architect and developer with over 15 years of experience, mainly in the consulting space. He is an 11-time Microsoft (2006-2016) MVP award recipient in Visual Studio and Development Technologies category (formerly, Visual C++), and he is currently a member of the Microsoft MVP Reconnect Program. Angel is also a TOGAF practitioner. He has deep knowledge of Microsoft and open source technologies (*nix Systems), and he's an expert in managed and native languages, C# and C++ being his favorites. He can be reached at http://www.angelhernand ezm.com.

I'd like to thank, first and foremost, God and his son Jesus; Packt and the author for giving me the opportunity to review this book; and my family, Mery, Miranda, and Mikaela (the 3Ms) for being understanding and patient with me.

www.PacktPub.com

For support files and downloads related to your book, please visit www.PacktPub.com.

Did you know that Packt offers eBook versions of every book published, with PDF and ePub files available? You can upgrade to the eBook version at www.PacktPub.com and as a print book customer, you are entitled to a discount on the eBook copy. Get in touch with us at service@packtpub.com for more details.

At www.PacktPub.com, you can also read a collection of free technical articles, sign up for a range of free newsletters and receive exclusive discounts and offers on Packt books and eBooks.

https://www.packtpub.com/mapt

Get the most in-demand software skills with Mapt. Mapt gives you full access to all Packt books and video courses, as well as industry-leading tools to help you plan your personal development and advance your career.

Why subscribe?

- Fully searchable across every book published by Packt
- Copy and paste, print, and bookmark content
- On demand and accessible via a web browser

Customer Feedback

Thanks for purchasing this Packt book. At Packt, quality is at the heart of our editorial process. To help us improve, please leave us an honest review on this book's Amazon page at https://www.amazon.com/dp/1787124940.

If you'd like to join our team of regular reviewers, you can e-mail us at customerreviews@packtpub.com. We award our regular reviewers with free eBooks and videos in exchange for their valuable feedback. Help us be relentless in improving our products!

Table of Contents

Preface

C++ has been used for 30 years, and during that time, many new languages have come and gone, but C++ has endured. The big question behind this book is: Why? Why use C++? The answer lies in the ten chapters you see in front of you but, as a spoiler, it is the flexibility and power of the language and the rich, broad Standard Library.

C++ has always been a powerful language, giving you direct access to memory while providing high-level features such as the ability to create new types—classes—and to override operators to suit your needs. However, the more modern C++ standards added to this, generic programming through templates, and functional programming through function objects and lambda expressions. You can use as much or as little of these features as you want; you can write event-driven code with abstract interface pointers, or C-like procedural code.

In this book, we will take you through the features of the 2011 standard of C++ and the Standard Library provided with the language. The text explains how to use these features with short code snippets, and each chapter has a worked example illustrating the concepts. At the end of this book, you will be aware of all the features of the language and what can be possible with the C++ Standard Library. You will start this book as a beginner, and finish it informed and equipped to use C++.

What this book covers

Chapter 1, *Starting with C++*, explains the files used to write C++ applications, file dependencies, and the basics of C++ project management.

Chapter 2, *Understanding Language Features*, covers C++ statements and expressions, constants, variables, operators, and how to control execution flow in applications.

Chapter 3, *Exploring C++ Types*, describes C++ built-in types, aggregated types, type aliases, initializer lists, and conversion between types.

Chapter 4, *Working with Memory, Arrays, and Pointers*, covers how memory is allocated and used in C++ applications, how to use built-in arrays, the role of C++ references, and how to use C++ pointers to access memory.

Chapter 5, *Using Functions*, explains how to define functions, how to pass parameters-by-reference and by-value using a variable number of parameters, creating and using pointers to functions, and defining template functions and overloaded operators.

Chapter 6, *Classes*, describes how to define new types through classes and the various special functions used in a class, how to instantiate a class as an object and how to destroy them, and how to access objects through pointers and how to write template classes.

Chapter 7, *Introduction to Object-Orientated Programming*, explains inheritance and composition, and how this affects using pointers and references to objects and the access levels of class members and how they affect inherited members. This chapter also explains polymorphism through virtual methods, and inheritance programming through abstract classes.

Chapter 8, *Using Standard Library Containers*, covers all the C++ Standard Library container classes and how to use them with iterators and the standard algorithms so that you can manipulate the data in containers.

Chapter 9, *Using Strings*, describes the features of the standard C++ string class, converting between numeric data and strings, internationalizing strings, and using regular expressions to search and manipulate strings.

Chapter 10, *Diagnostics and Debugging*, explains how to prepare your code to provide diagnostics and to enable it to be debugged, how applications are terminated, abruptly or gracefully, and how to use C++ exceptions.

What you need for this book

This book covers the C++11 standard, and the associated C++ Standard Library. For the vast majority of this book, any C++11 compliant compiler is suitable. This includes compilers from Intel, IBM, Sun, Apple, and Microsoft, as well as the open source GCC compiler.

This book uses Visual C++ 2017 Community Edition because it is a fully featured compiler and environment, and it is provided as a free download. This is a personal choice of the author, but it should not restrict readers who prefer using other compilers. Some of the sections of the last chapter on *Diagnostics and Debugging* describe Microsoft-specific features, but these sections are clearly marked.

Who this book is for

This book is intended for experienced programmers who are new to C++. The reader is expected to understand what high-level languages are for and basic concepts such as modularizing code and controlling execution flow.

Conventions

In this book, you will find a number of text styles that distinguish between different kinds of information. Here are some examples of these styles and an explanation of their meaning.

Code words in text, database table names, folder names, filenames, file extensions, pathnames, dummy URLs, user input, and Twitter handles are shown as follows: "We can include other contexts through the use of the `include` directive."

A block of code is set as follows:

```
class point
{
public:
    int x, y;
};
```

When we wish to draw your attention to a particular part of a code block, the relevant lines or items are set in bold:

```
class point
{
public:
    int x, y;
    point(int _x, int _y) : x(_x), y(_y) {}
};
```

Any command-line input or output is written as follows:

```
C:\> cl /EHsc test.cpp
```

New terms and **important words** are shown in bold. Words that you see on the screen, for example, in menus or dialog boxes, appear in the text like this: "Clicking the **Next** button moves you to the next screen."

Warnings or important notes appear in a box like this.

Tips and tricks appear like this.

Reader feedback

Feedback from our readers is always welcome. Let us know what you think about this book-what you liked or disliked. Reader feedback is important for us as it helps us develop titles that you will really get the most out of.

To send us general feedback, simply e-mail feedback@packtpub.com, and mention the book's title in the subject of your message.

If there is a topic that you have expertise in and you are interested in either writing or contributing to a book, see our author guide at www.packtpub.com/authors.

Customer support

Now that you are the proud owner of a Packt book, we have a number of things to help you to get the most from your purchase.

Downloading the example code

You can download the example code files for this book from your account at http://www.packtpub.com. If you purchased this book elsewhere, you can visit http://www.packtpub.com/support and register to have the files e-mailed directly to you.

You can download the code files by following these steps:

1. Log in or register to our website using your e-mail address and password.
2. Hover the mouse pointer on the **SUPPORT** tab at the top.
3. Click on **Code Downloads & Errata**.
4. Enter the name of the book in the **Search** box.
5. Select the book for which you're looking to download the code files.
6. Choose from the drop-down menu where you purchased this book from.
7. Click on **Code Download**.

Once the file is downloaded, please make sure that you unzip or extract the folder using the latest version of:

- WinRAR / 7-Zip for Windows
- Zipeg / iZip / UnRarX for Mac
- 7-Zip / PeaZip for Linux

The code bundle for the book is also hosted on GitHub at `https://github.com/PacktPubl ishing/Beginning-Cpp-Programming`. We also have other code bundles from our rich catalog of books and videos available at `https://github.com/PacktPublishing/`. Check them out!

Downloading the color images of this book

We also provide you with a PDF file that has color images of the screenshots/diagrams used in this book. The color images will help you better understand the changes in the output. You can download this file from `https://www.packtpub.com/sites/default/files/down loads/BeginningCppProgramming_ColorImages.pdf`.

Errata

Although we have taken every care to ensure the accuracy of our content, mistakes do happen. If you find a mistake in one of our books-maybe a mistake in the text or the code-we would be grateful if you could report this to us. By doing so, you can save other readers from frustration and help us improve subsequent versions of this book. If you find any errata, please report them by visiting `http://www.packtpub.com/submit-errata`, selecting your book, clicking on the **Errata Submission Form** link, and entering the details of your errata. Once your errata are verified, your submission will be accepted and the errata will be uploaded to our website or added to any list of existing errata under the Errata section of that title.

To view the previously submitted errata, go to `https://www.packtpub.com/books/conten t/support`and enter the name of the book in the search field. The required information will appear under the **Errata** section.

Piracy

Piracy of copyrighted material on the Internet is an ongoing problem across all media. At Packt, we take the protection of our copyright and licenses very seriously. If you come across any illegal copies of our works in any form on the Internet, please provide us with the location address or website name immediately so that we can pursue a remedy.

Please contact us at copyright@packtpub.com with a link to the suspected pirated material.

We appreciate your help in protecting our authors and our ability to bring you valuable content.

Questions

If you have a problem with any aspect of this book, you can contact us at questions@packtpub.com, and we will do our best to address the problem.

1
Starting with C++

Why C++? There will be as many reasons to use C++ as there will be readers of this book.

You may have chosen C++ because you have to support a C++ project. Over the 30 years of its lifetime there have been millions of lines of C++ written, and most popular applications and operating systems will be mostly written in C++, or will use components and libraries that are. It is nearly impossible to find a computer that does not contain some code that has been written in C++.

Or, you may have chosen C++ to write new code. This may be because your code will use a library written in C++, and there are thousands of libraries available: open source, shareware, and commercial.

Or it may be because you are attracted to the power and flexibility that C++ offers. Modern high-level languages have been designed to make it easy for programmers to perform actions; while C++ has such facilities, it also allows you to get as close to the machine as possible, gives you the (sometimes dangerous) power of direct memory access. Through language features such as classes and overloading, C++ is a flexible language that allows you to extend how the language works and write reusable code.

Whatever your reason for deciding on C++, you have made the right choice, and this book is the right place to start.

What will you find in this chapter?

Since this book is a hands-on book, it contains code that you can type, compile, and run. To compile the code, you will need a C++ compiler and linker, and in this book that means Visual Studio 2017 Community Edition, which provides Visual C++. This compiler was chosen because it is a free download, it is compliant with C++ standards and it has very wide range of tools to make writing code easier. Visual C++ provides C++11-compliant language features and almost all the language features of C++14 and C++17. Visual C++ is also provided with the C99 runtime library, C++11 standard library, and C++14 standard library. All of this mentions of **standard** means that the code that you learn to write in this book will compile with all other standard C++ compilers.

This chapter will start with details about how to obtain and install Visual Studio 2017 Community Edition. If you already have a C++ compiler, you can skip this section. Most of this book is vendor-neutral about the compiler and linker tools, but Chapter 10, *Diagnostics and Debugging*, which covers debugging and diagnostics, will cover some Microsoft-specific features. Visual Studio has a fully featured code editor, so even if you do not use it to manage your projects, you'll find it useful to edit your code.

After we've described the installation, you'll learn the basics of C++: how source files and projects are structured, and how you can manage projects with potentially thousands of files.

Finally, the chapter will finish with a step-by-step structured example. Here you will learn how to write simple functions that use the standard C++ library and one mechanism to manage files in the project.

What is C++?

The predecessor of C++ is C, which was designed by Dennis Richie at Bell Labs and first released in 1973. C is a widely used language and was used to write the early versions of Unix and Windows. Indeed, the libraries and software-development libraries of many operating systems are still written to have C interfaces. C is powerful because it can be used to write code that is compiled to a compact form, it uses a static type system (so the compiler does the work of type checking), and the types and structures of the language allow for direct memory access to computer architecture.

C, however, is procedural and based on functions, and although it has record types (`struct`) to encapsulate data, it does not have object-like behaviors to act on that encapsulated state. Clearly there was a need for the power of C but the flexibility and extensibility of object-oriented classes: a language that was C, with classes. In 1983, Bjarne Stroustrup released C++. The ++ comes from the C increment operator ++.

 Strictly, when postfixed to a variable, the ++ operator means *increment the variable, but return the variable's value before it was incremented*. So the C statements `int c = 1; int d = c++;` will result in variable `d` having a value of 1 and variable `c` having a value of 2. This does not quite express the idea that C++ is an increment on C.

Installing Visual C++

Microsoft's Visual Studio Community 2017 contains the Visual C++ compiler, the C++ standard libraries, and a collection of standard tools that you can use to write and maintain C++ projects. This book is not about how to write Windows code; it is about how to write standard C++ and how to use the C++ Standard Library. All the examples in this book will run on the command line. Visual Studio was chosen because it is a free download (although you do have to register an e-mail address with Microsoft), and it is standards-compliant. If you already have a C++ compiler installed, then you can skip this section.

Setting up

Before starting the installation, you should be aware that, as part of the agreement to install Visual Studio as part of Microsoft's community program, you should have a Microsoft account. You are given the option to create a Microsoft account the first time you run Visual Studio and if you skip this stage, you will be given a 30-day evaluation period. Visual Studio will be fully featured during this month, but if you want to use Visual Studio beyond this time you will have to provide a Microsoft account. The Microsoft account does not impose any obligation on you, and when you use Visual C++ after signing in, your code will still remain on your machine with no obligation to pass it to Microsoft.

Of course, if you read this book within one month, you will be able to use Visual Studio without having to sign in using your Microsoft account; you may view this as an incentive to be diligent about finishing the book!

Downloading the installation files

To download the Visual Studio Community 2017 installer go to `https://www.visualstudio.com/vs/ community/`.

When you click on the Download Community 2017 button, your browser will download a 1 MB file called `vs_community__1698485341.1480883588.exe`. When you run this application, it will allow you to specify the languages and libraries that you want installed, and then it downloads and installs all the necessary components.

Installing Visual Studio

Visual Studio 2017 treats Visual C++ as an optional component, so you have to explicitly indicate that you want to install it through custom options. When you first execute the installer, you will see the following dialog box:

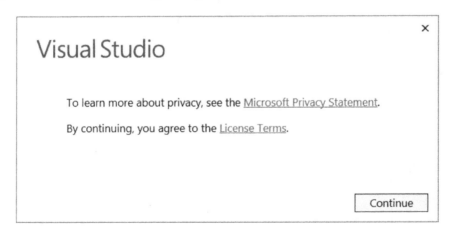

When you click on the **Continue** button the application will set up the installer, as shown here:

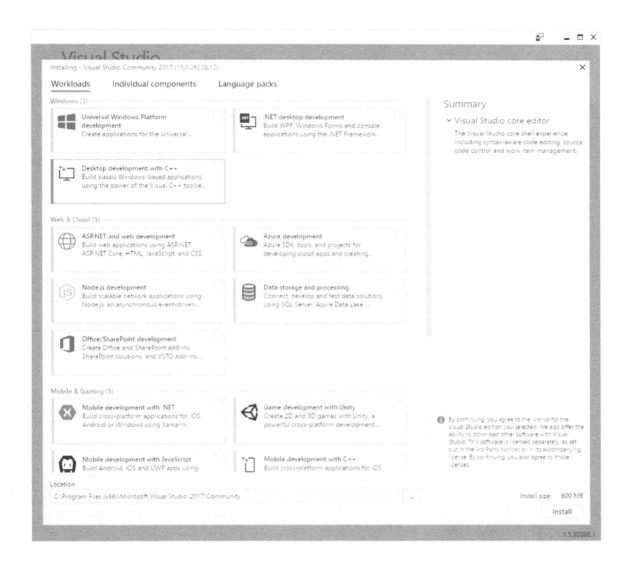

Along the top are three tabs labeled Workloads, Individual Components and Language Packs. Make sure that you have selected the Workloads tab (as shown in the screenshot) and check the checkbox in the item called **Desktop development with C++**.

The installer will check that you have enough disk space for the selected option. The maximum amount of space Visual Studio will require is 8 GB, although for Visual C++ you will use a lot less. When you check **Desktop development with C++** item, you will see the right side of the dialog change to list the options selected and the disk size required, as follows:

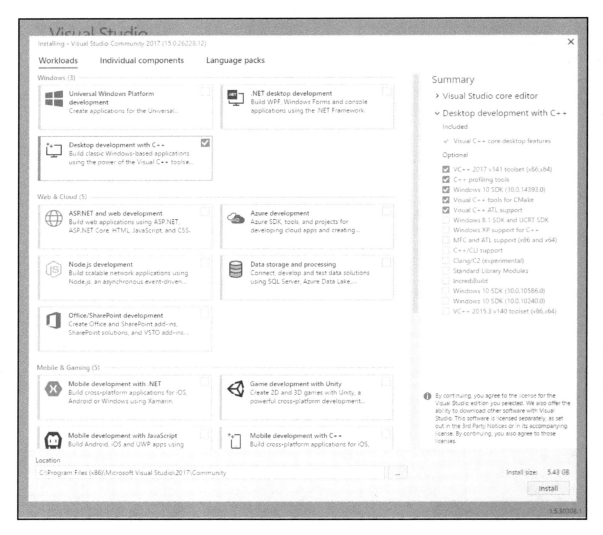

For this book, leave the options selected by the installer and then click the Install button in the bottom right hand corner. The installer will download all the code it needs and it will keep you updated with the progress with the following dialog box:

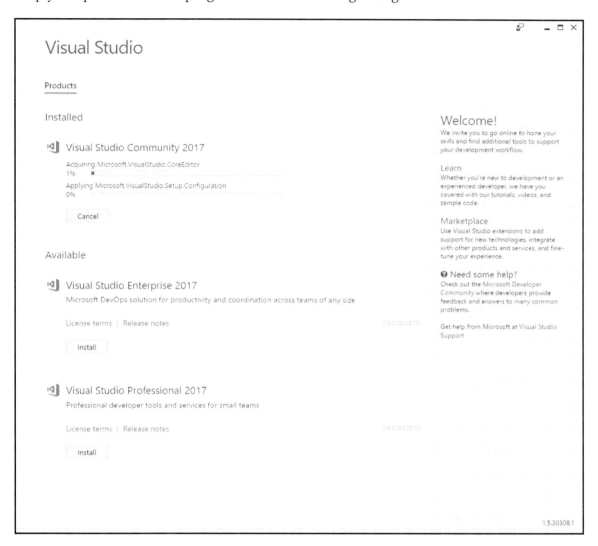

When the installation is complete the Visual Studio Community 2017 item will change to have two buttons, Modify and Launch, as showing here:

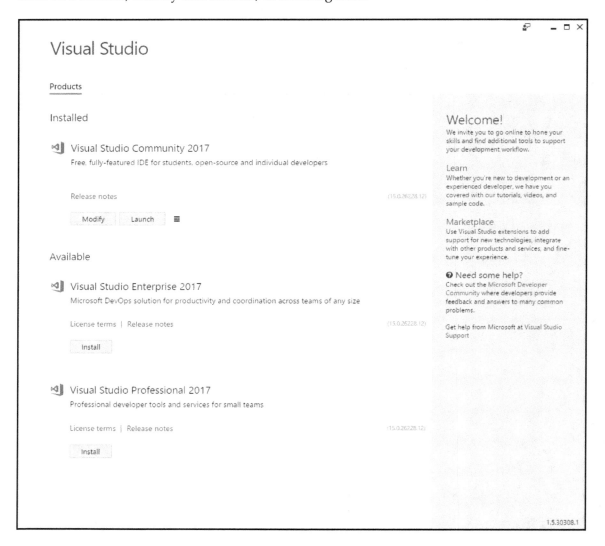

The **Modify** button allows you to add more components. Click on **Launch** to run Visual Studio for the first time.

Registering with Microsoft

The first time you run Visual Studio it will ask you to sign in to Microsoft services through the following dialog:

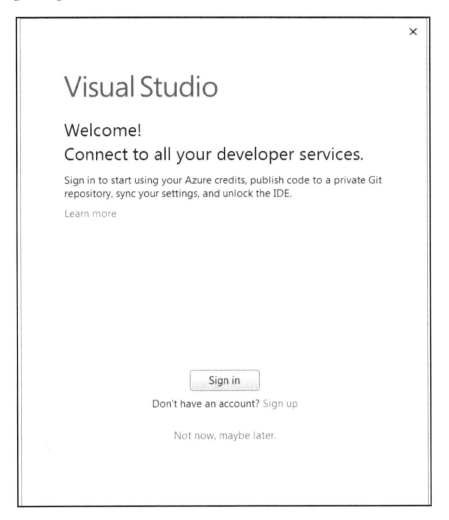

You do not have to register Visual Studio, but if you choose not to, Visual Studio will only work for 30 days. Registering with Microsoft places no obligations on you. If you are happy to register, then you may as well register now. Click on Sign in button provide your Microsoft credentials, or if you do not have an account then click on **Sign up** to create an account.

When you click on the **Launch** button a new window will open, but the installer window will remain open. You may find that the installer window hides the Welcome window, so check the Windows task bar to see if another window is open. Once Visual Studio has started you can close the installer window.

You will now be able to use Visual Studio to edit code, and will have the Visual C++ compiler and libraries installed on your machine, so you will be able to compile C++ code in Visual Studio or on the command line.

Examining C++ projects

C++ projects can contain thousands of files, and managing these files can be a task. When you build the project, should a file be compiled, and if so, by which tool? In what order should the files be compiled? What output will these compilers produce? How should the compiled files be combined to produce the executable?

Compiler tools will also have a large collection of options, as diverse as debug information, types of optimization, support for different language features, and processor features. Different combinations of compiler options will be used in different circumstances (for example, release builds and debug builds). If you compile from a command line, you have to make sure you choose the right options and apply them consistently across all the source code you compile.

Managing files and compiler options can get very complicated. This is why, for production code, you should use a make tool. Two are installed with Visual Studio: **MSBuild** and **nmake**. When you build a Visual C++ project in the Visual Studio environment, MSBuild will be used and the compilation rules will be stored in an XML file. You can also call MSBuild on the command line, passing it the XML project file. The nmake tool is Microsoft's version of the program maintenance utility common across many compilers. In this chapter, you will learn how to write a simple **makefile** to use with the nmake utility.

Before going through the basics of project management, first we have to examine the files that you will commonly find in a C++ project, and what a compiler will do to those files.

Compilers

C++ is a high-level language, designed to give you a wealth of language facilities and to be readable for you and other developers. The computer's processor executes low-level code, and it is the purpose of the compiler to translate C++ to the processor's machine code. A single compiler may be able to target several types of processor, and if the code is standard C++, it can be compiled with other compilers that support other processors.

However, the compiler does much more than this. As explained in Chapter 4, *Working With Memory, Arrays, and Pointers,* C++ allows you to split your code into functions, which take parameters and return a value, so the compiler sets up the memory used to pass this data. In addition, functions can declare variables that will only be used within that function (Chapter 5, *Using Functions,* will give more details), and will only exist while the function is executed. The compiler sets up this memory, called a **stack frame**. You have compiler options about how stack frames are created; for example, the Microsoft compiler options /Gd, /Gr, and /Gz determine the order in which function arguments are pushed onto the stack and whether the caller function or called function removes the arguments from the stack at the end of the call. These options are important when you write code that will be shared (but for the purpose of this book, the default stack construction should be used). This is just one area, but it should impress upon you that compiler settings give you access to a lot of power and flexibility.

The compiler compiles C++ code, and it will issue a compiler error if it comes across an error in your code. This is syntax checking of your code. It is important to point out that the code you write can be perfect C++ code from a syntax point of view, but it can still be nonsense. The syntax checking of the compiler is an important check of your code, but you should always use other checking. For example, the following code declares an integer variable and assigns it a value:

```
int i = 1 / 0;
```

The compiler will issue an error C2124 : divide or mod by zero. However, the following code will perform the same action using an additional variable, which is logically the same, but the compiler will issue no error:

```
int j = 0;
int i = 1 / j;
```

When the compiler issues an error it will stop compiling. This means two things. Firstly, you get no compiled output, so the error will not find its way into an executable. Secondly, it means that, if there are other errors in the source code, you will only find out about it once you have fixed the current error and recompiled. If you want to perform a syntax check and leave compilation to a later time, use the /Zs switch.

The compiler will also generate warning messages. A warning means that the code will compile, but there is, potentially, a problem in the code that will affect how the executable will run. The Microsoft compiler defines four levels of warnings: level 1 is the most severe (and should be addressed) and level 4 is informational.

Warnings are often used to indicate that the language feature being compiled is available, but it needs a specific compiler option that the developer has not used. During development of code, you will often ignore warnings, since you may be testing language features. However, when you get closer to producing production code you should pay more attention to warnings. By default, the Microsoft compiler will display level 1 warnings, and you can use the /W option with a number to indicate the levels that you wish to see (for example, /W2 means you wish to see level 2 warnings as well as level 1 warnings). In production code, you may use the /Wx option, which tells the compiler to treat warnings as errors so that you must fix the issues to be able to compile the code. You can also use the `pragmas` compiler (`pragmas` will be explained later) and compiler options to suppress specific warnings.

Linking the code

A compiler will produce an output. For C++ code, this will be object code, but you may have other compiler outputs, such as compiled resource files. On their own, these files cannot be executed; not least because the operating system will require certain structures to be set up. A C++ project will always be two-stage: compile the code into one or more object files and then link the object files into an executable. This means that your C++ compiler will provide another tool, called a linker.

The linker also has options to determine how it will work and specify its outputs and inputs, and it will also issue errors and warnings. Like the compiler, the Microsoft linker has an option, /WX, to treat warnings as errors in release builds.

Source files

At the very basic level, a C++ project will contain just one file: the C++ source file, typically with the extension cpp or cxx.

A simple example

The simplest C++ program is shown here:

```
#include <iostream>

// The entry point of the program
int main()
{
    std::cout << "Hello, world!n";
}
```

The first point to make is that the line starting with // is a comment. All the text until the end of the line is ignored by the compiler. If you want to have multiline comments, every line must start with //. You can also use C comments. A C comment starts with /* and ends with */ and everything between these two symbols is a comment, including line breaks.

C comments are a quick way to comment out a portion of your code.

The braces, {}, indicates a code block; in this case, the C++ code is for the function main. We know that this is a function because of the basic format: first, there is the type of the return value, then the name of the function with a pair of parentheses, which is used to declare the parameters passed to the function (and their types). In this example, the function is called main and the parentheses are empty, indicating that the function has no parameters. The identifier before the function name (int) says that the function will return an integer.

The convention with C++ is that a function called main is the **entry point** of the executable, that is, when you call the executable from the command line, this will be the first function in your code that will be called.

This simple example function immediately immerses you into an aspect of C++ that irritates programmers of other languages: the language may have rules, but the rules don't always appear to be followed. In this case, the main function is declared to return an integer, but the code returns no value. The rule in C++ is that, if the function declares that it returns a value, then it must return a value. However, there is a single exception to this rule: if the main function does not return a value, then a value of 0 will be assumed. C++ contains many quirks such as this, but you will soon learn what they are and get used to them.

The `main` function has just one line of code; this is a single statement starting with `std` and ending with the semicolon (`;`). C++ is flexible about the use of whitespace (spaces, tabs, and newlines) as will be explained in the next chapter. However, it is important to note that you have to be careful with literal strings (as used here), and every statement is delimited with a semicolon. Forgetting a required semicolon is a common source of compiler errors. An extra semicolon is simply an empty statement, so for a novice, having too many semicolons can be less fatal to your code than having too few.

The single statement prints the string `Hello, world!` (and a newline) to the console. You know that this is a string because it is enclosed in double quote marks (""). The string is *put to* the stream object `std::cout` using the operator `<<`. The `std` part of the name is a **namespace**, in effect, a collection of code with a similar purpose, or from a single vendor. In this case, `std` means that the `cout` stream object is part of the standard C++ library. The double colon `::` is the **scope resolution** operator, and indicates that you want to access the `cout` object declared in the `std` namespace. You can define namespaces of your own, and in a large project you should define your own namespaces, since it will allow you to use names that may have been declared in other namespaces, and this syntax allows you to disambiguate the symbol.

The `cout` object is an instance of the `ostream` class and this has already been created for you before the `main` function is called. The `<<` means that a function called `operator <<` is called and is passed the string (which is an array of `char` characters). This function prints each character in the string to the console until it reaches a `NUL` characte.

This is an example of the flexibility of C++, a feature called **operator overloading**. The `<<` operator is usually used with integers, and is used too shift the bits in the integer a specified number of places to the left; $x << y$ will return a value which has every bit in x shifted left by y places, in effect returning a value that has been multiplied by 2^y. However, in the preceding code, in place of the integer x there is the stream object `std::cout`, and in place of the left shift index there is a string. Clearly, this does not make any sense in the C++ definition of the `<<` operator. The C++ standard has effectively redefined what the `<<` operator means when used with an `ostream` object on the left-hand side. Furthermore, the `<<` operator in this code will print a string to the console, and so it takes a string on the right-hand side. The C++ Standard Library defines other `<<` operators that allow other data types to be printed to the console. They are all called the same way; the compiler determines which function is compiled dependent upon the type of the parameter used. Earlier we said that the `std::cout` object had already been created as an instance of the `ostream` class, but gave no indication of how this has occurred. This leads us to the last part of the simple source file not already explained: the first line starting with `#include`. The `#` here effectively indicates that a message of some kind will be given to the compiler.

There are various types of messages you can send (a few are `#define`, `#ifdef`, `#pragma`, which we will return to elsewhere in this book). In this case, `#include` tells the compiler to copy the contents of the specified file into the source file at this point, which essentially means the contents of that file will be compiled too. The specified file is called a **header file**, and is important in file management and the reuse of code through libraries.

The file `<iostream>` (note, no extension) is part of the Standard Library and can be found in the **include directory** provided with the C++ compiler. The angle brackets (`<>`) indicate that the compiler should look in the standard directories used to store header files, but you can provide the absolute location of a header file (or the location relative to the current file) using double quotes (`""`). The C++ Standard Library uses the convention of not using file extensions. You should use the extension `h` (or `hpp` and, rarely, `hxx`) when naming your own header files. The C Runtime Library (which is also available to your C++ code) also uses the extension `h` for its header files.

Creating source files

Start by finding the **Visual Studio 2017** folder on the Start Menu and click on the entry for **Developer Command Prompt for VS2017**. This will start a Windows command prompt and set up the environmental variables to use Visual C++ 2017. However, rather unhelpfully, it will also leave the command line in the Visual Studio folder under the Program Files folder. If you intend to do any development, you will want to move out of this folder to one where creating and deleting files will do no harm. Before you do that, move to the Visual C++ folder and list the files:

```
C:\Program Files\Microsoft Visual Studio\2017\Community>cd
%VCToolsInstallDir%
C:\Program Files\Microsoft Visual
Studio\2017\Community\VC\Tools\MSVC\14.0.10.2517>dir
```

Since the installer will place the C++ files in a folder that includes the current build of the compiler, it is safer to use the environment variable `VCToolsInstallDir` rather than specifying a specific version so that the latest version is used (in this case 14.0.10.2517). There are a few things to notice. First, the folders `bin`, `include`, and `lib`:

Folder	Description
bin	This contains, indirectly, the executables for Visual C++. The `bin` folder will contain separate folders for the CPU type you are using, so you will have to navigate below this to get to the actual folder containing the executables. The two main executables are `cl.exe`, which is the C++ compiler and `link.exe`, which is the linker.

include	This folder contains the header files for the C Runtime Library and the C++ Standard Library.
lib	This folder contains the static link library files for the C Runtime Library and the C++ Standard Library. Again, there will be separate folders for the CPU type

We will refer back to these folders later in this chapter.

The other thing to point out is the file vcvarsall.bat which is under the VC\Auxillary\Build folder. When you click on **Developer Command Prompt** for VS2017 on the Start menu, this batch file will be run. If you wish to use an existing command prompt to compile C++ code, you can set that up by running this batch file. The three most important actions of this batch file are to set up the PATH environment variable to contain a path to the bin folder, and to set up the INCLUDE and LIB environment variables to point to the include and lib folders, respectively.

Now navigate to the root directory and create a new folder, Beginning_C++, and move to that directory. Next, create a folder for this chapter called Chapter_01. Now you can switch to Visual Studio; if this is not already running, start it from the Start menu.

In Visual Studio, click the **File** menu, then **New,** and then the **File...** menu item to get the **New File** dialog, and in the left-hand tree-view, click on the **Visual C++** option. In the middle panel you'll see two options: **C++ File (.cpp)** and **Header File (.h)**, and C++ properties for Open folder, as shown in the following screenshot:

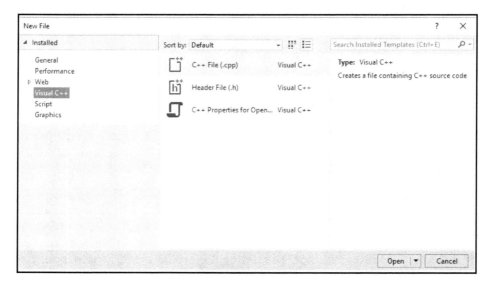

The first two file types are used for C++ projects, the third type creates a JSON file to aid Visual Studio IntelliSence (help as you type) and will not be used in this book.

Click on the first of these and then click the **Open** button. This will create a new empty file called **Source1.cpp**, so save this to the chapter project folder as **simple.cpp** by clicking on the **File** menu, then **Save Source1.cpp As,** and, navigating to the project folder, change the name in the **File name** box to **simple.cpp** before clicking on the **Save** button.

Now you can type in the code for the simple program, shown as following:

```cpp
#include <iostream>

int main()
{
    std::cout << "Hello, world!n";
}
```

When you have finished typing this code, save the file by clicking on the **File** menu and then the **Save simple.cpp** option in the menu. You are now ready to compile the code.

Compiling the code

Go to the command prompt and type `cl /?` command. Since the PATH environment is set up to include the path to the `bin` folder, you will see the help pages for the compiler. You can scroll through these pages by pressing the **Return** key until you get back to the command prompt. Most of these options are beyond the scope of this book, but the following table shows some that we will talk about:

Compiler Switch	Description
/c	Compile only, do not link.
/D<symbol>	Defines the constant or macro <symbol>.
/EHsc	Enable C++ exception handling but indicate that exceptions from extern "C" functions (typically operating system functions) are not handled.
/Fe:<file>	Provide the name of the executable file to link to.
/Fo:<file>	Provide the name of the object file to compile to.
/I <folder>	Provide the name of a folder to use to search for include files.
/link<linker options>	Pass <linker options> to the linker. This must come after the source file name and any switches intended for the compiler.

/Tp <file>	Compile <file> as a C++ file, even if it does not have .cpp or .cxx for its file extension.
/U<symbol>	Remove the previously defined <symbol> macro or constant.
/Zi	Enable debugging information.
/Zs	Syntax only, do not compile or link.

Note that some options need spaces between the switch and option, some must not have a space, and for others, the space is optional. In general, if you have the name of a file or folder that contains a space, you should enclose the name in double quotes. Before you use a switch, it is best to consult the help files to find out how it uses spaces.

At the command line, type the **cl simple.cpp** command. You will find that the compiler will issue warnings **C4530** and **C4577**. The reason is that the C++ Standard Library uses exceptions and you have not specified that the compiler should provide the necessary support code for exceptions. It is simple to overcome these warnings by using the /EHsc switch. At the command line, type the cl /EHsc simple.cpp command. If you typed in the code correctly it should compile:

```
C:\Beginning_C++\Chapter_01>cl /EHsc simple.cpp
Microsoft (R) C/C++ Optimizing Compiler Version 19.00.25017 for x86
Copyright (C) Microsoft Corporation.  All rights reserved

simple.cpp

Microsoft (R) Incremental Linker Version 14.10.25017.0
Copyright (C) Microsoft Corporation.  All rights reserved.
/out:simple.exe

simple.obj
```

By default, the compiler will compile the file to an object file and then pass this file to the linker to link as a command-line executable with the same name as the C++ file, but with the .exe extension. The line that says /out:simple.exe is generated by the linker, and /out is a linker option.

List the contents of the folder. You will find three files: `simple.cpp`, the source file; **simple.obj**, the object file which is the output of the compiler; and `simple.exe`, the output of the linker after it has linked the object file with the appropriate runtime libraries. You may now run the executable by typing `simple` on the command line:

```
C:\Beginning_C++\Chapter_01>simple
Hello, World!
```

Passing parameters between the command-line and an executable

Earlier, you found that the `main` function returned a value and by default this value is zero. When your application finishes, you can return an error code back to the command line; this is so that you can use the executable in batch files and scripts, and use the value to control the flow within the script. Similarly, when you run an executable, you may pass parameters from the command line, which will affect how the executable will behave.

Run the simple application by typing the **simple** command on the command line. In Windows, the error code is obtained through the pseudo environment variable ERRORLEVEL, so obtain this value through the **ECHO** command:

```
C:\Beginning_C++\Chapter_01>simple
Hello, World!

C:\Beginning_C++\Chapter_01>ECHO %ERRORLEVEL%
0
```

To show that this value is returned by the application, change the `main` function to return a value other than 0 (in this case, 99, shown highlighted):

```
int main()
{
    std::cout << "Hello, world!n";
    return 99;
}
```

Compile this code and run it, and then print out the error code as shown previously. You will find that the error code is now given as 99.

This is a very basic mechanism of communication: it only allows you to pass integer values, and the scripts that call your code must know what each value means.

You are much more likely to pass parameters to an application, and these will be passed through your code via parameters to the main function. Replace the main function with the following:

```cpp
int main(int argc, char *argv[])
{
    std::cout << "there are " << argc << " parameters" <<
    std::endl;
    for (int i = 0; i < argc; ++i)
    {
        std::cout << argv[i] << std::endl;
    }
}
```

When you write the main function to take parameters from the command line, the convention is that it has these two parameters.

The first parameter is conventionally called argc. It is an integer, and indicates how many parameters were passed to the application. *This parameter is very important.* The reason is that you are about to access memory through an array, and this parameter gives the limit of your access. If you access memory beyond this limit you will have problems: at best you will be accessing uninitialized memory, but at worst you could cause an access violation.

It is important that, whenever you access memory, you understand the amount of memory you are accessing and keep within its limits.

The second parameter is usually called argv and is an array of pointers to C strings in memory. You will learn more about arrays and pointers in Chapter 4, *Working With Memory, Arrays, and Pointers*, and about strings in Chapter 9, *Using Strings*, so we will not give a detailed discussion here. The square brackets ([]) indicate that the parameter is an array, and the type of each member of the array is given by the char *. The * means that each item is a pointer to memory. Normally, this would be interpreted as a pointer to a single item of the type given, but strings are different: the char * means that in the memory the pointer points to there will be zero or more characters followed by the NUL character (). The length of the string is the count of characters until the NUL character.

The third line shown here prints to the console the number of strings passed to the application. In this example, rather than using the newline escape character (n) to add a newline, we use the stream `std::endl`. There are several manipulators you can use, which will be discussed in Chapter 6, *Classes*. The `std::endl` manipulator will put the newline character into the output stream, and then it will flush the stream. This line shows that C++ allows you to chain the use of the << put operator into a stream. The line also shows you that the << put operator is overloaded, that is, there are different versions of the operator for different parameter types (in this case, three: one that takes an integer, used for `argv`, one that takes a string parameter, and another that takes manipulator as a parameter), but the syntax for calling these operators is exactly the same.

Finally, there is a code block to print out every string in the `argv` array, reproduced here:

```
for (int i = 0; i < argc; ++i)
{
    std::cout << argv[i] << std::endl;
}
```

The `for` statement means that the code block will be called until the variable i is less than the value of `argc`, and after each successful iteration of the loop, the variable i is incremented (using the prefix increment operator ++). The items in the array are accessed through the square bracket syntax ([]). The value passed is an *index* into the array.

Notice that the variable i has a starting value of 0, so the first item accessed is `argv[0]`, and since the `for` loop finishes when the variable i has a value of `argc`, it means that the last item in the array accessed is `argv[argc-1]`. This is a typical usage of arrays: the first index is zero and, if there are n items in the array, the last item has an index of n-1.

Compile and run this code as you have done before, with no parameters:

```
C:\Beginning_C++\Chapter_01>simple
there are 1 parameters
simple
```

Notice that, although you did not give a parameter, the program thinks there is one: the name of the program executable. In fact, this is not just the name, it is the command used to invoke the executable. In this case, you typed the **simple** command (without the extension) and got the value of the file `simple` as a parameter printed on the console. Try this again, but this time invoke the program with its full name, `simple.exe`. Now you will find the first parameter is `simple.exe`.

Try calling the code with some actual parameters. Type the **simple test parameters** command in the command line:

```
C:\Beginning_C++\Chapter_01>simple test parameters
there are 3 parameters
simple
test parameters
```

This time the program says that there are three parameters, and it has delimited them using the space character. If you want to use a space within a single parameter, you should put the entire string in double quotes:

```
C:\Beginning_C++\Chapter_01>simple "test parameters"
there are 2 parameters
simple
test parameters
```

Bear in mind that argv is an array of string pointers, so if you want to pass in a numeric type from the command line and you want to use it as a number in your program, you will have to convert from its string representation accessed through argv.

The preprocessor and symbols

The C++ compiler takes several steps to compile a source file. As the name suggests, the compiler preprocessor is at the beginning of this process. The preprocessor locates the header files and inserts them into the source file. It also substitutes macros and defined constants.

Defining constants

There are two main ways to define a constant via the preprocessor: through a compiler switch and in code. To see how this works, let's change the main function to print out the value of a constant; the two important lines are highlighted:

```
#include <iostream>
#define NUMBER 4

int main()
{
    std::cout << NUMBER << std::endl;
}
```

The line that starts with #define is an instruction to the preprocessor, and it says that, wherever in the text there is the exact symbol NUMBER, it should be replaced with 4. It is a text search and replace, but it will replace whole symbols only (so if there is a symbol in the file called NUMBER99 the NUMBER part will not be replaced). After the preprocessor has finished its work the compiler will see the following:

```
int main()
{
    std::cout << 4 << std::endl;
}
```

Compile the original code and run it, and confirm that the program simply prints 4 to the console.

The text search and replace aspect of the preprocessor can cause some odd results, for example, change your main function to declare a variable called NUMBER, as follows:

```
int main()
{
    int NUMBER = 99;
    std::cout << NUMBER << std::endl;
}
```

Now compile the code. You will get an error from the compiler:

```
C:\Beginning_C++\Chapter_01>cl /EHhc simple.cpp
Microsoft (R) C/C++ Optimizing Compiler Version 19.00.25017 for x86
Copyright (C) Microsoft Corporation.  All rights reserved.

simple.cpp
simple.cpp(7): error C2143: syntax error: missing ';' before 'constant'
simple.cpp(7): error C2106: '=': left operand must be l-value
```

This indicates that there is an error on line 7, which is the new line declaring the variable. However, because of the search and replace conducted by the preprocessor, what the compiler sees is a line that looks as follows:

```
int 4 = 99;
```

This is not correct C++!

In the code that you have typed, it is obvious what is causing the problem because you have a #define directive for the symbol within the same file. In practice, you will include several header files, and these may include files themselves, so the errant #define directive could be in one of many files. Equally, your constant symbols may have the same names as variables in header files included after your #define directive and may be replaced by the preprocessor.

Using #define as a way to define global constants is often not a good idea and there are much better ways in C++, as you'll see in Chapter 3, *Exploring C++ Types*.

If you have problems you think are coming from the preprocessor replacing symbols, you can investigate this by looking at the source file passed to the compiler after the preprocessor has done its work. To do this, compile with the /EP switch. This will suppress actual compilation and send the output of the preprocessor to stdout (the command line). Be aware that this could produce a lot of text, so it is usually better to direct this output to a file and examine that file with the Visual Studio editor.

Another way to provide the values used by the preprocessor is to pass them via a compiler switch. Edit the code and remove the line starting with #define. Compile this code as normal (**cl /EHsc simple.cpp**), run it, and confirm that the number printed on the console is **99**, the value assigned to the variable. Now compile the code again with the following line:

```
cl /EHsc simple.cpp /DNUMBER=4
```

Note that there is no space between the /D switch and the name of the symbol. This tells the preprocessor to replace every NUMBER symbol with the text 4 and this results in the same errors as above, indicating that the preprocessor is attempting to replace the symbol with the value provided.

Tools such as Visual C++ and nmake projects will have a mechanism to define symbols through the C++ compiler. The /D switch is used to define just one symbol, and if you want to define others they will have their own /D switch.

You are now wondering why C++ has such an odd facility that appears only to cause confusing errors. Defining symbols can be very powerful once you understand what the preprocessor is doing.

Using macros

One useful feature of preprocessor symbols is **macros**. A macro has parameters and the preprocessor will ensure that the search and replace will replace a symbol in the macro with the symbol used as a parameter to the macro.

Edit the `main` function to look as follows:

```
#include <iostream>

#define MESSAGE(c, v)
for(int i = 1; i < c; ++i) std::cout << v[i] << std::endl;

int main(int argc, char *argv[])
{
    MESSAGE(argc, argv);
    std::cout << "invoked with " << argv[0] << std::endl;
}
```

The `main` function calls a macro called `MESSAGE` and passes the command line parameters to it. The function then prints the first command line parameters (the invocation command) to the console. `MESSAGE` is not a function, it is a macro, which means that the preprocessor will replace every occurrence of `MESSAGE` with two parameters with the text defined previously, replacing the `c` parameter with whatever is passed as the first parameter of the macro, and replacing `v` with whatever is used as the second parameter. After the preprocessor has finished processing the file, `main` will look as follows:

```
int main(int argc, char *argv[])
{
    for(int i = 1; i < argc; ++i)
        std::cout << argv[i] << std::endl;
    std::cout << "invoked with " << argv[0] << std::endl;
}
```

Note that, in the macro definition, the backslash () is used as a line-continuation character, so you can have multiline macros. Compile and run this code with one or more parameters, and confirm that `MESSAGE` prints out the command-line parameters.

Using symbols

You can define a symbol without a value and the preprocessor can be told to test for whether a symbol is defined or not. The most obvious situation for this is compiling different code for debug builds than for release builds.

Edit the code to add the lines highlighted here:

```
#ifdef DEBUG
#define MESSAGE(c, v)
for(int i = 1; i < c; ++i) std::cout << v[i] << std::endl;
#else
#define MESSAGE
#endif
```

The first line tells the preprocessor to look for the DEBUG symbol. If this symbol is defined (regardless of its value), then the first definition of the MESSAGE macro will be used. If the symbol is not defined (a release build) then the MESSAGE symbol is defined, but it does nothing: essentially, occurrences of MESSAGE with two parameters will be removed from the code.

Compile this code and run the program with one or more parameters. For example:

```
C:\Beginning_C++\Chapter_01>simple test parameters
invoked with simple
```

This shows that the code has been compiled without DEBUG defined so MESSAGE is defined to do nothing. Now compile this code again, but this time with the **/DDEBUG** switch to define the DEBUG symbol. Run the program again and you will see that the command-line parameters are printed on the console:

```
C:\Beginning_C++\Chapter_01>simple test parameters
test parameters
invoked with simple
```

This code has used a macro, but you can use conditional compilation with symbols anywhere in your C++ code. Symbols used in this way allow you to write flexible code and choose the code to be compiled through a symbol defined on the compiler command line. Furthermore, the compiler will define some symbols itself, for example, __DATE__ will have the current date, __TIME__ will have the current time, and __FILE__ will have the current file name.

Microsoft, and other compiler producers, defines a long list of symbols that you can access, and you are advised to look these up in the manual. A few that you may find useful are as follows: __cplusplus will be defined for C++ source files (but not for C files) so you can identify code that needs a C++ compiler; _DEBUG is set for debug builds (note the preceding underscore), and _MSC_VER has the current version of the Visual C++ compiler, so you can use the same source for various versions of the compiler.

Using pragmas

Associated with symbols and conditional compilation is the compiler directive, #pragma once. Pragmas are directives specific to the compiler, and different compilers will support different pragmas. Visual C++ defines the #pragma once to solve the problem that occurs when you have multiple header files each including similar header files. The problem is that it may result in the same items being defined more than once and the compiler will flag this as an error. There are two ways to do this, and the <iostream> header file that you include next uses both of these techniques. You can find this file in the Visual C++ include folder. At the top of the file you will find the following:

```
// ostream standard header
#pragma once
#ifndef _IOSTREAM_
#define _IOSTREAM_
```

At the bottom, you will find the following line:

```
#endif /* _IOSTREAM_ */
```

First the conditional compilation: the first time this header is included, the symbol _IOSTREAM_ will not be defined, so the symbol is defined and then the rest of the file will be included until the #endif line.

This illustrates good practice when using conditional compilation. For every #ifndef, there must be a #endif, and often there may be hundreds of lines between them. It is a good idea, when you use #ifdef or #ifundef, to provide a comment with the corresponding #else and #endif, indicating the symbol it refers to.

If the file is included again then the symbol _IOSTREAM_ will be defined, so the code between the #ifndef and #endif will be ignored. However, it is important to point out that, even if the symbol is defined, the header file will still be loaded and processed because the instructions about what to do are contained within the file.

The #pragma once performs the same action as the conditional compilation, but it gets around the problem of using a symbol that could be duplicated. If you add this single line to the top of your header file, you are instructing the preprocessor to load and process this file once. The preprocessor maintains a list of the files that it has processed, and if a subsequent header tries to load a file that has already been processed, that file will not be loaded and will not be processed. This reduces the time it takes for the project to be preprocessed.

Before you close the `<iostream>` file, look at the number of lines in the file. For `<iostream>` version v6.50:0009 there are 55 lines. This is a small file, but it includes `<istream>` (1,157 lines), which includes `<ostream>` (1,036 lines), which includes `<ios>` (374 lines), which includes `<xlocnum>` (1,630 lines), and so on. The result of preprocessing could mean many tens of thousands of lines will be included into your source file even for a program that has one line of code!

Dependencies

A C++ project will produce an executable or library, and this will be built by the linker from object files. The executable or library is dependent upon these object files. An object file will be compiled from a C++ source file (and potentially one or more header files). The object file is dependent upon these C++ source and header files. Understanding dependencies is important because it helps you understand the order to compile the files in your project, and it allows you to make your project builds quicker by only compiling those files that have changed.

Libraries

When you include a file within your source file, the code within that header file will be accessible to your code. Your include file may contain whole function or class definitions (these will be covered in later chapters), but this will result in the problem mentioned previously: multiple definitions of a function or class. Instead, you can declare a class or **function prototype**, which indicates how calling code will call the function without actually *defining* it. Clearly, the code will have to be defined elsewhere, and this could be a source file or a library, but the compiler will be happy because it only sees one definition.

A library is code that has already been defined; it has been fully debugged and tested, and therefore, users should not need to have access to the source code. The C++ Standard Library is mostly shared via header files, which helps you when you debug your code, but you must resist any temptation to edit these files. Other libraries will be provided as compiled libraries.

There are essentially two types of compiled libraries: static libraries and dynamic link libraries. If you use a static library, then the compiler will copy the compiled code that you use from the static library and place it in your executable. If you use a dynamic link (or shared) library, then the linker will add information used during runtime (it may be when the executable is loaded, or it may even be delayed until the function is called) to load the shared library into memory and access the function.

Windows uses the extension `lib` for static libraries and `dll` for dynamic link libraries. GNU **gcc** uses the extension `a` for static libraries and `so` for shared libraries.

If you use library code in a static or dynamic link library, the compiler will need to know that you are calling a function correctly-to make sure your code calls a function with the correct number of parameters and correct types. This is the purpose of a function prototype: it gives the compiler the information it needs to know about calling the function without providing the actual body of the function, the function definition.

This book will not go into the details of how to write libraries, since it is compiler-specific; nor will it go into the details of calling library code, since different operating systems have different ways of sharing code. In general, the C++ Standard Library will be included in your code through the standard header files. The C Runtime Library (which provides some code for the C++ Standard Library) will be static-linked, but if the compiler provides a dynamic-linked version you will have a compiler option to use this.

Pre-compiled headers

When you include a file into your source file, the preprocessor will include the contents of that file (after taking into account any conditional compilation directives) and, recursively, any files included by that file. As illustrated previously, this could result in thousands of lines of code. As you develop your code, you will often compile the project so that you can test the code. Every time you compile your code, the code defined in the header files will also be compiled even though the code in library header files will not have changed. With a large project, this can make the compilation take a long time.

To get around this problem, compilers often offer an option to precompile headers that will not change. Creating and using precompiled headers is compiler-specific. For example, with the GNU C++ compiler, gcc, you compile a header as if it is a C++ source file (with the `/x` switch), and the compiler creates a file with an extension of `gch`. When gcc compiles source files that use the header it will search for the `gch` file, and if it finds the precompiled header, it will use that; otherwise, it will use the header file.

In Visual C++ the process is a bit more complicated because you have to specifically tell the compiler to look for a precompiled header when it compiles a source file. The convention in Visual C++ projects is to have a source file called `stdafx.cpp`, which has a single line that includes the file `stdafx.h`. You put all your stable header-file includes in `stdafx.h`. Next, you create a precompiled header by compiling `stdafx.cpp` using the `/Yc` compiler option to specify that `stdafx.h` contains the stable headers to compile. This will create a `pch` file (typically, Visual C++ will name it after your project) containing the code compiled up to the point of the inclusion of the `stdafx.h` header file. Your other source files must include the `stdafx.h` header file as the first header file, but they may also include other files. When you compile your source files, you use the `/Yu` switch to specify the stable header file (`stdafx.h`), and the compiler will use the precompiled header `pch` file instead of the header.

When you examine large projects, you will often find precompiled headers are used; as you can see, it alters the file structure of the project. The example later in this chapter will show how to create and use precompiled headers.

Project structure

It is important to organize your code into modules to enable you to maintain it effectively. `Chapter 7`, *Introduction to Object-Orientated Programming*, explains object orientation, which is one way to organize and reuse code. However, even if you are writing C-like procedural code (that is, your code involves calls to functions in a linear way) you will also benefit from organizing it into modules. For example, you may have functions that manipulate strings and other functions that access files, so you may decide to put the definition of the string functions in one source file, `string.cpp`, and the definition of the file functions in another file, `file.cpp`. So that other modules in the project can use these files, you must declare the prototypes of the functions in a header file and include that header in the module that uses the functions.

There is no absolute rule in the language about the relationship between the header files and the source files that contain the definition of the functions. You may have a header file called `string.h` for the functions in `string.cpp`; and a header file called `file.h` for the functions in `file.cpp`. Or you may have just one file called `utilities.h` that contains the declarations for all the functions in both files. The only rule that you have to abide by is that, at compile time, the compiler must have access to a declaration of the function in the current source file, either through a header file, or the function definition itself.

The compiler will not *look forward* in a source file, so if function A calls another function, B, in the same source file then function B must have already been defined before function A calls it, or there must be a prototype declaration. This leads to a typical convention of having a header file associated with each source file that contains the prototypes of the functions in the source file, and the source file includes this header. This convention becomes more important when you write classes.

Managing dependencies

When a project is built with a building tool, checks are performed to see if the output of the build exists and if not, the appropriate actions to build it are performed. The common terminology is that the output of a build step is called a **target** and the inputs of the build step (for example, source files) are the **dependencies** of that target. Each target's dependencies are the files used to make them. The dependencies may themselves be a target of a build action and have their own dependencies.

For example, the following diagram shows the dependencies in a project:

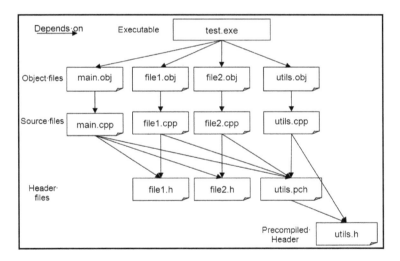

In this project, there are three source files (`main.cpp`, `file1.cpp`, and `file2.cpp`). Each of these includes the same header, `utils.h`, which is precompiled (hence there is a fourth source file, `utils.cpp`, that only contains `utils.h`). All of the source files depend on `utils.pch`, which in turn depends upon `utils.h`. The source file `main.cpp` has the `main` function and calls functions in the other two source files (`file1.cpp` and `file2.cpp`), and accesses the functions through the associated header files, `file1.h` and `file2.h`.

On the first compilation, the build tool will see that the executable depends on the four object files, and so it will look for the rule to build each one. In the case of the three C++ source files, this means compiling the `cpp` files, but since `utils.obj` is used to support the precompiled header, the build rule will be different to the other files. When the build tool has made these object files, it will then link them together along with any library code (not shown here).

Subsequently, if you change `file2.cpp` and build the project, the build tool will see that only `file2.cpp` has changed, and since only `file2.obj` depends on `file2.cpp`, all the make tool needs to do is compile `file2.cpp` and then link the new `file2.obj` with the existing object files to create the executable. If you change the header file, `file2.h`, the build tool will see that two files depend on this header file, `file2.cpp` and `main.cpp`, and so the build tool will compile these two source files and link the new two object files `file2.obj` and `main.obj` with the existing object files to form the executable. If, however, the precompiled header source file, `util.h`, changes, it means that *all* of the source files will have to be compiled.

For a small project, dependencies are easy to manage, and as you have seen, for a single source file project you do not even have to worry about calling the linker, because the compiler will do that automatically. As a C++ project gets bigger, managing dependencies gets more complex, and this is where development environments such as Visual C++ become vital.

Makefiles

If you are supporting a C++ project, you are likely to come across a makefile. This is a text file containing the targets, dependencies, and rules for building the targets in the project. The makefile is invoked through the make tool, nmake on Windows and **make** on Unix-like platforms.

A makefile is a series of rules that look as follows:

```
targets : dependents
    commands
```

The targets are one or more files that depend on the dependents (which may be several files), so that if one or more of the dependents is newer than one or more of the targets (and hence has changed since the targets were last built), then the targets need to be built again, which is done by running the commands. There may be more than one command, and each one is on a separate line prefixed with a tab character. A target may have no dependents, in which case the commands will always be called.

For example, using the preceding example, the rule for the executable, `test.exe` will be as follows:

```
test.exe : main.obj file1.obj file2.obj utils.obj
    link /out:test.exe main.obj file1.obj file2.obj utils.obj
```

Since the `main.obj` object file depends on the source file `main.cpp`, the headers `File1.h` and `File2.h`, and the precompiled header `utils.pch`, the rule for this file will be as follows:

```
main.obj : main.cpp file1.h file2.h utils.pch
    cl /c /Ehsc main.cpp /Yuutils.h
```

The compiler is called with the `/c` switch, which indicates that the code is compiled to an object file, but the compiler should not invoke the linker. The compiler is told to use the precompiled header file `utils.pch` through the header file `utils.h` with the `/Yu` switch. The rules for the other two source files will be similar.

The rule to make the precompiled header file is as follows:

```
utils.pch : utils.cpp utils.h
    cl /c /EHsc utils.cpp /Ycutils.h
```

The `/Yc` switch tells the compiler to create the precompiled header using the header file, `utils.h`.

Makefiles are often much more complicated than this. They will contain macros, which group targets, dependents, or command switches. They will contain general rules for target types rather than the specific rules shown here, and they will have conditional tests. If you need to support or write a makefile, then you should look up all of the options in the manual for the tool.

Writing a simple project

This project will illustrate the features of C++ and projects that you have learned in this chapter. The project will use several source files so that you can see the effect of dependencies and how the build tool will manage changes to the source files. The project is simple: it will ask you to type your first name, and then it will print your name and the time and date to the command line.

The project structure

The project uses three functions: the `main` function, which calls two functions `print_name` and `print_time`. These are in three separate source files and, since the `main` function will call the other two functions in other source files, this means the `main` source file will have to have prototypes of those functions. In this example, that means a header for each of those files. The project will also use a precompiled header, which means a source file and a header file. In total, this means three headers and four source files will be used.

Creating the precompiled header

The code will use the C++ Standard Library to input and output via streams, so it will use the `<iostream>` header. The code will use the C++ `string` type to handle input, so it will use the `<string>` header. Finally, it accesses the C runtime time and date functions, so the code will use the `<ctime>` header. These are all standard headers that will not change while you develop the project, so they are good candidates for precompiling.

In Visual Studio create a C++ header file and add the following lines:

```
#include <iostream>
#include <string>
#include <ctime>
```

Save the file as `utils.h`.

Now create a C++ source file and add a single line to include the header file you just created:

```
#include "utils.h"
```

Save this as `utils.cpp`. You will need to create a makefile for the project, so in the **New File** dialog, select **Text File** as your file type. Add the following rules for building the precompiled header:

```
utils.pch utils.obj :: utils.cpp utils.h
    cl /EHsc /c utils.cpp /Ycutils.h
```

Save this file as `makefile.` with the appended period. Since you created this file as a text file, Visual Studio will normally automatically give it an extension of `txt`, but since we want no extension, you need to add the period to indicate no extension. The first line says that the two files, `utils.pch` and `utils.obj`, depend on the source file and header file being specified. The second line (prefixed with a tab) tells the compiler to compile the C++ file, not to call the linker, and it tells the compiler to save the precompiled code included into `utils.h`. The command will create `utils.pch` and `utils.obj`, the two targets specified.

When the make utility sees that there are two targets, the default action (when a single colon is used between targets and dependencies) is to call the command once for each target (there are macros that you can use to determine which target is being built). This would mean that the same compiler command would be called twice. We do not want this behavior, because both targets are created with a single call to the command. The double colon, `::`, is a work around: it tells nmake not to use the behavior of calling the command for each target. The result is that, when the make utility has called the command once, to make `utils.pch`, it then tries to make `utils.obj` but sees that it has already been made, and so realizes that it does not need to call the command again.

Now test this out. At the command line, in the folder that contains your project, type `nmake`.

If you do not give the name of a makefile, the program maintenance tool will automatically use a file called `makefile` (if you want to use a makefile with another name, use the `/f` switch to provide the name):

```
C:\Beginning_C++\Chapter_01\Code>nmake
Microsoft (R) Program Maintenance Utility Version 14.00.24210.0
Copyright (C) Microsoft Corporation.  All rights reserved.

cl /EHsc /c utils.cpp /Ycutils.h
Microsoft (R) C/C++ Optimizing Compiler Version 19.00.24210 for x86
Copyright (C) Microsoft Corporation.  All rights reserved.

utils.cpp
```

Do a directory listing to confirm that `utils.pch` and `utils.obj` have been made.

Creating the main file

Now create a C++ source file and add the following code:

```cpp
#include "utils.h"
#include "name.h"
#include "time.h"

void main()
{
    print_name();
    print_time();
}
```

Save this file as `main.cpp`.

The first include file is the precompiled header for the Standard Library headers. The other two files provide function prototype declarations for the two functions that are called in the `main` function.

You now need to add a rule for the `main` file to the makefile. Add the following highlighted line to the top of the file:

```
main.obj : main.cpp name.h time.h utils.pch
    cl /EHsc /c main.cpp /Yuutils.h

utils.pch utils.obj :: utils.cpp utils.h
    cl /EHsc /c utils.cpp /Ycutils.h
```

This new line says that the `main.obj` target depends on two header files: a source file and the precompiled header file, `utils.pch`. At this point, the `main.cpp` file will not compile, because the header files do not exist yet. So that we can test the makefile, create two C++ header files; in the first header file, add the function prototype:

```cpp
void print_name();
```

Save this file as `name.h`. In the second header file, add the function prototype:

```cpp
void print_time();
```

Save this file as `time.h`.

You can now run the make utility, which will compile only the `main.cpp` file. Test this out: delete all of the target files by typing `del main.obj utils.obj utils.pch` on the command line and then run the make utility again. This time, you'll see that the make utility compiles `utils.cpp` first and then compiles `main.cpp`. The reason for this order is because the first target is `main.obj`, but since this depends on `utils.pch`, the make tool moves to the next rule and uses this to make the precompiled header, before returning to the rule to create `main.obj`.

Note that you have not defined `print_name` nor `print_time`, yet the compiler does not complain. The reason is that the compiler is only creating object files, and it is the responsibility of the linker to resolve the links to the functions. The function prototypes in the header files satisfy the compiler that the function will be defined in another object file.

Using input and output streams

So far, we have seen how to output data to the console via the `cout` object. The Standard Library also provides a `cin` stream object to allow you to input values from the command line.

Create a C++ source file and add the following code:

```
#include "utils.h"
#include "name.h"

void print_name()
{
    std::cout << "Your first name? ";
    std::string name;
    std::cin >> name;
    std::cout << name;
}
```

Save this file as `name.cpp`.

The first include file is the precompiled header, which will include the two Standard Library headers `<iostream>` and `<string>`, so you can use types declared in those files. The first line of the function prints the string **Your first name?** on the console. Note that there is a space after the query, so the cursor will remain on the same line, ready for the input.

The next line declares a C++ `string` object variable. Strings are zero or more characters, and each character will take up memory. The `string` class does all the work of allocating and freeing the memory that will be used by the string. This class will be described in more detail in `Chapter 8`, *Using the Standard Library Containers*. The `cin` overloads the `>>` operator to get input from the console. When you press the **Enter** key the `>>` operator will return the characters you typed into the `name` variable (treating the space character as a delimiter). The function then prints out the contents of the `name` variable to the console without a newline.

Now add a rule for this source file to the makefile; add the following lines to the top of the file:

```
name.obj : name.cpp name.h utils.pch
        cl /EHsc /c name.cpp /Yuutils.h
```

Save this file and run the make tool to confirm that it will make the `name.obj` target.

Using time functions

The final source file will obtain the time and print this on the console. Create a C++ source file and add the following lines:

```
#include "utils.h"
#include "time.h"

void print_time()
{
    std::time_t now = std::time(nullptr);
    std::cout << ", the time and date are "
              << std::ctime(&now) << std::endl;
}
```

The two functions, `std::time` and `std::gmtime`, are C functions, and `std::time_t` is a C type; all are available through the C++ Standard Library. The `std::time` function obtains the time as the number of seconds since midnight on January 1, 1970. The function returns a value of type `std::time_t`, which is a 64-bit integer. The function can optionally copy this value to another variable if you pass a pointer to where, in memory, the variable is stored. In this example, we do not need this facility, so we pass the C++ `nullptr` to the function to indicate that a copy should not be performed.

Next, we need to convert the number of seconds to a string that has the time and date in a format you can understand. This is the purpose of the `std::ctime` function, which takes as a parameter a pointer to the variable that holds the number of seconds. The `now` variable has the number of seconds, and the `&` operator is used to obtain the address of this variable in memory. Memory and pointers are covered in more detail in `Chapter 4`, *Working With Memory, Arrays, and Pointers*. This function returns a string, but you have not allocated any memory for this string, nor should you attempt to free the memory used by this string. The `std::ctime` function creates a **statically allocated** memory buffer, which will be used by all the code running on the current execution thread. Every time you call the `std::ctime` function on the same thread of execution, the memory location used will be the same, although the contents of the memory may change.

This function illustrates how important it is to check the manual to see who has responsibility for allocating and freeing memory. `Chapter 4`, *Working With Memory, Arrays, and Pointers*, goes into more detail about memory allocation.

The string returned from `std::ctime` is printed to the console using several calls to the put `<<` operator to format the output.

Now add a build rule to the makefile. Add the following to the top of the file:

```
time.obj : time.cpp time.h utils.pch
    cl /EHsc /c time.cpp /Yuutils.h
```

Save this file and run the make tool, and confirm that it builds the `time.obj` target.

Building the executable

You now have all the object files needed for your project, so the next task is to link them together. To do this, add the following line to the top of the makefile:

```
time_test.exe : main.obj name.obj time.obj utils.obj
    link /out:$@ $**
```

The target here is the executable, and the dependents are the four object files. The command to build the executable calls the link tool and uses a special syntax. The `$@` symbol is interpreted by the make tool as use the target, and so the `/out` switch will actually be `/out:time_test.out`. The `$**` symbol is interpreted by the make tool as *use all the dependencies* so that all the dependencies are linked.

Save this file and run the make utility. You should find that only the link tool will be called, and it will link together the object files to create the executable.

Finally, add a rule to clean the project. It is good practice to provide a mechanism to remove all of the files created by the compile process and leave the project clean, with only the source files. After the line to link the object files, add the following lines:

```
time_test.exe : main.obj name.obj time.obj utils.obj
    link /out:$@ $**
clean : @echo Cleaning the project...
    del main.obj name.obj time.obj utils.obj utils.pch
    del time_test.exe
```

The target `clean` is a pseudo target: no file is actually made, and for this reason, there are no dependencies. This illustrates a feature of the make utility: if you call nmake with the name of a target, the utility will make just that target. If you do not specify a target then the utility will make the first target mentioned in the makefile, in this case `time_test.exe`.

The `clean` pseudo target has three commands. The first command prints `Cleaning the project...` to the console. The @ symbol here tells the make utility to run the command without printing the command to the console. The second and third commands call the command-line tool `del` to delete the files. Clean the project now by typing `nmake clean` on the command line, and confirm that the directory has just the header files, source files, and the makefile.

Testing the code

Run the make utility again so that the executable is built. On the command line, run the example by typing the **time_test** command. You will be asked to type your first name; do this, and press the **Enter** key. You should find that your name, the time, and date are printed on the console:

```
C:\Beginning_C++\Chapter_01>time_test
Your first name? Richard
Richard, the time and date are Tue Sep  6 19:32:23 2016
```

Changing the project

Now that you have the basic project structure, with a makefile you can make changes to the files and be reassured that, when the project is rebuilt, only the files that have changed will be compiled. To illustrate this, change the print_name function in name.cpp to ask for your name in a more polite way. Change the first line in the function body as highlighted here:

```
void print_name()
{
    std::cout << "Please type your first name and press [Enter] ";
    std::string name;
```

Save the file and then run the make utility. This time, only the name.cpp source file is compiled, and the resulting file, name.obj, is linked with the existing object files.

Now change the name.h header file and add a comment in the file:

```
// More polite version
void print_name();
```

Make the project. What do you find? This time, *two* source files are compiled, name.cpp and main.cpp, and they are linked with the existing object files to create the executable. To see why these two files are compiled, take a look at the dependency rules in the makefile. The only file that was changed was name.h, and this file is named in the dependency list of name.obj and main.obj, hence, these two files are rebuilt. Since these two files are in the dependency list of time_test.exe, the executable will be rebuilt, too.

Summary

This chapter was a gentle, but thorough, introduction to C++. You learned about the reasons to use the language and how to install the compiler from one vendor. You learned how C++ projects are structured, about source files and header files, and how code is shared through libraries. You also learned how to maintain projects using makefiles, and, through a simple example, you have had hands-on experience of editing and compiling code.

You have a compiler, an editor, and a tool to manage projects, so now you are ready to learn more details about C++, starting in the following chapter with C++ statements and controlling execution flow in an application.

2
Understanding Language Features

In the previous chapter, you installed a C++ compiler and developed a simple application. You also explored the basic structure of C++ projects and how to manage them. In this chapter, you will dive deeper into language, and learn the various language features to control flow in your code.

Writing C++

C++ is a very flexible language when it comes to formatting and writing code. It is also a strongly typed language, meaning there are rules about declaring the types of variables, which you can use to your advantage by making the compiler help you write better code. In this section, we will cover how to format C++ code and rules on declaring and scoping variables.

Using white space

Other than string literals, you have free usage of white space (spaces, tabs, newlines), and are able to use as much or as little as you like. C++ statements are delimited by semicolons, so in the following code there are three statements, which will compile and run:

```
int i = 4;
i = i / 2;
std::cout << "The result is" << i << std::endl;
```

The entire code could be written as follows:

```
int i=4;i=i/2; std::cout<<"The result is "<<i<<std::endl;
```

There are some cases where white space is needed (for example, when declaring a variable you must have white space between the type and the variable name), but the convention is to be as judicious as possible to make the code readable. And while it is perfectly correct, language-wise, to put all the statements on one line (like JavaScript), it makes the code almost completely unreadable.

If you are interested in some of the more creative ways of making code unreadable, have a look at the entries for the annual International Obfuscated C Code Contest (http://www.ioccc.org/). As the progenitor of C++, many of the lessons in C shown at IOCCC apply to C++ code too.

Bear in mind that, if the code you write is viable, it may be in use for decades, which means you may have to come back to the code years after you have written it, and it means that other people will support your code, too. Making your code readable is not only a courtesy to other developers, but unreadable code is always a likely target for replacement.

Formatting code

Inevitably, whoever you are writing code for will dictate how you format code. Sometimes it makes sense, for example, if you use some form of preprocessing to extract code and definitions to create documentation for the code. In many cases, the style that is imposed on you is the personal preference of someone else.

Visual C++ allows you to place XML comments in your code. To do this you use a three--slash comment (///) and then compile the source file with the /doc switch. This creates an intermediate XML file called an xdc file with a <doc> root element and containing all the three--slash comments. The Visual C++ documentation defines standard XML tags (for example, <param>, <returns> to document the parameters and return value of a function). The intermediate file is compiled to the final document XML file with the xdcmake utility.

There are two broad styles in C++: **K&R** and **Allman**.

Kernighan and Ritchie (K&R) wrote the first, and most influential, book about C (Dennis Ritchie was the author of the C language). The K&R style is used to describe the formatting style used in that book. In general, K&R places the opening brace of a code block on the same line of the last statement. If your code has nested statements (and typically, it will) then this style can get a bit confusing:

```
if (/* some test */) {
    // the test is true
    if (/* some other test */) {
        // second test is true
    } else {
        // second test is false
    }
} else {
    // the test is false
}
```

This style is typically used in Unix (and Unix-like) code.

The Allman style (named after the developer Eric Allman) places the opening brace on a new line, so the nested example looks as follows:

```
if (/* some test */)
{
    // the test is true
    if (/* some other test */)
    {
        // second test is true
    }
    else
    {
        // second test is false
    }
}
else
{
    // the test is false
}
```

The Allman style is typically used by Microsoft.

Remember that your code is unlikely to be presented on paper, so the fact that K&R is more compact will save no trees. If you have the choice, you should choose the style that is the most readable; the decision of this author, for this book, is that Allman is the more readable.

If you have multiple nested blocks, the indents can give you an idea of which block the code resides in. However, comments can help. In particular, if a code block has a large amount of code, it is often helpful to comment the reason for the code block. For example, in an `if` statement, it is helpful to put the result of the test in the code block so you know what the variable values are in that block. It is also useful to put a comment on the closing brace of the test:

```
if (x < 0)
{
    // x < 0
    /* lots of code */
}   // if (x < 0)

else
{
    // x >= 0
    /* lots of code */
}   // if (x < 0)
```

If you put the test as a comment on a closing brace, it means that you have a search term that you can use to find the test that resulted in the code block. The preceding lines make this commenting redundant, but when you have code blocks with many tens of lines of code, and with many levels of nesting, comments like this can be very helpful.

Writing statements

A statement can be a declaration of a variable, an expression that evaluates to a value, or it can be a definition of a type. A statement may also be a control structure to affect the flow of the execution through your code.

A statement ends with a semicolon. Other than that, there are few rules about how to format statements. You can even use a semicolon on its own, and this is called a null statement. A null statement does nothing, so having too many semicolons is usually benign.

Working with expressions

An expression is a sequence of operators and operands (variables or literals) that results in some value. Consider the following:

```
int i;
i = 6 * 7;
```

On the right side `6 * 7` is an expression, and the assignment (from `i` on the left-hand side to the semicolon on the right) is a statement.

Every expression is either an **lvalue** or an **rvalue**. You are most likely to see these keywords used in error descriptions. In effect, an lvalue is an expression that refers to some memory location. Items on the left-hand side of an assignment must be lvalues. However, an lvalue can appear on the left- or right-hand side of an assignment. All variables are lvalues. An rvalue is a temporary item that does not exist longer than the expression that uses it; it will have a value, but cannot have a value assigned to it, so it can only exist on the right-hand side of an assignment. Literals are rvalues. The following shows a simple example of lvalues and rvalues:

```
int i;
i = 6 * 7;
```

In the second line, `i` is an lvalue, and the expression `6 * 7` results in an rvalue (`42`). The following will not compile because there is an rvalue on the left:

```
6 * 7 = i;
```

Broadly speaking, an expression becomes a statement by when you append a semicolon. For example, the following are both statements:

```
42;
std::sqrt(2);
```

The first line is an rvalue of `42`, but since it is temporary it has no effect. A C++ compiler will optimize it away. The second line calls the standard library function to calculate the square root of 2. Again, the result is an rvalue and the value is not used, so the compiler will optimize this away. However, it illustrates that a function can be called without using its return value. Although it is not the case with `std::sqrt`, many functions have a lasting effect other than their return value. Indeed, the whole point of a function is usually to do something, and the return value is often used merely to indicate if the function was successful; often developers assume that a function will succeed and ignore the return value.

Using the comma operator

Operators will be covered later in this chapter; however, it is useful to introduce the comma operator here. You can have a sequence of expressions separated by a comma as a single statement. For example, the following code is legal in C++:

```
int a = 9;
int b = 4;
int c;
c = a + 8, b + 1;
```

The writer intended to type `c = a + 8 / b + 1;` and : they pressed comma instead of a /. The intention was for `c` to be assigned to 9 + 2 + 1, or 12. This code will compile and run, and the variable `c` will be assigned with a value of 17 (`a + 8`). The reason is that the comma separates the right-hand side of the assignment into two expressions, `a + 8` and `b + 1`, and it uses the value of the first expression to assign `c`. Later in this chapter, we will look at operator precedence. However, it is worth saying here that the comma has the lowest precedence and + has a higher precedence than =, so the statement is executed in the order of the addition: the assignment and then the comma operator (with the result of `b + 1` thrown away).

You can change the precedence using parentheses to group expressions. For example, the mistyped code could have been as follows:

```
c = (a + 8, b + 1);
```

The result of this statement is: variable `c` is assigned to 5 (or `b + 1`). The reason is that with the comma operator expressions are executed from left to right so the value of the group of expressions is the tight-most one. There are some cases, for example, in the initialization or loop expression of a `for` loop, where you will find the comma operator useful, but as you can see here, even used intentionally, the comma operator produces hard-to-read code.

Using types and variables

Types will be covered in more detail in the next chapter, but it is useful to give basic information here. C++ is a strongly typed language, which means that you have to declare the type of the variables that you use. The reason for this is that the compiler needs to know how much memory to allocate for the variable, and it can determine this by the type of the variable. In addition, the compiler needs to know how to initialize a variable, if it has not been explicitly initialized, and to perform this initialization the compiler needs to know the type of the variable.

C++11 provides the `auto` keyword, which relaxes this concept of strong typing, and it will be covered in the next chapter. However, the type checking of the compiler is so important that you should use type checking as much as possible.

C++ variables can be declared anywhere in your code as long as they are declared before they are used. *Where* you declare a variable determines *how* you use it (this is called the **scope** of the variable). In general, it is best to declare the variable as close as possible to where you will use it, and within the most restrictive scope. This prevents *name clashes*, where you will have to add additional information to disambiguate two or more variables.

You may, *and should*, give your variables descriptive names. This makes your code much more readable and easier to understand. C++ names must start with an alphabetic character, or an underscore. They can contain alphanumeric characters except spaces, but can contain underscores. So, the following are valid names:

```
numberOfCustomers
NumberOfCustomers
number_of_customers
```

C++ names are case-sensitive, and the first `2,048` characters are significant. You can start a variable name with an underscore, but you cannot use two underscores, nor can you use an underscore followed by a capital letter (these are reserved by C++). C++ also reserves keywords (for example, `while` and `if`), and clearly you cannot use type names as variable names, neither built in type names (`int`, `long`, and so on) nor your own custom types.

You declare a variable in a statement, ending with a semicolon. The basic syntax of declaring a variable is that you specify the type, then the name, and, optionally, any initialization of the variable.

Built-in types must be initialized before you use them:

```
int i;
i++;            // C4700 uninitialized local variable 'i' used
std::cout << i;
```

There are essentially three ways to initialize variables. You can assign a value, you can call the type constructor (constructors for classes will be defined in `Chapter 6`, *Classes*) or you can initialize a variable using function syntax:

```
int i = 1;
int j = int(2);
int k(3);
```

These three are all legal C++, but stylistically the first is the better because it is more obvious: the variable is an integer, it is called i, and it is assigned a value of 1. The third looks confusing; it looks like the declaration of a function when it is actually declaring a variable. The next chapter will show a variation of assigning a value using the initialization list syntax. The reasons why you will want to do this will be left to that chapter.

Chapter 6, *Classes* will cover classes, your own custom types. A custom type may be defined to have a default value, which means that you may decide not to initialize a variable of a custom type before using it. However, this will result in poorer performance, because the compiler will initialize the variable with the default value and subsequently your code will assign a value, resulting in an assignment being performed twice.

Using constants and literals

Each type will have a literal representation. An integer will be a numeric represented without a decimal point and, if it is a signed integer, the literal can also use the plus or minus symbol to indicate the sign. Similarly, a real number can have a literal value that contains a decimal point, and you may even use the scientific (or engineering) format including an exponent. C++ has various rules to use when specifying literals in code, and these will be covered in the next chapter. Some examples of literals are shown here:

```
int pos = +1;
int neg = -1;
double micro = 1e-6;
double unit = 1.;
std::string name = "Richard";
```

Note that for the unit variable, the compiler knows that the literal is a real number because the value has a decimal point. For integers, you can provide a hexadecimal literal in your code by prefixing the number with 0x, so 0x100 is 256 in decimal. By default, the output stream will print numeric values in base 10; however, you can insert a **manipulator** into an output stream to tell it to use a different number base. The default behavior is std::dec, which means the numbers should be displayed as base 10, std::oct means display as octal (base 8), and std::hex means display as hexadecimal (base 16). If you prefer to see the prefix printed, then you use the stream manipulator std::showbase (more details will be given in Chapter 8, *Using the Standard Library Containers*).

C++ defines some literals. For bool, the logic type, there are true and false constants, where false is zero and true is 1. There is also the nullptr constant, again, zero, which is used as an invalid value for any pointer type.

Defining constants

In some cases, you will want to provide constant values that can be used throughout your code. For example, you may decide to declare a constant for π. You should not allow this value to be changed because it will change the underlying logic in your code. This means that you should mark the variable as being constant. When you do this, the compiler will check the use of the variable and if it is used in code that changes the value of the variable the compiler will issue an error:

```
const double pi = 3.1415;
double radius = 5.0;
double circumference = 2 * pi * radius;
```

In this case the symbol `pi` is declared as being constant, so it cannot change. If you subsequently decide to change the constant, the compiler will issue an error:

```
// add more precision, generates error C3892
pi += 0.00009265359;
```

Once you have declared a constant, you can be assured that the compiler will make sure it remains so. You can assign a constant with an expression as follows:

```
#include <cmath>
const double sqrtOf2 = std::sqrt(2);
```

In this code, a global constant called `sqrtOf2` is declared and assigned with a value using the `std::sqrt` function. Since this constant is declared outside a function, it is global to the file and can be used throughout the file.

In the last chapter, you learned that one way to declare a constant is to use `#define` symbols. The problem with this approach is that the preprocessor does a simple replacement. With constants declared with `const`, the C++ compiler will perform type checking to ensure that the constant is being used appropriately.

You can also use `const` to declare a constant that will be used as a **constant expression**. For example, you can declare an array using the square bracket syntax (more details will be given in `Chapter 4`, *Working with Memory, Arrays, and Pointers*):

```
int values[5];
```

This declares an array of five integers on the stack and these items are accessed through the `values` array variable. The 5 here is a constant expression. When you declare an array on the stack, you have to provide the compiler with a constant expression so it knows how much memory to allocate and this means the size of the array must be known at compile time. (You can allocate an array with a size known only at runtime, but this requires dynamic memory allocation, explained in Chapter 4, *Working with Memory, Arrays, and Pointers*.) In C++, you can declare a constant to do the following:

```
const int size = 5;
int values[size];
```

Elsewhere in your code, when you access the `values` array, you can use the `size` constant to make sure that you do not access items past the end of the array. Since the `size` variable is declared in just one place, if you need to change the size of the array at a later stage, you have just one place to make this change.

The `const` keyword can also be used on pointers and references (see Chapter 4, *Working with Memory, Arrays, and Pointers*) and on objects (see Chapter 6, *Classes*); often, you'll see it used on parameters to functions (see Chapter 5, *Using Functions*). This is used to get the compiler to help ensure that pointers, references, and objects are used appropriately, as you intended.

Using constant expressions

C++11 introduces a keyword called `constexpr`. This is applied to an expression, and indicates that the expression should be evaluated at compile type rather than at runtime:

```
constexpr double pi = 3.1415;
constexpr double twopi = 2 * pi;
```

This is similar to initializing a constant declared with the `const` keyword. However, the `constexpr` keyword can also be applied to functions that return a value that can be evaluated at compile time, and so this allows the compiler to optimize the code:

```
constexpr int triang(int i)
{
    return (i == 0) ? 0 : triang(i - 1) + i;
}
```

In this example, the function `triang` calculates triangular numbers recursively. The code uses the conditional operator. In the parentheses, the function parameter is tested to see if it is zero, and if so the function returns zero, in effect ending the recursion and returning the function to the original caller. If the parameter is not zero, then the return value is the sum of the parameter and the return value of `triang` called with the parameter is decremented.

This function, when called with a literal in your code, can be evaluated at compile time. The `constexpr` is an indication to the compiler to check the usage of the function to see if it can determine the parameter at compile time. If this is the case, the compiler can evaluate the return value and produce code more efficiently than by calling the function at runtime. If the compiler cannot determine the parameter at compile-time, the function will be called as **normal**. A function marked with the `constexpr` keyword must only have one expression (hence the use of the conditional operator `? :` in the `triang` function).

Using enumerations

A final way to provide constants is to use an `enum` variable. In effect, an `enum` is a group of named constants, which means that you can use an `enum` as a parameter to a function. For example:

```
enum suits {clubs, diamonds, hearts, spades};
```

This defines an enumeration called `suits`, with named values for the suits in a deck of cards. An enumeration is an integer type and by default the compiler will assume an `int`, but you can change this by specifying the integer type in the declaration. Since there are just four possible values for card suits, it is a waste of memory to use `int` (usually 4 bytes) and instead we can use `char` (a single byte):

```
enum suits : char {clubs, diamonds, hearts, spades};
```

When you use an enumerated value, you can use just the name; however, it is usual to scope it with the name of the enumeration, making the code more readable:

```
suits card1 = diamonds;
suits card2 = suits::diamonds;
```

Both forms are allowed, but the latter makes it more explicit that the value is taken from an enumeration. To force developers to specify the scope, you can apply the keyword `class`:

```
enum class suits : char {clubs, diamonds, hearts, spades};
```

With this definition and the preceding code, the line declaring `card2` will compile, but the line declaring `card1` will not. With a scoped `enum`, the compiler treats the enumeration as a new type and has no inbuilt conversion from your new type to an integer variable. For example:

```
suits card = suits::diamonds;
char c = card + 10; // errors C2784 and C2676
```

The `enum` type is based on `char` but when you define the `suits` variable as being scoped (with `class`) the second line will not compile. If the enumeration is defined as not being scoped (without `class`) then there is an inbuilt conversion between the enumerated value and `char`.

By default, the compiler will give the first enumerator a value of 0 and then increment the value for the subsequent enumerators. Thus `suits::diamonds` will have a value of 1 because it is the second value in `suits`. You can assign values yourself:

```
enum ports {ftp=21, ssh, telnet, smtp=25, http=80};
```

In this case, `ports::ftp` has a value of 21, `ports::ssh` has a value of 22 (21 incremented), `ports::telnet` is 22, `ports::smtp` is 25, and `ports::http` is 80.

Often the point of enumerations is to provide named symbols within your code and their values are unimportant. Does it matter what value is assigned to `suits::hearts`? The intention is usually to ensure that it is different from the other values. In other cases, the values are important because they are a way to provide values to other functions.

Enumerations are useful in a `switch` statement (see later) because the named value makes it clearer than using just an integer. You can also use an enumeration as a parameter to a function and hence restrict the values passed via that parameter:

```
void stack(suits card)
{
    // we know that card is only one of four values
}
```

Declaring pointers

Since we are covering the use of variables, it is worth explaining the syntax used to define pointers and arrays because there are some potential pitfalls. Chapter 4, *Working with Memory, Arrays, and Pointers*, covers this in more detail, so we will just introduce the syntax so that you are familiar with it.

In C++, you will access memory using a typed pointer. The type indicates the type of the data that is held in the memory that is pointed to. So, if the pointer is an (4 byte) integer pointer, it will point to four bytes that can be used as an integer. If the integer pointer is incremented, then it will point to the next four bytes, which can be used as an integer.

 Don't worry if you find pointers confusing at this point. `Chapter 4`, *Working with Memory, Arrays, and Pointers*, will explain this in more detail. The purpose of introducing pointers at this time is to make you aware of the syntax.

In C++, pointers are declared using the * symbol and you access a memory address with the & operator:

```
int *p;
int i = 42;
p = &i;
```

The first line declares a variable, p, which will be used to hold the memory address of an integer. The second line declares an integer and assigns it a value. The third line assigns a value to the pointer p to be the address of the integer variable just declared. It is important to stress that the value of p *is not* 42; it will be a memory address where the value of 42 is stored.

Note how the declaration has the * on the variable name. This is common convention. The reason is that if you declare several variables in one statement, the * applies only to the immediate variable. So, for example:

```
int* p1, p2;
```

Initially this looks like you are declaring two integer pointers. However, this line does not do this; it declares just one pointer to integer called p1. The second variable is an integer called p2. The preceding line is equivalent to the following:

```
int *p1;
int p2;
```

If you wish to declare two integers in one statement, then you should do it as follows:

```
int *p1, *p2;
```

Using namespaces

Namespaces give you one mechanism to modularize code. A namespace allows you to label your types, functions, and variables with a unique name so that, using the scope resolution operator, you can give a *fully qualified name*. The advantage is that you know exactly which item will be called. The disadvantage is that using a fully qualified name you are in effect switching off C++'s *argument-dependent lookup* mechanism for overloaded functions where the compiler will choose the function that has the best fit according to the arguments passed to the function.

Defining a namespace is simple: you decorate the types, functions, and global variables with the `namespace` keyword and the name you give to it. In the following example, two functions are defined in the `utilities` namespace:

```cpp
namespace utilities
{
    bool poll_data()
    {
        // code that returns a bool
    }
    int get_data()
    {
        // code that returns an integer
    }
}
```

Do not use semicolon after the closing bracket.

Now when you use these symbols, you need to qualify the name with the namespace:

```cpp
if (utilities::poll_data())
{
    int i = utilities::get_data();
    // use i here...
}
```

The namespace declaration may just declare the functions, in which case the actual functions would have to be defined elsewhere, and you will need to use a qualified name:

```cpp
namespace utilities
{
    // declare the functions
    bool poll_data();
```

```
        int get_data();
}

//define the functions
bool utilities::poll_data()
{
    // code that returns a bool
}

int utilities::get_data()
{
    // code that returns an integer
}
```

One use of namespaces is to version your code. The first version of your code may have a side-effect that is not in your functional specification and is technically a bug, but some callers will use it and depend on it. When you update your code to fix the bug, you may decide to allow your callers the option to use the old version so that their code does not break. You can do this with a namespace:

```
namespace utilities
{
    bool poll_data();
    int get_data();

    namespace V2
    {
        bool poll_data();
        int get_data();
        int new_feature();
    }
}
```

Now callers who want a specific version can call the fully qualified names, for example, callers could use utilities::V2::poll_data to use the newer version and utilities::poll_data to use the older version. When an item in a specific namespace calls an item in the same namespace, it does not have to use a qualified name. So, if the new_feature function calls get_data, it will be utilities::V2::get_data that is called. It is important to note that, to declare a nested namespace, you have to do the nesting manually (as shown here); you cannot simply declare a namespace called utilities::V2.

The preceding example has been written so that the first version of the code will call it using the namespace `utilities`. C++11 provides a facility called an **inline** namespace that allows you to define a nested namespace, but allows the compiler to treat the items as being in the parent namespace when it performs an argument-dependent lookup:

```
namespace utilities
{
    inline namespace V1
    {
        bool poll_data();
        int get_data();
    }

    namespace V2
    {
        bool poll_data();
        int get_data();
        int new_feature();
    }
}
```

Now to call the first version of `get_data`, you can use `utilities::get_data` or `utilities::V1::get_data`.

Fully qualified names can make the code difficult to read, especially if your code will only use one namespace. To help here you have several options. You can place a `using` statement to indicate that symbols declared in the specified namespace can be used without a fully qualified name:

```
using namespace utilities;
int i = get_data();
int j = V2::get_data();
```

You can still use fully qualified names, but this statement allows you to ease the requirement. Note that a nested namespace is a member of a namespace, so the preceding `using` statement means that you can call the second version of `get_data` with either `utilities::V2::get_data` or `V2::get_data`. If you use the unqualified name, then it means that you will call `utilities::get_data`.

A namespace can contain many items, and you may decide that you only want to relax the use of fully qualified names with just a few of them. To do this, use `using` and give the name of the item:

```
using std::cout;
using std::endl;
cout << "Hello, World!" << endl;
```

This code says that, whenever `cout` is used, it refers to `std::cout`. You can use `using` within a function, or you can put it as file scope and make the intention global to the file.

You do not have to declare a namespace in one place, you can declare it over several files. The following could be in a different file to the previous declaration of `utilities`:

```
namespace utilities
{
    namespace V2
    {
        void print_data();
    }
}
```

The `print_data` function is still part of the `utilities::V2` namespace.

You can also put an `#include` in a namespace, in which case the items declared in the header file will now be part of the namespace. The standard library header files that have a prefix of `c` (for example, `cmath`, `cstdlib`, and `ctime`) give access to the C runtime functions by including the appropriate C header in the `std` namespace.

The great advantage of a namespace is to be able to define your items with names that may be common, but are hidden from other code that does not know the namespace name of. The namespace means that the items are still available to your code via the fully qualified name. However, this only works if you use a unique namespace name, and the likelihood is that, the longer the namespace name, the more unique it is likely to be. Java developers often name their classes using a URI, and you could decide to do the same thing:

```
namespace com_packtpub_richard_grimes
{
    int get_data();
}
```

The problem is that the fully qualified name becomes quite long:

```
int i = com_packtpub_richard_grimes::get_data();
```

You can get around this issue using an alias:

```
namespace packtRG = com_packtpub_richard_grimes;
int i = packtRG::get_data();
```

C++ allows you to define a namespace without a name, an **anonymous** namespace. As mentioned previously, namespaces allow you to prevent name clashes between code defined in several files. If you intend to use such a name in only one file you could define a unique namespace name. However, this could get tedious if you had to do it for several files. A namespace without a name has the special meaning that it has **internal linkage**, that is, the items can only be used in the current translation unit, the current file, and not in any other file.

Code that is not declared in a namespace will be a member of the `global` namespace. You can call the code without a namespace name, but you may want to explicitly indicate that the item is in the `global` namespace using the scope resolution operator without a namespace name:

```
int version = 42;

void print_version()
{
    std::cout << "Version = " << ::version << std::endl;
}
```

C++ scoping of variables

As you saw in the previous chapter the compiler will compile your source files as individual items called **translation units**. The compiler will determine the objects and variables you declare and the types and functions you define, and once declared you can use any of these in the subsequent code within the scope of the declaration. At its very broadest, you can declare an item at the global scope by declaring it in a header file that will be used by all of the source files in your project. If you do not use a namespace it is often wise when you use such global variables to name them as being part of the global namespace:

```
// in version.h
extern int version;

// in version.cpp
#include "version.h"
version = 17;

// print.cpp
#include "version.h"
void print_version()
{
    std::cout << "Version = " << ::version << std::endl;
}
```

This code has the C++ for two source files (`version.cpp` and `print.cpp`) and a header file (`version.h`) included by both source files. The header file declares the global variable `version`, which can be used by both source files; it declares the variable, but does not define it. The actual variable is defined and initialized in `version.cpp`; it is here that the compiler will allocate memory for the variable. The `extern` keyword used on the declaration in the header indicates to the compiler that `version` has **external linkage**, that is, the name is visible in files other than where the variable is defined. The `version` variable is used in the `print.cpp` source file. In this file, the scope resolution operator (`::`) is used without a namespace name and hence indicates that the variable `version` is in the global namespace.

You can also declare items that will only be used within the current translation unit, by declaring them within the source file before they are used (usually at the top of the file). This produces a level of modularity and allows you to hide implementation details from code in other source files. For example:

```
// in print.h
void usage();

// print.cpp
#include "version.h"
std::string app_name = "My Utility";
void print_version()
{
    std::cout << "Version = " << ::version << std::endl;
}

void usage()
{
    std::cout << app_name << " ";
    print_version();
}
```

The `print.h` header contains the interface for the code in the file `print.cpp`. Only those functions declared in the header will be callable by other source files. The caller does not need to know about the implementation of the `usage` function, and as you can see here it is implemented using a call to a function called `print_version` that is only available to code in `print.cpp`. The variable `app_name` is declared at file scope, so it will only be accessible to code in `print.cpp`.

If another source file declares a variable at file scope, that is called `app_name`, and is also a `std::string` the file will compile, but the linker will complain when it tries to link the object files. The reason is that the linker will see the same variable defined in two places and it will not know which one to use.

A function also defines a scope; variables defined within the function can only be accessed through that name. The parameters of the function are also included as variables within the function, so when you declare other variables, you have to use different names. If a parameter is not marked as `const` then you can alter the value of the parameter in your function.

You can declare variables anywhere within a function as long as you declare them before you use them. Curly braces (`{ }`) are used to define code blocks, and they also define local scope; if you declare a variable within a code block then you can only use it there. This means that you can declare variables with the same name outside the code block and the compiler will use the variable closest to the scope it is accessed.

Before finishing this section, it is important to mention one aspect of the C++ **storage class**. A variable declared in a function means that the compiler will allocate memory for the variable on the stack frame created for the function. When the function finishes, the stack frame is torn down and the memory recycled. This means that, after a function returns, the values in any local variables are lost; when the function is called again, the variable is created anew and initialized again.

C++ provides the `static` keyword to change this behavior. The `static` keyword means that the variable is allocated when the program starts just like variables declared at global scope. Applying `static` to a variable declared in a function means that the variable has internal linkage, that is, the compiler restricts access to that variable to that function:

```cpp
int inc(int i)
{
    static int value;
    value += i;
    return value;
}

int main()
{
    std::cout << inc(10) << std::endl;
    std::cout << inc(5) << std::endl;
}
```

By default, the compiler will initialize a static variable to 0, but you can provide an initialization value, and this will be used when the variable is first allocated. When this program starts, the `value` variable will be initialized to 0 before the `main` function is called. The first time the `inc` function is called, the `value` variable is incremented to 10, which is returned by the function and printed to the console. When the `inc` function returns the `value` variable is retained, so that when the `inc` function is called again, the `value` variable is incremented by 5 to a value of 15.

Using operators

Operators are used to compute a value from one or more operands. The following table groups all of the operators with equal *precedence* and lists their *associativity*. The higher in the table, the higher precedence of execution the operator has in an expression. If you have several operators in an expression, the compiler will perform the higher--precedence operators before the lower--precedence operators. If an expression contains operators of equal precedence, then the compiler will use the associativity to decide whether an operand is grouped with the operator to its left or right.

There are some ambiguities in this table. A pair of parentheses can mean a function call or a cast and in the table these are listed as `function()` and `cast()`; in your code you will simply use `()`. The + and – symbols are either used to indicate sign (unary plus and unary minus, given in the table as +x and –x), or addition and subtraction (given in the table as + and –). The & symbol means either "take the address of" (listed in the table as &x) or bitwise `AND` (listed in the table as &). Finally, the postfix increment and decrement operators (listed in the table as x++ and x--) have a higher precedence than the prefix equivalents (listed as ++x and --x).

Precedence and Associativity	Operators
1: No associativity	`::`
2: Left to right associativity	`.` or `->` `[]` `function()` `{}` `x++` `x--` `typeid` `const_cast` `dynamic_cast` `reinterpret_cast` `static_cast`
3: Right to left associativity	`sizeof` `++x` `--x` `~` `!` `-x` `+x` `&x` `*` `new` `delete` `cast()`
4: Left to right associativity	`.*` or `->*`
5: Left to right associativity	`*` `/` `%`
6: Left to right associativity	`+` `-`
7: Left to right associativity	`<<` `>>`
8: Left to right associativity	`<` `>` `<=` `>=`
9: Left to right associativity	`==` `!=`
10: Left to right associativity	`&`

11: Left to right associativity	^
12: Left to right associativity	|
13: Left to right associativity	&&
14: Left to right associativity	||
15: Right to left associativity	? :
16: Right to left associativity	= *= /= %= += -= <<= >>= &= |= ^=
17: Right to left associativity	throw
18: Left to right associativity	,

For example, take a look at the following code:

```
int a = b + c * d;
```

This is interpreted as the multiplication being performed first, and then the addition. A clearer way to write the same code is:

```
int a = b + (c * d);
```

The reason is that * has a higher precedence than + so that the multiplication is carried out first, and then the addition is performed:

```
int a = b + c + d;
```

In this case, the + operators have the same precedence, which is higher than the precedence of assignment. Since + has left to right associativity the statement is interpreted as follows:

```
int a = ((b + c) + d);
```

That is, the first action is the addition of b and c, and the result is added to d and it is this result that is used to assign a. This may not seem important, but bear in mind that the addition could be between function calls (a function call has a higher precedence than +):

```
int a = b() + c() + d();
```

This means that the three functions are called in the order b, c, d, and then their return values are summed according to the left-to-right associativity. This may be important because d may depend on global data altered by the other two functions.

It makes your code more readable and easier to understand if you explicitly specify the precedence by grouping expressions with parentheses. Writing b + (c * d) makes it immediately clear which expression is executed first, whereas b + c * d means you have to know the precedence of each operator.

The built-in operators are overloaded, that is, the same syntax is used regardless of which built-in type is used for the operands. The operands must be the same type; if different types are used, the compiler will perform some default conversions, but in other cases (in particular, when operating on types of different sizes), you will have to perform a cast to indicate explicitly what you mean. The next chapter will explain this in more detail.

Exploring the built-in operators

C++ comes with a wide range of built-in operators; most are arithmetic or logic operators, which will be covered in this section. The casting operators will be covered in the next chapter; memory operators will be covered in Chapter 4, *Working with Memory, Arrays, and Pointers,* and the object-related operators in Chapter 6, *Classes.*

Arithmetic operators

The arithmetic operators +, −, /, *, and % need little explanation other than perhaps the division and modulus operators. All of these operators act upon integer and real numeric types except for %, which can only be used with integer types. If you mix the types (say, add an integer to a floating-point number) then the compiler will perform an automatic conversion, as explained in the next chapter. The division operator / behaves as you expect for floating point variables: it produces the result of the division of the two operands. When you perform the division between two integers a / b, the result is the whole number of the divisor (b) in the dividend (a). The remainder of the division is obtained by the modulus %. So, for any integer, b (other than zero), one could say that, an integer a can be expressed as follows:

```
(a / b) * b + (a % b)
```

Note that the modulus operator can only be used with integers. If you want to get the remainder of a floating-point division, use the standard function, std::remainder.

Be careful when using division with integers, since fractional parts are discarded. If you need the fractional parts, then you may need to explicitly convert the numbers into real numbers. For example:

```
int height = 480;
int width = 640;
float aspect_ratio = width / height;
```

This gives an aspect ratio of 1 when it should be 1.3333 (or 4 : 3). To ensure that floating-point division is performed, rather than integer division, you can cast either (or both) the dividend or divisor to a floating-point number as explained in the next chapter.

Increment and decrement operators

There are two versions of these operators, prefix and postfix. As the name suggests, prefix means that the operator is placed on the left of the operand (for example, ++i), and a postfix operator is placed to the right (i++). The ++ operator will increment the operand and the -- operator will decrement it. The prefix operator means "return the value *after* the operation," and the postfix operator means "return the value *before* the operation." So the following code will increment one variable and use it to assign another:

```
a = ++b;
```

Here, the prefix operator is used so the variable b is incremented and the variable a is assigned to the value after b has been incremented. Another way of expressing this is:

```
a = (b = b + 1);
```

The following code assigns a value using the postfix operator:

```
a = b++;
```

This means that the variable b is incremented, but the variable a is assigned to the value before b has been incremented. Another way of expressing this is:

```
int t;
a = (t = b, b = b + 1, t);
```

Note that this statement uses the comma operator, so a is assigned to the temporary variable t in the right-most expression.

The increment and decrement operators can be applied to both integer and floating point numbers. The operators can also be applied to pointers, where they have a special meaning. When you increment a pointer variable it means *increment the pointer by the size of the type pointed to by the operator*.

Bitwise operators

Integers can be regarded as a series of bits, 0 or 1. Bitwise operators act upon these bits compared to the bit in the same position in the other operand. Signed integers use a bit to indicate the sign, but bitwise operators act on every bit in an integer, so it is usually only sensible to use them on unsigned integers. In the following, all the types are marked as unsigned, so they are treated as not having a sign bit.

The & operator is bitwise AND, which means that each bit in the left-hand operand is compared with the bit in the right-hand operand in the same position. If both are 1, the resultant bit in the same position will be 1; otherwise, the resultant bit is zero:

```
unsigned int a = 0x0a0a; // this is the binary 0000101000001010
unsigned int b = 0x00ff; // this is the binary 0000000000001111
unsigned int c = a & b;  // this is the binary 0000000000001010
std::cout << std::hex << std::showbase << c << std::endl;
```

In this example, using bitwise & with 0x00ff has the same effect as providing a mask that masks out all but the lowest byte.

The bitwise OR operator | will return a value of 1 if either or both bits in the same position are 1, and a value of 0 only if both are 0:

```
unsigned int a = 0x0a0a; // this is the binary 0000101000001010
unsigned int b = 0x00ff; // this is the binary 0000000000001111
unsigned int c = a & b;  // this is the binary 0000101000001111
std::cout << std::hex << std::showbase << c << std::endl;
```

One use of the & operator is to find if a particular bit (or a specific collection of bits) is set:

```
unsigned int flags = 0x0a0a; // 0000101000001010
unsigned int test = 0x00ff;  // 0000000000001111

// 0000101000001111 is (flags & test)
if ((flags & test) == flags)
{
    // code for when all the flags bits are set in test
}
if ((flags & test) != 0)
{
```

```
        // code for when some or all the flag bits are set in test
    }
```

The `flags` variable has the bits we require, and the `test` variable is a value that we are examining. The value (`flags & test`) will have only those bits in the `test` variables that are also set in `flags`. Thus, if the result is non-zero, it means that at least one bit in `test` is also set in `flags`; if the result is exactly the same as the `flags` variable then all the bits in `flags` are set in `test`.

The exclusive OR operator `^` is used to test when the bits are different; the resultant bit is `1` if the bits in the operands are different, and `0` if they are the same. Exclusive OR can be used to flip specific bits:

```
int value = 0xf1;
int flags = 0x02;
int result = value ^ flags; // 0xf3
std::cout << std::hex << result << std::endl;
```

The final bitwise operator is the bitwise complement `~`. This operator is applied to a single integer operand and returns a value where every bit is the complement of the corresponding bit in the operand; so if the operand bit is 1, the bit in the result is 0, and if the bit in the operand is 0, the bit in the result is 1. Note that all bits are examined, so you need to be aware of the size of the integer.

Boolean operators

The `==` operator tests whether two values are exactly the same. If you test two integers then the test is obvious; for example, if x is 2 and y is 3, then x `==` y is obviously `false`. However, two real numbers may not be the same even when you think so:

```
double x = 1.000001 * 1000000000000;
double y = 1000001000000;
if (x == y) std::cout << "numbers are the same";
```

The `double` type is a floating-point type held in 8 bytes, but this is not enough for the precision being used here; the value stored in the x variable is `1000000999999.9999` (to four decimal places).

The != operator tests if two values are not true. The operators > and <, test two values to see if the left-hand operand is greater than, or less than, the right-hand operand, the >= operator tests if the left-hand operand is greater than or equal to the right-hand operand, and the <= operator tests if the left-hand operand is less than or equal to the right-hand operand. These operators can be used in the if statement similarly to how == is used in the preceding example. The expressions using the operators return a value of type bool and so you can use them to assign values to Boolean variables:

```
int x = 10;
int y = 11;
bool b = (x > y);
if (b) std::cout << "numbers same";
else   std::cout << "numbers not same";
```

The assignment operator (=) has a higher precedence than the greater than (>=) operator, but we have used the parentheses to make it explicit that the value is tested before being used to assign the variable. You can use the ! operator to negate a logical value. So, using the value of b obtained previously, you can write the following:

```
if (!b) std::cout << "numbers not same";
else    std::cout << "numbers same";
```

You can combine two logical expressions using the && (AND) and || (OR) operators. An expression with the && operator is true only if both operands are true, whereas an expression with the || operator is true if either, or both, operands are true:

```
int x = 10, y = 10, z = 9;
if ((x == y) || (y < z))
    std::cout << "one or both are true";
```

This code involves three tests; the first tests if the x and y variables have the same value, the second tests if the variable y is less than z, and then there is a test to see if either or both of the first two tests are true.

In a || expression such as this, where the first operand (x==y) is true, the total logical expression will be true regardless of the value of the right operand (here, y < z). So there is no point in testing the second expression. Correspondingly, in an && expression, if the first operand is false then the entire expression must be false, and so the right-hand part of the expression need not be tested. The compiler will provide code to perform this *short-circuiting* for you:

```
if ((x != 0) && (0.5 > 1/x))
{
    // reciprocal is less than 0.5
```

}

This code tests to see if the reciprocal of x is less than 0.5 (or, conversely, that x is greater than 2). If the x variable has value 0 then the test 1/x is an error but, in this case, the expression will never be executed because the left operand to && is false.

Bitwise shift operators

Bitwise shift operators shift the bits in the left-hand operand integer the specified number of bits given in the right-hand operand, in the specified direction. A shift by one bit left multiplies the number by two, a shift one bit to the right divides by 2. In the following a 2-byte integer is bit-shifted:

```
unsigned short s1 = 0x0010;
unsigned short s2 = s1 << 8;
std::cout << std::hex << std::showbase;
std::cout << s2 << std::endl;
// 0x1000
s2 = s2 << 3;
std::cout << s2 << std::endl;
// 0x8000
```

In this example, the s1 variable has the fifth bit set (0x0010 or 16). The s2 variable has this value, shifted left by 8 bits, so the single bit is shifted to the 13th bit, and the bottom 8 bits are all set to 0 (0x10000 or 4,096). This means that 0x0010 has been multiplied by 2^8, or 256, to give 0x1000. Next, the value is shifted left by another 3 bits, and the result is 0x8000; the top bit is set.

The operator discards any bits that overflow, so if you have the top bit set and shift the integer one bit left, that top bit will be discarded:

```
s2 = s2 << 1;
std::cout << s2 << std::endl;
// 0
```

A final shift left by one bit results in a value 0.

It is important to remember that, when used with a stream, the operator << means *insert into the stream*, and when used with integers, it means *bitwise shift*.

Assignment operators

The assignment operator = assigns an lvalue (a variable) on the left with the result of the rvalue (a variable or expression) on the right:

```
int x = 10;
x = x + 10;
```

The first line declares an integer and initializes it to 10. The second line alters the variable by adding another 10 to it, so now the variable x has a value of 20. This is assignment. C++ allows you to change the value of a variable based on the variable's value using an abbreviated syntax. The previous lines can be written as follows:

```
int x = 10;
x += 10;
```

An increment operator such as this (and the decrement operator) can be applied to integers and floating-point types. If the operator is applied to a pointer, then the operand indicates how many whole item addresses the pointer is changed by. For example, if an int is 4 bytes and you add 10 to an int pointer, the actual pointer value is incremented by 40 (10 times 4 bytes).

In addition to the increment (+=) and decrement (−=) assignments, you can have assignments for multiply (*=), divide (/=), and remainder (%=). All of these except for the last one (%=) can be used for both floating-point types and integers. The remainder assignment can only be used on integers.

You can also perform bitwise assignment operations on integers: left shift (<<=), right shift (>>=), bitwise AND (&=), bitwise OR (|=), and bitwise exclusive OR (^=). It usually only makes sense to apply these to unsigned integers. So, multiplying by eight can be carried out by both of these two lines:

```
i *= 8;
i <<= 3;
```

Controlling execution flow

C++ provides many ways to test values and loop through code.

Using conditional statements

The most frequently used conditional statement is `if`. In its simplest form, the `if` statement takes a logical expression in a pair of parentheses and is immediately followed by the statement that is executed if the condition is `true`:

```
int i;
std::cin >> i;
if (i > 10) std::cout << "much too high!" << std::endl;
```

You can also use the `else` statement to catch occasions when the condition is `false`:

```
int i;
std::cin >> i;
if (i > 10) std::cout << "much too high!" << std::endl;
else        std::cout << "within range" << std::endl;
```

If you want to execute several statements, you can use braces (`{ }`) to define a code block.

The condition is a logical expression and C++ will convert from numeric types to a `bool`, where 0 is `false` and anything not 0 is `true`. If you are not careful, this can be a source of an error that is not only difficult to notice, but also can have an unexpected side-effect. Consider the following code, which asks for input from the console and then tests to see if the user enters -1:

```
int i;
std::cin >> i;
if (i == -1) std::cout << "typed -1" << endl;
std::cout << "i = " << i << endl;
```

This is contrived, but you may be asking for values in a loop and then performing actions on those values, except when the user enters -1, at which point the loop finishes. If you mistype, you may end up with the following code:

```
int i;
std::cin >> i;
if (i = -1) std::cout << "typed -1" << endl;
std::cout << "i = " << i << endl;
```

In this case, the assignment operator (=) is used instead of the *equality* operator (==). There is just one character difference, but this code is still correct C++ and the compiler is happy to compile it.

The result is that, regardless of what you type at the console, the variable i is assigned to -1, and since -1 is not zero, the condition in the if statement is true, hence the true clause of the statement is executed. Since the variable has been assigned to -1, this may alter logic further on in your code. The way to avoid this bug is to take advantage of the requirement that in an assignment the left-hand side must be an lvalue. Perform your test as follows:

```
if (-1 == i) std::cout << "typed -1" << endl;
```

Here, the logical expression is (-1 == i), and since the == operator is commutative (the order of the operands does not matter; you get the same result), this is exactly the same as you intended in the preceding test. However, if you mistype the operator, you get the following:

```
if (-1 = i) std::cout << "typed -1" << endl;
```

In this case, the assignment has an rvalue on the left-hand side, and this will cause the compiler to issue an error (in Visual C++ this is C2106 '=' : left operand must be l-value).

You are allowed to declare a variable in an if statement, and the scope of the variable is in the statement blocks. For example, a function that returns an integer can be called as follows:

```
if (int i = getValue()) {
    // i != 0     // can use i here
} else {
    // i == 0     // can use i here
}
```

While this is perfectly legal C++, there are few reasons why you would want to do this.

In some cases, the conditional operator ?: can be used instead of an if statement. The operator executes the expression to the left of the ? operator and, if the conditional expression is true, it executes the expression to the right of the ?. If the conditional expression is false, it executes the expression to the right of the :. The expression that the operator executes provides the return value of the conditional operator.

For example, the following code determines the maximum of two variables, a and b:

```
int max;
if (a > b) max = a;
else       max = b;
```

This can be expressed with the following single statement:

```
int max = (a > b) ? a : b;
```

The main choice is which ever is most readable in the code. Clearly, if the assignment expressions are large it may well be best to split them over lines in an `if` statement. However, it is useful to use the conditional statement in other statements. For example:

```
int number;
std::cin  >> number;
std::cout << "there "
          << ((number == 1) ? "is " : "are ")
          << number << " item"
          << ((number == 1) ? "" : "s")
          << std::endl;
```

This code determines if the variable `number` is 1 and if so it prints on the console `there is 1 item`. This is because in both conditionals, if the value of the `number` variable is 1, the test is `true` and the first expression is used. Note that there is a pair of parentheses around the entire operator. The reason is that the stream `<<` operator is overloaded, and you want the compiler to choose the version that takes a string, which is the type returned by the operator rather than `bool`, which is the type of the expression (`number == 1`).

If the value returned by the conditional operator is an lvalue then you can use it on the left-hand side of an assignment. This means that you can write the following, rather odd, code:

```
int i = 10, j = 0;
((i < j) ? i : j) = 7;
// i is 10, j is 7

i = 0, j = 10;
((i < j) ? i : j) = 7;
// i is 7, j is 10
```

The conditional operator checks to see if `i` is less than `j` and if so it assigns a value to `i`; otherwise, it assigns `j` with that value. This code is terse, but it lacks readability. It is far better in this case to use an `if` statement.

Selecting

If you want to test to see if a variable is one of several values, using multiple `if` statements becomes cumbersome. The C++ `switch` statement fulfills this purpose much better. The basic syntax is shown here:

```
int i;
std::cin >> i;
switch(i)
{
```

```
    case 1:
        std::cout << "one" << std::endl;
        break;
    case 2:
        std::cout << "two" << std::endl;
        break;
    default:
        std::cout << "other" << std::endl;
}
```

Each `case` is essentially a label as to the specific code to be run if the selected variable is the specified value. The `default` clause is for values where there exists no `case`. You do not have to have a `default` clause, which means that you are testing only for specified cases. The `default` clause could be for the most common case (in which case, the cases filter out the less likely values) or it could be for exceptional values (in which case, the cases handle the most likely values).

A `switch` statement can only test integer types (which includes `enum`), and you can only test for constants. The `char` type is an integer, and this means that you can use characters in the `case` items, but only individual characters; you cannot use strings:

```
char c;
std::cin >> c;
switch(c)
{
    case 'a':
        std::cout << "character a" << std::endl;
        break;
    case 'z':
        std::cout << "character z" << std::endl;
        break;
    default:
        std::cout << "other character" << std::endl;
}
```

The `break` statement indicates the end of the statements executed for a `case`. If you do not specify it, execution will *fall through* and the following `case` statements will be executed even though they have been specified for a different case:

```
switch(i)
{
    case 1:
        std::cout << "one" << std::endl;
        // fall thru
    case 2:
        std::cout << "less than three" << std::endl;
```

```
            break;
        case 3:
            std::cout << "three" << std::endl;
            break;
        case 4:
            break;
            default:
            std::cout << "other" << std::endl;
    }
```

This code shows the importance of the break statement. A value of 1 will print both one and less than three to the console, because execution *falls through* to the preceding case, even though that case is for another value.

It is usual to have different code for different cases, so you will most often finish a case with break. It is easy to miss out a break by mistake, and this will lead to unusual behavior. It is good practice to document your code when deliberately missing out the break statement so that you know that if a break is missing, it is likely to be a mistake.

You can provide zero or more statements for each case. If there is more than one statement, they are all executed for that specific case. If you provide no statements (as for case 4 in this example) then it means that no statements will be executed, not even those in the default clause.

The break statement means *break out of this code block,* and it behaves like this in the loop statements while and for as well. There are other ways that you can break out of a switch. A case could call return to finish the function where the switch is declared; it can call goto to jump to a label, or it can call throw to throw an exception that will be caught by an exception handler outside the switch, or even outside the function.

So far, the cases are in numeric order. This is not a requirement, but it does make the code more readable, and clearly, if you want to *fall through* the case statements (as in case 1 here), you should pay attention to the order the case items.

If you need to declare a temporary variable in a case handler then you must define a code block using braces, and this will make the scope of the variable localized to just that code block. You can, of course, use any variable declared outside of the switch statement in any of the case handlers.

Since enumerated constants are integers, you can test an `enum` in a `switch` statement:

```
enum suits { clubs, diamonds, hearts, spades };

void print_name(suits card)
{
    switch(card)
    {
        case suits::clubs:
            std::cout << "card is a club";
            break;
        default:
            std::cout << "card is not a club";
    }
}
```

Although the `enum` here is not scoped (it is neither `enum class` nor `enum struct`), it is not required to specify the scope of the value in the `case`, but it makes the code more obvious what the constant refers to.

Looping

Most programs will need to loop through some code. C++ provides several ways to do this, either by iterating with an indexed value or testing a logical condition.

Looping with iteration

There are two versions of the `for` statement, iteration and range-based. The latter was introduced in C++11. The iteration version has the following format:

```
for (init_expression; condition; loop_expression)
    loop_statement;
```

You can provide one or more loop statements, and for more than one statement, you should provide a code block using braces. The purpose of the loop may be served by the loop expression, in which case you may not want a loop statement to be executed; here, you use the null statement, ; which means *do nothing*.

Within the parentheses are three expressions separated by semicolons. The first expression allows you to declare and initialize a loop variable. This variable is scoped to the `for` statement, so you can only use it in the `for` expressions or in the loop statements that follow. If you want more than one loop variable, you can declare them in this expression using the comma operator.

The `for` statement will loop while the condition expression is `true`; so if you are using a loop variable, you can use this expression to check the value of the loop variable. The third expression is called at the end of the loop, after the loop statement has been called; following this, the condition expression is called to see if the loop should continue. This final expression is often used to update the value of the loop variable. For example:

```
for (int i = 0; i < 10; ++i)
{
    std::cout << i;
}
```

In this code, the loop variable is `i` and it is initialized to zero. Next, the condition is checked, and since `i` will be less than 10, the statement will be executed (printing the value to the console). The next action is the loop expression; `++i`, is called, which increments the loop variable, `i`, and then the condition is checked, and so on. Since the condition is `i < 10`, this means that this loop will run ten times with a value of `i` between 0 and 9 (so you will see **0123456789** on the console).

The loop expression can be any expression you like, but often it increments or decrements a value. You do not have to change the loop variable value by 1; for example, you can use `i -= 5` as the loop expression to decrease the variable by 5 on each loop. The loop variable can be any type you like; it does not have to be integer, it does not even have to be numeric (for example, it could be a pointer, or an **iterator object** described in Chapter 8, *Using the Standard Library Containers*), and the condition and loop expression do not have to use the loop variable. In fact, you do not have to declare a loop variable at all!

If you do not provide a loop condition then the loop will be infinite, unless you provide a check in the loop:

```
for (int i = 0; ; ++i)
{
    std::cout << i << std::endl;
    if (i == 10) break;
}
```

This uses the `break` statement introduced earlier with the `switch` statement. It indicates that execution exits the `for` loop, and you can also use `return`, `goto`, or `throw`. You will rarely see a statement that finishes using `goto`; however, you may see the following:

```
for (;;)
{
    // code
}
```

In this case, there is no loop variable, no loop expression, and no conditional. This is an everlasting loop, and the code within the loop determines when the loop finishes.

The third expression in the `for` statement, the loop expression, can be anything you like; the only property is that it is executed at the end of a loop. You may choose to change another variable in this expression, or you can even provide several expressions separated by the comma operator. For example, if you have two functions, one called `poll_data` that returns `true` if there is more data available and `false` when there is no more data, and a function called `get_data` that returns the next available data item, you could use `for` as follows (bear in mind; this is a contrived example, to make a point):

```
for (int i = -1; poll_data(); i = get_data())
{
    if (i != -1) std::cout << i << std::endl;
}
```

When `poll_data` returns a `false` value, the loop will end. The `if` statement is needed because the first time the loop is called, `get_data` has not yet been called. A better version is as follows:

```
for (; poll_data() ;)
{
    int i = get_data();
    std::cout << i << std::endl;
}
```

Keep this example in mind for the following section.

There is one other keyword that you can use in a `for` loop. In many cases, your `for` loop will have many lines of code and at some point, you may decide that the current loop has completed and you want to start the next loop (or, more specifically, execute the loop expression and then test the condition). To do this, you can call `continue`:

```
for (float divisor = 0.f; divisor < 10.f; ++divisor)
{
    std::cout << divisor;
    if (divisor == 0)
    {
        std::cout << std::endl;
        continue;
    }
    std::cout << " " << (1 / divisor) << std::endl;
}
```

In this code, we print the reciprocal of the numbers 0 to 9 (`0.f` is a 4-byte floating-point literal). The first line in the `for` loop prints the loop variable, and the next line checks to see if the variable is zero. If it is, it prints a new line and continues, that is, the last line in the `for` loop is not executed. The reason is that the last line prints the reciprocal and it would be an error to divide any number by zero.

C++11 introduces another way to use the `for` loop, which is intended to be used with containers. The C++ standard library contains **templates** for container classes. These classes contain collections of objects, and provide access to those items in a standard way. The standard way is to iterate through collections using an **iterator** object. More details about how to do this will be given in Chapter 8, *Using the Standard Library Containers*; the syntax requires an understanding of pointers and iterators, so we will not cover them here. The range-based `for` loop gives a simple mechanism to access items in a container without explicitly using iterators.

The syntax is simple:

```
for (for_declaration : expression) loop_statement;
```

The first thing to point out is that there are only two expressions and they are separated by a colon (`:`). The first expression is used to declare the loop variable, which is of the type of the items in the collection being iterated through. The second expression gives access to the collection.

 In C++ terms, the collections that can be used are those that define a `begin` and `end` function that gives access to iterators, and also to stack-based arrays (that the compiler knows the size of).

The Standard Library defines a container object called a `vector`. The `vector` template is a class that contains items of the type specified in the angle brackets (`<>`); in the following code, the `vector` is initialized in a special way that is new to C++11, called **list initialization**. This syntax allows you to specify the initial values of the vector in a list between curly braces. The following code creates and initializes a `vector`, and then uses an iteration `for` loop to print out all the values:

```
using namespace std;
vector<string> beatles = { "John", "Paul", "George", "Ringo" };

for (int i = 0; i < beatles.size(); ++i)
{
    cout << beatles.at(i) << endl;
}
```

Here a `using` statement is used so that the classes `vector` and `string` do not have to be used with fully qualified names.

The `vector` class has a member function called `size` (called through the `.` operator, which means "call this function on this object") that returns the number of items in the `vector`. Each item is accessed using the `at` function passing the item's index. The one big problem with this code is that it uses random access, that is, it accesses each item using its index. This is a property of `vector`, but other Standard Library container types do not have random access. The following uses the range-based `for`:

```
vector<string> beatles = { "John", "Paul", "George", "Ringo" };

for (string musician : beatles)
{
    cout << musician << endl;
}
```

This syntax works with any of the standard container types and for arrays allocated on the stack:

```
int birth_years[] = { 1940, 1942, 1943, 1940 };

for (int birth_year : birth_years)
{
    cout << birth_year << endl;
}
```

In this case, the compiler knows the size of the array (because the compiler has allocated the array) and so it can determine the range. The range-based `for` loop will iterate through all the items in the container, but as with the previous version you can leave the `for` loop using `break`, `return`, `throw`, or `goto`, and you can indicate that the next loop should be executed using the `continue` statement.

Conditional loops

In the previous section we gave a contrived example, where the condition in the `for` loop polled for data:

```
for (; poll_data() ;)
{
    int i = get_data();
    std::cout << i << std::endl;
}
```

In this example, there is no loop variable used in the condition. This is a candidate for the `while` conditional loop:

```
while (poll_data())
{
    int i = get_data();
    std::cout << i << std::endl;
}
```

The statement will continue to loop until the expression (`poll_data` in this case) has a value of `false`. As with `for`, you can exit the `while` loop with `break`, `return`, `throw`, or `goto`, and you can indicate that the next loop should be executed using the `continue` statement.

The first time the `while` statement is called, the condition is tested before the loop is executed; in some cases you may want the loop executed at least once, and then test the condition (most likely dependent upon the action in the loop) to see if the loop should be repeated. The way to do this is to use the `do-while` loop:

```
int i = 5;
do
{
    std::cout << i-- << std::endl;
} while (i > 0);
```

Note the semicolon after the `while` clause. This is required.

This loop will print 5 to 1 in reverse order. The reason is that the loop starts with `i` initialized to 5. The statement in the loop decrements the variable through a postfix operator, which means the value before the decrement is passed to the stream. At the end of the loop, the `while` clause tests to see if the variable is greater than zero. If this test is `true`, the loop is repeated. When the loop is called with `i` assigned to 1, the value of 1 is printed to the console and the variable decremented to zero, and the `while` clause will test an expression that is `false` and the looping will finish.

The difference between the two types of loop is that the condition is tested before the loop is executed in the `while` loop, and so the loop may not be executed. In a `do-while` loop, the condition is called after the loop, which means that, with a `do-while` loop, the loop statements are always called at least once.

Jumping

C++ supports jumps, and in most cases, there are better ways to branch code; however, for completeness, we will cover the mechanism here. There are two parts to a jump: a labeled statement to jump to and the `goto` statement. A label has the same naming rules as a variable; it is declared suffixed with a colon, and it must be before a statement. The `goto` statement is called using the label's name:

```
int main()
{
    for (int i = 0; i < 10; ++i)
    {
        std::cout << i << std::endl;
        if (i == 5) goto end;
    }

end:
    std::cout << "end";
}
```

The label must be in the same function as the calling `goto`.

Jumps are rarely used, because they encourage you to write non-structured code. However, if you have a routine with highly nested loops or `if` statements, it may make more sense and be more readable to use a `goto` to jump to clean up code.

Using C++ language features

Let's now use the features you have learned in this chapter to write an application. This example is a simple command-line calculator; you type an expression such as *6 * 7*, and the application parses the input and performs the calculation.

Start Visual C++ and click the **File** menu, and then **New**, and finally, click on the **File...** option to get the **New File** dialog. In the left-hand pane, click on **Visual C++**, and in the middle pane, click on **C++ File (.cpp)**, and then click on the **Open** button. Before you do anything else, save this file. Using a Visual C++ console (a command line, which has the Visual C++ environment), navigate to the `Beginning_C++` folder you created in the previous chapter and create a new folder called `Chapter_02`. Now, in Visual C++, on the **File** menu, click **Save Source1.cpp As...** and in the **Save File As** dialog locate the `Chapter_02` folder you just created. In the **File name** box, type **calc.cpp** and click on the **Save** button.

The application will use `std::cout` and `std::string`; so at the top of the file, add the headers that define these and, so that you do not have to use fully qualified names, add a `using` statement:

```
#include <iostream>
#include <string>

using namespace std;
```

You will pass the expression via the command-line, so add a `main` function that takes command line parameters at the bottom of the file:

```
int main(int argc, char *argv[])
{
}
```

The application handles expressions in the form `arg1 op arg2` where `op` is an operator and `arg1` and `arg2` are the arguments. This means that, when the application is called, it must have four parameters; the first is the command used to start the application and the last three are the expression. The first code in the `main` function should ensure that the right number of parameters is provided, so at the top of this function add a condition, as follows:

```
if (argc != 4)
{
    usage();
    return 1;
}
```

If the command is called with more or less than four parameters, a function `usage` is called, and then the `main` function returns, stopping the application.

Add the `usage` function before the `main` function, as follows:

```
void usage()
{
    cout << endl;
    cout << "calc arg1 op arg2" << endl;
    cout << "arg1 and arg2 are the arguments" << endl;
    cout << "op is an operator, one of + - / or *" << endl;
}
```

This simply explains how to use the command and explains the parameters. At this point, you can compile the application. Since you are using the C++ Standard Library, you will need to compile with support for C++ exceptions, so type the following at the command-line:

```
C:\Beginning_C++Chapter_02\cl /EHsc calc.cpp
```

If you typed in the code without any mistakes, the file should compile. If you get any errors from the compiler, check the source file to see if the code is exactly as given in the preceding code. You may get the following error:

```
'cl' is not recognized as an internal or external command,
operable program or batch file.
```

This means that the console is not set up with the Visual C++ environment, so either close it down and start the console via the Windows Start menu, or run the **vcvarsall.bat** batch file. The steps to do both of these were given in the previous chapter.

Once the code has compiled you may run it. Start by running it with the correct number of parameters (for example, `calc 6 * 7`), and then try it with an incorrect number of parameters (for example, `calc 6 * 7 / 3`). Note that the space between the parameters is important:

```
C:\Beginning_C++Chapter_02>calc 6 * 7

C:\Beginning_C++Chapter_02>calc 6 * 7 / 3

calc arg1 op arg2
arg1 and arg2 are the arguments
op is an operator, one of + - / or *
```

In the first case, the application does nothing, so all you see is a blank line. In the second example, the code has determined that there are not enough parameters, and so it prints the usage information to the console.

Next, you need to do some simple parsing of the parameters to check that the user has passed valid values. At the bottom of the `main` function, add the following:

```
string opArg = argv[2];
if (opArg.length() > 1)
{
    cout << endl << "operator should be a single character" << endl;
    usage();
    return 1;
}
```

The first line initializes a C++ `std::string` object with the third command-line parameter, which should be the operator in the expression. This simple example only allows a single character for the operator, so the subsequent lines check to make sure that the operator is a single character. The C++ `std::string` class has a member function called `length` that returns the number of characters in the string.

The `argv[2]` parameter will have a length of at least one character (a parameter with no length will not be treated as a command-line parameter!), so we have to check if the user typed an operator longer than one character.

Next you need to test to ensure that the parameter is one of the restricted set allowed and, if the user types another operator, print an error and stop the processing. At the bottom of the `main` function, add the following:

```
char op = opArg.at(0);
if (op == 44 || op == 46 || op < 42 || op > 47)
{
    cout << endl << "operator not recognized" << endl;
    usage();
    return 1;
}
```

The tests are going to be made on a character, so you need to extract this character from the `string` object. This code uses the `at` function, which is passed the index of the character you need. (*Chapter 8, Using the Standard Library Containers*, will give more details about the members of the `std::string` class.) The next line checks to see if the character is not supported. The code relies on the following values for the characters that we support:

Character	Value
+	42
*	43
–	45
/	47

As you can see, if the character is less than 42 or greater than 47 it will be incorrect, but between 42 and 47 there are two characters that we also want to reject: , (44) and . (46). This is why we have the preceding conditional: "if the character is less than 42 or greater than 47, or it is 44 or 46, then reject it."

The `char` data type is an integer, which is why the test uses integer literals. You could have used character literals, so the following change is just as valid:

```
if (op == ',' || op == '.' || op < '+' || op > '/')
{
    cout << endl << "operator not recognized" << endl;
    usage();
    return 1;
}
```

You should use whichever you find the most readable. Since it makes less sense to check whether one character is *greater than* another, this book will use the former.

At this point, you can compile the code and test it. First try with an operator that is more than one character (for example, **) and confirm that you get the message that the operator should be a single character. Secondly, test with a character that is not a recognized operator; try any character other than +, *, –, or /, but it is also worth trying . and ,.

Bear in mind that the command prompt has special actions for some symbols, such as "&" and "|", and the command prompt may give you an error from it by parsing the command-line before even calling your code.

The next thing to do is to convert the arguments into a form that the code can use. The command-line parameters are passed to the program in an array of strings; however, we are interpreting some of those parameters as floating-point numbers (in fact, double-precision floating-point numbers). The C runtime provides a function called atof, which is available through the C++ Standard Library (in this case, <iostream> includes files that include <cmath>, where atof is declared).

It is a bit counter-intuitive to get access to a math function such as atof through including a file associated with stream input and output. If this makes you uneasy, you can add a line after the include lines to include the <cmath> file. As mentioned in the previous chapter, the C++ Standard Library headers have been written to ensure that a header file is only included once, so including <cmath> twice has no ill effect. This was not done in the preceding code, because it was argued that atof is a string function and the code includes the <string> header and, indeed, <cmath> is included via the files the <string> header includes.

Add the following lines to the bottom of the main function. The first two lines convert the second and fourth parameters (remember, C++ arrays are zero-based indexed) to double values. The final line declares a variable to hold the result:

```
double arg1 = atof(argv[1]);
double arg2 = atof(argv[3]);
double result = 0;
```

Now we need to determine which operator was passed and perform the requested action. We will do this with a switch statement. We know that the op variable will be valid, and so we do not have to provide a default clause to catch the values we have not tested for. Add a switch statement to the bottom of the function:

```
double arg1 = atof(argv[1]);
double arg2 = atof(argv[3]);
double result = 0;

switch(op)
{
}
```

The first three cases, +, −, and *, are straightforward:

```
switch (op)
{
    case '+':
        result = arg1 + arg2;
        break;
    case '-':
        result = arg1 - arg2;
        break;
    case '*':
        result = arg1 * arg2;
        break;
}
```

Again, since char is an integer, you can use it in a switch statement, but C++ allows you to check for the character values. In this case, using characters rather than numbers makes the code much more readable.

After the switch, add the final code to print out the result:

```
cout << endl;
cout << arg1 << " " << op << " " << arg2;
cout << " = " << result << endl;
```

You can now compile the code and test it with calculations that involve +, −, and *.

Division is a problem, because it is invalid to divide by zero. To test this out, add the following lines to the bottom of the switch:

```
case '/':
    result = arg1 / arg2;
    break;
```

Compile and run the code, passing zero as the final parameter:

```
C:\Beginning_C++Chapter_02>calc 1 / 0
1 / 0 = inf
```

The code ran successfully, and printed out the expression, but it says that the result is an odd value of inf. What is happening here?

The division by zero assigned `result` to a value of NAN, which is a constant defined in <math.h> (included via <cmath>), and means "not a number." The `double` overload of the insertion operator for the `cout` object tests to see if the number has a valid value, and if the number has a value of NAN, it prints the string **inf**. In our application, we can test for a zero divisor, and we treat the user action of passing a zero as being an error. Thus, change the code so that it reads as follows:

```
case '/':
if (arg2 == 0) {
    cout << endl << "divide by zero!" << endl;
    return 1;
} else {
    result = arg1 / arg2;
}
break;
```

Now when the user passes zero as a divisor, you will get a `divide by zero!` message.

You can now compile the full example and test it out. The application supports floating-point arithmetic using the +, −, *, and / operators, and will handle the case of dividing by zero.

Summary

In this chapter, you have learned how to format your code, and how to identify expressions and statements. You have learned how to identify the scope of variables, and how to group collections of functions and variables into namespaces so that you can prevent name clashes. You have also learned the basic plumbing in C++ of looping and branching code, and how the built-in operators work. Finally, you put all of this together in a simple application that allows you to perform simple calculations at the command line.

In the following chapter, you will learn about C++ types and how to convert values from one type to another.

3
Exploring C++ Types

In the last two chapters, you have learned how to put together a C++ program, learned about the files you use, and the ways to control execution flow. This chapter is about the data that you will use in your program: the type of data and the variables that will hold that data.

A variable can handle data of a particular format and with a particular behavior, and that is determined by the type of the variable. The type of the variable determines the operations you can perform on the data and on the format of the data when inputted or viewed by the user.

Essentially, you can view three general categories of types: built-in types, custom types, and pointers. Pointers in general will be covered in the next chapter, and custom types, or classes, and pointers to them, will be covered in Chapter 6, *Classes*. This chapter will cover the types that are provided as part of the C++ language.

Exploring built-in types

C++ provides integer, floating point, and Boolean types. The `char` type is an integer but it can be used to hold individual characters and so its data can be viewed as a number or as a character. The C++ Standard Library provides the `string` class to allow you to use and manipulate strings of characters. Strings will be covered in depth in Chapter 9, *Using Strings*.

As the name suggests, integer types contain integral values where there are no fractional parts. If you perform calculations with integers you should expect that any fractional parts will be discarded unless you take steps to retain them (for example, through the remainder operator %). Floating point types hold numbers that may have a fractional part; because floating point types can hold numbers in a mantissa exponent format, they can hold exceptionally large or exceptionally small numbers.

A variable is an instance of a type; it is the memory allocated to hold the data that the type can hold. Integer and floating point variable declarations can be modified to tell the compiler how much memory to allocate, and thus the limits of the data that the variable can hold and the precision of the calculations performed on the variable. In addition, you can also indicate if the variable will hold a number where the sign is important. If the number is being used to hold bitmaps (where the bits do not make up a number, but have a separate meaning of their own) then it usually makes no sense to use a signed type.

In some cases, you will be using C++ to unpack data from a file or a network stream so that you can manipulate it. In this case, you will need to know whether the data is a floating point or integral, signed or unsigned, how many bytes are used and what order those bytes will be in. The order of the bytes (whether the first byte in a multi-byte number is the low or high part of the number) is determined by the processor which you are compiling for, and in most cases, you will not need to worry about it.

Similarly, sometimes you may need to know about the size of a variable and how it is aligned in memory; in particular, when you are using records of data, known in C++ as structs. C++ provides the sizeof operator to give the number of bytes used to hold a variable and the alignof operator to determine the alignment of the type in memory. For basic types, the sizeof and alignof operators return the same value; it is only necessary to call the alignof operator on custom types where it will return the alignment of the largest data member in the type.

Integers

As the name suggests, an integer holds integral data, numbers that have no fractional part. For this reason, it makes little sense to do any arithmetic with an integer where the fractional part is important; in this case, you should use floating point numbers. An example of this was shown in the last chapter:

```
int height = 480;
int width = 640;
int aspect_ratio = width / height;
```

This gives an aspect ratio of 1, which is clearly untrue and serves no purpose. Even if you assign the result to a floating-point number, you will get the same result:

```
float aspect_ratio = width / height;
```

The reason is that the arithmetic is performed in the expression `width / height`, which will use the division operator for integers that will throw away any fractional part of the result. To use the floating-point division operator you will have to cast one or other of the operands to a floating-point number so the floating-point operator is used:

```
float aspect_ratio = width / (float)height;
```

This will assign a value of 1.3333 (or 4 : 3) to the `aspect_ratio` variable. The cast operator used here is the C cast operator, which forces data of one type to be used as data of another type. (It is used because we have not yet introduced the C++ cast operators, and the syntax of C cast operators is clear.) There is no type safety in this cast. C++ provides cast operators, which are discussed in the following text, some of which will cast in a type-safe way, which becomes important when you use pointers to objects of custom types.

C++ provides integer types of various sizes, as summarized in the following table. These are the five standard integer types. The standard says that an `int` is the natural size of the processor and will have a value between (and including) `INT_MIN` and `INT_MAX` (defined in the `<climits>` header file). The size of the integer type has *at least as much storage as those preceding it in the list*, so an `int` is, at least, as big as a `short int` and a `long long int` types, which is at least as big as a `long int` type. The phrase *at least as big as* is not much use if the types are all the same size, so the `<climits>` header file defines ranges for the other fundamental integer types too. It is implementation-specific how many bytes are needed to store these integer ranges. This table gives the ranges of the fundamental types and the sizes on x86, 32-bit processors:

Type	Range	Size in bytes
signed char	-128 to 127	1
short int	-32768 to 32767	2
int	-2147483648 to 2147483647	4
long int	-2147483648 to 2147483647	4
long long int	-9223372036854775808 to 9223372036854775807	8

In practice, rather than the `short int` type, you will use `short`; for `long int`, you will use `long`; and for `long long int`, you will typically use `long long`. As you can see from this table, the `int` and `long int` types are the same size, but they are still two different types.

Other than the `char` type, by default integer types are signed, that is, they can hold negative as well as positive numbers (for example, a variable of type `short` can have a value between -32,768 and 32,767). You can use the `signed` keyword to explicitly indicate that the type is signed. You can also have unsigned equivalents by using the `unsigned` keyword, which will give you an extra bit, but will also mean that bitwise operators and shift operators will work as you expect. You may find `unsigned` used without a type, in which case it refers to `unsigned int`. Similarly, `signed` used without a type refers to `signed int`.

The `char` type is a separate type to both `unsigned char` and `signed char`. The standard says that every bit in a `char` is used to hold character information, and so it is implementation-dependent as to whether a `char` can be treated as being able to hold negative numbers. If you want a `char` to hold a signed number, you should specifically use `signed char`.

The standard is imprecise about the size of the standard integer types and this may be an issue if you are writing code (for example, accessing data in a file, or a network stream) that contains a stream of bytes. The `<cstdlib>` header file defines named types that will hold specific ranges of data. These types have names which have the number of bits used in the range (although the actual type may require more bits). So, there are types with names such as `int16_t` and `uint16_t`, where the first type is a signed integer that will hold a range of 16-bit values and the second type is an unsigned integer. There are also types declared for 8-, 32-, and 64-bit values.

The following shows the actual sizes of these types determined by the `sizeof` operator on an x86 machine:

```
// #include <cstdint>
using namespace std;              // Values for x86
cout << sizeof(int8_t)  << endl;  // 1
cout << sizeof(int16_t) << endl;  // 2
cout << sizeof(int32_t) << endl;  // 4
cout << sizeof(int64_t) << endl;  // 8
```

In addition, the <cstdlib> header file defines types with names such as int_least16_t and uint_least16_t using the same naming scheme as before, and with versions for 8-, 16-,32-, and 64-bits. The least part of the name means that the type will hold values with at least the specified number of bits, but there could be more. There are also types with names such as int_fast16_t and uint_fast16_t with versions for 8-, 16-, 32-, and 64-bits which are regarded as the fastest types that can hold that number of bits.

Specifying integer literals

To assign a value to an integer variable you provide a number that has no fractional part. The compiler will identify the type with the nearest precision that the number represents and attempt to assign the integer, performing a conversion if necessary.

To explicitly specify that a literal is a long value, you use the l or L suffix. Similarly, for an unsigned long, you use the suffix ul or UL. For long long values, you use ll or LL suffix, and use ull or ULL for unsigned long long. The u (or U) suffix is for unsigned (that is, unsigned int) and you do not need a suffix for int. The following illustrates this, using uppercase suffixes:

```
int i = 3;
signed s = 3;
unsigned int ui = 3U;
long l = 3L;
unsigned long ul = 3UL;
long long ll = 3LL;
unsigned long long ull = 3ULL;
```

Using a 10-based number system to specify a number that is a bitmap is confusing and cumbersome. The bits in a bitmap are the powers of 2, so it makes more sense to use a number system that is a power of 2. C++ allows you to provide numbers in octal (base 8) or hexadecimal (base 16). To provide a literal in an octal you prefix the number with a zero character (0). To provide a literal in a hexadecimal you prefix the number with the 0x character sequence. Octal numbers use the digits 0 through 7, but hexadecimal numbers need 16 digits, which means 0 through 9 and a through f (or A through F), where A is 10 in base 10 and F is 15 in base 10:

```
unsigned long long every_other = 0xAAAAAAAAAAAAAAAA;
unsigned long long each_other  = 0x5555555555555555;
cout << hex << showbase << uppercase;
cout << every_other << endl;
cout << each_other  << endl;
```

In this code, two 64-bit (in Visual C++) integers are assigned bitmap values, with every other bit set to 1. The first variable starts with the bottom bit set, the second variable starts with the bottom bit unset, and the second lowest bit set. Before inserting the numbers, the stream is modified with three manipulators. The first `hex` indicates that integers should be printed on the console as hexadecimals, and `showbase` means that the leading `0x` will be printed. By default, the alphabetic digits (A to F) will be given in lowercase and, to specify that uppercase must be used, you use `uppercase`. Once the stream has been modified, the setting remains until it is changed. To change the stream subsequently to use lowercase for alphabetic hexadecimal digits you insert `nouppercase` into the stream and to print the number without the base, insert the `noshowbase` manipulator. To use octal digits, you insert the `oct` manipulator and to use decimals, insert the `dec` manipulator.

When you specify large numbers like this, it becomes difficult to see if you have specified the right number of digits. You can group together digits using a single quote (`'`):

```
unsigned long long every_other = 0xAAAA'AAAA'AAAA'AAAA;
int billion = 1'000'000'000;
```

The compiler ignores the quote; it is just used as a visual aid. In the first example, the quote groups the digits into two byte groups; in the second case the quote groups a decimal number in thousands and millions.

Using bitset to show bit patterns

There is no manipulator to tell the `cout` object to print an integer as a bitmap, but you can simulate the behavior using a `bitset` object:

```
// #include <bitset>
unsigned long long every_other = 0xAAAAAAAAAAAAAAAA;
unsigned long long each_other  = 0x5555555555555555;
bitset<64> bs_every(every_other);
bitset<64> bs_each(each_other);
cout << bs_every << endl;
cout << bs_each << endl;
```

The result is:

```
1010101010101010101010101010101010101010101010101010101010101010
0101010101010101010101010101010101010101010101010101010101010101
```

Here the `bitset` class is **parameterized,** which means that you provide a parameter through the angle brackets (`<>`) and in this case, 64 is used, indicating that the `bitset` object will accommodate 64-bits. In both cases, the initialization of the `bitset` object is carried out using a syntax that looks like a function call (in fact, it does call a function called a **constructor**) and this is the preferred way to initialize an object. Inserting the `bitset` object into the stream, prints out each bit starting with the highest bit. (The reason for this is that there is an `operator <<` function defined, which takes a `bitset` object, as is the case for most of the standard library classes).

The `bitset` class is useful for accessing and setting individual bits as an alternative to using bitwise operators:

```
bs_every.set(0);
every_other = bs_every.to_ullong();
cout << bs_every << endl;
cout << every_other << endl;
```

The `set` function will set the bit in the specified position to a value of 1. The `to_ullong` function will return a `long long` number that the `bitset` represents.

The call to the `set` function and the assignment has the same result as the following:

```
every_other |= 0x0000000000000001;
```

Determining integer byte order

The order of bytes in an integer is implementation-dependent; it depends on how the processor handles integers. In most cases, you do not need to know. However, if you are reading bytes from a file in binary mode, or bytes from a network stream, and you need to interpret two or more bytes as parts of an integer, you will need to know what order they are in, and if necessary convert them to the order recognized by the processor.

The C network library (on Windows, it is called the **Winsock** library) contains a collection of functions that convert `unsigned short` and `unsigned long` types from the network order to the host order (that is, the order used by the processor on the current machine) and vice versa. The network order is big endian. **Big endian** means that the first byte will be the highest byte in the integer, whereas **little endian** means that the first byte is the smallest byte. When you transmit an integer to another machine you first convert from the order used by the processor of the source machine (the host order) to the network order and the receiving machine converts the integer from network order to the host order of the receiving machine before using the data.

The functions to change the byte order are `ntohs` and `ntohl`; for converting `unsigned short` and `unsigned long` from the network order to the host order and `htons` and `htonl` for the conversion from the host order to the network order. Knowing the byte order will be important when you view memory when you are debugging code (for example, as in `Chapter 10`, *Diagnostics and Debugging*).

It is easy to write code to reverse the byte order:

```
unsigned short reverse(unsigned short us)
{
    return ((us & 0xff) << 8) | ((us & 0xff00) >> 8);
}
```

This uses bitwise operators to separate the two bytes that are assumed to make up the `unsigned short` into the lower byte, which is shifted eight bits left, and the upper byte that is shifted eight bits right and these two numbers are recombined as an `unsigned short` using the bitwise OR operator, `|`. It is simple to write versions of this function for 4-byte and 8-byte integers.

Floating point types

There are three basic floating point types:

- `float` (single precision)
- `double` (double precision)
- `long double` (extended precision)

All of these are signed. The actual format of the number in memory, and the number of bytes used, is specific to the C++ implementation, but the `<cfloat>` header file gives the ranges. The following table gives the positive ranges and number of bytes used on x86, 32-bit processors:

Type	Range	Size in bytes
float	1.175494351e-38 to 3.402823466e+38	4
double	2.2250738585072014e-308 to 1.7976931348623158e+308	8
long double	2.2250738585072014e-308 to 1.7976931348623158e+308	8

As you can see, in Visual C++ `double` and `long double` have the same ranges, but they are still two distinct types.

Specifying floating point literals

A literal used to initialize a `double` is specified as a floating point by using either the scientific format, or simply by providing a decimal point:

```
double one = 1.0;
double two = 2.;
double one_million = 1e6;
```

The first example indicates that the variable `one` is assigned to a floating-point value of 1.0. The trailing zero is not important, as shown in the second variable, `two`; however, the trailing zero does make the code more readable since the period is easy to overlook. The third example uses scientific notation. The first part is the mantissa and can be signed and the part after the `e` is the exponent. The exponent is the power-of-10 magnitude of the number (which can be negative). The variable is assigned to a value of the mantissa multiplied by 10 and raised to the exponent. Although it is not recommended, you can write the following:

```
double one = 0.0001e4;
double one_billion = 1000e6;
```

The compiler will interpret the numbers appropriately. The first example is perverse, but the second makes some sense; it shows in your code that a billion is a thousand million.

These examples assign double precision floating point values to `double` variables. To specify a value for single precision variables so that you can assign a `float` variable, use the `f` (or `F`) suffix. Similarly, for a `long double` literal use the `l` (or `L`) suffix:

```
float one = 1.f;
float two = 2f; // error
long double one_million = 1e6L;
```

If you use these suffixes, you still have to provide the number in the right format. A literal of `2f` is incorrect; you have to provide a decimal point, `2.f`. When you specify floating point numbers with a large number of digits you can use the single quote (`'`) to group digits. As stated before, this is just a visual aid to the programmer:

```
double one_billion = 1'000'000'000.;
```

Characters and strings

The `string` class and C string functions will be covered in `Chapter 9`, *Using String*; this section covers the basic use of character variables in your code.

Character types

The `char` type is an integer, so `signed char` and `unsigned char` exist too. These are three distinct types; the `signed char` and `unsigned char` types should be treated as numeric types. The `char` type is used to hold a single character in the implementation's character set. In Visual C++, this is an eight-bit integer that can hold characters from the ISO-8859 or UTF-8 character set. These character sets are able to represent the characters used in English and most European languages. Characters from other languages take up more than one byte and C++ provides the `char16_t` type to hold 16-bit characters and `char32_t` to hold 32-bit characters.

There is also a type called `wchar_t` (wide character) that will be able to hold characters from the largest extended character set. In general, when you see a C Runtime Library or C++ Standard Library function with a `w` prefix, it will use wide character strings rather than `char` strings. So, the `cout` object will allow you to insert `char` strings and the `wcout` object will allow you to insert wide character strings.

The C++ standard says that every bit in a `char` is used to hold character information, and so it is implementation-dependent as to whether a `char` can be treated as being able to hold negative numbers. The following illustrates this:

```
char c = '~';
cout << c << " " << (signed short)c << endl;
c += 2;
cout << c << " " << (signed short)c << endl;
```

The range of a `signed char` is -128 to 127, but this code uses the separate type `char` and attempts to use it in the same way. The variable `c` is first assigned to the ASCII character ~ (126). When you insert a character into an output stream it will attempt to print a character rather than a number, so the next line prints this character to the console, to get the numeric value the code converts the variable to a `signed short` integer. (Again, a C cast is used for clarity.) Next, the variable is incremented by two, that is, the character is two characters further in the character set, which means the first character in the extended ASCII character set; the result is this:

```
~ 126
C -128
```

The first character in the extended character set is C-cedilla.

It is rather counter-intuitive that a value of 126 incremented by two results is a value of -128, and this comes about from overflow calculations with signed types. Even if this is intentional, it is best to avoid doing this.

In Visual C++, the C-cedilla character is treated as -128 so you can write the following to have the same effect:

```
char c = -128;
```

This is implementation-specific, so for portable code you should not rely upon it.

Using character macros

The `<cctype>` header contains various macros that you can use to examine the type of character a `char` holds. These are the C runtime macros declared in `<ctype.h>`. Some of the more useful macros to test character values are explained in the following table. Bear in mind that, since these are C routines, they will not return `bool` values; instead they return an `int` with a value of non-zero for `true` and zero for `false`.

Macro	Tests if the character is:
isalnum	An alphanumeric character, A to Z, a to z, 0 to 9
isalpha	An alphabetic character, A to Z, a to z
isascii	An ASCII character, 0x00 to 0x7f
isblank	A space or horizontal tab
iscntrl	A control character, 0x00 to 0x1f or 0x7f
isdigit	A decimal digit 0 to 9
isgraph	A printable character other than space, 0x21 to 0x7e
islower	A lowercase character, a to z
isprint	A printable character, 0x20 to 0x7e
ispunct	A punctuation character, ! " # $ % & ' ( ) * + , - . / : ; < = > ? @ [ ] ^ _ ` { | } ~ \
isspace	A space
isupper	An uppercase character, A to Z
isxdigit	A hexadecimal digit, 0 to 9, a to f, A to F

For example, the following code loops while reading in a single character from the input stream (after each character, you need to press the *Enter* key). The loop finishes when a non-numeric value is provided:

```
char c;
do
{
    cin >> c
} while(isdigit(c));
```

There are also macros to change characters. Again, these will return an int value, which you should convert to a char.

Macro	Returns
toupper	The uppercase version of the character
tolower	The lowercase version of the character

In the following code, the character typed at the console is echoed back until the user types q or Q. If the character typed is a lowercase character, the echoed character is converted to uppercase:

```
char c;
do
{
    cin >> c;
    if (islower(c)) c = toupper(c);
    cout << c << endl;
} while (c != 'Q');
```

Specifying character literals

You can initialize a char variable with literal characters. This will be a character from the supported character set. The ASCII character set includes some unprintable characters, and so that you can use these, C++ provides two character sequences using the backslash character (\).

Name	ASCII name	C++ sequence
Newline	LF	\n
Horizontal tab	HT	\t
Vertical tab	VT	\v

Backspace	BS	\b
Carriage return	CR	\r
Form feed	FF	\f
Alert	BEL	\a
Backslash	\	\\
Question mark	?	\?
Single quote	'	\'
Double quote	"	\"

In addition, you can give the numeric value of that character as an octal or hexadecimal number. To provide an octal number you give the number as three characters (prefixed with one or two 0 characters if necessary) prefixed with a backslash. For a hexadecimal number, you prefix it with \x. The character M, is the character number 77 in decimal, 115 in octal, and 4d in hexadecimal, so you can initialize a character variable with an M character in three ways:

```
char m1 = 'M';
char m2 = '\115';
char m3 = '\x4d';
```

For completeness, it is worth pointing out that you can initialize a char as an integer, so the following will also initialize each variable to an M character:

```
char m4 = 0115; // octal
char m5 = 0x4d; // hexadecimal
```

All of these methods are valid.

Specifying string literals

Strings are made up of one or more characters, and you can use the escaped characters in string literals too:

```
cout << "This is \x43\x2b\05\3n";
```

This rather unreadable string will be printed on the console as `This is C++` followed by a newline. The capital C is 43 in hexadecimal and the + symbol is 2b in hexadecimal and 53 in octal. The `\n` character is a newline. Escaped characters are useful for printing characters that are not in the character set your C++ compiler uses and for some unprintable characters (for example, `\t` to insert a horizontal tab). The `cout` object buffers the characters before writing them to the output stream. If you use `\n` as a newline it is treated like any other character in the buffer. The `endl` manipulator will insert `\n` into the buffer and then flush it so the characters are immediately written to the console.

The *empty*, or NULL character, is a `\0`. This is an important character because it is unprintable, and it has no use other than to mark the end of a sequence of characters in a string. The empty string is `""`, but since strings are delimited by the NULL character the memory taken up by a string variable initialized with the empty string will have one character, that is `\0`.

The newline character allows you to put a newline within a string. This is useful if the only formatting you'll do is with paragraphs and you are printing short paragraphs:

```
cout << "Mary had a little lamb,n its fleece was white as snow."
     << endl;
```

This prints two lines on the console:

```
Mary had a little lamb,
its fleece was white as snow.
```

However, you may want to initialize a string with a long sequence of characters and the limitations of the editor you are using may mean you want to split the string over several lines. You do this by putting each fragment of the string within double quotes:

```
cout << "And everywhere that Mary went, "
        "the lamb was sure to go."
     << endl;
```

You will see the following on the console:

```
And everywhere that Mary went, the lamb was sure to go.
```

There is no newline printed other than the one explicitly requested at the end with `endl`. This syntax allows you to make long strings more readable in your code; you can, of course, use the newline characters `\n`, in such strings.

Unicode literals

A `wchar_t` variable can also be initialized with a character and the compiler will promote the character to a wide character essentially by using the character's byte and assigning the remaining (higher) bytes to zero. However, it makes more sense to assign such a variable with a wide character, and you do this using the `L` prefix.

```
wchar_t dollar = L'$';
wchar_t euro = L'\u20a0';
wcout << dollar;
```

Notice that, rather than using the `cout` object, this code uses `wcout`, the wide character version. The syntax of using the `\u` prefix within the quotes indicates that the following character is a Unicode character.

Bear in mind that, to show the Unicode character, you need to use a console that will show Unicode characters and, by default, the Windows console is set to **Code Page 850** which will not show Unicode characters. You can change the mode of the output console by calling `_setmode` (defined in `<io.h>`) on the standard output stream, `stdout`, specifying the UTF-16 file mode (using `_O_U16TEXT` defined in `<fcntl.h>`):

```
_setmode(_fileno(stdout), _O_U16TEXT);
```

You can find a list of all of the characters supported by Unicode at `http://unicode.org/charts/`.

UTF-16 characters can also be assigned to `char16_t` variables, and UTF-32 characters can be assigned to `char32_t` variables.

Raw strings

When you use a raw string literal you essentially switch off the meaning of escape characters. Whatever you type into a raw string becomes its content, even if you use whitespace including newlines. The raw string is delimited with `R"(` and `)"`. That is, the string is between the inner parentheses.

```
cout << R"(newline is \n in C++ and "quoted text" use quotes)";
```

Note that, the `()` is part of the syntax and is not part of the string. The preceding code prints the following to the console:

```
newline is \n in C++ and "quoted text" use quotes
```

Normally in a string \n is an escaped character and will be translated as a newline, but in a raw string it is not translated and is printed as two characters.

In a normal C++ string, you will have to escape some of the characters; for example, the double quote will have to be escaped to \" and the backslash escaped to \\. The following will give the same result without using a raw string:

```
cout << "newline is \\n in C++ and \"quoted text\" use quotes";
```

You can also have newlines in raw strings:

```
cout << R"(Mary had a little lamb,
               its fleece was white as snow)"
cout << endl;
```

In this code, the newline after the comma will be printed to the console. Unfortunately, all whitespace will be printed on the console, so assuming that in the preceding code the indentation is three spaces and the cout is indented once, you will see the following on the console:

```
Mary had a little lamb,
               its fleece was white as snow
```

There are 14 spaces in front of its because there were 14 spaces in front of its in the source code. For this reason, you should be wary about using raw strings.

Perhaps, the best use for raw strings is to initialize variables with file paths on Windows. The folder separation character in Windows is a backslash, which means that for a literal string that represents a file path you will have to escape each of these separators; thus, the string will have a lot of double backslashes, with the possibility of missing one. With raw strings this escaping is not necessary. The two string variables in the following represent the same string:

```
string path1 = "C:\\Beginning_C++\\Chapter_03\\readme.txt";
string path2 = R"(C:\Beginning_C++\Chapter_03\readme.txt)";
```

These two strings have the same contents, but the second one is more readable since the C++ literal string does not have escaped backslashes.

The requirement for escaping backslashes is only needed for literal strings declared in your code; it is an indication to the compiler of how to interpret the character. If you obtain a file path from a function (or via argv[0]), the separator will be backslashes.

String byte order

Extended character sets use more than one byte per character. If such characters are stored in a file, the order of the bytes becomes important. In this situation, the writer of the character must use the same order that will be used by potential readers.

One way to do this is to use a **Byte Order Mark** (**BOM**). This is a known number of bytes with a known pattern, and is typically placed as the first item in a stream so that the reader of the stream can use it to determine the byte order of the remaining characters in the stream. Unicode defines the 16-bit character, \uFEFF, and the non-character, \uFFFE, as byte order marks. In the case of \uFEFF, all bits are set except for bit 8 (if the lowest bit is labeled as bit 0). This BOM can be prefixed to data that is passed between machines. The destination machine can read the BOM into a 16-bit variable and test the bits. If bit 8 is zero it means the two machines have the same byte order and so the characters can be read as two byte values in the order in the stream. If bit 0 is zero then it means that the destination machine reads 16-bit variables in the opposite order to the source, and so action must be taken to ensure that, with 16-bit characters, the bytes are read in the right order.

The Unicode byte order mark (BOM) is serialized as follows (in hexadecimal):

Character set	Byte order mark
UTF-8	EF BB BF
UTF-16 big endian	FE FF
UTF-16 little endian	FF FE
UTF-32 big endian	00 00 FE FF
UTF-32 little endian	FF FE 00 00

Bear this in mind that, when you read data from a file. The character sequence, FE FF, will be very rare in a non-Unicode file, and so if you read these as the first two bytes in a file it means that the file is Unicode. Since \uFEFF and \uFFFE are not printable Unicode characters, it means that a file that starts with either of these has a byte order mark, and you can then use the BOM to determine how to interpret the remaining bytes in the file.

Boolean

The `bool` type holds a Boolean value, that is, just one of two values: `true` or `false`. C++ allows you to treat 0 (zero) as being `false` and anything non-zero as being `true` but this can lead to mistakes, so it is better to get in to the habit of explicitly checking values:

```
int use_pointer(int *p)
{
    if (p)              { /* not a null pointer */ }
    if (p != nullptr) { /* not a null pointer */ }
    return 0;
}
```

The second of these two is preferable, since it is clearer what you are comparing.
Note that, even if a pointer is not a `nullptr`, it still may not be a valid pointer, but it is common practice to assign a pointer to `nullptr` to convey some other meaning, perhaps to say that the pointer operation is not appropriate.

You can insert Boolean values into an output stream. However, the default behavior is to treat a Boolean as an integer. If you want `cout` to output `bool` values with string names, then insert the manipulator `boolalpha` in to the stream; this will make the stream print `true` or `false` to the console. The default behavior can be achieved by using the `noboolalpha` manipulator.

void

In some cases, you need to indicate that a function does not have parameters or will not return a value; in both cases, you can use the keyword `void`:

```
void print_message(void)
{
    cout << "no inputs, no return value" << endl;
}
```

The use of `void` in the parameter list is optional; an empty pair of parentheses is acceptable and is preferable. This is the only way to indicate that a function returns no value other than returning `void`.

Note that `void` is not really a type because you cannot create a `void` variable; it is the absence of a type. As you'll find out in the next chapter, you can create pointers of the type `void`, but you will not be able to use the memory that such pointers point to without casting to a typed pointer: to use the memory you have to decide the type of the data that the memory holds.

Initializers

Initializers were touched upon in the last chapter, but we will go into more depth here. For built-in types, you must initialize a variable before you use it. For custom types, it is possible for the type to define a default value, but there are some issues in doing this, which will be covered in `Chapter 6`, *Classes*.

In all versions of C++, there are three ways to initialize a built-in type: assignment, function syntax, or calling a constructor. In C++11 another way to initialize variables was introduced: construction through a list initializer. These four ways are shown here:

```
int i = 1;
int j = int(2);
int k(3);
int m{4};
```

The first of these three is the clearest; it shows, using an easy to understand syntax, that the variable is being initialized to a value. The second example initializes a variable by calling the type as if it is a function. The third example calls the constructor of the `int` type. This is a typical way to initialize custom types, so it is best to reserve this syntax just for custom types.

The fourth syntax is new to C++11 and initializes the variable using an initialize list between curly braces (`{ }`). Just to confuse things slightly, you can also initialize a built-in type using the same syntax as an assignment to a single item list:

```
int n = { 5 };
```

This is really confusing things, the type `n` is an integer, not an array. Recall that, in the last chapter, we created an array with the birth dates of The Beatles:

```
int birth_years[] = { 1940, 1942, 1943, 1940 };
```

This creates an array of four integers; the type of each item is `int` but the type of the array variable is `int *`. The variable points to memory that holds four integers. Similarly, you can also initialize a variable to be an array of one item:

```
int john[] = { 1940 };
```

This is exactly the same initialization code that C++11 allows to initialize a single integer. In addition, the same syntax is used to initialize instances of record types (`structs`), adding another level of potential confusion about what the syntax means.

It is best to avoid using the curly brace syntax for variable initialization and use it exclusively for initializing lists. However, there are advantages to this syntax for casting, as explained shortly.

The curly brace syntax can be used to provide the initial values for any of the collection classes in the C++ Standard Library, as well as for C++ arrays. Even when used to initialize a collection object, there is a potential for confusion. For example, consider the `vector` collection class. This can hold a collection of the type provided through a pair of angled brackets (<>). The capacity of an object of this class can grow as you add more items to the object, but you can optimize its use by specifying an initial capacity:

```
vector<int> a1 (42);
cout << " size " << a1.size() << endl;
for (int i : a1) cout << i << endl;
```

The first line of this code says: create a `vector` object that can hold integers and start by reserving space for 42 integers, each initialized to a value of zero. The second line prints the size of the vector to the console (42) and the third line prints all the items in the array to the console and it will print 42 zeros.

Now consider the following:

```
vector<int> a2 {42};
cout << " size " << a2.size() << endl;
for (int i : a2) cout << i << endl;
```

There is only one change here: the parentheses have been changed to braces but it means that the initialization has been changed entirely. The first line now means: create a `vector` that can hold integers and initialize it with the single integer, 42. The size of a2 is 1 and the last line will print just one value, 42.

The great power of C++ is that it should be easy to write correct code, and to persuade the compiler to help you to avoid mistakes. The use of braces for single item initialization increases the possibility of hard-to-find errors.

Default values

Variables of built-in types should be initialized before you first use them, but there are some situations when the compiler will provide a default value.

If you declare a variable at file scope, or globally in your project, and you do not give it an initial value, the compiler will give it a default value. For example:

```
int outside;

int main()
{
    outside++;
    cout << outside << endl;
}
```

This code will compile and run, printing a value of 1; the compiler has initialized outside to 0, which is then incremented to 1. The following code will not compile:

```
int main()
{
    int inside;
    inside++;
    cout << inside << endl;
}
```

The compiler will complain that the increment operator is being used on an uninitialized variable.

In the last chapter, we saw another example of the compiler providing a default value: static.

```
int counter()
{
    static int count;
    return ++count;
}
```

This is a simple function that maintains a count. The variable count is marked with the static storage class modifier, meaning that the variable has the same lifetime as the application (allocated when the code starts and deallocated when the program ends); however, it has internal linkage, meaning the variable can only be used within the scope of where it is declared, the counter function. The compiler will initialize the count variable with a default value of zero, so that the first time the counter function is called it will return a value of 1.

The new initialize list syntax of C++11 provides a way for you to declare a variable and specify that you want it initialized by the compiler to the default value for that type:

```
int a {};
```

Of course, when reading this code, you have to know what the default value for an int is (it is zero). Again, it is much easier and more explicit to simply initialize the variable to a value:

```
int a = 0;
```

The rules for default values are simple: a value of zero. Integers and floating point numbers have a default value of 0, for a character the default value is \0, for a bool it is false, and for a pointer the default is the constant, nullptr.

Declarations without a type

C++11 introduces a mechanism for declaring that a variable's type should be determined from the data it is initialized with, that is, auto.

There is a minor confusion here because prior to C++11, the auto key was used to declare **automatic** variables, that is, variables that are automatically allocated on the stack in a function. Other than variables declared at file scope or as static, all the other variables in this book so far have been automatic variables and automatic variables are the most widely used **storage class** (explained shortly). Since it was optional and applicable to most variables, the auto keyword was rarely used in C++, so C++11 took advantage of this, removed the old meaning, and gave auto a new meaning.

If you are compiling old C++ code with a C++11 compiler and that old code uses auto, you will get errors because the new compiler will assume auto will be used with variables with no specified type. If this happens, simply search and delete each instance of auto; it was redundant in C++ prior to C++11, and there was little reason for a developer to use it.

The auto keyword means that the compiler should create a variable with the type of the data that is assigned to it. The variable can only have a single type, the type the compiler decides is the type it needs for the data assigned to it, and you cannot use the variable elsewhere to hold data of a different type. Because the compiler needs to determine the type from an initializer, it means that all auto variables must be initialized:

```
auto i  = 42;      // int
auto l  = 421;     // long
auto ll = 4211;    // long long
auto f  = 1.0f;    // float
auto d  = 1.0;     // double
auto c  = 'q';     // char
auto b  = true;    // bool
```

Note that there is no syntax to specify that an integer value is a single byte or two bytes, so you cannot create `unsigned char` variables or `short` variables this way.

This is a trivial use of the `auto` keyword and you should not use it this way. The power of auto is when you use containers that can result in some fairly complicated looking types:

```
// #include <string>
// #include <vector>
// #include <tuple>

vector<tuple<string, int> > beatles;
beatles.push_back(make_tuple("John", 1940));
beatles.push_back(make_tuple("Paul", 1942));
beatles.push_back(make_tuple("George", 1943));
beatles.push_back(make_tuple("Ringo", 1940));

for (tuple<string, int> musician : beatles)
{
    cout << get<0>(musician) << " " << get<1>(musician) << endl;
}
```

This code uses the `vector` container we have used before, but it stores two value items using a `tuple`. The `tuple` class is simple; you declare a list of the types of items in the `tuple` object in the declaration between the angle brackets. So, the `tuple<string, int>` declaration says that the object will hold a string and an integer, in that order. The `make_tuple` function is provided by the C++ Standard Library and will create a `tuple` object containing the two values. The `push_back` function will put the item into the vector container. After the four calls to the `push_back` function, the `beatles` variable will contain four items and each one is a `tuple` with a name and birth year.

The range `for` loops through the container and on each loop assigns the `musician` variable with the next item in the container. The values in the `tuple` are printed to the console in the statements in the `for` loop. An item in the `tuple` is accessed using the `get` parameterized function (from `<tuple>`) where the parameter in the angle brackets indicates the index of the item (indexed from zero) to get from the `tuple` object passed as a parameter in the parentheses. In this example, the call to `get<0>` gets the name which is printed out, then a space, and then `get<1>` gets the year item in the `tuple`. The result of this code is:

```
John 1940
Paul 1942
George 1943
Ringo 1940
```

This text has poor formatting because it does not take into account the length of the names. This can be addressed using manipulators explained in `Chapter 9`, *Using String*.

Take another look at the `for` loop:

```
for (tuple<string, int> musician : beatles)
{
    cout << get<0>(musician) << " " << get<1>(musician) << endl;
}
```

The type of musician is `tuple<string, int>;`, this is a fairly simple type, and as you use the standard template more you could end up with some complicated types (particularly when you use **iterators**). This is where `auto` becomes useful. The following code is the same, but easier to read:

```
for (auto musician : beatles)
{
    cout << get<0>(musician) << " " << get<1>(musician) << endl;
}
```

The musician variable is still typed, it is a `tuple<string, int>`, but `auto` means you do not have to explicitly code this.

Storage classes

When declaring a variable, you can specify its storage class which indicates the lifetime, linkage (what other code can access it), and memory location of the variable.

You have already seen one storage class, `static`, which when applied to a variable in a function means that the variable can only be accessed within that function, but its lifetime is the same as the program. However, `static` can be used on variables declared at file scope, in which case it indicates that the variable can only be used in the current file, which is called **internal linkage**. If you omit the `static` keyword on a variable, defined at file scope, then it has an **external linkage,** which means the name of the variable is visible to code in other files. The `static` keyword can be used on a data member of a class, and on methods defined on a class, both of which have interesting effects that will be described in `Chapter 6`, *Classes*.

The `static` keyword says that the variable can only be used in the current file. The `extern` keyword indicates the opposite; the variable (or function) has external linkage and can be accessed in other files in the project. In most cases, you will define a variable in one source file, and then declare it as `extern` in a header file so that the same variable can be used in other source files.

The final storage class specifier is `thread_local`. This is new to C++11 and it only applies to multithreaded code. This book does not cover threading, so only a brief description will be given here.

A thread is a unit of execution and concurrency. You can have more than one thread running in a program, and it is possible to have two or more threads running the same code at the same time. This means that two different threads of execution could access and alter the same variable. Since concurrent access may have undesirable effects, multithreaded code often involves taking action to ensure that only one thread can access data at any time. If such code is not written carefully there is a danger of deadlocks, where the execution of threads is paused (in the worst cases, indefinitely) for exclusive access to the variable, negating the benefit of using threads.

The `thread_local` storage class indicates that each thread will have its own copy of a variable. So, if two threads access the same function and a variable in that function is marked as `thread_local,` it means that each thread only sees the changes it makes.

You will sometimes see the storage class `register` used in older C++ code. This is now deprecated. It was used as a hint to the compiler that the variable has important consequences on the performance of the program and suggests to the compiler that if possible it should use a CPU register to hold the variable. The compiler could ignore this suggestion. In fact, in C++11 the compiler literally does ignore the keyword; code with `register` variables will compile with no errors or warnings and the compiler will optimize the code however it feels is necessary.

Although it is not a storage class specifier, the `volatile` keyword has an effect on compiler code optimization. The `volatile` keyword indicates that a variable (perhaps through **Direct Memory Access** (**DMA**) to some hardware) can be altered by an external action, and so it is important that the compiler *does not* apply any optimizations.

There is one other storage class modifier called `mutable`. This can only be used on class members and so it will be covered in `Chapter 6`, *Classes*.

Using type aliases

Sometimes the names of types can become quite cumbersome. If you use nested namespaces, the name of a type includes all of the namespaces used. If you define parameterized types (examples used so far in this chapter are vector and tuple), the parameters increase the name of the type. For example, earlier we saw a container for the names and birth years of musicians:

```
// #include <string>
// #include <vector>
// #include <tuple>

vector<tuple<string, int> > beatles;
```

Here, the container is a vector and it holds items that are tuple items, each of which will hold a string and an integer. To make the type easier to use you could define a preprocessor symbol:

```
#define name_year tuple<string, int>
```

Now you can use name_year instead of the tuple in your code, and the preprocessor will replace the symbol with the type before the code is compiled:

```
vector<name_year> beatles;
```

However, because #define is a simple search and replace, there can be problems as explained earlier in this book. C++ provides the typedef statement to create an alias for a type:

```
typedef tuple<string, int> name_year_t;
vector<name_year_t> beatles;
```

Here, an alias called name_year_t is created for tuple<string, int>.

With a typedef, the alias usually comes at the end of the line preceded by the type it aliases. This is the opposite order to #define, where the symbol you are defining comes after #define, followed by its definition. Note also typedef is terminated with a semicolon. It becomes much more complicated with function pointers, as you'll see in Chapter 5, *Using Functions*.

Now, wherever you want use the `tuple`, you can use the alias:

```
for (name_year_t musician : beatles)
{
    cout << get<0>(musician) << " " << get<1>(musician) << endl;
}
```

You can `typedef` aliases:

```
typedef tuple<string, int> name_year_t;
typedef vector<name_year_t> musician_collection_t;
musician_collection_t beatles2;
```

The type of the `beatles2` variable is `vector<tuple<string, int>>`. It is important to note that `typedef` creates an alias; it does not create a new type, so you can switch between the original type and its alias.

The `typedef` keyword is a well-established way to create aliases in C++.

C++11 introduces another way to create a type alias, the `using` statement:

```
using name_year = tuple<string, int>;
```

Again, this does not create a new type, it creates a new name for the same type, and semantically, this is the same as `typedef`. The `using` syntax can be more readable than using a `typedef` and it also allows you to use templates.

The `using` method of creating an alias is more readable than `typedef` because the use of the assignment follows the convention used for variables, that is, the new name on the left is used for the type on the right of the =.

Aggregating data in record types

Often you will have data that is related and must be used together: an aggregated type. Such a record type allows you to encapsulate data into a single variable. C++ inherits from C `struct` and `union`, as ways of providing records.

Structures

In most applications, you will want to associate several data items together. For example, you may want to define a time record that has an integer for each of the following: the hour, the minute, and the second of the specified time. You can declare them like this:

```
// start work
int start_sec = 0;
int start_min = 30;
int start_hour = 8;

// end work
int end_sec = 0
int end_min = 0;
int end_hour = 17;
```

This approach becomes quite cumbersome and error-prone. There is no encapsulation, that is, the _min variables can be used in isolation to the other variables. Does the *minutes past the hour* make sense when it is used without the hour that it refers to? You can define a structure that associates these items:

```
struct time_of_day
{
    int sec;
    int min;
    int hour;
};
```

Now you have the three values as part of one record, which means that you can declare variables of this type; although you can access individual items it is clear that the data is associated with the other members:

```
time_of_day start_work;
start_work.sec = 0;
start_work.min = 30;
start_work.hour = 8;

time_of_day end_work;
end_work.sec = 0;
end_work.min = 0;
end_work.hour = 17;

print_time(start_work);
print_time(end_work);
```

Now we have two variables: one that represents the start time, and the other that represents the end time. The members of a `struct` are encapsulated within the `struct`, that is, you access the member through the instance of the `struct`. To do this, you use the dot operator. In this code, `start_work.sec` means that you are accessing the `sec` member of the instance of the `time_of_day` structure called `start_work`. The members of a structure are `public` by default, that is, code outside the `struct` has access to the members.

> Classes and structures can indicate the level of member access, and `Chapter 6`, *Classes*, will show how to do this. For example, it is possible to mark some members of a `struct` as `private`, which means that only code that is a member of the type can access the member.

A helper function called `print_time` is called to print the data to the console:

```
void print_time(time_of_day time)
{
    cout << setw(2) << setfill('0') << time.hour << ":";
    cout << setw(2) << setfill('0') << time.min << ":";
    cout << setw(2) << setfill('0') << time.sec << endl;
}
```

In this case, the `setw` and `setfill` manipulators are used to set the width of the next inserted item to two characters and to fill any unfilled places with zeros (more details will be given in `Chapter 9`, *Using String*; in effect, `setw` gives the size of the column occupied by the next inserted data, and `setfill` specifies the padding character used).

`Chapter 5`, *Using Functions*, will go into more detail about the mechanism of passing structures to functions and the most efficient way to do it, but for the purpose of this section we will use the simplest syntax here. The important point is that the caller has associated the three items of data together using a `struct` and all the items can be passed to a function as a unit.

Initializing

There are several ways to initialize an instance of a structure. The preceding code shows one method: accessing the member using the dot operator, and assigning it a value. You can also assign values to an instance of a `struct` through a specially provided function called a constructor. Since there are special rules about how to name a constructor and what you can do in them, this will be left until `Chapter 6`, *Classes*.

You can also initialize structures using the list initializer syntax using curly braces ({ }). The items in the braces should match the members of the `struct` in the order of the members as declared. If you provide fewer values than there are members, the remaining members are initialized to zero. Indeed, if you provide no items between the curly braces then all members are set to zero. It is an error to provide more initializers than there are members. So, use the `time_of_day` record type defined previously:

```
time_of_day lunch {0, 0, 13};
time_of_day midnight {};
time_of_day midnight_30 {0, 30};
```

In the first example, the `lunch` variable is initialized to 1 PM. Notice that, because the `hour` member is declared as the third member in the type, it is initialized using the third item in the initialize list. In the second example, all members are set to zero, and of course, zero hours is midnight. The third example provides two values, so these are used to initialize `sec` and `min`.

You can have a member of a `struct` that is a `struct` itself, and this is initialized using nested braces:

```
struct working_hours
{
    time_of_day start_work;
    time_of_day end_work;
};

working_hours weekday{ {0, 30, 8}, {0, 0, 17} };
cout << "weekday:" << endl;
print_time(weekday.start_work);
print_time(weekday.end_work);
```

Structure fields

A structure can have members that are as small as a single bit, called a **bit-field**. In this case, you declare an integer member with the number of bits that the member will take up. You are able to declare unnamed members. For example, you may have a structure that holds information about the length of an item, and whether the item has been changed (is dirty). The item this refers to has a maximum size of 1,023, so you need an integer with at least 10 bits of width to hold this. You could use an `unsigned short` to hold both the length and the dirty information:

```
void print_item_data(unsigned short item)
{
    unsigned short size = (item & 0x3ff);
    char *dirty = (item > 0x7fff) ? "yes" : "no";
```

```
        cout << "length " << size << ", ";
        cout << "is dirty: " << dirty << endl;
    }
```

This code separates the two pieces of information, and then prints them out. A bitmap like this is quite unfriendly to code. You can use a `struct` to hold this information using an `unsigned short` to hold the 10 bits of length information and a `bool` to hold the dirty information. Using bit fields you can define the structure like this:

```
    struct item_length
    {
        unsigned short len : 10;
        unsigned short : 5;
        bool dirty : 1;
    };
```

The `len` member is marked as `unsigned short` but only 10 bits are needed, so this is mentioned using the colon syntax. Similarly, a Boolean yes/no value can be held in just one bit. The structure indicates that there are five bits between the two values that are not used, and so have no name.

Fields are simply a convenience. Although it looks like the `item_length` structure should only take up 16 bits (`unsigned short`), there is no guarantee that the compiler will do this. If you receive an `unsigned short` from a file or network stream you will have to extract the bits yourself:

```
    unsigned short us = get_length();
    item_length slen;
    slen.len = us & 0x3ff;
    slen.dirty = us > 0x7fff;
```

Using structure names

In some cases, you may need to use a type before you have actually defined it. As long as you do not use the members, you can declare a type before defining it:

```
    struct time_of_day;
    void print_day(time_of_day time);
```

This could be declared in a header, where it says that there is a function defined somewhere else that takes a `time_of_day` record and prints it out. To be able to declare the `print_day` function, you have to have declared the `time_of_day` name. The `time_of_day` struct must be defined somewhere else in your code before the function is defined, otherwise you will get an *undefined type* error.

There is, however, an exception: a type can hold pointers to instances of the same type before the type is fully declared. This is because the compiler knows the size of a pointer, so it can allocate sufficient memory for the member. It is not until the entire type has been defined before you can create an instance of the type. The classic example of this is a linked list, but since this requires using pointers and dynamic allocation, that will be left to the next chapter.

Determining alignment

One of the uses of structs is that if you know how data is held in memory you can deal with a struct as a block of memory. This is useful if you have a hardware device that is mapped into memory, where different memory locations refer to values controlling or returning values from the device. One way to access the device would be to define a struct that matches the memory layout of the device's direct memory access to C++ types. Further, structs are also useful for files, or for packets of data that need to be transmitted over the network: you manipulate the struct and then copy the memory occupied by the struct to the file or to the network stream.

The members of the struct are arranged in memory in the order that they are declared in the type. The items will take up *at least* as much memory as each type requires. A member may take more memory than the type requires, and the reason for this is a mechanism called **alignment**.

The compiler will place variables in memory in the way that is the most efficient, in terms of memory usage, or speed of access. The various types will be aligned to alignment boundaries. For example, a 32-bit integer will be aligned to a four-byte boundary, and if the next available memory location is not on this boundary the compiler will skip a few bytes and put the integer at the next alignment boundary. You can test the alignment of a specific type using the `alignof` operator passing the type name:

```
cout << "alignment boundary for int is "  0
    << alignof(int) << endl;                    // 4
cout << "alignment boundary for double is "
    << alignof(double) << endl;                 // 8
```

The alignment of an `int` is 4 and this means that an `int` variable will be placed at the next four-byte boundary in memory. The alignment of a `double` is 8 and this makes sense because in Visual C++ a `double` occupies eight bytes. So far, it looks like the result of `alignof` is the same as `sizeof`; however, this is not so.

```
cout << "alignment boundary for time_of_day is "
    << alignof(time_of_day) << endl;            // 4
```

This example prints the alignment of the `time_of_day` struct, which we previously defined to be three integers. The alignment of this `struct` is 4, that is, the alignment of the largest item in the `struct`. This means that an instance of `time_of_day` will be placed on a 4-byte boundary; it does not say how the items within the `time_of_day` variable will be aligned.

As an example, consider the following `struct`, which has four members that occupy respectively one, two, four, and eight bytes:

```
struct test
{
    uint8_t   uc;
    uint16_t  us;
    uint32_t  ui;
    uint64_t  ull;
}
```

The compiler will tell you that the alignment is 8 (the alignment of the largest item, `ull`), but that the size is 16, which may appear a little odd. If every item were aligned on 8-byte boundaries, then the size would have to be 32 (four times eight). If the items were stored in memory and packed as efficiently possible, then the size would be 15. Instead, what is happening is that the second item is aligned on a two-byte boundary, which means that there is one byte of unused space between `uc` and `us`.

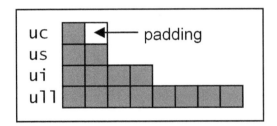

If you want to align the internal items onto, say, the same boundaries as used by a `uint32_t` variable, you can mark an item with `alignas` and give the alignment that you need. Note that, because 8 is bigger than 4, any item aligned on an 8-byte boundary will also be aligned on a 4-byte boundary:

```
struct test
{
    uint8_t   uc;
    alignas(uint32_t)  uint16_t us;
    uint32_t  ui;
    uint64_t  ull;
}
```

The uc item will be aligned on a 4-byte boundary already (alignof(test) will be 8), and it will occupy one byte. The us member is a uint16_t but it is marked with alignas(uint32_t) to say that it should be aligned in the same way as a uint32_t, that is, on a 4-byte boundary. This means that both uc and us will be on 4-byte boundaries with padding provided. Of course, the ui member will also be aligned on a 4-byte boundary because it is a uint32_t.

If the struct has just these first three members, then the size would be 12. However, the struct has another member, the 8-byte ull member. This must be aligned on an 8-byte boundary, which means 16 bytes from the beginning of the struct, and to do this there needs to be 4 bytes of padding between ui and ull. As a consequence, the size of test is now reported as 24: 4 bytes for uc and for us (because the following item ui has to be aligned on the next four-byte boundary), 8 bytes for ull (because it is an 8-byte integer), and 8 bytes for ui because the following item (ull) has to be on the next 8-byte boundary.

The following diagram shows the location in memory of the various members of the test type:

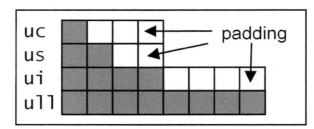

You cannot use alignas to relax alignment requirements, so you cannot mark a uint64_t variable to be aligned on a two-byte boundary that is not also an eight-byte boundary.

In most cases, you will not need to worry about alignment; however, if you are accessing memory-mapped devices, or binary data from files, it is convenient if you can directly map this data to a struct and in this case, you will find that you will have to pay close attention to alignment. This is known as **plain old data** and you will often see structs referred to as **POD types**.

POD is an informal description, and sometimes it is used to describe types that have a simple construction and do not have virtual members (see `Chapter 6`, *Classes* and `Chapter 7`, *Introduction to Object-Oriented Programming*). The standard library provides a function in `<type_traits>` called `is_pod` that tests a type for these members.

Storing data in the same memory with unions

A union is a struct where all the members occupy the same memory. The size of such a type is the size of the largest member. Since a union can only hold one item of data, it is a mechanism to interpret the data in more than one way.

An example of a union is in the `VARIANT` type that is used to pass data between **Object Linking and Embedding (OLE)** objects in Microsoft's **Component Object Model (COM)**. The `VARIANT` type can hold data of any of the data types that COM is able to transmit between OLE objects. Sometimes OLE objects will be in the same process, but it is possible for them to be in different processes on the same machine or on different machines. COM guarantees that it can transmit `VARIANT` without the developer providing any additional networking code. The structure is complicated, but an edited version is shown here:

```
// edited version
struct VARIANT
{
    unsigned short vt;
    union
    {
        unsigned char bVal;
        short iVal;
        long lVal;
        long long llVal;
        float fltVal;
        double dblVal;
    };
};
```

Notice that you can use a union without a name: this is an anonymous `union` and from a member access point of view you access a member of the union as if it is a member of the `VARIANT` that contains it. The `union` contains a member for every type that can be transmitted between OLE objects, and the `vt` member indicates which one is used. When you create a `VARIANT` instance, you have to set `vt` to the appropriate value and then initialize the related member:

```
enum VARENUM
{
    VT_EMPTY = 0,
    VT_NULL = 1,
    VT_UI1 = 17,
    VT_I2 = 2,
    VT_I4 = 3,
    VT_I8 = 20,
    VT_R4 = 4,
    VT_R8 = 5
};
```

This record ensures that only the memory that is needed is used, and the code that transmits the data from one process to another will be able to read the `vt` member to determine how the data needs to be processed so that it can be transmitted:

```
// pseudo code, real VARIANT should not be handled like this
VARIANT var {}; // clear all items
var.vt = VT_I4; // specify the type
var.lVal = 42;  // set the appropriate member
pass_to_object(var);
```

Note that you must be disciplined and only initialize the appropriate member. When your code receives a `VARIANT`, you must read `vt` to see which member you should use to access the data.

In general, when using unions you should access only the item that you initialize:

```
union d_or_i {double d; long long i};
d_or_i test;
test.i = 42;
cout << test.i << endl; // correct use
cout << test.d << endl; // nonsense printed
```

Accessing runtime type information

C++ provides an operator called `typeid` that will return type information about a variable (or a type) at runtime. **Runtime Type Information (RTTI)** is significant when you use custom types that can be used in a **polymorphic** way; details will be left until later chapters. RTTI allows you to check at runtime the type of a variable and process the variable accordingly. RTTI is returned through a `type_info` object (in the `<typeinfo>` header file):

```
cout << "int type name: " << typeid(int).name() << endl;
int i = 42;
cout << "i type name: " << typeid(i).name() << endl;
```

In both cases, you'll see **int** printed as the type. The `type_info` class defines comparison operators (`==` and `!=`) so you can compare types:

```
auto a = i;
if (typeid(a) == typeid(int))
{
    cout << "we can treat a as an int" << endl;
}
```

Determining type limits

The `<limits>` header contains a template class called `numeric_limits` and this is used through the specializations provided for each of the built-in types. The way to use these classes is to provide the type you want information for in the angle brackets and then call the `static` members on the class using the scope resolution operator (`::`). (Full details of `static` functions on classes will be given in `Chapter 6`, *Classes*). The following prints the limits of the `int` type to the console:

```
cout << "The int type can have values between ";
cout << numeric_limits<int>::min() << " and  ";
cout << numeric_limits<int>::max() << endl;
```

Converting between types

Even if you try exceptionally hard to use the correct types in your code, at some point you will find that you will have to convert between types. For example, you may be using library functions that return a value of a particular type, or you may be reading in data from an external source that is a different type to your routine.

With built-in types, there are standard rules about conversion between different types, some of which will be automatic. For example, if you have an expression like a + b, and a and b are different types, then, if it is possible, the compiler will automatically convert one variable's value to the type of the other and the + operator for that type will be called.

In other cases, you may need to force one type to another type so that the right operator is called and this will require a cast of some kind. C++ allows you to use C-like casts, but these do not have runtime tests, so it is far better to use C++ casts, which have various levels of runtime checks and type safety.

Type conversions

Built-in conversions can have one of two outcomes: promotion or narrowing. A promotion is when a smaller type is promoted to a larger type and you will not lose data. A narrowing conversion happens when a value from a larger type is converted to a smaller type with potential loss of data.

Promoting conversions

In a mixed type expression, the compiler will attempt to promote smaller types to the larger type. So, a char or a short can be used in an expression where an int is needed because it can be promoted to the larger type with no loss of data.

Consider a function declared as taking a parameter that is an int:

```
void f(int i);
```

We can write:

```
short s = 42;
f(s); // s is promoted to int
```

Here the variable s is silently converted to an int. There are some cases that may appear odd:

```
bool b = true;
f(b); // b is promoted to int
```

Again, the conversion is silent. The compiler assumes you know what you are doing and that your intention is that you want false treated as 0 and true treated as 1.

Narrowing conversions

In some cases, *narrowing* occurs. Be very careful of this because it loses data. In the following, an attempt is made to convert a `double` into an `int`.

```
int i = 0.0;
```

This is allowed, but the compiler will issue a warning:

> C4244: 'initializing': conversion from 'double' to 'int', possible loss of data

This code is clearly wrong, but the mistake is not an error because it may be intentional. For example, in the following code we have a function that has a parameter that is a floating point, and within the routine the parameter is used to initialize an `int`:

```
void calculation(double d)
{
    // code
    int i = d;

    // use i
    // other code
}
```

This may be intentional, but because there will be a loss of precision you should document why you are doing this. At the very least, use a cast operator so that it is obvious that you understand the consequence of the action.

Narrowing to bool

As mentioned previously, pointers, integers, and floating point values can be implicitly converted to `bool` where a nonzero value converts to `true` and a zero value converts to `false`. This can result in a nasty bug that is difficult to notice:

```
int x = 0;
if (x = 1) cout << "not zero" << endl;
else       cout << "is zero" << endl;
```

Here, the compiler sees the assignment expression x = 1, which is a bug; it should be the comparison x == 1. However, this is valid C++ because the value of the expression is 1 and the compiler, helpfully, converts this to a `bool` value of `true`. This code will compile without even a warning, and not only will it produce a result that is the opposite of what you expect (you'll see `not zero` printed on the console), but also the assignment will have changed the value of the variable propagating the error throughout the program.

It is easy to avoid this bug by getting into the habit of always constructing a comparison so that the rvalue of a potential assignment is on the left. In a comparison, there will be no concept of rvalue or lvalue, so this uses the compiler to catch an assignment when it is not intended:

```
if (1 = x) // error
cout << "not zero" << endl;
```

Converting signed types

Signed to unsigned conversions can happen and can cause unexpected results. For example:

```
int s = -3;
unsigned int u = s;
```

The `unsigned short` variable will be assigned with a value of `0xfffffffd`, that is, the two's compliment of 3. This may be the result you want, but it is an odd way of getting it.

Interestingly, if you try and compare these two variables, the compiler will issue a warning:

```
if (u < s) // C4018
cout << "u is smaller than s" << endl;
```

The Visual C++ warning C4018 given here is `'<': signed/unsigned mismatch`, which says that you cannot compare a signed and unsigned type, and to do so would need a cast.

Casting

In some cases, you will have to convert between types. For example, this may be because the data is provided in a different type to the routines that you use to process it. You may have a library that processes floating point numbers as `float`, but your data is inputted as `double`. You are aware that the conversion will lose precision but know that this will have little effect on the final result so you do not want the compiler warning you. What you want to do is tell the compiler that the coercion of one type to another is acceptable.

The following table summarizes the various cast operations you can use in C++11:

Name	Syntax
Construction	{}
Remove `const` requirement	const_cast
Cast with no runtime checks	static_cast

Bitwise casting of types	`reinterpret_cast`
Cast between class pointers, with runtime checks	`dynamic_cast`
C style	`()`
Function style	`()`

Casting away const-ness

As mentioned in the last chapter, the `const` specifier is used to indicate to the compiler that an item will not change, and that any attempt by your code to change the item is an error. There is another way to use this specifier, which will be explored in the next chapter. When `const` is applied to a pointer, it indicates that the memory that the pointer points to cannot be changed:

```
char *ptr = "0123456";
// possibly lots of code
ptr[3] = '\0'; // RUNTIME ERROR!
```

This badly written code tells the compiler to create a string constant with the value `0123456` and then put the address of this memory into the string pointer `ptr`. The final line attempts to write to the string. This will compile but it will cause an access violation at runtime. Applying `const` to the pointer declaration will ensure that the compiler will check for such situations:

```
const char *ptr = "0123456";
```

More typical cases are applying `const` to pointers that are function parameters and the intention is the same: it indicates to the compiler that the data the pointer points to should be read-only. However, there may be situations when you want to remove the `const` property of such a pointer, and this is carried out using the `const_cast` operator:

```
char * pWriteable = const_cast<char *>(ptr);
pWriteable[3] = '\0';
```

The syntax is simple. The type that you want to convert to is given in the angle brackets (<>) and the variable (which is a `const` pointer) is provided in the parentheses.

You can also cast a pointer *to* a `const` pointer. This means that you can have one pointer that you can use to access the memory so that you can write to it, and then after you have made changes, you create a `const` pointer to the memory, in effect making the memory read-only through the pointer.

Clearly, once you have cast away the const-ness of a pointer you take responsibility for the damage that you do by writing to the memory, so the `const_cast` operator in your code is a good marker for you to examine code during a code review.

Casting without runtime checks

Most casts are performed using the `static_cast` operator, and this can be used to convert pointers to related pointer types as well as converting between numeric types. There are no runtime checks performed so you should be certain that the conversion is acceptable:

```
double pi = 3.1415;
int pi_whole = static_cast<int>(pi);
```

Here a `double` is converted to an `int`, which means that the fractional part is discarded. Normally the compiler would issue a warning that data is lost, but the `static_cast` operator shows that this is your intention and hence the warning is not given.

The operator is often used to convert `void*` pointers to a typed pointer. In the following code the `unsafe_d` function assumes that the parameter is a pointer to a double value in memory, and so it can convert the `void*` pointer to a `double*` pointer. The `*` operator used with the pd pointer *dereferences* the pointer to give the data that it points to. Thus, the `*pd` expression will return a `double`.

```
void unsafe_d(void* pData)
{
    double* pd = static_cast<double*>(pData);
    cout << *pd << endl;
}
```

This is unsafe because you rely on the caller to ensure that the pointer actually points to a `double`. It could be called like this:

```
void main()
{
    double pi = 3.1415;
    unsafe_d(&pi);         // works as expected

    int pi_whole = static_cast<int>(pi);
    unsafe_d(&pi_whole); // oops!
}
```

The `&` operator returns the memory address of the operand as a typed pointer. In the first case, a `double*` pointer is obtained and passed to the `unsafe_d` function. The compiler will automatically convert this pointer to the `void*` parameter. The compiler does this automatically with no checks that the pointer will be used correctly in the function. This is illustrated by the second call to `unsafe_d` where the `int*` pointer is converted to the `void*` parameter and then in the `unsafe_d` function it is cast by `static_cast` to a `double*` even though the pointer points to an `int`. Consequently, the dereference will return unpredictable data and `cout` will print nonsense.

Casting pointers without runtime checks

The `reinterpret_cast` operator allows pointers to one type to be converted to pointers of another type, and it can convert from a pointer to an integer and an integer to a pointer:

```
double pi = 3.1415;
int i = reinterpret_cast<int>(&pi);
cout << hex << i << endl;
```

Unlike `static_cast`, this operator always involves a pointer: converting between pointers, converting from a pointer to an integral type, or converting from an integral type to a pointer. In this example, a pointer to a `double` variable is converted to an `int` and the value printed to the console. In effect, this prints out the memory address of the variable.

Casting with runtime checks

The `dynamic_cast` operator is used to convert pointers between related classes, and for this reason it will be explained in `Chapter 6`, *Classes*. This operator involves runtime checks so that the conversion is only performed if the operand can be converted to the specified type. If the conversion is not possible then the operator returns `nullptr`, giving you an opportunity to only use converted pointers that point to an actual object of that type.

Casting with list initializer

The C++ compiler will allow some implicit conversions; in some cases, they may be intentional and in some cases, they may not be. For example, the following code is similar to code shown before: a variable is initialized to a `double` value and then later in the code it is used to initialize an `int`. The compiler will perform the conversion, and will issue a warning:

```
double pi = 3.1415;
// possibly loss of code
int i = pi;
```

If you ignore warnings then you may not notice this loss of precision, which may cause a problem. One way to get around this issue is to use initialization using curly braces:

```
int i = {pi};
```

In this case, if `pi` can be converted to an `int` without loss (for example, if `pi` is a `short`) then the code will compile without even a warning. However, if `pi` is an incompatible type (in this case, a `double`) the compiler will issue an error:

C2397: conversion from 'double' to 'int' requires a narrowing conversion

Here's an interesting example. The `char` type is an integer, but the `<<` operator for `char` from the `osteam` class interprets a `char` variable as being a character, not a number, as per the following:

```
char c = 35;
cout << c << endl;
```

This will print # on the console, not 35, because 35 is the ASCII code for "#". To get the variable to be treated as a number you can use one of the following:

```
cout << static_cast<short>(c) << endl;
cout << short{ c } << endl;
```

As you can see, the second version (construction) is just as readable, but is shorter than the first.

Using C casts

Finally, you can use C style casts, but these are provided only so that you can compile legacy code. You should use one of the C++ casts instead. For completeness, the C style casts are shown here:

```
double pi = 3.1415;
float f1 = (float)pi;
float f2 = float(pi);
```

There are two versions: the first cast operator has the parentheses around the type to cast to, and in the second one the cast looks like a function call. In both cases, it would be better to use `static_cast` so that there is compile-time checking.

Using C++ types

In this final part of the chapter, we will develop a command-line application that allows you to print out the contents of a file in a mixed alphanumeric and hex format.

The application must be run with the name of a file, but optionally you can specify how many lines to print. The application will print on the console the contents of the file, 16 bytes per line. On the left, it gives the hex representation and on the right, it gives the printable representation (or a dot if the character is not in the printable non-extended ASCII range).

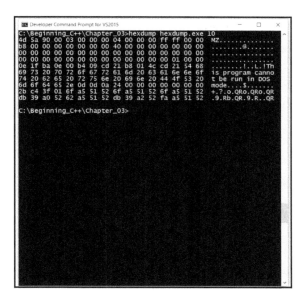

Create a new folder under `C:\Beginning_C++` called `Chapter_03`. Start Visual C++ and create a C++ source file, and save it to the folder you just created as `hexdump.cpp`. Add a simple `main` function that allows the application to accept parameters, and provides support for input and output using C++ streams:

```
#include <iostream>

using namespace std;

int main(int argc, char* argv[])
{
}
```

The application will have up to two parameters: the first is the name of the file and the second is the number of 16-byte blocks to print on the command-line. This means that you'll need to check that the parameters are valid. Start by adding a `usage` function to give the application parameters and, if called with a non-null parameter, print out an error message:

```
void usage(const char* msg)
{
    cout << "filedump filename blocks" << endl;
    cout << "filename (mandatory) is the name of the file to dump"
        << endl;
    cout << "blocks (option) is the number of 16 byte blocks "
        << endl;
    if (nullptr == msg) return;
    cout << endl << "Error! ";
    cout << msg << endl;
}
```

Add this function before the `main` function so that you can call it from there. The function can be called with a pointer to a C string or with `nullptr`. The parameter is `const`, indicating to the compiler that the string will not be changed in the function, so if there is any attempt to change the string, the compiler will generate an error.

Add the following lines to the `main` function:

```
int main(int argc, char* argv[])
{
    if (argc < 2)    {
        usage("not enough parameters");
        return 1;
    }
    if (argc > 3)    {
        usage("too many parameters");
        return 1;
```

```
}    // the second parameter is file name
string filename = argv[1];
}
```

Compile the file and confirm that there are no typos. Since this application uses the C++ Standard Library, you have to provide support for C++ exceptions with the /EHsc switch:

```
cl /EHsc hexdump.cpp
```

You can test the application invoking it from the command-line with zero, one, two, and then three parameters. Confirm that the application will only allow it to be called with one or two parameters on the command-line (which actually means two or three parameters since argc and argv include the application name).

The next task is to determine if the user provided a number to indicate how many 16-byte blocks to dump to the console and, if so, convert the string provided by the command line into an integer. This code will perform the conversion from a string to a number using the istringstream class, so you need to include the header file where this class is defined. Add the following to the top of the file:

```
#include <iostream>
#include <sstream>
```

After the declaration of the filename variable add the following highlighted code:

```
string filename = argv[1];
int blocks = 1;  // default value
if (3 == argc)    {
    // we have been passed the number of blocks
    istringstream ss(argv[2]);
    ss >> blocks;
    if (ss.fail() || 0 >= blocks)        {
        // cannot convert to a number
        usage("second parameter: must be a number," "and greater than
zero");
        return 1;
    }
}
```

By default, the application will dump one line of data (up to 16 bytes) from the file. If the user provided a different number of lines, the string-formatted number is converted to an integer by using an istringstream object. This is initialized with the argument and then the number is extracted from the stream object. If the user typed a value of zero, or if they typed a value that cannot be interpreted as a string, the code prints an error message. The error string is split over two lines, but it is still one string.

Notice that, the `if` statement uses short-circuiting; that is, if the first part of the expression (`ss.fail()`, meaning the conversion failed), is `true`, then the second expression (`0 >= blocks`, that is `blocks` must be greater than zero) will not be evaluated.

Compile this code and try it several times. For example:

```
hexdump readme.txt
hexdump readme.txt 10
hexdump readme.txt 0
hexdump readme.txt -1
```

The first two should run without an error; the second two should generate an error.

Don't worry that `readme.txt` does not exist, as it is only here as a test parameter.

Next, you'll add the code to open a file and process it. Since you'll use the `ifstream` class to input data from a file, add the following header file to the top of the file:

```
#include <iostream>
#include <sstream>
#include <fstream>
```

Then at the bottom of the `main` function add the code to open the file:

```
ifstream file(filename, ios::binary);
if (!file.good())
{
    usage("first parameter: file does not exist");
    return;
}

while (blocks-- && read16(file) != -1);
file.close();
```

The first line creates a stream object called `file` and this is attached to the file specified through the path given in `filename`. If the file cannot be found, the `good` function will return `false`. This code negates the value using the `!` operator so that if the file *does not exist* the statements in the braces following the `if` are executed. If the file exists and the `ifstream` object can open it, the data is read 16 bytes at a time in a `while` loop. Notice that at the end of this code the `close` function is called on the `file` object. It is good practice to explicitly close resources when you have finished with them.

The file will be accessed by the `read16` function on a byte-by-byte basis, including non-printable bytes, so that control characters like \r or \n have no special meaning and are still read in. However, the stream class treats the \r character in a special way: this is treated as the end of a line and normally the stream will silently consume this character. To prevent this, we open the file in binary mode using `ios::binary`.

Review the `while` statement again:

```
while (blocks-- && read16(file) != -1);
```

There are two expressions here. The first expression decrements the `blocks` variable, which holds the number of 16-byte blocks that will be printed. The postfix decrement means that the value of the expression is the value of the variable *before* the decrement, so if the expression is called when `blocks` is zero the whole expression is short-circuited and the `while` looping ends. If the first expression is non-zero, then the `read16` function is called and if this returns a value of -1 (the end of the file is reached), the looping finishes. The actual work of the loop occurs within the `read16` function, so the `while` loop statement is the empty statement.

Now you must implement the `read16` function just above the `main` function. This function will use a constant that defines the length of each block, so add the following declaration near the top of the file:

```
using namespace std;
const int block_length = 16;
```

Just before the `main` function, add this code:

```
int read16(ifstream& stm)
{
    if (stm.eof()) return -1;
    int flags = cout.flags();
    cout << hex;

    string line;

    // print bytes

    cout.setf(flags);
    return line.length();
}
```

This is just skeleton code for the function. You'll add more code in a moment.

This function will read up to 16 bytes at a time and print the contents of those bytes to the console. The return value is the number of bytes that were read or -1 if the end of the file was reached. Notice the syntax used to pass the stream object to the function. This is a **reference**, a type of pointer to the actual object. The reason why a reference is used is because if we do not do this the function will get a *copy* of the stream. References will be covered in the next chapter and using object references as function parameters will be covered in Chapter 5, *Using Functions*.

The first line of this function test is to verify whether the end of the file has been reached, and if so, no more processing can be done and the value of -1 is returned. The code will manipulate the cout object (for example, inserting the hex manipulator); and so that you always know the state of this object outside of the function, the function ensures that when it returns the cout object is in the same state as when the function was called. The initial formatting state of the cout object is obtained by calling the flags function, and this is used to reset the cout object just before the function returns by calling the setf function.

This function does nothing, so it is safe to compile the file and confirm that you have no typos.

The read16 function does three things:

1. It reads in, byte-by-byte, up to 16 bytes.
2. It prints out the hex value of each byte.
3. It prints out the printable value of the byte.

This means that each line has two parts: the hex part on the left, and the printable part on the right. Replace the comment in the function with the highlighted code:

```
string line;
for (int i = 0; i < block_length; ++i) {
    // read a single character from the stream
    unsigned char c = stm.get();
    if (stm.eof())
        break;
    // need to make sure that all hex are printed
    // two character padded with zeros
    cout << setw(2) << setfill('0');
    cout << static_cast<short>(c) << " ";
    if (isprint(c) == 0) line += '.';
    else                 line += c;
}
```

The `for` loop will loop for a maximum of `block_length` times. The first statement reads a single character from the stream. This byte is read in as raw data. If `get` finds that there are no more characters in the stream, it will set a flag in the stream object, and this is tested by calling the `eof` function. If the `eof` function returns `true` it means that the end of the file has been reached and so the `for` loop finishes, but the function does not return immediately. The reason is that *some* bytes may have been read so more processing must be carried out.

The remainder of the statements in the loop do two things:

- There are statements to print the hex value of the character on the console
- There's a statement to store the character in a printable form in the `line` variable

We have already set the `cout` object to output hex values, but if the byte is less that 0x10 the value will not be printed prefixed with a zero. To get this format, we insert the `setw` manipulator to say that the data inserted will take up two character positions and `setfill` to say that a `0` character is used to pad the string. These two manipulators are available in the `<iomanip>` header, so add them to the top of the file:

```
#include <fstream>
#include <iomanip>
```

Normally, when you insert a `char` into a stream the character value is shown, so the `char` variable is cast to a `short` so that the stream will print the hex numeric value. Finally, a single space is printed between each item.

The final lines in the `for` loop are shown here:

```
if (isprint(c) == 0) line += '.';
else                 line += c;
```

This code checks to see if the byte is a printable character (" " to "~") using the `isprint` macro and if the character is printable it is appended to the end of the `line` variable. If the byte is not printable, a dot is appended to the end of the `line` variable as a placeholder.

The code so far will print the hex representation of the bytes to the console one after the other and the only formatting is the space between bytes. If you want to test the code, you can compile this and run it on the source file:

```
hexdump hexdump.cpp 5
```

You will see something unintelligible, such as the following:

```
C:\Beginning_C++\Chapter_03>hexdump hexdump.cpp 5

23 69 6e 63 6c 75 64 65 20 3c 69 6f 73 74 72 65 61 6d 3e 0d 0a
23 69 6e 63 6c 75 64 65 20 3c 73 73 74 72 65 61 6d 3e 0d 0a 23
69 6e 63 6c 75 64 65 20 3c 66 73 74 72 65 61 6d 3e 0d 0a 23 69
6e 63 6c 75 64 65 20 3c 69 6f 6d 61 6e 69 70 3e 0d
```

The 23 values are #, 20 are spaces, and 0d and 0a are returns and newlines.

We now need to print the character representations in the `line` variable and carry out some formatting, and add line breaks. After the `for` loop, add the following:

```
string padding = " ";
if (line.length() < block_length)
{
    padding += string(
        3 * (block_length - line.length()), ' ');
}

cout << padding;
cout << line << endl;
```

There will be at least *two* spaces between the hex display and the character display. One space will come from the last character printed out in the `for` loop, and the second space is provided in the initialization of the `padding` variable.

The maximum number of bytes on each line should be 16 bytes (`block_length`) and thus 16 hex values printed on the console. If a fewer number of bytes are read then extra padding is required so that over successive lines the character representations align. The actual number of bytes read, will be the length of the `line` variable obtained by calling the `length` function, so the number of missing bytes is the expression `block_length – line.length()`. Since every hex representation takes up three characters (two for the digits and one space), the padding needed is three times the number of missing bytes. To create the appropriate number of spaces, the string constructor is called with two parameters: the number of copies and the character to copy.

Finally, this padding string is printed to the console followed by the character representation of the bytes.

At this point you should be able to compile the code with no errors or warnings. When you run the code on the source file, you should see something like this:

```
C:\Beginning_C++\Chapter_03>hexdump hexdump.cpp 5
```

```
23 69 6e 63 6c 75 64 65 20 3c 69 6f 73 74 72 65    #include <iostre
61 6d 3e 0d 0a 23 69 6e 63 6c 75 64 65 20 3c 73    am>..#include <s
73 74 72 65 61 6d 3e 0d 0a 23 69 6e 63 6c 75 64    stream>..#includ
65 20 3c 66 73 74 72 65 61 6d 3e 0d 0a 23 69 6e    e <fstream>..#in
63 6c 75 64 65 20 3c 69 6f 6d 61 6e 69 70 3e 0d    clude <iomanip>.
```

Now the bytes make more sense. Since the application does not change the files it dumps, it is safe to use this tool on binary files, including itself:

```
C:\Beginning_C++\Chapter_03>hexdump hexdump.exe 17
```

```
4d 5a 90 00 03 00 00 00 04 00 00 00 ff ff 00 00    MZ..............
b8 00 00 00 00 00 00 00 40 00 00 00 00 00 00 00    ........@.......
00 00 00 00 00 00 00 00 00 00 00 00 00 00 00 00    ................
00 00 00 00 00 00 00 00 00 00 00 00 01 00 00 00    ................
0e 1f ba 0e 00 b4 09 cd 21 b8 01 4c cd 21 54 68    ........!..L.!Th
69 73 20 70 72 6f 67 72 61 6d 20 63 61 6e 6e 6f    is program canno
74 20 62 65 20 72 75 6e 20 69 6e 20 44 4f 53 20    t be run in DOS
6d 6f 64 65 2e 0d 0d 0a 24 00 00 00 00 00 00 00    mode....$.......
2b c4 3f 01 6f a5 51 52 6f a5 51 52 6f a5 51 52    +.?.o.QRo.QRo.QR
db 39 a0 52 62 a5 51 52 db 39 a2 52 fa a5 51 52    .9.Rb.QR.9.R..QR
db 39 a3 52 73 a5 51 52 b2 5a 9a 52 6a a5 51 52    .9.Rs.QR.Z.Rj.QR
6f a5 50 52 30 a5 51 52 8a fc 52 53 79 a5 51 52    o.PR0.QR..RSy.QR
8a fc 54 53 54 a5 51 52 8a fc 55 53 2f a5 51 52    ..TST.QR..US/.QR
9d fc 54 53 6e a5 51 52 9d fc 53 53 6e a5 51 52    ..TSn.QR..SSn.QR
52 69 63 68 6f a5 51 52 00 00 00 00 00 00 00 00    Richo.QR........
00 00 00 00 00 00 00 00 00 00 00 00 00 00 00 00    ................
50 45 00 00 4c 01 05 00 6b e7 07 58 00 00 00 00    PE..L..k..X....
```

The MZ indicates that this is the DOS header part of Microsoft's **Portable Executable** (PE) file format. The actual PE header starts on the bottom line with the characters, PE.

Summary

In this chapter, you have learned about the various built-in types in C++, how to initialize them, and how to use them. You also learned how to convert variables to different types using casting operators. The chapter also introduced you to record types, a topic that will be expanded on in `Chapter 6`, *Classes*. Finally, you have seen various examples of pointers, a topic that will be examined in greater detail in the next chapter.

4

Working with Memory, Arrays, and Pointers

C++ allows you to have direct access to memory through pointers. This gives you a lot of flexibility, and potentially it allows you to improve the performance of your code by eliminating some unnecessary copying of data. However, it also provides an extra source of errors; some can be fatal for your application or worse (yes, worse than fatal!) because poor use of memory buffers can open security holes in your code that can allow malware to take over the machine. Clearly pointers are an important aspect of C++.

In this chapter, you'll see how to declare pointers and initialize them to memory locations, how to allocate memory on the stack and, C++ free store, and how to use C++ arrays.

Using memory in C++

C++ uses the same syntax as C to declare pointer variables and assign them to memory addresses, and it has C-like pointer arithmetic. Like C, C++ also allows you to allocate memory on the stack, so there is automatic memory cleanup when the stack frame is destroyed, and dynamic allocation (on the C++ free store) where the programmer has the responsibility to release memory. This section will cover these concepts.

Using C++ pointer syntax

The syntax to access memory in C++ is straightforward. The & operator returns the address of an object. That *object* can be a variable, a built-in type or the instance of a custom type, or even a function (function pointers will be covered in the next chapter). The address is assigned a typed pointer variable or a void* pointer. A void* pointer should be treated as merely storage for the memory address because you cannot access data and you cannot perform pointer arithmetic (that is, manipulate the pointer value using arithmetic operators) on a void* pointer. Pointer variables are usually declared using a type and the * symbol. For example:

```
int i = 42;
int *pi = &i;
```

In this code, the variable i is an integer, and the compiler and linker will determine where this variable will be allocated. Usually, a variable in a function will be on a stack frame, as described in a later section. At runtime, the stack will be created (essentially a chunk of memory will be allocated) and space will be reserved in the stack memory for the variable i. The program then puts a value (42) in that memory. Next, the address of the memory allocated for the variable i is placed in the variable pi. The memory usage of the previous code is illustrated in the following diagram:

The pointer holds a value of 0x007ef8c (notice that the lowest byte is stored in the lowest byte in memory; this is for an x86 machine). The memory location 0x007ef8c has a value of 0x0000002a, that is, a value of 42, the value of the variable i. Since pi is also a variable, it also occupies space in memory, and in this case the compiler has put the pointer *lower* in memory than the data it points to and, in this case, the two variables are not contiguous.

With variables allocated on the stack like this, you should make no assumptions about where in memory the variables are allocated, nor their location in relation to other variables.

This code assumes a 32-bit operating system, and so the pointer `pi` occupies 32 bits and contains a 32-bit address. If the operating system is 64 bits then the pointer will be 64 bits wide (but the integer may still be 32 bits). In this book, we will use 32-bit pointers for the simple convenience that 32-bit addresses take less typing than 64-bit addresses.

The typed pointer is declared with a `*` symbol and we will refer to this as an `int *` pointer because the pointer points to memory that holds an `int`. When declaring a pointer, the convention is to put the `*` next to the variable name rather than next to the type. This syntax emphasizes that the *type pointed* to is an `int`. However, it is important to use this syntax if you declare more than one variable in a single statement:

```
int *pi, i;
```

It is clear that the first variable is an `int *` pointer and the second is an `int`. The following is not so clear:

```
int* pi, i;
```

You might interpret this to mean that the type of both variables is `int *`, *but this is not the case*, as this declares a pointer and an `int`. If you want to declare two pointers, then apply `*` to each variable:

```
int *p1, *p2;
```

It is probably better just to declare the two pointers on separate lines.

When you apply the `sizeof` operator to a pointer, you will get the size of the pointer, not what it points to. Thus, on an x86 machine, `sizeof(int *)` will return 4; and on an x64 machine, it will return 8. This is an important observation, especially when we discuss C++ built-in arrays in a later section.

To access the data pointed to by a pointer, you must **dereference** it using the `*` operator:

```
int i = 42;
int *pi = &i;
int j = *pi;
```

Used like this on the right-hand side of an assignment, the dereferenced pointer gives access to the value pointed to by the pointer, so `j` is initialized to 42. Compare this to the declaration of a pointer, where the `*` symbol is also used, but has a different meaning.

The dereference operator does more than give read access to the data at the memory location. As long as the pointer does not restrict it (using the `const` keyword; see later), you can dereference the pointer to write to a memory location too:

```
int i = 42;
cout << i << endl;
int *pi { &i };
*pi = 99;
cout << i << endl;
```

In this code, the pointer `pi` points to the location in memory of the variable `i` (in this case, using the brace syntax). Assigning the dereferenced pointer assigns the value to the location that the pointer points to. The result is that on the last line, the variable `i` will have a value of 99 and not 42.

Using null pointers

A pointer could point to anywhere in the memory installed in your computer, and assignment through a dereferenced pointer means that you could potentially write over sensitive memory used by your operating system, or (through direct memory access) write to memory used by hardware on your machine. However, operating systems will usually give an executable a specific memory range that it can access, and attempts to access memory out of this range will cause an operating system memory access violation.

For this reason, you should almost always obtain pointer values using the `&` operator or from a call to an operating system function. You should not give a pointer an absolute address. The only exception to this is the C++ constant for an invalid memory address, `nullptr`:

```
int *pi = nullptr;
// code
int i = 42;
pi = &i;
// code
if (nullptr != pi) cout << *pi << endl;
```

This code initializes the pointer `pi` to `nullptr`. Later in the code, the pointer is initialized to the address of an integer variable. Still later in the code, the pointer is used, but rather than calling it immediately, the pointer is first checked to ensure that it has been initialized to a non-null value. The compiler will check to see if you are about to use a variable that has not been initialized, but if you are writing library code, the compiler will not know whether the callers of your code will use pointers correctly.

The type of constant `nullptr` is not an integer, it is `std::nullptr_t`. All pointer types can be implicitly converted to this type, so `nullptr` can be used to initialize variables of all pointer types.

Types of memory

In general, you can regard memory as being one of four types:

- Static or global
- String pool
- Automatic or stack
- Free store

When you declare a variable at the global level, or if you have a variable declared in a function as `static`, then the compiler will ensure that the variable is allocated from memory that has the same lifetime as the application--the variable is created when the application starts and deleted when the application ends.

When you use a string literal, the data will also, effectively, be a global variable, but stored in a different part of the executable. For a Windows executable, string literals are stored in the `.rdata` PE/COFF section of the executable. The `.rdata` section of the file is for read-only initialized data, and hence you cannot change the data. Visual C++ allows you to go a step further and gives you an option of **string pooling**. Consider this:

```
char *p1 { "hello" };
char *p2 { "hello" };
cout << hex;
cout << reinterpret_cast<int>(p1) << endl;
cout << reinterpret_cast<int>(p2) << endl;
```

In this code, two pointers are initialized with the address of the string literal `hello`. In the following two lines, the address of each pointer is printed on the console. Since the `<<` operator for `char*` treats the variable as a pointer to a string, it will print the string rather than the address of the pointer. To get around this, we call the `reinterpret_cast` operator to convert the pointer to an integer and print the value of the integer.

If you compile the code at the command line using the Visual C++ compiler, you will see two different addresses printed. These two addresses are in the .rdata section and are both read-only. If you compile this code with the /GF switch to enable string pooling (which is default for Visual C++ projects), the compiler will see that the two string literals are the same and will only store one copy in the .rdata section, so the result of this code will be that a single address will be printed on the console twice.

In this code, the two variables p1 and p2 are automatic variables, that is, they are created on the stack created for the current function. When a function is called, a chunk of memory is allocated for the function and this contains space for the parameters passed to the function and the return address of the code that called the function, as well as space for the automatic variables declared in the function. When the function finishes, the stack frame is destroyed.

The **calling convention** of the function determines whether the calling function or the called function has the responsibility to do this. In Visual C++, the default is the __cdecl calling convention, which means the calling function cleans up the stack. The __stdcall calling convention is used by Windows operating system functions and the stack clean up is carried out by the called function. More details will be given in the next chapter.

Automatic variables only last as long as the function and the address of such variables only make any sense within the function. Later in this chapter, you will see how to create arrays of data. Arrays allocated as automatic variables are allocated on the stack to a fixed size determined at compile time. It is possible with large arrays that you could exceed the size of the stack, particularly with functions that are called recursively. On Windows, the default stack size is 1 MB, and on x86 Linux, it is 2 MB. Visual C++ allows you to specify a bigger stack with the /F compiler switch (or the /STACK linker switch). The gcc compiler allows you to change the default stack size with the --stack switch.

The final type of memory is **dynamic memory** created on the **free store** or sometimes known as the **heap**. This is the most flexible way of using memory. As the name suggests, you allocate memory at runtime of a size determined at runtime. The implementation of the free store depends on the C++ implementation but you should regard the free store as having the same lifetime as your application, so memory allocated from the free store should last at least as long as your application.

However, there are potential dangers here, particularly for long-lived applications. All memory allocated from the free store should be returned back to the free store when you have finished with it so that the free store manager can reuse the memory. If you do not return memory appropriately, then potentially the free store manager could run out of memory, which will prompt it to ask the operating system for more memory, and consequently, the memory usage of your application will grow over time, causing performance issues due to memory paging.

Pointer arithmetic

A pointer points to memory, and the type of the pointer determines the type of the data that can be accessed through the pointer. So, an `int*` pointer will point to an integer in memory, and you dereference the pointer (`*`) to get the integer. If the pointer allows it (it is not marked as `const`), you can change its value through pointer arithmetic. For example, you can increment or decrement a pointer. What happens to the value of the memory address depends on the type of the pointer. Since a typed pointer points to a type, any pointer arithmetic will change the pointer in units of the *size* of that type.

If you increment an `int*` pointer, it will point to the *next* integer in memory and the change in the memory address depends on the size of the integer. This is equivalent to array indexing, where an expression such as `v[1]` means you should start at the memory location of the first item in `v` and then move one item further in memory and return the item there:

```
int v[] { 1, 2, 3, 4, 5 };
int *pv = v;
*pv = 11;
v[1] = 12;
pv[2] = 13;
*(pv + 3) = 14;
```

The first line allocates an array of five integers on the stack and initializes the values to the numbers 1 to 5. In this example, because an initialization list is used, the compiler will create space for the required number of items, hence the size of the array is not given. If you give the size of the array between the brackets, then the initialization list must not have more items than the array size. If the list has fewer items, then the rest of the items in the array are initialized to the default value (usually zero).

The next line in this code obtains a pointer to the first item in the array. This line is significant: an array name is treated as a pointer to the first item in the array. The following lines alter array items in various ways. The first of these (`*pv`) changes the first item in the array by dereferencing the pointer and assigning it a value. The second (`v[1]`) uses array indexing to assign a value to the second item in the array. The third (`pv[2]`) uses indexing, but this time with a pointer, and assigns a value to the third value in the array. And the final example (`*(pv + 3)`) uses pointer arithmetic to determine the address of the fourth item in the array (remember the first item has an index of 0) and then dereferences the pointer to assign the item a value. After these, the array contains the values `{ 11, 12, 13, 14, 5 }` and the memory layout is illustrated here:

If you have a memory buffer containing values (in this example, allocated via an array) and you want to multiply each value by 3, you can do this using pointer arithmetic:

```
int v[] { 1, 2, 3, 4, 5 };
int *pv = v;
for (int i = 0; i < 5; ++i)
{
    *pv++ *= 3;
}
```

The loop statement is complicated, and you will need to refer back to the operator precedence given in Chapter 2, *Understanding Language Features*. The postfix increment operator has the highest precedence, the next highest precedence is the dereference operator (`*`), and finally, the `*=` operator has the lowest of the three operators, so the operators are run in this order: `++`, `*`, `*=`. The postfix operator returns the value *before* the increment, so although the pointer is incremented to the next item in memory, the expression uses the address before the increment. This address is then dereferenced which is assigned by the assignment operator that replaces the item with the value multiplied by 3. This illustrates an important difference between pointers and array names; you can increment a pointer but you cannot increment an array:

```
pv += 1; // can do this
v += 1; // error
```

You can, of course use indexing (with `[]`) on both array names and pointers.

Using arrays

As the name suggests, a C++ built-in array is zero or more items of data of the same type. In C++, square brackets are used to declare arrays and to access array elements:

```
int squares[4];
for (int i = 0; i < 4; ++i)
{
    squares[i] = i * i;
}
```

The `squares` variable is an array of integers. The first line allocates enough memory for *four* integers and then the `for` loop initializes the memory with the first four squares. The memory allocated by the compiler from the stack is contiguous and the items in the array are sequential, so the memory location of `squares[3]` is `sizeof(int)` following on from `squares[2]`. Since the array is created on the stack, the size of the array is an instruction to the compiler; this is not dynamic allocation, so the size has to be a constant.

There is a potential problem here: the size of the array is mentioned twice, once in the declaration and then again in the `for` loop. If you use two different values, then you may initialize too few items, or you could potentially access memory outside the array. The ranged `for` syntax allows you to get access to each item in the array; the compiler can determine the size of the array and will use this in the ranged `for` loop. In the following code, there is a deliberate mistake that shows an issue with array sizes:

```
int squares[5];
for (int i = 0; i < 4; ++i)
{
    squares[i] = i * i;
}
for(int i : squares)
{
    cout << i << endl;
}
```

The size of the array and the range of the first `for` loop do not agree and consequently the last item will not be initialized. The ranged `for` loop, however, will loop through all five items and so will print out some random value for the value of the last value. What if the same code is used but the `squares` array is declared to have three items? It depends on the compiler you are using and whether you are compiling a debug build, but clearly you will be writing to memory *outside* of that allocated to the array.

There are some ways to mitigate these issues. The first one has been mentioned in an earlier chapter: declare a constant for the size of the array and use that whenever your code needs to know the array size:

```
constexpr int sq_size = 4;
int squares[sq_size];
for (int i = 0; i < sq_size; ++i)
{
    squares[i] = i * i;
}
```

The array declaration must have a constant for the size, and that is managed by using the `sq_size` constant variable.

You may also want to calculate the size of an already allocated array. The `sizeof` operator, when applied to an array, returns the size in bytes of the *entire* array, so you can determine the size of the array by dividing this value by the size of a single item:

```
int squares[4];
for (int i = 0; i < sizeof(squares)/sizeof(squares[0]); ++i)
{
    squares[i] = i * i;
}
```

This is safer code, but clearly it is verbose. The C runtime library contains a macro called `_countof` that performs this calculation.

Function parameters

As illustrated, there is an automatic conversion of an array to the appropriate pointer type and this occurs if you pass an array to a function, or return it from a function. This decay to a dumb pointer means that other code can make no assumption about an array size. A pointer could point to memory allocated on the stack where the memory lifetime is determined by the function, or a global variable where the memory lifetime is that of the program, or it could be to memory that is dynamically allocated and the memory is determined by the programmer. There is nothing in a pointer declaration that indicates the type of memory or who is responsible for the deallocation of the memory. Nor is there any information in a dumb pointer of how much memory the pointer points to. When you write code using pointers, you have to be disciplined about how you use them.

A function can have an array parameter, but this means a lot less than it appear to indicate:

```
// there are four tires on each car
bool safe_car(double tire_pressures[4]);
```

This function will check that each member of the array has a value between the minimum and maximum values allowed. There are four tires in use at any one time on a car, so the function *should* be called with an array of four values. The problem is that although it appears that the compiler *should* check that the array passed to the function is the appropriate size, it doesn't. You can call this function like this:

```
double car[4] = get_car_tire_pressures();
if (!safe_car(car)) cout << "take off the road!" << endl;
double truck[8] = get_truck_tire_pressures();
if (!safe_car(truck)) cout << "take off the road!" << endl;
```

Of course, it should have been obvious to the developer that a truck is not a car, and so this developer should not have written this code, but the usual advantage of a compiled language is that the compiler will perform some *sanity checks* for you. In the case of array parameters, it won't.

The reason is that the array is passed as a pointer, so although the parameter appears to be a built-in array, you cannot use facilities you are used to using with arrays like ranged `for`. In fact, if the `safe_car` function calls `sizeof(tire_pressures)`, it will get the size of a double pointer and not 16, the size in bytes of a four `int` array.

This *decay to a pointer* feature of array parameters means that functions will only ever know the size of an array parameter if you explicitly tell it the size. You can use an empty pair of square brackets to indicate that the item should be passed an array, but it really is just the same as a pointer:

```
bool safe_car(double tire_pressures[], int size);
```

Here the function has a parameter that indicates the size of the array. The preceding function is exactly the same as declaring the first parameter to be a pointer. The following is not an overload of the function; it is the *same* function:

```
bool safe_car(double *tire_pressures, int size);
```

The important point is that when you pass an array to a function, the *first dimension* of the array is treated as a pointer. So far arrays have been single dimensional, but they may have more than one dimension.

Multidimensional arrays

Arrays can be multidimensional and to add another dimension you add another set of square brackets:

```
int two[2];
int four_by_three[4][3];
```

The first example creates an array of two integers, the second creates a two-dimensional array with 12 integers arranged so that there are four rows of three columns. Of course, *row* and *column* are arbitrary and treat the two-dimensional array like a conventional spreadsheet table, but it helps to visualize how the data is arranged in memory.

Note that there are square brackets around every dimension. C++ is different to other languages in this respect, so a declaration of int x[10,10] will be reported as an error by the C++ compiler.

Initializing multidimensional arrays involves a pair of braces and the data in the order that it will be used to initialize the dimensions:

```
int four_by_three[4][3] { 11,12,13,21,22,23,31,32,33,41,42,43 };
```

In this example, the values having the highest digit reflect the left-most index and the lower digit reflect, the right-most index (in both cases, one more than the actual index). Clearly, you can split this over several lines and use whitespace to group values together to make this more readable. You can also use nested braces. For example:

```
int four_by_three[4][3] = { {11,12,13}, {21,22,23},
                            {31,32,33}, {41,42,43} };
```

If you read the dimensions going left to right, you can read the initialization going into deeper levels of nesting. There are four rows, so within the outer braces there are four sets of nested braces. There are three columns, and so within the nested braces there are three initialization values.

Nested braces are not just a convenience for formatting your C++ code, because if you provide an empty pair of braces the compiler will use the default value:

```
int four_by_three[4][3] = { {11,12,13}, {}, {31,32,33}, {41,42,43} };
```

Here, the second-row items are initialized to 0.

When you increase the dimensions, the principle applies: increase the nesting for the right most dimension:

```
int four_by_three_by_two[4][3][2]
    = { { {111,112}, {121,122}, {131,132} },
        { {211,212}, {221,222}, {231,232} },
        { {311,312}, {321,322}, {331,332} },
        { {411,412}, {421,422}, {431,432} }
      };
```

This is four rows of three columns of pairs (as you can see, when the dimensions increase it becomes apparent that the terms **rows** and **columns** are largely arbitrary).

You access items using the same syntax:

```
cout << four_by_three_by_two[3][2][0] << endl; // prints 431
```

In terms of the memory layout, the compiler interprets the syntax in the following way. The first index determines the offset from the beginning of the array in chunks of six integers (3 * 2), the second index indicates the offset within one of these six integer *chunks* itself in chunks of two integers, and the third index is the offset in terms of individual integers. Thus `[3][2][0]` is *(3 * 6) + (2 * 2) + 0 = 22* integers from the beginning, treating the first integer as index zero.

A multidimensional array is treated as arrays of arrays, so the type of each "row" is `int[3][2]` and we know from the declaration that there are four of them.

Passing multidimensional arrays to functions

You can pass a multidimensional array to a function:

```
// pass the torque of the wheel nuts of all wheels
bool safe_torques(double nut_torques[4][5]);
```

This compiles and you can access the parameter as a 4x5 array, assuming that this vehicle has four wheels with five nuts on each one.

As stated earlier, when you pass an array, the first dimension will be treated as a pointer, so while you can pass a 4x5 array to this function, you can also pass a 2x5 array and the compiler will not complain. However, if you pass a 4x3 array (that is, the second dimension is not the same as declared in the function), the compiler will issue an error that the array is incompatible. The parameter may be more accurately described as being `double row[][5]`. Since the size of the first dimension is not available, the function should be declared with the size of that dimension:

```
bool safe_torques(double nut_torques[][5], int num_wheels);
```

This says that `nut_torques` is one or more "rows", each of which has five items. Since the array does not provide information about the number of rows it has, you should provide it. Another way to declare this is:

```
bool safe_torques(double (*nut_torques)[5], int num_wheels);
```

The brackets are important here, if you omit them and use `double *nut_torques[5]`, then it means the `*` will refer to the type in the array, that is, the compiler will treat `nut_torques` as a five-element array of `double*` pointers. We have seen an example of such an array before:

```
void main(int argc, char *argv[]);
```

The `argv` parameter is an array of `char*` pointers. You can also declare the `argv` parameter as `char**` which has the same meaning.

In general, if you intend to pass arrays to a function it is best to use custom types, or use the C++ array types.

Using ranged `for` with multidimensional arrays is a bit more complicated than appears on first sight, and requires the use of a reference as explained in the section later in this chapter.

Using arrays of characters

Strings will be covered in more detail in Chapter 9, *Using Strings*, but it is worth pointing out here that C strings are arrays of characters and are accessed through pointer variables. This means that if you want to manipulate strings, you must manipulate the memory that the pointer points to, and not manipulate the pointer itself.

Comparing strings

The following allocates two string buffers and it calls the `strcpy_s` function to initialize each with the same string:

```
char p1[6];
strcpy_s(p1, 6, "hello");
char p2[6];
strcpy_s(p2, 6, p1);
bool b = (p1 == p2);
```

The `strcpy_c` function will copy characters from the pointer given in the last parameter (until the terminating `NUL`), into the buffer given in the first parameter, whose maximum size is given in the second parameter. These two pointers are compared in the final line, and this will return a value of `false`. The problem is that the compare function is comparing the values of the pointers, not what the pointers point to. The two buffers have the same string, but the pointers are different, so `b` will be `false`.

The correct way to compare strings is to compare the data character by character to see if they are equal. The C runtime provides `strcmp` that compares two string buffers character by character, and the `std::string` class defines a function called `compare` that will also perform such a comparison; however, be wary of the value returned from these functions:

```
string s1("string");
string s2("string");
int result = s1.compare(s2);
```

The return value is not a `bool` type indicating if the two strings are the same; it is an `int`. These compare functions carry out a lexicographical compare and return a negative value if the parameter (`s2` in this code) is greater than the operand (`s1`) lexicographically, and a positive number if the operand is greater than the parameter. If the two strings are the same, the function returns 0. Remember that a `bool` is `false` for a value of 0 and `true` for non-zero values. The standard library provides an overload for the `==` operator for `std::string`, so it is safe to write code like this:

```
if (s1 == s2)
{
    cout << "strings are the same" << endl;
}
```

The operator will compare the strings contained in the two variables.

Preventing buffer overruns

The C runtime library for manipulating strings is notorious for allowing buffer overruns. For example, the `strcpy` function copies one string to another, and you get access to this through the `<cstring>` header, which is included by the `<iostream>` header. You may be tempted to write something like this:

```
char pHello[5];          // enough space for 5 characters
strcpy(pHello, "hello");
```

The problem is that `strcpy` will copy all the character up to, and including the terminating NULL character and so you will be copying six characters into an array with space for only *five*. You could be taking a string from the user input (say, from a text box on a web page) and think that the array you have allocated is big enough, but a malicious user could provide an excessively long string deliberately bigger than the buffer so that it overwrites other parts of your program. Such *buffer overruns* have caused a lot of programs to be subjected to hackers taking control of servers, so much so that the C string functions have all been replaced by safer versions. Indeed, if you are tempted to type the preceding code, you'll find that `strcpy` is available, but the Visual C++ compiler will issue an error:

```
error C4996: 'strcpy': This function or variable may be unsafe.
Consider using strcpy_s instead. To disable deprecation, use
_CRT_SECURE_NO_WARNINGS. See online help for details.
```

If you have existing code that uses `strcpy`, and you need to make that code compile, you can define the symbol before `<cstring>`:

```
#define _CRT_SECURE_NO_WARNINGS
#include <iostream>
```

An initial attempt to prevent this issue is to call `strncpy`, which will copy a specific number of characters:

```
char pHello[5];             // enough space for 5 characters
strncpy(pHello, "hello", 5);
```

The function will copy up to five characters and then stop. The problem is that the string to copy has five characters and so the result will be no NULL termination. The safer version of this function has a parameter that you can use to say how big the destination buffer is:

```
size_t size = sizeof(pHello)/sizeof(pHello[0]);
strncpy_s(pHello, size, "hello", 5);
```

At runtime this will still cause a problem. You have told the function that the buffer is five characters in size and it will determine that this is not big enough to hold the six characters that you have asked it to copy. Rather than allowing the program to silently continue and the buffer overrun to cause problems, the safer string functions will call a function called the **constraint handler** and the default version will shut down the program on the rationale that a buffer overrun means that the program is compromised.

The C runtime library strings functions were originally written to return the result of the function, the safer versions now return an error value. The `strncpy_s` function can also be told to truncate the copy rather than call the constraint handler:

```
strncpy_s(pHello, size, "hello", _TRUNCATE);
```

The C++ `string` class protects you from such issues.

Using pointers in C++

Pointers are clearly very important in C++, but as with any powerful feature, there are issues and dangers, so it is worth pointing out some of the major issues. A pointer points to a single location in memory, and the type of the pointer indicates how the memory location should be interpreted. The very most you can assume is the number of bytes at that position in memory is the size of the type of the pointer. That's it. This means that pointers are inherently unsafe. However, in C++ they are the quickest way to enable code within your process to access large amounts of data.

Accessing out of bounds

When you allocate a buffer, whether on the stack or on the free store, and you get a pointer, there is little to stop you from accessing memory you have not allocated--either before or after the position of the buffer. This means that when you use pointer arithmetic, or indexed access on arrays, that you check carefully that you are not going to access data out of bounds. Sometimes the error may not be immediately obvious:

```
int arr[] { 1, 2, 3, 4 };
for (int i = 0; i < 4; ++i)
{
    arr[i] += arr[i + 1]; // oops, what happens when i == 3?
}
```

When you use indexing, you have to keep reminding yourself that arrays are indexed from zero so the highest index is the size of the array minus 1.

Pointers to deallocated memory

This applies to memory allocated on the stack and to memory dynamically allocated. The following is a poorly written function that returns a string allocated on the stack in a function:

```
char *get()
{
    char c[] { "hello" };
    return c;
}
```

The preceding code allocates a buffer of six characters and then initializes it with the five characters of the string literal hello, and the NULL termination character. The problem is that once the function finishes the stack frame is torn down so that the memory can be re-used, and the pointer will point to memory that could be used by something else. This error is caused by poor programming, but it may not be as obvious as in this example. If the function uses several pointers and performs a pointer assignment, you may not immediately notice that you have returned a pointer to a stack-allocated object. The best course of action is simply not to return raw pointers from functions, but if you do want to use this style of programming, make sure that the memory buffer is passed in through a parameter (so the function does not own the buffer) or is dynamically allocated and you are passing ownership to the caller.

This leads on to another issue. If you call delete on a pointer and then later in your code, try to access the pointer, you will be accessing memory that is potentially being used by other variables. To alleviate this problem, you can get into the habit of assigning a pointer to null_ptr when you delete it and check for null_ptr before using a pointer. Alternatively, you can use a smart pointer object which will do this for you. Smart pointers will be covered in Chapter 6, *Classes*.

Converting pointers

You can either have typed pointers, or the void* pointer. Typed pointers will access the memory as if it is the specified type (this has interesting consequences when you have inheritance with classes, but that will be left for Chapter 6, *Classes* and Chapter 7, *Introduction to Object-Oriented Programming*). Thus, if you cast a pointer to a different type and dereference it, the memory will be treated as containing the cast type. It rarely makes sense to do this. The void* pointer cannot be dereferenced, so you can never access data through a void* pointer, to access the data you have to cast the pointer.

The whole reason for the `void*` pointer type is that it can point to anything. In general, `void*` pointers should only be used when the type does not matter to that function. For example, the C `malloc` function returns a `void*` pointer because the function merely allocates memory; it does not care what that memory will be used for.

Constant pointers

Pointers can be declared as `const` which, depending on where you apply it, means that the memory the pointer points to is read-only through the pointer, or the value of the pointer is read-only:

```
char c[] { "hello" }; // c can be used as a pointer
*c = 'H';             // OK, can write thru the pointer
const char *ptc {c};  // pointer to constant
cout << ptc << endl;  // OK, can read the memory pointed to
*ptc =  'Y';          // cannot write to the memory
char *const cp {c};   // constant pointer
*cp = 'y';            // can write thru the pointer
cp++;                 // cannot point to anything else
```

Here, `ptc` is a pointer to constant `char`, that is, although you can change what `ptc` points to, and you can read what it points to, you cannot use it to change the memory. On the other hand, `cp` is a constant pointer, which means you can both read and write the memory which the pointer points to, but you cannot change where it points to. It is typical to pass the `const char*` pointers to functions because the functions do not know where the string has been allocated or the size of the buffer (the caller may pass a literal which cannot be changed). Note that there is no `const*` operator so `char const*` is treated as `const char*`, a pointer to a constant buffer.

You can make a pointer constant, change it, or remove it using casts. The following does some fairly pointless changing around of the `const` keyword to prove the point:

```
char c[] { "hello" };
char *const cp1 { c }; // cannot point to any other memory
*cp1 = 'H';            // can change the memory
const char *ptc = const_cast<const char*>(cp1);
ptc++;                 // change where the pointer points to
char *const cp2 = const_cast<char *const>(ptc);
*cp2 = 'a';            // now points to Hallo
```

The pointers cp1 and cp2 can be used to change the memory they point to, but once assigned neither can point to other memory. The first const_cast casts away the const-ness to a pointer that can be changed to point to other memory, but cannot be used to alter that memory, ptc. The second const_cast casts away the const-ness of ptc so that the memory can be changed through the pointer, cp2.

Changing the type pointed to

The static_cast operator is used to convert with a compile time check, but not a runtime check, so this means that the pointers must be related. The void* pointer can be converted to any pointer, so the following compiles and makes sense:

```
int *pi = static_cast<int*>(malloc(sizeof(int)));
*pi = 42;
cout << *pi << endl;
free(pi);
```

The C malloc function returns a void* pointer so you have to convert it to be able to use the memory. (Of course, the C++ new operator removes the need for such casting.) The built-in types are not "related" enough for static_cast to convert between pointer types, so you cannot use static_cast to convert an int* pointer to a char* pointer, even though int and char are both integer types. For custom types that are related through inheritance, you can cast pointers using static_cast, but there is no runtime check that the cast is correct. To cast with runtime checks you should use dynamic_cast, and more details will be given in Chapters 6, *Classes* and Chapter 7, *Introduction to Object-Oriented Programming*.

The reinterpret_cast operator is the most flexible, and dangerous, of the cast operators because it will convert between any pointer types without any type checks. It is inherently unsafe. For example, the following code initializes a wide character array with a literal. The array wc will have six characters, hello followed by NULL. The wcout object interprets a wchar_t* pointer as a pointer to the first character in a wchar_t string, so inserting wc will print the string (every character until the NUL). To get the actual memory location, you have to convert the pointer to an integer:

```
wchar_t wc[] { L"hello" };
wcout << wc << " is stored in memory at ";
wcout << hex;
wcout << reinterpret_cast<int>(wc) << endl;
```

Similarly, if you insert a `wchar_t` into the `wcout` object, it will print the character, not the numeric value. So, to print out the codes for the individual characters, we need to cast the pointer to a suitable integer pointer. This code assumes that a `short` is the same size as a `wchar_t`:

```
wcout << "The characters are:" << endl;
short* ps = reinterpret_cast<short*>(wc);
do
{
    wcout << *ps << endl;
} while (*ps++);
```

Allocating memory in code

C++ defines two operators, `new` and `delete`, that allocate memory from the free store and release memory back into the free store.

Allocating individual objects

The `new` operator is used with the type to allocate memory, and it will return a typed pointer to that memory:

```
int *p = new int; // allocate memory for one int
```

The `new` operator will call the *default constructor* for custom types for every object it creates (as explained in `Chapter 6`, *Classes*). Built-in types do not have constructors, so instead a type initialization will occur and this will usually initialize the object to zero (in this example, a zero integer).

In general, you should not use memory allocated for built-in types without explicitly initializing it. In fact, in Visual C++ the debug version of the `new` operator will initialize memory to a value of `0xcd` for every byte, as a visual reminder in the debugger that you have not initialized the memory. For custom types, it is left to the author of the type to initialize allocated memory.

It is important that when you have finished with memory that you return it back to the free store so that the allocator can reuse it. You do this by calling the `delete` operator:

```
delete p;
```

When you delete a pointer, the **destructor** for the object is called. For built-in types, this does nothing. It is good practice to initialize a pointer to `nullptr`, after you have deleted it, and if you use the convention of checking the value of a pointer before using it, this will protect you from using a deleted pointer. The C++ standard says that the `delete` operator will have no effect if you delete a pointer that has a value of `nullptr`.

C++ allows you to initialize a value at the time you call the `new` operator, in two ways:

```
int *p1 = new int (42);
int *p2 = new int {42};
```

For a custom type, the `new` operator will call a constructor on the type; for a built in type, the end result is the same, and is carried out by initializing the item to the value provided. You can also use initialized list syntax, as shown in the second line in the preceding code. It is important to note that the initialization is the memory pointed to, not the pointer variable.

Allocating arrays of objects

You can also create arrays of objects in dynamic memory using the `new` operator. You do this by providing the number of items you want created in a pair of square brackets. The following code allocates memory for two integers:

```
int *p = new int[2];
p[0] = 1;
*(p + 1) = 2;
for (int i = 0; i < 2; ++i) cout << p[i] << endl;
delete [] p;
```

The operator returns a pointer to the type allocated, and you can use pointer arithmetic or array indexing to access the memory. You cannot initialize the memory in the `new` statement; you have to do that after creating the buffer. When you use `new` to create a buffer for more than one object, you must use the appropriate version of the `delete` operator: the `[]` is used to indicate that more than one item is deleted and the destructor for each object will be called. It is important that you always use the right version of `delete` appropriate to the version of `new` used to create the pointer.

Custom types can define their own operator `new` and operator `delete` for individual objects, as well as operator `new[]` and operator `delete[]` for arrays of objects. The custom type author can use these to use custom memory allocation schemes for their objects.

Handling failed allocations

If the `new` operator cannot allocate the memory for an object, it will throw the `std::bad_alloc` exception and the pointer returned will be `nullptr`. Exceptions are covered in `Chapter 10`, *Diagnostics and Debugging*, so only a brief outline of the syntax will be given here. It is important that you check for failure to allocate memory in production code. The following code shows how to guard the allocation so that you can catch the `std::bad_alloc` exception and handle it:

```
// VERY_BIG_NUMER is a constant defined elsewhere
int *pi;
try
{
    pi = new int[VERY_BIG_NUMBER];
    // other code
}
catch(const std::bad_alloc& e)
{
    cout << "cannot allocate" << endl;
    return;
}
// use pointer
delete [] pi;
```

If any code in the `try` block throws an exception control it is passed to the `catch` clause, ignoring any other code that has not been executed yet. The `catch` clause checks the type of the exception object and if it is the correct type (in this case an allocation fault), it creates a reference to that object and passes control to the `catch` block, and the scope of the exception reference is this block. In this example, the code merely prints an error, but you would use it to take action to ensure that the memory allocation failure does not affect subsequent code.

Using other versions of the new operator

Further, a custom type can define a placement operator `new`, which allows you to provide one or more parameters to the custom `new` function. The syntax of the placement `new` is to provide the placement fields through parentheses.

The C++ Standard Library version of the `new` operator provides a version that can take the constant `std::nothrow` as a placement field. This version will not throw an exception if the allocation fails, instead, the failure can only be assessed from the value of the returned pointer:

```
int *pi = new (std::nothrow) int [VERY_BIG_NUMBER];
if (nullptr == pi)
{
    cout << "cannot allocate" << endl;
}
else
{
    // use pointer
    delete [] pi;
}
```

The parentheses before the type are used to pass placement fields. If you use parentheses after the type, these will give a value to initialize the object if the allocation is successful.

Memory lifetime

The memory allocated by `new` will remain valid until you call `delete`. This means that you may have memory with long lifetimes, and the code may be passed around various functions in your code. Consider this code:

```
int *p1 = new int(42);
int *p2 = do_something(p1);
delete p1;
p1 = nullptr;
// what about p2?
```

This code creates a pointer and initializes the memory it points to and then passes the pointer to a function, which itself returns a pointer. Since the `p1` pointer is no longer needed, it is deleted and assigned to `nullptr` so that it cannot be used again. This code looks fine, but the problem is what do you do with the pointer returned by the function? Imagine that the function simply manipulates the data pointed to by the pointer:

```
int *do_something(int *p)
{
    *p *= 10;
    return p;
}
```

In effect, calling `do_something` creates a copy of a pointer, but not a copy of what it points to. This means that when the `p1` pointer is deleted, the memory it points to is no longer available, and so the pointer `p2` points to the invalid memory.

This problem can be addressed using a mechanism called **Resource Acquisition Is Initialization** (**RAII**), which means using the features of C++ objects to manage resources. RAII in C++ needs classes and in particular, copy constructors and destructors. A smart pointer class can be used to manage a pointer so that when it is copied, the memory it points to is also copied. A destructor is a function that is called automatically when the object goes out of scope and so a smart pointer can use this to free memory. Smart pointers and destructors will be covered in `Chapter 6`, *Classes*.

The Windows SDK and pointers

Returning a pointer from a function has its inherent dangers: the responsibility for the memory is passed to the caller, and the caller must ensure that the memory is appropriately de-allocated, otherwise this could cause a memory leak with a corresponding loss of performance. In this section, we will look at some ways that the Window's **Software Development Kit** (**SDK**) provides access to memory buffers and learn some techniques used in C++.

First, it is worth pointing out that any function in the Windows SDK that returns a string, or has a string parameter, will come in two versions. The version suffixed with `A` indicates that the function uses ANSI strings, and the `W` version will use wide character strings. For the purpose of this discussion, it is easier to use the ANSI functions.

The `GetCommandLineA` function has the following prototype (taking into account the Windows SDK `typedef`):

```
char * __stdcall GetCommandLine();
```

All Windows functions are defined as using the `__stdcall` calling convention. Usually, you will see the `typedef` of `WINAPI` used for the `__stdcall` calling convention.

The function can be called like this:

```
//#include <windows.h>
cout << GetCommandLineA() << endl;
```

Notice that we are making no effort to do anything about freeing the returned buffer. The reason is that the pointer points to memory that lives the lifetime of your process, so you *should not* release it. Indeed, if you were to release it, how would you do it? You cannot guarantee that the function was written with the same compiler, or the same libraries that you are using, so you cannot use the C++ `delete` operator or the C `free` function.

When a function returns a buffer, it is important to consult the documentation to see who allocated the buffer, and who should release it.

Another example is `GetEnvironmentStringsA`:

```
char * __stdcall GetEnvironmentStrings();
```

This also returns a pointer to a buffer, but this time the documentation is clear that after using the buffer you should release it. The SDK provides a function to do this called `FreeEnvironmentStrings`. The buffer contains one string for each environment variable in the form `name=value` and each string is terminated by a `NUL` character. The last string in the buffer is simply a `NUL` character, that is, there are two `NUL` characters at the end of the buffer. These functions can be used like this:

```
char *pBuf = GetEnvironmentStringsA();
if (nullptr != pBuf)
{
    char *pVar = pBuf;
    while (*pVar)
    {
        cout << pVar << endl;
        pVar += strlen(pVar) + 1;
    }

    FreeEnvironmentStringsA(pBuf);
}
```

The `strlen` function is part of the C runtime library and it returns the length of a string. You do not need to know how the `GetEnvironmentStrings` function allocates the buffer because the `FreeEnvironmentStrings` will call the correct deallocation code.

There are cases when the developer has the responsibility of allocating a buffer. The Windows SDK provides a function called `GetEnvironmentVariable` to return the value of a named environment variable. When you call this function, you do not know if the environment variable is set, or if it is set, or how big its value is, so this means that you will most likely have to allocate some memory. The prototype of the function is:

```
unsigned long __stdcall GetEnvironmentVariableA(const char *lpName,
    char *lpBuffer, unsigned long nSize);
```

There are two parameters that are pointers to C strings. There is a problem here, a `char*` pointer could be passing *in* a string to the function, or it could be used to pass in a buffer for a string to be returned *out*. How do you know what a `char*` pointer is intended to be used for?

You are given a clue with the full parameter declaration. The `lpName` pointer is marked `const` so the function will not alter the string it points to; this means that it is an *in* parameter. This parameter is used to pass in the name of the environment variable you want to obtain. The other parameter is simply a `char*` pointer, so it could be used to pass a string *in* to the function or *out*, or indeed, both *in* and *out*. The only way to know how to use this parameter is to read the documentation. In this case, it is an *out* parameter; the function will return the value of the environment variable in `lpBuffer` if the variable exists, or if the variable does not exist, the function will leave the buffer untouched and return the value 0. It is your responsibility to allocate this buffer in whatever way you see fit, and you pass the size of this buffer in the last parameter, `nSize`.

The function's return value has two purposes. It is used to indicate that an error has occurred (just one value, 0, which means you have to call the `GetLastError` function to get the error), and it is also used to give you information about the buffer, `lpBuffer`. If the function succeeds, then the return value is the number of characters copied into the buffer excluding the `NULL` terminating character. However, if the function determines that the buffer is too small (it knows the size of the buffer from the `nSize` parameter) to hold the environment variable value, no copy will happen, and the function will return the required size of the buffer, which is the number of characters in the environment variable including the `NULL` terminator.

A common way to call this function is to call it twice, first with a zero-sized buffer and then use the return value to allocate a buffer before calling it again:

```
unsigned long size = GetEnvironmentVariableA("PATH", nullptr, 0);
if (0 == size)
{
    cout << "variable does not exist " << endl;
}
else
{
    char *val = new char[size];
    if (GetEnvironmentVariableA("PATH", val, size) != 0)
    {
        cout << "PATH = ";
        cout << val << endl;
    }
    delete [] val;
}
```

In general, as with all libraries, you have to read the documentation to determine how the parameters are used. The Windows documentation will tell you if a pointer parameter is in, out, or in/out. It will also tell you who owns the memory and whether you have the responsibility for allocating and/or freeing the memory.

Whenever you see a pointer parameter for a function, take special care to check the documentation as to what the pointer is used for and how the memory is managed.

Memory and the C++ Standard Library

The C++ Standard Library provides various classes to allow you to manipulate collections of objects. These classes, called the **Standard Template Library** (STL), provide a standard way to insert items into collection objects and ways to access the items and iterate through entire collections (called iterators). The STL defines collection classes that are implemented as queues, stacks, or as vectors with random access. These classes will be covered in depth Chapter 8, *Using the Standard Library Containers*, so in this section we will limit the discussion to just two classes that behave like C++ built in arrays.

Standard Library arrays

The C+ Standard Library provides two containers that give random access via an indexer to the data. These two containers also allow you to access the underlying memory and since they guarantee to store the items sequentially and contiguous in memory, they can be used when you are required to provide a pointer to a buffer. These two types are both templates, which means that you can use them to hold built-in and custom types. These two collection classes are `array` and `vector`.

Using the stack-based array class

The `array` class is defined in the `<array>` header file. The class allows you to create fixed sized arrays on the stack and, as with built-in arrays, they cannot shrink or expand at runtime. Since they are allocated on the stack, they do not require a call to a memory allocator at runtime, but clearly, they should be smaller than the stack frame size. This means that an `array` is a good choice for small arrays of items. The size of an `array` must be known at compile time and it is passed as a template parameter:

```
array<int, 4> arr { 1, 2, 3, 4 };
```

In this code, the first template parameter in the angle brackets (<>) is the type of each item in the array, and the second parameter is the number of items. This code initializes the array with an initialize list, but note that you still have to provide the size of the array in the template. This object will work like a built-in array (or indeed, any of the Standard Library containers) with ranged `for`:

```
for (int i : arr) cout << i << endl;
```

The reason is that `array` implements the `begin` and `end` functions that are required for this syntax. You can also use indexing to access items:

```
for (int i = 0; i < arr.size(); ++i) cout << arr[i] << endl;
```

The `size` function will return the size of the array and the square bracket indexer gives random access to members of the array. You can access memory outside of the bounds of the array, so for the previously defined array that has four members, you can access `arr[10]`. This may cause unexpected behavior at runtime, or even some kind of memory fault. To guard against this, the class provides a function, `at`, which will perform a range check and if the index is out of range the class will throw the C++ exception `out_of_range`.

The main advantage of using an `array` object is that you get compile time checks to see if you are inadvertently passing the object to a function as a dumb pointer. Consider this function:

```
void use_ten_ints(int*);
```

At runtime, the function does not know the size of the buffer passed to it, and in this case the documentation says that you must pass a buffer with 10 `int` type variables, but, as we have seen, C++ allows a built-in array to be used as a pointer:

```
int arr1[] { 1, 2, 3, 4 };
use_ten_ints(arr1); // oops will read past the end of the buffer
```

There is no compiler check, nor any runtime check to catch this error. The `array` class will not allow such an error to happen because there is no automatic conversion into a dumb pointer:

```
array<int, 4> arr2 { 1, 2, 3, 4 };
use_ten_ints(arr2); // will not compile
```

If you really insist in obtaining a dumb pointer, you can do this and be guaranteed to have access to the data as a contiguous block of memory where the items are stored sequentially:

```
use_ten_ints(&arr2[0]);    // compiles, but on your head be it
use_ten_ints(arr2.data()); // ditto
```

The class is not just a wrapper around a built-in array, it also provides some additional functionality. For example:

```
array<int, 4> arr3;
arr3.fill(42);    // put 42 in each item
arr2.swap(arr3); // swap items in arr2 with items in arr3
```

Using the dynamically allocated vector class

The Standard Library also provides the `vector` class in the `<vector>` header. Again, this class is a template, so you can use it with built-in and custom types. However, unlike `array`, the memory is dynamically allocated, which means that a `vector` can be expanded or shrunk at runtime. The items are stored contiguously so you can access the underlying buffer by calling the `data` function or accessing the address of the first item (to support resizing the collection, the buffer may change, so such pointers should only be used temporarily). And, of course, as with `array`, there is no automatic conversion to a dumb pointer. The `vector` class provides indexed random access with square bracket syntax and a range check with the `at` function. The class also implements the methods to allow the container to be used with Standard Library functions and with ranged `for`.

The `vector` class has more flexibility than the `array` class because you can insert items, and move items around, but this does come with some overhead. Because instances of the class allocate memory dynamically at runtime there is a cost of using an allocator and there is some extra overhead in initialization and destruction (when the `vector` object goes out of scope). Objects of the `vector` class also take more memory than the data it holds. For this reason, it is not suitable for small numbers of items (when `array` is a better choice).

References

A reference is an alias to an object. That is, it is another name for the object, and so access to the object is the same through a reference as it is through the object's variable name. A reference is declared using a `&` symbol on the reference name and it is initialized and accessed in exactly the same way as a variable:

```
int i = 42;
```

```
int *pi = &i;    // pointer to an integer
int& ri1 = i;    // reference to a variable
i = 99;          // change the integer thru the variable
*pi = 101;       // change the integer thru the pointer
ri1 = -1;        // change the integer thru the reference
int& ri2 {i};    // another reference to the variable
int j = 1000;
pi = &j;         // point to another integer
```

In this code, a variable is declared and initialized, then a pointer is initialized to point to this data, and a reference is initialized as an alias for the variable. Reference `ri1` is initialized with an assignment operator, whereas reference `ri2` is initialized using initializer list syntax.

 The pointer and reference have two different meanings. The reference is not initialized to the value of the variable, the variable's data; it is an alias for the variable name.

Wherever the variable is used, the reference can be used; whatever you do to the reference is actually the same as performing the same operation on the variable. A pointer points to data, so you can change the data by dereferencing the pointer, but equally so, you can make the pointer point to any data and change that data by dereferencing the pointer (this is illustrated in the last two lines of the preceding code). You can have several aliases for a variable, and each must be initialized to the variable at the declaration. Once declared, you cannot make a reference refer to a different object.

The following code will not compile:

```
int& r1;             // error, must refer to a variable
int& r2 = nullptr;   // error, must refer to a variable
```

Since a reference is an alias for another variable, it cannot exist without being initialized to a variable. Likewise, you cannot initialize it to anything other than a variable name, so there is no concept of a *null reference*.

Once initialized, a reference is only ever an alias to the one variable. Indeed, when you use a reference as an operand to any operator, the operation is performed on the variable:

```
int x = 1, y = 2;
int& rx = x; // declaration, means rx is an alias for x
rx = y;      // assignment, changes value of x to the value of y
```

In this code, `rx` is an alias to the variable `x`, so the assignment in the last line simply assigns `x` with the value of `y`: the assignment is performed on the aliased variable. Further, if you take the address of a reference, you are returned the address of the variable it references. While you can have a reference to an array, you cannot have an array of references.

Constant references

The reference used so far allows you to change the variable it is an alias for, therefore it has lvalue semantics. There are also `const` lvalue references, that is, a reference to an object that you can read, but not write to.

As with `const` pointers, you declare a `const` reference using the `const` keyword on a lvalue reference. This essentially makes the reference read-only: you can access the variable's data to read it, but not to change it.

```
int i = 42;
const int& ri = i;
ri = 99;              // error!
```

Returning references

Sometimes an object will be passed to a function and the semantics of the function is that the object should be returned. An example of this is the << operator used with the stream objects. Calls to this operator are *chained*:

```
cout << "The value is " << 42;
```

This is actually a series of calls to functions called `operator<<`, one that takes a `const char*` pointer, and another that takes an `int` parameter. These functions also have an `ostream` parameter for the stream object that will be used. However, if this is simply an `ostream` parameter then it would mean that a copy of the parameter would be made, and the insertion would be performed on the copy. Stream objects often use buffering, so changes to a copy of a stream object may not have the desired effect. Further, to enable the *chaining* of the insertion operators, the insertion functions will return the stream object passed as a parameter. The intention is to pass the same stream object through multiple function calls. If such a function returned an object then it would be a copy and not only would this means that a series of insertions would involve lots of copies being made, these copies would also be temporary and so any changes to the stream (for example, manipulators such as `std::hex`) would not persist. To address these issues, references are used. A typical prototype of such a function is:

```
ostream& operator<<(ostream& _Ostr, int _Val);
```

Clearly you have to be careful about returning a reference since you have to ensure that the object lifetime lasts as long as the reference. This `operator<<` function will return the reference passed in the first parameter, but in the following code a reference is returned to an automatic variable:

```
string& hello()
{
    string str ("hello");
    return str; // don't do this!
}   // str no longer exists at this point
```

In the preceding code, the `string` object only lives as long as the function, so the reference returned by this function will refer to an object that does not exist. Of course, you can return a reference to a `static` variable declared in a function.

Returning a reference from a function is a common idiom, but whenever you consider doing this make sure that the lifetime of the aliased variable is not the scope of the function.

Temporaries and references

The lvalue references must refer to a variable, but C++ has some odd rules when it comes to `const` references declared on the stack. If the reference is a `const`, the compiler will extend the lifetime of a temporary for the lifetime of the reference. For example, if you use the initialization list syntax, the compiler will create a temporary:

```
const int& cri { 42 };
```

In this code, the compiler will create a temporary `int` and initialize it to a value and then alias it to the `cri` reference (it is important that this reference is `const`). The temporary is available through the reference while it is in scope. This may look a little odd, but consider using a `const` reference in this function:

```
void use_string(const string& csr);
```

You can call this function with a `string` variable, a variable that will explicitly convert to a `string` or with a `string` literal:

```
string str { "hello" };
use_string(str);       // a std::string object
const char *cstr = "hello";
use_string(cstr);      // a C string can be converted to a std::string
use_string("hello");   // a literal can be converted to a std::string
```

In most cases, you'll not want to have a `const` reference to a built-in type, but with custom types where there will be an overhead in making copies there is an advantage and, as you can see here, the compiler will fall back to creating a temporary if required.

The rvalue references

C++11 defines a new type of reference, rvalue references. Prior to C++11, there was no way that code (like an assignment operator) could tell if the rvalue passed to it was a temporary object or not. If such a function is passed a reference to an object, then the function has to be careful not to change the reference because this would affect the object it refers to. If the reference is to a temporary object, then the function can do what it likes to the temporary object because the object will not live after the function completes. C++11 allows you to write code specifically for temporary objects, so in the case of the assignment, the operator for temporary objects can just *move* the data from the temporary into the object being assigned. In contrast, if the reference is not to a temporary object then the data will have to be *copied*. If the data is large, then this prevents a potentially expensive allocation and copy. This enables so-called *move semantics*.

Consider this rather contrived code:

```
string global{ "global" };

string& get_global()
{
    return global;
}

string& get_static()
{
    static string str { "static" };
    return str;
}

string get_temp()
{
    return "temp";
}
```

The three functions return a `string` object. In the first two cases, the `string` has the lifetime of the program and so a reference can be returned. In the last function, the function returns a string literal, so a temporary `string` object is constructed. All three can be used to provide a `string` value. For example:

```
cout << get_global() << endl;
cout << get_static() << endl;
cout << get_temp() << endl;
```

All three can provide a string that can be used to assign a `string` object. The important point is that the first two functions return along a lived object, but the third function returns a temporary object, but these objects can be used the same.

If these functions returned access to a large object, you would not want to pass the object to another function, so instead, in most cases, you'll want to pass the objects returned by these functions as references. For example:

```
void use_string(string& rs);
```

The reference parameter prevents another copy of the string. However, this is just half of the story. The `use_string` function could manipulate the string. For example, the following function creates a new `string` from the parameter, but replaces the letters a, b, and o with an underscore (indicating the gaps in words without those letters, replicating what life would be like without donations of the blood types A, B, and O). A simple implementation would look like this:

```
void use_string(string& rs)
{
    string s { rs };
    for (size_t i = 0; i < s.length(); ++i)
    {
        if ('a' == s[i] || 'b' == s[i] || 'o' == s[i])
        s[i] = '_';
    }
    cout << s << endl;
}
```

The string object has an index operator (`[]`), so you can treat it like an array of characters, both reading the values of characters and assigning values to character positions. The size of the `string` is obtained through the `length` function, which returns an `unsigned int` (`typedef` to `size_t`). Since the parameter is a reference, it means that any change to the `string` will be reflected in the `string` passed to the function. The intention of this code is to leave other variables intact, so it first makes a copy of the parameter. Then on the copy, the code iterates through all of the characters changing the a, b, and o characters to an underscore before printing out the result.

This code clearly has a copy overhead--creating the string, s, from the reference, rs; but this is necessary if we want to pass strings like those from get_global or get_static to this function because otherwise the changes would be made to the actual global and static variables.

However, the temporary string returned from get_temp is another situation. This temporary object only exists until the end of the statement that calls get_temp. Thus, it is possible to make changes to the variable knowing that it will affect nothing else. This means that you can use move semantics:

```cpp
void use_string(string&& s)
{
    for (size_t i = 0; i < s.length(); ++i)
    {
        if ('a' == s[i] || 'b' == s[i] || 'o' == s[i]) s[i] = '_';
    }
    cout << s << endl;
}
```

There are just two changes here. The first is that the parameter is identified as an rvalue reference using the && suffix to the type. The other change is that the changes are made on the object that the reference refers to because we know that it is a temporary and the changes will be discarded, so it will affect no other variables. Note that there are now *two* functions, overloads with the same name: one with an lvalue reference, and one with an rvalue reference. When you call this function, the compiler will call the right one according to the parameter passed to it:

```cpp
use_string(get_global()); // string&  version
use_string(get_static()); // string&  version
use_string(get_temp());   // string&& version
use_string("C string");   // string&& version
string str{"C++ string"};
use_string(str);          // string&  version
```

Recall that get_global and get_static return references to objects that will live the lifetime of the program, and for this reason the compiler chooses the use_string version that takes an lvalue reference. The changes are made on a temporary variable within the function, and this has a copy overhead. The get_temp returns a temporary object and so the compiler calls the overload of use_string that takes an rvalue reference. This function alters the object that the reference refers to, but this does not matter because the object will not last beyond the semicolon at the end of the line. The same can be said for calling use_string with a C-like string literal: the compiler will create a temporary string object and call the overload that has an rvalue reference parameter. In the final example in this code, a C++ string object is created on the stack and passed to use_string.

The compiler sees that this object is an lvalue and potentially can be altered, so it calls the overload that takes an lvalue reference that is implemented in a way that only alters a temporary local variable in the function.

This example shows that the C++ compiler will detect when a parameter is a temporary object and will call the overload with an rvalue reference. Typically, this facility is used when writing *copy constructors* (special functions used to create a new custom type from an existing instance) and assignment operators so that these functions can implement the lvalue reference overload to copy the data from the parameter, and the rvalue reference overload to move the data from the temporary to the new object. Other uses are for writing custom types that are *move only*, where they use resources that cannot be copied, for example file handles.

Ranged for and references

As an example of what you can do with references, it is worth looking at the ranged `for` facility in C++11. The following code is quite straightforward; the array `squares` is initialized with the squares of 0 to 4:

```
constexpr int size = 4;
int squares[size];

for (int i = 0; i < size; ++i)
{
    squares[i] = i * i;
}
```

The compiler knows the size of the array so you can use ranged `for` to print out the values in the array. In the following, on each iteration, the local variable `j` is a copy of the item in the array. As a copy, it means that you can read the value, but any changes made to the variable will not be reflected to the array. So, the following code works as expected; it prints out the contents of the array:

```
for (int j : squares)
{
    cout << J << endl;
}
```

If you want to change the values in the array, then you have to have access to the actual values, and not a copy. The way to do this in a ranged `for` is to use a reference as the loop variable:

```
for (int& k : squares)
{
    k *= 2;
}
```

Now, on every iteration, the `k` variable is an alias to an actual member in the array, so whatever you do to the `k` variable is actually performed on the array member. In this example, every member of the `squares` array is multiplied by 2. You cannot use `int*` for the type of k because the compiler sees that the type of the items in the array is `int` and will use this as the loop variable in the ranged `for`. Since a reference is an alias for a variable, the compiler will allow a reference as the loop variable, and moreover, since the reference is an alias, you can use it to change the actual array member.

Ranged `for` becomes interesting for multidimensional arrays. For example, in the following, a two-dimensional array is declared and an attempt is made to use nested loops using `auto` variables:

```
int arr[2][3] { { 2, 3, 4 }, { 5, 6, 7} };
for (auto row : arr)
{
    for (auto col : row) // will not compile
    {
        cout << col << " " << endl;
    }
}
```

Since a two-dimensional array is an array of arrays (each row is a one-dimensional array), the intention is to obtain each row in the outer loop and then in the inner loop access each item in the row. There are several issues with this approach, but the immediate issue is that this code will not compile.

The compiler will complain about the inner loop, saying that it cannot find a `begin` or `end` function for the type `int*`. The reason is that ranged `for` uses iterator objects and for arrays it uses the C++ Standard Library functions, `begin` and `end,` to create these objects. The compiler will see from the `arr` array in the outer ranged for that each item is an `int[3]` array, and so in the outer `for` loop the loop variable will be a *copy* of each element, in this case an `int[3]` array. You cannot copy arrays like this, so the compiler will provide a pointer to the first element, an `int*`, and this is used in the inner `for` loop.

The compiler will attempt to obtain iterators for `int *`, but this is not possible because an `int *` contains no information about how many items it points to. There is a version of `begin` and `end` defined for `int[3]` (and all sizes of arrays) but not for `int *`.

A simple change makes this code compile. Simply turn the `row` variable into a reference:

```
for (auto& row : arr)
{
    for (auto col : row)
    {
        cout << col << " " << endl;
    }
}
```

The reference parameter indicates that an alias is used for the `int[3]` array and, of course, an alias is the same as the element. Using `auto` hides the ugliness of what is actually going on. The inner loop variable is, of course, an `int` since this is the type of the item in the array. The outer loop variable is in fact `int (&)[3]`. That is, it is a reference to an `int[3]` (the parentheses used to indicate that it references an `int[3]` and is not an array of `int&`).

Using pointers in practice

A common requirement is to have a collection that can be an arbitrary size and can grow and shrink at runtime. The C++ Standard Library provides various classes to allow you to do this, as will be described in `Chapter 8`, *Using the Standard Library Containers*. The following example illustrates some of the principles of how these standard collections are implemented. In general, you should use the C++ Standard Library classes rather than implementing your own. Further, the Standard Library classes *encapsulate* code together in a class and since we have not covered classes yet, the following code will use functions that potentially can be called incorrectly. So, you should regard this example as just that, example code. A linked list is a common data structure. These are typically used for queues where the order of items is important. For example, a first-in-first-out queue where tasks are performed in the order that they are inserted in the queue. In this example, each task is represented as a structure that contains the task description and a pointer to the next task to be performed.

If the pointer to the next task is `nullptr` then this means the current task is the last task in the list:

```
struct task
{
    task* pNext;
    string description;
};
```

Recall from the last chapter that you access members of a structure using the dot operator through an instance:

```
task item;
item.descrription = "do something";
```

In this case, the compiler will create a `string` object initialized with the string literal `do something` and assign it to the `description` member of the instance called `item`. You can also create a `task` on the free store using the `new` operator:

```
task* pTask = new task;
// use the object
delete pTask;
```

In this case, the members of the object have to be accessed through a pointer, and C++ provides the `->` operator to give you this access:

```
task* pTask = new task;
pTask->descrription = "do something";
// use the object
delete pTask;
```

Here the `description` member is assigned to the string. Note that since `task` is a structure there are no access restrictions, something that is important with classes and described in Chapter 6, *Classes*.

Creating the project

Create a new folder under C:\Beginning_C++ called Chapter_04. Start Visual C++ and create a C++ source file and save it to the folder you just created, as tasks.cpp. Add a simple main function without parameters, and provide support for input and output using C++ streams:

```
#include <iostream>
#include <string>
using namespace std;

int main()
{
}
```

Above the main function, add a definition for the structure that represents a task in the list:

```
using namespace std;
struct task {
    task* pNext;
    string description;
};
```

This has two members. The guts of the object is the description item. In our example, executing a task will involve printing the description item to the console. In an actual project, you'll most likely have many data items associated with the task, and you may even have member functions to execute the task, but we have not yet covered member functions; that's a topic for Chapter 6, *Classes*.

The plumbing of the linked list is the other member, pNext. Note that the task structure has not been completely defined at the point that the pNext member is declared. This is not a problem because pNext is a *pointer*. You cannot have a data member of an undefined, or a partially defined type, because the compiler will not know how much memory to allocate for it. You can have a pointer member to a partially defined type because a pointer member is the same size irrespective of what it points to.

If we know the first link in a list, then we can access the whole list and, in our example, this will be a global variable. When constructing the list, the construction functions need to know the end of the list so that they can attach a new link to the list. Again, for convenience, we will make this a global variable. Add the following pointers after the definition of the task structure:

```
task* pHead = nullptr;
task* pCurrent = nullptr;
int main()
{
}
```

As it stands, the code does nothing, but it is a good opportunity to compile the file to test that there are no typos:

```
cl /EHsc tasks.cpp
```

Adding a task object to the list

The next thing to do to provide the code is to add a new task to the task list. This needs to create a new task object and initialize it appropriately and then add it to the list by altering the last link in the list to point to the new link.

Above the main function, add the following function:

```
void queue_task(const string& name)
{
    . . .
}
```

The parameter is a const reference because we will not change the parameter and we do not want the overhead of a copy being made. The first thing this function must do is create a new link, so add the following lines:

```
void queue_task(const string& name)
{
    task* pTask = new task;
    pTask->description = name;
    pTask->pNext = nullptr;
}
```

The first line creates a new link on the free store, and the following lines initialize it. This is not necessarily the best way of initializing such an object, and a better mechanism, a constructor, will be covered in Chapter 6, *Classes*. Notice that the pNext item is initialized to nullptr; this indicates that the link will be at the end of the list.

The final part of this function adds the link to the list, that is, it makes the link the last in the list. However, if the list is empty, it means that this link is also the *first* link in the list. The code must perform both actions. Add the following code to the end of the function:

```
if (nullptr == pHead)
{
    pHead = pTask;
    pCurrent = pTask;
}
else
{
    pCurrent->pNext = pTask;
    pCurrent = pTask;
}
```

The first line checks to see if the list is empty. If pHead is nullptr, it means that there are no other links and so the current link is the first link, and so both pHead and pCurrent are initialized to the new link pointer. If there are existing links in the list, the link has to be added to the last link, so in the else clause the first line makes the last link point to the new link and the second line initializes pCurrent with the new link pointer, making the new link the last link for any new insertions to the list.

The items are added to the list by calling this function in the main function. In this example, we will queue the tasks to wallpaper a room. This involves removing the old wallpaper, filling any holes in the wall, sizing the wall (painting it with diluted paste to make the wall sticky), and then hanging the pasted wallpaper to the wall. You have to do these tasks in this order, you cannot change the order, so these tasks are ideal for a linked list. In the main function add the following lines:

```
queue_task("remove old wallpaper");
queue_task("fill holes");
queue_task("size walls");
queue_task("hang new wallpaper");
```

After the last line, the list has been created. The pHead variable points to the first item in the list and you can access any other item in the list simply by following the pNext member from one link to the next.

You can compile the code, but there is no output. Worse, as the code stands, there is a memory leak. The program has no code to `delete` the memory occupied by the `task` objects created on the free store by the `new` operator.

Deleting the task list

Iterating through the list is simple, you follow the `pNext` pointer from one link to the next. Before doing this, let's first fix the memory leak introduced in the last section. Above the `main` function, add the following function:

```
bool remove_head()
{
    if (nullptr == pHead) return false;
    task* pTask = pHead;
    pHead = pHead->pNext;
    delete pTask;
    return (pHead != nullptr);
}
```

This function will remove the link at the beginning of the list and make sure that the `pHead` pointer points to the next link, which will become the new beginning of the list. The function returns a `bool` value indicating if there are any more links in the list. If this function returns `false` then it means the entire list has been deleted.

The first line checks to see if this function has been called with an empty list. Once we are reassured that the list has at least one link, we create a temporary copy of this pointer. The reason is that the intention is to delete the first item and make `pHead` point to the next item, and to do that we have to do those steps in reverse: make `pHead` point to the next item and then delete the item that `pHead` previously pointed to.

To delete the entire list, you need to iterate through the links, and this can be carried out using a `while` loop. Below the `remove_head` function, add the following:

```
void destroy_list()
{
    while (remove_head());
}
```

To delete the entire list, and address the memory leak, add the following line to the bottom of the main function

```
    destroy_list();
}
```

You can now compile the code, and run it. However, you'll see no output because all the code does is create a list and then delete it.

Iterating the task list

The next step is to iterate the list from the first link following each pNext pointer until we get to the end of the list. For each link accessed, the task should be executed. Start by writing a function that performs the execution by printing out the description of the task and then returning a pointer to the next task. Just above the main function, add the following code:

```
task *execute_task(const task* pTask)
{
    if (nullptr == pTask) return nullptr;
    cout << "executing " << pTask->description << endl;
    return pTask->pNext;
}
```

The parameter here is marked as const because we will not change the task object pointed to by the pointer. This indicates to the compiler that if the code does try to change the object there is an issue. The first line checks to make sure that the function is not called with a null pointer. If it was then the following line would dereference an invalid pointer and cause a memory access fault. The last line returns the pointer to the next link (which could be nullptr for the last link in the list), so that the function can be called in a loop. After this function, add the following to iterate the entire list:

```
void execute_all()
{
    task* pTask = pHead;
    while (pTask != nullptr)
    {
        pTask = execute_task(pTask);
    }
}
```

This code starts at the beginning, pHead, and calls execute_task on each link in the list until the function returns a nullptr. Add a call to this function towards the end of the main function:

```
    execute_all();
    destroy_list();
}
```

You can now compile and run the code. The result will be:

```
    executing remove old wallpaper
  executing fill holes
      executing size walls
      executing hang new wallpaper
```

Inserting items

One of the advantages of linked lists is that you can insert items into the list by only allocating one new item and changing the appropriate pointers to point to it, and make it point to the next item in the list. Contrast this to allocating an array of task objects; if you want to insert a new item somewhere in the middle, you would have to allocate a new array big enough for the old items and the new one and then copy the old items to the new array, copying in the new item in the right position.

The problem with the wallpaper task list is that the room has some painted wood and, as any decorator knows, it is best to paint the woodwork before hanging the wallpaper, and usually before sizing the walls. We need to insert a new task between filling any holes and sizing the walls. Further, before you do any decorating, you should cover any furniture in the room before doing anything else, so you need to add a new task to the beginning.

The first step is to find the position where we want to put our new task to paint the woodwork. We will look for the task that we want to be before the task we are inserting. Before main add the following:

```
task *find_task(const string& name)
{
    task* pTask = pHead;

    while (nullptr != pTask)
    {
        if (name == pTask->description) return pTask;
        pTask = pTask->pNext;
    }
    return nullptr;
}
```

This code searches the entire list for a link with the description that matches the parameter. This is carried out through a loop which uses the string comparison operator, and if the required link is found, a pointer to that link is returned. If the comparison fails, the loop initializes the loop variable to the address of the next link and if this address is nullptr it means that the required task is not in the list.

After the list is created in the main function, add the following code to search for the `fill holes` task:

```
queue_task("hang new wallpaper");

// oops, forgot to paint
woodworktask* pTask = find_task("fill holes");
if (nullptr != pTask) {
    // insert new item after pTask
}
execute_all();
```

If the `find_task` function returns a valid pointer, then we can add an item at this point.

The function to do this will allow you to add a new item after any item in the list that you pass to it and, if you pass `nullptr`, it will add the new item to the beginning. It's called `insert_after`, but clearly, if you pass `nullptr` it also means *insert before the beginning*. Add the following just above the `main` function:

```
void insert_after(task* pTask, const string& name)
{
    task* pNewTask = new task;
    pNewTask->description = name;
    if (nullptr != pTask)
    {
        pNewTask->pNext = pTask->pNext;
        pTask->pNext = pNewTask;
    }
}
```

The second parameter is a `const` reference because we will not change the `string`, but the first parameter is not a `const` pointer because we will be changing the object that it points to. This function creates a new `task` object and initializes the `description` member to the new task name. It then checks to see if the `task` pointer passed to the function is null. If it is not, then the new item can be inserted *after* the specified link in the list. To do this, the new link `pNext` member is initialized to be the next item in the list, and the `pNext` member of the previous link is initialized to the address of the new link.

What about inserting an item at the beginning, when the function is passed `nullptr` as the item to insert after? Add the following `else` clause.

```
void insert_after(task* pTask, const string& name)
{
    task* pNewTask = new task;
    pNewTask->description = name;
    if (nullptr != pTask)
    {
        pNewTask->pNext = pTask->pNext;
        pTask->pNext = pNewTask;
    }
    else {
        pNewTask->pNext = pHead;
        pHead = pNewTask;
    }
}
```

Here, we make the `pNext` member of the new item to point to the old beginning of the list and then change `pHead` to point to the new item.

Now, in the `main` function, you can add a call to insert a new task to paint the woodwork, and since we also forgot to indicate that it is best to decorate a room after covering all furniture with dustsheets, add a task to do that first in the list:

```
task* pTask = find_task("fill holes");
if (nullptr != pTask)
{
    insert_after(pTask, "paint woodwork");
}
insert_after(nullptr, "cover furniture");
```

You can now compile the code. When you run the code, you should see the tasks performed in the required order:

```
    executing cover furniture
    executing remove old wallpaper
executing fill holes
executing paint woodwork
executing size walls
executing hang new wallpaper
```

Summary

It can be argued that one of the main reasons to use C++ is that you have direct access to memory using pointers. This is a feature that programmers of most other languages are prevented from doing. This means that as a C++ programmer, you are a special type of programmer: someone who is trusted with memory. In this chapter, you have seen how to obtain and use pointers and some examples of how inappropriate use of pointers can make your code go horribly wrong.

In the next chapter, we will cover functions which will include the description of another type of pointer: function pointers. If you are trusted with pointers to data and function pointers, you really are a special type of programmer.

5
Using Functions

Functions are the basic infrastructure of C++; code is contained in functions and to execute that code you have to call a function. C++ is remarkably flexible in the ways that you can define and call functions: you can define functions with a fixed number of parameters or a variable number of parameters; you can write generic code so that the same code can be used with different types; and you can even write generic code with a variable number of types.

Defining C++ functions

At the most basic level, a function has parameters, has code to manipulate the parameters, and returns a value. C++ gives you several ways to determine these three aspects. In the following section, we will cover those parts of a C++ function from the left to the right of the declaration. Functions can also be **templated**, but this will be left to a later section.

Declaring and defining functions

A function must be defined exactly once, but through overloading, you can have many functions with the same name that differ by their parameters. Code that uses a function has to have access to the name of the function, and so it needs to have access to either the function definition (for example, the function is defined earlier in the source file) or the declaration of the function (also called the function prototype). The compiler uses the prototype to type-check that the *calling code* is calling the function, using the right types.

Typically, libraries are implemented as separate compiled library files and prototypes of the library functions are provided in header files so that many source files can use the functions by including the headers. However, if you know the function name, parameters, and return type, you can type the prototype yourself in your file.

Whichever you do, you are simply providing the information for the compiler to type-check the expression that calls function. It is up to the linker to locate the function in the library and either copy the code into the executable or set up the infrastructure to use the function from a shared library. Including the header file for a library does not mean that you will be able to use the functions from that library because in standard C++, the header file does not have information about the library that contains a function.

Visual C++ provides a `pragma` called `comment`, which can be used with the `lib` option as a message to the linker to link with a specific library. So `#pragma comment(lib, "mylib")` in a header file will tell the linker to link with `mylib.lib`. In general, it is better to use project management tools, such as **nmake** or **MSBuild**, to ensure that the right libraries are linked in the project.

Most of the C Runtime Library is implemented this way: the function is compiled in a static library or a dynamic link library, and the function prototypes are provided in a header file. You provide the library in the linker command line, and typically you will include the header file for the library so that the function prototypes are available to the compiler. As long as the linker knows about the library, you can type the prototype in your code (and describe it as *external linkage* so the compiler knows the function is defined elsewhere). This can save you from including some large files into your source files, files that will mostly have prototypes of functions that you will not use.

However, much of the C++ Standard Library is implemented in header files, which means that these files can be quite large. You can save compile time by including these header files in a precompiled header, as explained in `Chapter 1`, *Starting with C++*.

So far in this book, we have used one source file so all the functions are defined in the same file as where they are used, and we have defined the function before calling it, that is, the function is defined *above* the code that calls it. You do not have to define the function before it is used as long as the function prototype is defined before the function is called:

```
int mult(int, int);

int main()
{
    cout << mult(6, 7) << endl;
    return 0;
}

int mult(int lhs, int rhs)
{
    return lhs * rhs;
}
```

The `mult` function is defined after the `main` function, but this code will compile because the prototype is given before the `main` function. This is called a **forward declaration**. The prototype does not have to have the parameter names. This is because the compiler only needs to know the types of the parameters, not their names. However, since parameter names should be self-documenting, it is usually a good idea to give the parameter names so that you can see the purpose of the function.

Specifying linkage

In the previous example, the function is defined in the same source file, so there is *internal linkage*. If the function is defined in another file, the prototype will have *external linkage* and so the prototype will have to be defined like this:

```
extern int mult(int, int);        // defined in another file
```

The `extern` keyword is one of many specifiers that you can add to a function declaration, and in the previous chapters we have seen others. For example, the `static` specifier can be used on a prototype to indicate that the function has internal linkage and the name can only be used in the current source file. In the preceding example, it is appropriate to mark the function as `static` in the prototype.

```
static int mult(int, int);        // defined in this file
```

You can also declare a function as `extern "C"`, which affects how the name of the function is stored in the object file. This is important for libraries, and will be covered shortly.

Inlining

If a function calculates a value that can be calculated at compile time, you can mark it on the left of the declaration with `constexpr` to indicate that the compiler can optimize the code by computing the value at compile time. If the function value can be calculated at compile time, it means that the parameters in the function call must be known at compile time and so they must be literals. The function must also be a single line. If these restrictions are not met, then the compiler is free to ignore the specifier.

Related is the `inline` specifier. This can be placed on the left of a function declaration as a suggestion to the compiler that, when other code calls the function, rather than the compiler inserting a jump to the function in memory (and the creation of a stack frame), the compiler should put a copy of the actual code in the calling function. Again, the compiler is free to ignore this specifier.

Determining the return type

Functions may be written to run a routine and not return a value. If this is the case, you must specify that the function returns `void`. In most cases, a function will return a value, if only to indicate that the function has completed correctly. There is no requirement that the calling function obtains the return value or does anything with it. The calling function can simply ignore the return value.

There are two ways to specify the return type. The first way is to give the type before the function name. This is the method used in most of the examples so far. The second way is called the **trailing return type** and requires that you place `auto` as the return type before the function name and use the `->` syntax to give the actual return type after the parameter list:

```
inline auto mult(int lhs, int rhs) -> int
{
    return lhs * rhs;
}
```

This function is so simple that it is a good candidate to be inlined. The return type on the left is given as `auto`, meaning that the actual return type is specified after the parameter list. The `-> int` means that the return type is `int`. This syntax has the same effect as using `int` on the left. This syntax is useful when a function is templated and the return type may not be noticeable.

In this trivial example, you can omit the return type entirely and just use `auto` on the left of the function name. This syntax means that the compiler will deduce the return type from the actual value returned. Clearly the compiler will only know what the return type is from the function body, so you cannot provide a prototype for such functions.

Finally, if a function does not return at all (for example, if it goes into a never-ending loop to poll some value) you can mark it with the C++11 attribute `[[noreturn]]`. The compiler can use this attribute to write more efficient code because it knows that it does not need to provide code to return a value.

Naming the function

In general, function names have the same rules for variables: they must begin with a letter or an underscore and cannot contain spaces or other punctuation characters. Following the general principle of self-documenting code, you should name the function according to what it does. There is one exception and these are the special functions used to provide overloads for operators (which are mostly punctuation symbols). These functions have a name in the form of `operatorx`, where `x` is the operator that you will use in your code. A later section will explain how to implement operators with global functions.

Operators are one example of overloading. You can overload any function, that is, use the same name but provide implementations with different parameter types or different numbers of parameters.

Function parameters

Functions may have no parameters, in which case the function is defined with a pair of empty parentheses. A function definition must give the type and name of the parameters between the parentheses. In many cases, functions will have a fixed number of parameters, but you can write functions with a variable number of parameters. You can also define functions with default values for some of the parameters, in effect, providing a function that overloads itself on the number of parameters passed to the function. Variable argument lists and default arguments will be covered later.

Specifying exceptions

Functions can also be marked to indicate whether they will throw an exception. More details about exceptions will be given in `Chapter 10`, *Diagnostics and Debugging*, but there are two syntaxes you need to be aware of.

Earlier versions of C++ allowed you to use the `throw` specifier on a function in three ways: firstly, you can provide a comma separated list of the types of the exceptions that may be thrown by code in the function; secondly, you can provide an ellipsis (. . .) which means that the function may throw any exception; and thirdly, you can provide an empty pair of parentheses, which means the function will not throw exceptions. The syntax looks like this:

```
int calculate(int param) throw(overflow_error)
{
    // do something which potentially may overflow
}
```

The `throw` specifier has been deprecated in C++11 largely because the ability to indicate the type of exception was not useful. However, the version of `throw` that indicates that no exception will be thrown was found to be useful because it enables a compiler to optimize code by providing no code infrastructure to handle exceptions. C++11 retains this behavior with the `noexcept` specifier:

```cpp
// C++11 style:
int increment(int param) noexcept
{
    // check the parameter and handle overflow appropriately
}
```

Function body

After the return type, function name, and parameters have been determined, you then need to define the body of the function. The code for a function must appear between a pair of braces (`{ }`). If the function returns a value, then the function must have at least one line (the last line in the function) with the `return` statement. This must return the appropriate type or a type that can be implicitly converted to the return type of the function. As mentioned before, if the function is declared as returning `auto`, then the compiler will deduce the return type. In this case, all the `return` statements *must* return the same type.

Using function parameters

When a function is called, the compiler checks all the overloads of the function to find one that matches the parameters in the calling code. If there is no exact match then standard and user-defined type conversions are performed, so the values provided by the calling code may be a different type from the parameters.

By default, parameters are passed by value and a copy is made, which means that the parameters are treated as local variables in the function. The writer of the function can decide to pass a parameter by reference, either through a pointer or a C++ reference. **Pass-by-reference** means that the variable in the calling code can be altered by the function, but this can be controlled by making the parameters `const`, in which case the reason for pass-by-reference is to prevent a (potentially costly) copy being made. Built-in arrays are always passed as a pointer to the first item to the array. The compiler will create temporaries when needed. For example, when a parameter is a `const` reference and the calling code passes a literal, a temporary object is created, and is only available to code in the function:

```cpp
void f(const float&);
```

```
f(1.0);                  // OK, temporary float created
double d = 2.0;
f(d);                    // OK, temporary float created
```

Passing Initializer lists

You can pass an initializer list as a parameter if that list can be converted to the type of the parameter. For example:

```
struct point { int x; int y; };

void set_point(point pt);

int main()
{
    point p;
    p.x = 1; p.y = 1;
    set_point(p);
    set_point({ 1, 1 });
    return 0;
}
```

This code defines a structure that has two members. In the `main` function, a new instance of `point` is created on the stack and it is initialized by accessing the members directly. The instance is then passed to a function that has a `point` parameter. Since the parameter of `set_point` is pass-by-value, the compiler creates a copy of the structure on the stack of the function. The second call of `set_point` does the same: the compiler will create a temporary `point` object on the stack of the function and initialize it with the values in the initializer list.

Using default parameters

There are situations when you have one or more parameters that have values that are so frequently used that you want them to be treated as a default value for the parameter, while still having the option of allowing the caller to provide a different value if necessary. To do this, you provide the default value in the parameter list of the definition:

```
void log_message(const string& msg, bool clear_screen = false)
{
    if (clear_screen) clear_the_screen();
    cout << msg << endl;
}
```

In most cases, this function is expected to be used to print a single message, but occasionally the user may want to have the screen cleared first (say, for the first message, or after a pre-determined count of lines). To accommodate this use of the function, the `clear_screen` parameter is given a default value of `false`, but the caller still has the option of passing a value:

```
log_message("first message", true);
log_message("second message");
bool user_decision = ask_user();
log_message("third message", user_decision);
```

Note that the default values occur in the function definition, not in a function prototype, so if the `log_message` function is declared in a header file the prototype should be:

```
extern void log_message(const string& msg, bool clear_screen);
```

The parameters that can have default values are the right-most parameters.

You can treat each parameter with a default value as representing a separate overload of the function, so conceptually the `log_message` function should be treated as two functions:

```
extern void log_message(const string& msg, bool clear_screen);
extern void log_message(const string& msg); // conceptually
```

If you define a `log_message` function that has just a `const string&` parameter, then the compiler will not know whether to call that function or the version where `clear_screen` is given a default value of `false`.

Variable number of parameters

A function with default parameter values can be regarded as having a variable number of user-provided parameters, where you know at compile time the maximum number of parameters and their values if the caller chooses not to provide values. C++ also allows you to write functions where there is less certainty about the number of parameters, and the values passed to the function.

There are three ways to have a variable number of parameters: initializer lists, C-style variable argument lists, and variadic templated functions. The latter of these three will be addressed later in the chapter once templated functions have been covered.

Initializer lists

So far in this book, initializer lists have been treated as a kind of C++11 construct, a bit like built-in arrays. In fact, when you use the initializer list syntax using braces, the compiler actually creates an instance of the templated `initialize_list` class. If an initializer list is used to initialize another type (for example, to initialize a `vector`), the compiler creates an `initialize_list` object with the values given between the braces, and the container object is initialized using the `initialize_list` iterators. This ability to create an `initialize_list` object from a braced initializer list can be used by to give a function a variable number of parameters, albeit all of the parameters must be of the same type:

```cpp
#include <initializer_list>

int sum(initializer_list<int> values)
{
    int sum = 0;
    for (int i : values) sum += i;
    return sum;
}

int main()
{
    cout << sum({}) << endl;                        // 0
    cout << sum({-6, -5, -4, -3, -2, -1}) << endl; // -21
    cout << sum({10, 20, 30}) << endl;             // 60
    return 0;
}
```

The `sum` function has a single parameter of `initializer_list<int>`, which can only be initialized with a list of integers. The `initializer_list` class has very few functions because it only exists to give access to the values in the braced list. Significantly, it implements a `size` function that returns the number of items in the list, and `begin` and `end` functions that return a pointer to the first item in the list, and to the position after the last item. These two functions are needed to give iterator access to the list, and it enables you to use the object with the ranged-`for` syntax.

 This is typical in the C++ Standard Library. If a container holds data in a contiguous block of memory, then pointer arithmetic can use the pointer to the first item and a pointer immediately after the last item to determine how many items are in the container. Incrementing the first pointer gives sequential access to every item, and pointer arithmetic allows random access. All containers implement a `begin` and `end` function to give access to the container *iterators*.

In this example, the `main` function calls this function three times, each time with a braced initializer list, and the function will return a sum of the items in the list.

Clearly this technique means that each item in the *variable* parameter list has to be the same type (or a type that can be converted to the specified type). You would have the same result if the parameter had been a `vector`; the difference is that an `initializer_list` parameter requires less initialization.

Argument lists

C++ inherits from C the idea of argument lists. To do this, you use the ellipses syntax (. . .) as the last parameter to indicate that the caller can provide zero or more parameters. The compiler will check how the function is called and will allocate space on the stack for these extra parameters. To access the extra parameters, your code must include the `<cstdarg>` header file, which has macros that you can use to extract the extra parameters off the stack.

This is inherently type-unsafe because the compiler cannot check that the parameters that the function will get off the stack at runtime will be the same type as the parameters put on the stack by the calling code. For example, the following is an implementation of a function that will sum integers:

```
int sum(int first, ...)
{
    int sum = 0;
    va_list args;
    va_start(args, first);
    int i = first;
    while (i != -1)
    {
        sum += i;
        i = va_arg(args, int);
    }
    va_end(args);
    return sum;
}
```

The definition of the function must have at least one parameter so that the macros work; in this case the parameter is called `first`. It is important that your code leaves the stack in a consistent state and this is carried out using a variable of the `va_list` type. This variable is initialized at the beginning of the function by calling the `va_start` macro and the stack is restored to its previous state at the end of the function by calling the `va_end` macro.

The code in this function simply iterates through the argument list, and maintains a sum, and the loop finishes when the parameter has a value of -1. There are no macros to give information about how many parameters there are on the stack, nor are there any macros to give an indication of the type of the parameter on the stack. Your code has to assume the type of the variable and provide the desired type in the va_arg macro. In this example, va_arg is called, assuming that every parameter on the stack is an int.

Once all parameters have been read off the stack, the code calls va_end before returning the sum. The function can be called like this:

```
cout << sum(-1) << endl;                       // 0
cout << sum(-6, -5, -4, -3, -2, -1) << endl;   // -20 !!!
cout << sum(10, 20, 30, -1) << endl;           // 60
```

Since −1 is used to indicate the end of the list, it means that to sum a zero number of parameters, you have to pass at least one parameter, that is −1. In addition, the second line shows that you have a problem if you are passing a list of negative numbers (in this case −1 cannot be a parameter). This problem could be addressed in this implementation by choosing another *marker value*.

Another implementation could eschew the use of a marker for the end of the list, and instead use the first, required, argument to give the count of the parameters that follow:

```
int sum(int count, ...)
{
    int sum = 0;
    va_list args;
    va_start(args, count);
    while(count--)
    {
        int i = va_arg(args, int);
        sum += i;
    }
    va_end(args);
    return sum;
}
```

This time, the first value is the *number of arguments* that follow, and so the routine will extract this exact number of integers off the stack and sum them. The code is called like this:

```
cout << sum(0) << endl;                            // 0
cout << sum(6, -6, -5, -4, -3, -2, -1) << endl; // -21
cout << sum(3, 10, 20, 30) << endl;                // 60
```

There is no convention for how to handle the issue of determining how many parameters have been passed.

The routine assumes that every item on the stack is an `int`, but there is no information about this in the prototype of the function, so the compiler cannot do type checking on the parameters actually used to call the function. If the caller provides a parameter of a different type, the wrong number of bytes could be read off the stack, making the results of all the other calls to `va_arg` invalid. Consider this:

```
cout << sum(3, 10., 20, 30) << endl;
```

It is easy to press both, the comma and period keys, at the same time, and this has happened after typing the `10` parameter. The period means that the `10` is a `double`, and so the compiler puts a `double` value on the stack. When the function reads values off the stack with the `va_arg` macro, it will read the 8-byte `double` as two 4-byte `int` values and for code produced by Visual C++ this results in a total sum of `1076101140`. This illustrates the type unsafe aspect of argument lists: you cannot get the compiler to do type checks of the parameters passed to the function.

If your function has different types passed to it then you have to implement some mechanism to determine what those parameters are. A good example of argument lists is the C `printf` function:

```
int printf(const char *format, ...);
```

The required parameter of this function is a format string, and importantly this has an ordered list of variable parameters and their types. The format string provides the information that is not available via the `<cstdarg>` macros: the number of variable parameters and the type of each one. The implementation of the `printf` function will iterate through the format string and when it comes across a format specifier for a parameter (a character sequence starting with %) it will read the expected type off the stack with `va_arg`. It should be clear that C-style argument lists are not as flexible as they appear on first sight; moreover, they can be quite dangerous.

Function features

Functions are modularized pieces of code defined as part of your application, or in a library. If a function is written by another vendor it is important that your code calls the function in the way intended by the vendor. This means understanding the calling convention used and how it affects the stack.

Call stack

When you call a function, the compiler will create a stack frame for the new function call and it will push items on to the stack. The data put on the stack depends on your compiler and whether the code is compiled for the debug or release build; however, in general there will be information about the parameters passed to the function, the return address (the address after the function call), and the automatic variables allocated in the function.

This means that, when you make a function call at runtime, there will be a memory overhead and performance overhead from creating the stack frame before the function runs, and a performance overhead in cleaning up, after the function completes. If a function is inlined, this overhead does not occur because the function call will use the current stack frame rather than a new one. Clearly, inlined functions should be small, both in terms of code and the memory used on the stack. The compiler can ignore the `inline` specifier and call the function with a separate stack frame.

Specifying calling conventions

When your code uses your own functions, you do not need to pay any attention to *calling conventions* because the compiler will make sure the appropriate convention is used. However, if you are writing library code that can be used by other C++ compilers, or even by other languages, then the calling convention becomes important. Since this book is not about interoperable code we won't go into much depth, but instead will look at two aspects: function naming and stack maintenance.

Using C linkage

When you give a C++ function a name, this is the name that you will use to call the function in your C++ code. However, under the covers, the C++ compiler will *decorate* the name with extra symbols for the return type and parameters so that overloaded functions all have different names. To C++ developers, this is also known as **name mangling**.

If you need to export a function through a shared library (in Windows, a **dynamic linked library**), you must use types and names that other languages can use. To do this, you can mark a function with `extern "C"`. This means that the function has C linkage and the compiler will not use C++ name mangling. Clearly, you should use this only on functions that will be used by external code and you should not use it with functions that have return values and parameters that use C++ custom types.

However, if such a function does return a C++ type, the compiler will only issue a warning. The reason is that C is a flexible language and a C programmer will be able to work out how to turn the C++ type into something usable, but it is poor practice to abuse them like this!

 The `extern "C"` linkage can also be used with global variables, and you can use it on a single item or (using braces) on many items.

Specifying how the stack Is maintained

Visual C++ supports six calling conventions that you can use on a function. The `__clrcall` specifier means that the function should be called as a .NET function and allows you to write code that has mixed native code and managed code. C++/CLR (Microsoft's language extensions to C++ to write .NET code) is beyond the scope of this book. The other five are used to indicate how parameters are passed to a function (on the stack or using CPU registers) and whose responsibility it is to maintain the stack. We will cover just three: `__cdecl`, `__stdcall`, and `__thiscall`.

You will rarely explicitly use `__thiscall`; it is the calling convention used for functions defined as members of custom types, and indicates that the function has a hidden parameter that is a pointer to the object that can be accessed through the `this` keyword in the function. More details will be given in the next chapter, but it is important to realize that such member functions have a different calling convention, especially when you need to initialize function pointers.

By default, C++ global functions will use the `__cdecl` calling convention. The stack is maintained by the calling code, so in the calling code each call to a `__cdecl` function is followed by code to clean up the stack. This makes each function call a little larger, but it is needed for variable argument lists to be used. The `__stdcall` calling convention is used by most of the Windows SDK functions and it indicates that the called function cleans up the stack so there is no need for such code to be generated in the calling code. Clearly, it is important that the compiler knows that a function uses `__stdcall` because, otherwise, it will generate code to clean up a stack frame that has already been cleaned up by the function. You will usually see Windows functions marked with `WINAPI`, which is a `typedef` for `__stdcall`.

Using recursion

In most cases the memory overhead of a call stack is unimportant. However, when you use recursion it is possible to build up a long chain of stack frames. As the name suggests, recursion is when a function calls itself. A simple example is a function that calculates a factorial:

```
int factorial(int n)
{
    if (n > 1) return n * factorial(n - 1);
    return 1;
}
```

If you call this for 4, the following calls are made:

```
factorial(4) returns 4 * factorial(3)
    factorial(3) returns 3 * factorial(2)
        factorial(2) returns 2 * factorial(1)
            factorial(1) returns 1
```

The important point is that in the recursive function there must be at least one way to leave the function without recursion. In this case, it will be when factorial is called with a parameter of 1. In practice, a function like this should be marked as inline to avoid creating any stack frames at all.

Overloading functions

You can have several functions with the same name, but where the parameter list is different (the number of parameters and/or the type of the parameters). This is *overloading* the function name. When such a function is called, the compiler will attempt to find the function that best fits the parameters provided. If there is not a suitable function, the compiler will attempt to convert the parameters to see if a function with those types exists. The compiler will start with trivial conversions (for example, an array name to a pointer, a type to a const type), and if this fails the compiler will try to promote the type (for example, bool to int). If that fails, the compiler will try standard conversions (for example, a reference to a type). If such conversions results in more than one possible candidate, then the compiler will issue an error that the function call is ambiguous.

Functions and scope

The compiler will also take the scope of the function into account when looking for a suitable function. You cannot define a function within a function, but you can provide a function prototype within the scope of a function and the compiler will attempt (if necessary through conversions) to call a function with such a prototype first. Consider this code:

```
void f(int i)    { /*does something*/ }
void f(double d) { /*does something*/ }

int main()
{
    void f(double d);
    f(1);
    return 0;
}
```

In this code, the function f is overloaded with one version that takes an int and the other with a double. Normally, if you call f(1) then the compiler will call the first version of the function. However, in main there is a prototype for the version that takes a double, and an int can be converted to a double with no loss of information. The prototype is in the same scope as the function call, so in this code the compiler will call the version that takes a double. This technique essentially *hides* the version with an int parameter.

Deleted functions

There is a more formal way to hide functions than using the scope. C++ will attempt to explicitly convert built-in types. For example:

```
void f(int i);
```

You can call this with an int, or anything that can be converted to an int:

```
f(1);
f('c');
f(1.0); // warning of conversion
```

In the second case, a `char` is an integer, so it is promoted to an `int` and the function is called. In the third case, the compiler will issue a warning that the conversion can cause a loss of data, but it is a warning and so the code will compile. If you want to prevent this implicit conversion you can *delete* the functions that you do not want callers to use. To do this, provide a prototype and use the syntax = `delete`:

```
void f(double) = delete;

void g()
{
    f(1);    // compiles
    f(1.0); // C2280: attempting to reference a deleted function
}
```

Now, when the code attempts to call the function with a `char` or a `double` (or `float`, which will be implicitly converted to a `double`), the compiler will issue an error.

Passing by value and passing by reference

By default, the compiler will pass parameters by value, that is, a copy is made. If you pass a custom type, then its *copy constructor* is called to create a new object. If you pass a pointer to an object of a built-in type or custom type, then the *pointer* will be passed by value, that is, a new pointer is created on the function stack for the parameter and it is initialized with the memory address passed to the function. This means that, in the function, you can change the pointer to point to other memory (this is useful if you want to use pointer arithmetic on that pointer). The data that the pointer points to will be passed by a reference, that is, the data remains where it is, outside of the function, but the function can use the pointer to change the data. Similarly, if you use a reference on a parameter then it means that the object is passed by the reference. Clearly, if you use `const` on a pointer or reference parameter then this will affect whether the function can change the data pointed to or referenced.

In some cases, you may want to return several values from a function, and you may choose to use the return value of the function to indicate if the function executed correctly. One way to do this is to make one of the parameters an *out* parameter, that is, it is either a pointer or a reference to an object or container that the function will alter:

```
// don't allow any more than 100 items
bool get_items(int count, vector<int>& values)
{
    if (count > 100) return false;
    for (int i = 0; i < count; ++i)
    {
```

```
            values.push_back(i);
        }
        return true;
    }
```

To call this function, you must create a `vector` object and pass it to the function:

```
vector<int> items {};
get_items(10, items);
for(int i : items) cout << i << ' ';
cout << endl
```

Because the `values` parameter is a reference it means that when `get_values` calls `push_back` to insert a value in the `values` container it is actually inserting that value into the `items` container.

If an out parameter is passed via a pointer it is important to look at the pointer declaration. A single `*` means that the variable is a pointer, two means that it is a pointer to a pointer. The following function returns an `int` through an out parameter:

```
bool get_datum(/*out*/ int *pi);
```

The code is called like this:

```
int value = 0;
if (get_datum(&value)) { cout << "value is " << value << endl; }
else                   { cout << "cannot get the value" << endl;}
```

This pattern of returning a value indicating success is frequently used, particularly with code that accesses data across process or machine boundaries. The function return value can be used to give detailed information about why the call failed (no network access?, invalid security credentials?, and so on), and indicates that the data in the out parameters should be discarded.

If the out parameter has a double `*` then it means the return value is itself a pointer, either to a single value or to an array:

```
bool get_data(/*in/out*/ int *psize, /*out*/ int **pi);
```

In this case, you pass in the size of the buffer you want using the first parameter and on return you receive the actual size of the buffer via this parameter (it is in/out) and a pointer to the buffer in the second parameter:

```
int size = 10;
int *buffer = nullptr;
if (get_data(&size, &buffer))
{
```

```
for (int i = 0; i < size; ++i)
{
    cout << buffer[i] << endl;
}
delete [] buffer;
}
```

Any function that returns a memory buffer must document who has the responsibility of deallocating the memory. In most cases, it is usually the caller, as assumed in this example code.

Designing functions

Often functions will act upon global data, or data passed in by the caller. It is important that when the function completes, it leaves this data in a consistent state. Equally so, it is important that, the function can make assumptions about the data before it accesses it.

Pre- and post-conditions

A function will typically alter some data: values passed into the function, data returned by the function, or some global data. It is important when designing a function that you determine what data will be accessed and changed and that these rules are documented.

A function will have pre-conditions, assumptions about the data that it will use. For example, if a function is passed a filename, with the intention that the function will extract some data from the file, whose responsibility is it to check that the file exists? You can make it the responsibility of the function, and so the first few lines will check that the name is a valid path to a file and call operating system functions to check that the file exists. However, if you have several functions that will perform actions on the file, you will be replicating this checking code in each function and it may be better to put that responsibility on the calling code. Clearly such actions can be expensive, so it is important to avoid both the calling code and the function to perform the checks.

Chapter 10, *Diagnostics and Debugging*, will describe how to add debugging code, called **asserts**, that you can place in your functions to check the values of the parameters to make sure that the calling code is following the pre-condition rules you have set. Asserts are defined using conditional compilation and so will only appear in **debug builds** (that is, C++ code compiled with debugging information). **Release builds** (completed code that will be delivered to the end user) will conditionally compile asserts away; this makes the code faster, and if your testing is thorough enough, you can be assured that pre-conditions are met.

You should also document the post-conditions of your function. That is, assumptions about the data returned by the function (through the function return value, out parameters, or parameters passed by a reference). Post-conditions are the assumptions that the calling code will make. For example, you may return a signed integer where the function is meant to return a positive value, but a negative value is used to indicate an error. Often functions that return pointers will return `nullptr` if the function fails. In both cases, the calling code knows that it needs to check the return value and only use it if it is either positive or not `nullptr`.

Using invariants

You should be careful to document how a function uses data external to the function. If the intention of the function is to change external data, you should document what the function will do. If you don't explicitly document what the function does to external data, then you must ensure that when the function finishes such data is left untouched. The reason is that the calling code will only assume what you have said in the documentation and the side-effects of changing global data may cause problems. Sometimes it is necessary to store the state of global data and return the item back to that state before the function returns.

We have already seen an example of this in Chapter 3, *Exploring C++ Types*, with the `cout` object. The `cout` object is global to your application, and it can be changed through manipulators to make it interpret numeric values in certain ways. If you change it in a function (say, by inserting the `hex` manipulator), then this change will remain when the `cout` object is used outside the function.

Chapter 3, *Exploring C++ Types*, shows how to address such an issue. In that chapter, you created a function called `read16` that reads 16 bytes from a file and prints the values out to the console both in hexadecimal form and interpreted as an ASCII character:

```
int read16(ifstream& stm)
{
    if (stm.eof()) return -1;

    int flags = cout.flags();
    cout << hex;
    string line;

    // code that changes the line variable

    cout.setf(flags);
    return line.length();
}
```

This code stores the state of the `cout` object in a temporary variable, `flags`. The `read16` function can change the `cout` object in any way necessary, but because we have the stored state it means that the object can be restored to its original state before returning.

Function pointers

When an application is run, the functions it will call will exist in memory somewhere. This means that you can get the address of a function. C++ allows you to use the function call operator (a pair of parentheses enclosing the parameters `()`) to call a function through a function pointer.

Remember the parentheses!

First, a simple example of how function pointers can cause difficult to notice bugs in your code. A global function called `get_status` performs various validation actions to determine if the state of the system is valid. The function returns a value of zero to mean that the system state is valid and values over zero are error codes:

```
// values over zero are error codes
int get_status()
{
    int status = 0;
    // code that checks the state of data is valid
    return status;
}
```

The code could be called like this:

```
if (get_status > 0)
{
    cout << "system state is invalid" << endl;
}
```

This is an error because the developer has missed off the `()`, so the compiler does not treat this as a function call. Instead, it treats this as a test of the memory address of the function, and since the function will never be located at a memory address of zero, the comparison will always be `true` and the message will be printed even if the system state is valid.

Declaring function pointers

The last section highlights how easy it is to get the address of a function: you just use the name of the function without the parentheses:

```
void *pv = get_status;
```

The pointer `pv` is only of mild interest; you now know where in memory the function is stored, but to print this address you still need to cast it to an integer. To make the pointer useful, you need to be able to declare a pointer through which the function can be called. To look at how to do this, let's go back to the function prototype:

```
int get_status()
```

The function pointer must be able to call the function passing no parameters and expecting a return value of an integer. The function pointer is declared like this:

```
int (*fn)() = get_status;
```

The `*` indicates that the variable `fn` is a pointer; however, this binds to the left, so without the parentheses surrounding `*fn` the compiler would interpret this to mean that the declaration is for an `int*` pointer. The rest of the declaration indicates how this function pointer is called: taking no parameters and returning an `int`.

Calling through a function pointer is simple: you give the name of the pointer where you would normally give the name of the function:

```
int error_value = fn();
```

Note again how important the parentheses are; they indicates that the function at the address held in the function pointer, `fn`, is called.

Function pointers can make code look rather cluttered, especially when you use them to point to templated functions, so often code will define an alias:

```
using pf1 = int(*)();
typedef int(*pf2)();
```

These two lines declare aliases for the type of the function pointer needed to call the `get_status` function. Both are valid, but the `using` version is more readable since it is clear that `pf1` is the alias being defined. To see why, consider this alias:

```
typedef bool(*MyPtr)(MyType*, MyType*);
```

The type alias is called `MyPtr` and it is to a function that returns a `bool` and takes two `MyType` pointers. This is much clearer with `using`:

```
using MyPtr = bool(*)(MyType*, MyType*);
```

The tell-tale sign here is the `(*)`, which indicates that the type is a function pointer because you are using the parenthesis to break the associatively of the `*`. You can then read outwards to see the prototype of the function: to the left to see the return type, and to the right to get the parameter list.

Once you have declared an alias, you can create a pointer to a function and call it:

```
using two_ints = void (*)(int, int);

void do_something(int l, int r){/* some code */}

void caller()
{
    two_ints fn = do_something;
    fn(42, 99);
}
```

Notice that, because the `two_ints` alias is declared as a pointer, you do not use a `*` when declaring a variable of this type.

Using function pointers

A function pointer is merely a pointer. This means that you can use it as a variable; you can return it from a function, or pass it as a parameter. For example, you may have some code that performs some lengthy routine and you want to provide some feedback during the routine. To make this flexible, you could define your function to take a **callback pointer** and periodically in the routine call the function to indicate progress:

```
using callback = void(*)(const string&);

void big_routine(int loop_count, const callback progress)
{
    for (int i = 0; i < loop_count; ++i)
    {
```

```
                    if (i % 100 == 0)
                    {
                        string msg("loop ");
                        msg += to_string(i);
                        progress(msg);
                    }
                    // routine
            }
        }
```

Here `big_routine` has a function pointer parameter called `progress`. The function has a loop that will be called many times and every one hundredth loop it calls the callback function, passing a `string` that gives information about the progress.

 Note that the `string` class defines a += operator that can be used to append a string to the end of the `string` in the variable and the `<string>` header file defines a function called `to_string` that is overloaded for each of the built-in types to return a `string` formatted with the value of the function parameter.

This function declares the function pointer as `const` merely so that the compiler knows that the function pointer should not be changed to a pointer to another function in this function. The code can be called like this:

```
void monitor(const string& msg)
{
    cout << msg << endl;
}

int main()
{
    big_routine(1000, monitor);
    return 0;
}
```

The `monitor` function has the same prototype as described by the `callback` function pointer (if, for example, the function parameter was `string&` and not `const string&`, then the code will not compile). The `big_routine` function is then called, passing a pointer to the `monitor` function as the second parameter.

If you pass callback functions to library code, you must pay attention to the calling convention of the function pointer. For example, if you pass a function pointer to a Windows function, such as `EnumWindows`, it must point to a function declared with the `__stdcall` calling convention.

The C++ standards uses another technique to call functions defined at runtime, which is, functors. It will be covered shortly.

Templated functions

When you write library code, you often have to write several functions that differ only between the types that are passed to the function; the routine action is the same, it's just the types that have changed. C++ provides *templates* to allow you to write more generic code; you write the routine using a *generic type* and at compile time the compiler will generate a function with the appropriate types. The templated function is marked as such using the `template` keyword and a list of parameters in angle brackets (<>) that give placeholders for the types that will be used. It is important to understand that these template parameters are types and refer to the types of the parameters (and return a value of the function) that will be replaced with the actual types used by calling the functions. They are not parameters of the function, and you do not (normally) provide them when you call the function.

It is best to explain template functions with an example. A simple `maximum` function can be written like this:

```
int maximum(int lhs, int rhs)
{
    return (lhs > rhs) ? lhs : rhs;
}
```

You can call this with other integer types, and smaller types (`short`, `char`, `bool`, and so on) will be promoted to an `int`, and values of larger types (`long long`) will be truncated. Similarly, variables of `unsigned` types will be converted to the `signed int` which could cause problems. Consider this call of the function:

```
unsigned int s1 = 0xffffffff, s2 = 0x7fffffff;
unsigned int result = maximum(s1, s2);
```

What is the value of the `result` variable: s1 or s2? It is s2. The reason is that both values are converted to `signed int` and when converted to a signed type s1 will be a value of −1 and s2 will be a value of 2147483647.

To handle unsigned types, you need to *overload* the function and write a version for signed and unsigned integers:

```
int maximum(int lhs, int rhs)
{
    return (lhs > rhs) ? lhs : rhs;
}

unsigned maximum(unsigned lhs, unsigned rhs)
{
    return (lhs > rhs) ? lhs : rhs;
}
```

The routine is the same, but the types have changed. There is another issue--what if the caller mixes types? Does the following expression make any sense:

```
int i = maximum(true, 100.99);
```

This code will compile because a `bool` and a `double` can be converted to an `int` and the first overload will be called. Since such a call is nonsense, it would be much better if the compiler caught this error.

Defining templates

Returning back to the two versions of the `maximum` function, the routine is the same for both; all that has changed is the type. If you had a generic type, let's call it `T`, where `T` could be any type that implements an `operator>`, the routine could be described by this pseudocode:

```
T maximum(T lhs, T rhs)
{
    return (lhs > rhs) ? lhs : rhs;
}
```

This will not compile because we have not defined the type `T`. Templates allow you to tell the compiler that the code uses a type and will be determined from the parameter passed to the function. The following code will compile:

```
template<typename T>
T maximum(T lhs, T rhs)
{
    return (lhs > rhs) ? lhs : rhs;
}
```

The template declaration specifies the type that will be used using the `typename` identifier. The type `T` is a placeholder; you can use any name you like as long as it is not a name used elsewhere at the same scope, and of course, it must be used in the parameter list of the function. You can use `class` instead of `typename`, but the meaning is the same.

You can call this function, passing values of any type, and the compiler will create the code for that type, calling the `operator>` for that type.

It is important to realize that, the first time the compiler comes across a templated function, it will create a version of the function for the specified type. If you call the templated function for several different types, the compiler will create, or instantiate, a *specialized* function for each of these types.

The definition of this template indicates that only one type will be used, so you can only call it with two parameters of the same type:

```
int i = maximum(1, 100);
double d = maximum(1.0, 100.0);
bool b = maximum(true, false);
```

All of these will compile and the first two will give the expected results. The last line will assign b to a value of `true` because `bool` is an integer and `true` has a value of `1`+ and `false` has a value of `0`. This may not be what you would want, so we will return to this issue later. Note that, since the template says that both parameters must be the same type, the following will not compile:

```
int i = maximum(true, 100.99);
```

The reason is that the `template` parameter list only gives a single type. If you want to define a function with parameters of different types, then you will have to provide extra parameters to the template:

```
template<typename T, typename U>
T maximum(T lhs, U rhs)
{
    return (lhs > rhs) ? lhs : rhs;
}
```

This is done to illustrate how templates work; it really does not make sense to define a maximum function that takes two different types.

This version is written for two different types, the template declaration mentions two types, and these are used for the two parameters. But notice that the function returns `T`, the type of the first parameter. The function can be called like this:

```
cout << maximum(false, 100.99) << endl; // 1
cout << maximum(100.99, false) << endl; // 100.99
```

The output from the first is 1 (or if you use the `bool alpha` manipulator, `true`) and the result of the second line is `100.99`. The reason is not immediately obvious. In both cases, the comparison will return `100.99` from the function, but because the type of the return value is `T`, the returned value type will be the type of the first parameter. In the first case, `100.99` is first converted to a `bool`, and since `100.99` is not zero, the value returned is `true` (or 1). In the second case, the first parameter is a `double`, so the function returns a `double` and this means that `100.99` is returned. If the template version of `maximum` is changed to return `U` (the type of the second parameter) then the values returned by the preceding code are reversed: the first line returns `100.99` and the second returns `1`.

Note that when you *call* the template function, you do not have to give the types of the template parameters because the compiler will deduce them. It is important to point out that this applies only to the parameters. The return type is not determined by the type of the variable the caller assigns to the function value because the function can be called without using the return value.

Although the compiler will deduce the template parameters from how you call the function, you can explicitly provide the types in the called function to call a specific version of the function and (if necessary) get the compiler to perform implicit conversions:

```
// call template<typename T> maximum(T,T);
int i = maximum<int>(false, 100.99);
```

This code will call the version of `maximum` that has two `int` parameters and returns an `int`, so the return value is `100`, that is, `100.99` converted to an `int`.

Using template parameter values

The templates defined so far have had types as the parameters of the template, but you can also provide integer values. The following is a rather contrived example to illustrate the point:

```
template<int size, typename T>
T* init(T t)
{
    T* arr = new T[size];
```

```
        for (int i = 0; i < size; ++i) arr[i] = t;
        return arr;
    }
```

There are two template parameters. The second parameter provides the name of a type where T is a placeholder used for the type of the parameter of the function. The first parameter looks like a function parameter because it is used in a similar way. The parameter size can be used in the function as a local (read-only) variable. The function parameter is T and so the compiler can deduce the second template parameter from the function call, but it cannot deduce the first parameter, so you *must* provide a value in the call. Here is an example of calling this template function for an int for T and a value of 10 for size:

```
    int *i10 = init<10>(42);
    for (int i = 0; i < 10; ++i) cout << i10[i] << ' ';
    cout << endl;
    delete [] i10;
```

The first line calls the function with 10 as the template parameter and 42 as the function parameter. Since 42 is an int, the init function will create an int array with ten members and each one is initialized to a value of 42. The compiler deduced int as the second parameter, but this code could have called the function with init<10,int>(42) to explicitly indicate that you require an int array.

The non-type parameters must be constant at compile time: the value can be integral (including an enumeration), but not a floating point. You can use arrays of integers, but these will be available through the template parameter as a pointer.

Although in most cases the compiler cannot deduce the value parameter, it can if the value is defined as the size of an array. This can be used to make it appear that a function can determine the size of a built-in array, but of course, it can't because the compiler will create a version of the function for each size needed. For example:

```
    template<typename T, int N> void print_array(T (&arr)[N])
    {
        for (int i = 0; i < N; ++i)
        {
            cout << arr[i] << endl;
        }
    }
```

Here, there are two template parameters: one is the type of the array, and the other is the size of the array. The parameter of the function looks a little odd, but it is just a built-in array being passed by a reference. If the parentheses are not used then the parameter is `T&` `arr[N]`, that is, an N-sized built-in array of references to objects of type `T`, which is not what we want. We want an N-sized built-in array objects of type `T`. This function is called like this:

```
int squares[] = { 1, 4, 9, 16, 25 };
print_array(squares);
```

The interesting thing about the preceding code is that the compiler sees that there are five items in the initializer list. The built-in array has five items, thus calls the function like this:

```
print_array<int,5>(squares);
```

As mentioned, the compiler will instantiate this function for every combination of `T` and `N` that your code calls. If the template function has a large amount of code, then this may be an issue. One way around this is to use a helper function:

```
template<typename T> void print_array(T* arr, int size)
{
    for (int i = 0; i < size; ++i)
    {
        cout << arr[i] << endl;
    }
}

template<typename T, int N> inline void print_array(T (&arr)[N])
{
    print_array(arr, N);
}
```

This does two things. First, there is a version of `print_array` that takes a pointer and the number of items that the pointer points to. This means that the `size` parameter is determined at runtime, so versions of this function are only instantiated at compile time for the types of the arrays used, not for both type and array size. The second thing to note is that the function that is templated with the size of the array is declared as `inline` and it calls the first version of the function. Although there will be a version of this for each combination of type and array size, the instantiation will be inline rather than a complete function.

Specialized templates

In some cases, you may have a routine that works for most types (and a candidate for a templated function), but you may identify that some types need a different routine. To handle this, you can write a specialized template function, that is, a function that will be used for a specific type and the compiler will use this code when a caller uses types that fit this specialization. As an example, here is a fairly pointless function; it returns the size of a type:

```
template <typename T> int number_of_bytes(T t)
{
    return sizeof(T);
}
```

This works for most built-in types, but if you call it with a pointer, you will get the size of the pointer, not what the pointer points to. So, `number_of_bytes("x")` will return 4 (on a 32-bit system) rather than 2 for the size of the `char` array. You may decide that you want a specialization for `char*` pointers that uses the C function, `strlen`, to count the number of characters in the string until the `NUL` character. To do this, you need a similar prototype to the templated function, replacing the template parameter with the actual type, and since the template parameter is not needed you miss this out. Since this function is for a specific type, you need to add the specialized type to the function name:

```
template<> int number_of_bytes<const char *>(const char *str)
{
    return strlen(str) + 1;
}
```

Now when you call `number_of_bytes("x")` the specialization will be called and it will return a value of 2.

Earlier, we defined a templated function to return a maximum of two parameters of the same type:

```
template<typename T>
T maximum(T lhs, T rhs)
{
    return (lhs > rhs) ? lhs : rhs;
}
```

Using specialization, you can write versions for types that are not compared using the `>` operator. Since it makes no sense to find the maximum of two Booleans, you can delete the specialization for `bool`:

```
template<> bool maximum<bool>(bool lhs, bool rhs) = delete;
```

This now means that, if the code calls `maximum` with `bool` parameters, the compiler will generate an error.

Variadic templates

A variadic template is when there is a variable number of template parameters. The syntax is similar to variable arguments to a function; you use ellipses, but you use them on the left of the argument in the parameter list, which declares it a *parameter pack*:

```
template<typename T, typename... Arguments>
void func(T t, Arguments... args);
```

The `Arguments` template parameter is zero or more types, which are the types of the corresponding number of arguments, `args`, of the function. In this example, the function has at least one parameter, of type `T`, but you can have any number of fixed parameters, including none at all.

Within the function, you need to unpack the parameter pack to get access to the parameters passed by the caller. You can determine how many items there are in the parameter pack using the special operator, `sizeof...` (note the ellipses are part of the name); unlike the `sizeof` operator, this is the item count and not the size in bytes. To unpack the parameter pack, you need to use the ellipses on the right of the name of the parameter pack (for example, `args...`). The compiler will expand the parameter pack at this point, replacing the symbol with the contents of the parameter pack.

However, you will not know at design time how many parameters there are or what types they are, so there are some strategies to address this. The first uses recursion:

```
template<typename T> void print(T t)
{
    cout << t << endl;
}

template<typename T, typename... Arguments>
void print(T first, Arguments ... next)
{
    print(first);
    print(next...);
}
```

The variadic templated `print` function can be called with one or more parameters of any type that can be handled by the `ostream` class:

```
print(1, 2.0, "hello", bool);
```

When this is called, the parameter list is split into two: the first parameter (1) in the first parameter, `first`, and the other three are put in the parameter pack, `next`. The function body then calls the first version of `print` which, prints the `first` parameter to the console. The next line in the variadic function then expands the parameter pack in a call to `print`, that is, this calls itself recursively. In this call, the `first` parameter will be 2.0, and the rest will be put in the parameter pack. This continues until the parameter pack has been expanded so much that there are no more parameters.

Another way to unpack the parameter pack is to use an initializer list. In this case, the compiler will create an array with each parameter:

```
template<typename... Arguments>
void print(Arguments ... args)
{
    int arr [sizeof...(args)] = { args... };
    for (auto i : arr) cout << i << endl;
}
```

The array, `arr`, is created with the size of the parameter pack and the unpack syntax used with the initializer braces will fill the array with the parameters. Although this will work with any number of parameters, all the parameters have to be the same type of the array, `arr`.

One trick is to use the comma operator:

```
template<typename... Arguments>
void print(Arguments ... args)
{
    int dummy[sizeof...(args)] = { (print(args), 0)... };
}
```

This creates a dummy array called `dummy`. This array is not used, other than in the expansion of the parameter pack. The array is created in the size of the `args` parameter pack and the ellipsis expands the parameter pack using the *expression* between the parentheses. The expression uses the comma operator, which will return the right side of the comma. Since this is an integer, it means that each entry of `dummy` has a value of zero. The interesting part is the left side of the comma operator. Here the version of `print` with a single templated parameter is called with each item in the `args` parameter pack.

Overloaded operators

Earlier we said that function names should not contain punctuation. That is not strictly true because, if you are writing an operator, you *only* use punctuation in the function name. An operator is used in an expression acting on one or more operands. A unary operator has one operand, a binary operator has two operands, and an operator returns the result of the operation. Clearly this describes a function: a return type, a name, and one or more parameters.

C++ provides the keyword `operator` to indicate that the function is not used with the function call syntax, but instead is called using the syntax associated with the operator (usually, a unary operator the first parameter is on the right of the operator, and for a binary operator the first parameter is on the left and the second is on the right, but there are exceptions to this).

In general, you will provide the operators as part of a custom type (so the operators act upon variables of that type) but in some cases, you can declare operators at a global scope. Both are valid. If you are writing a custom type (classes, as explained in the next chapter), then it makes sense to encapsulate the code for an operator as part of the custom type. In this section, we will concentrate on the other way to define an operator: as a global function.

You can provide your own versions of the following unary operators:

```
! & + - * ++ -- ~
```

You can also provide your own versions of the following binary operators:

```
!= == < <= > >= && ||
% %= + += - -= * *= / /= & &= | |= ^ ^= << <<= = >> =>>
-> ->* ,
```

You can also write versions of the function call operator `()`, array subscript `[]`, conversion operators, the cast operator `()`, and `new` and `delete`. You cannot redefine the `.`, `.*`, `::`, `?:`, `#` or `##` operators, nor the "named" operators, `sizeof`, `alignof` or `typeid`.

When defining the operator, you write a function where the function name is
operator*x* and *x* is the operator symbol (note that there is no space). For example, if you
define a struct that has two members defining a Cartesian point, you may want to
compare two points for equality. The struct can be defined like this:

```
struct point
{
    int x;
    int y;
};
```

Comparing two point objects is easy. They are the same if x and y of one object are equal
to the corresponding values in the other object. If you define the == operator, then you
should also define the != operator using the same logic because != should give the exact
opposite result of the == operator. This is how these operators can be defined:

```
bool operator==(const point& lhs, const point& rhs)
{
    return (lhs.x == rhs.x) && (lhs.y == rhs.y);
}

bool operator!=(const point& lhs, const point& rhs)
{
    return !(lhs == rhs);
}
```

The two parameters are the two operands of the operator. The first one is the operand on
the left-hand side and the second parameter is the operand on the right-hand side of the
operator. These are passed as references so that a copy is not made, and they are marked as
const because the operator will not alter the objects. Once defined, you can use the point
type like this:

```
point p1{ 1,1 };
point p2{ 1,1 };
cout << boolalpha;
cout << (p1 == p2) << endl; // true
cout << (p1 != p2) << endl; // false
```

You could have defined a pair of functions called equals and not_equals and use these
instead:

```
cout << equals(p1,p2) << endl;     // true
cout << not_equals(p1,p2) << endl; // false
```

However, defining operators makes the code more readable because you use the type like the built-in types. Operator overloading is often referred to as *syntactic sugar*, syntax that makes the code easier to read--but this trivializes an important technique. For example, smart pointers are a technique that involves class **destructors** to manage resource lifetime, and are only useful because you can call the objects of such classes as if they are pointers. You can do this because the smart pointer class implements the -> and * operators. Another example is **functors**, or function objects, where the class implements the () operator so that objects can be accessed as if they are functions.

When you write a custom type, you should ask yourself if overloading an operator for your type makes sense. If the type is a numeric type, for example, a complex number or a matrix - then it makes sense to implement arithmetic operators, but would it make sense to implement the logical operators since the type does not have a logical aspect? There is a temptation to redefine the *meaning* of operators to cover your specific operation, but this will make your code less readable.

In general, a unary operator is implemented as a global function that takes a single parameter. The postfix increment and decrement operators are an exception to allow for a different implementation from prefix operators. Prefix operators will have a reference to the object as a parameter (which the operator will increment or decrement) and return a reference to this changed object. The postfix operator, however, has to return the value of the object before the increment or decrement. Thus, the operator function has two parameters: a reference to an object that will be changed and an integer (which will always be a value of 1); it will return a copy of the original object.

A binary operator will have two parameters and return an object or a reference to an object. For example, for the struct we defined previously, we could define an insertion operator for ostream objects:

```
struct point
{
    int x;
    int y;
};

ostream& operator<<(ostream& os, const point& pt)
{
    os << "(" << pt.x << "," << pt.y << ")";
    return os;
}
```

This means that you can now insert a `point` object to the `cout` object to print it on the console:

```
point pt{1, 1};
cout << "point object is " << pt << endl;
```

Function objects

A function object, or **functor**, is a custom type that implements the function call operator: (`operator()`). This means that a function operator can be called in a way that looks like it is a function. Since we haven't covered classes yet, in this section we will just explore the function objects types that are provided by the Standard Library and how to use them.

The `<functional>` header file contains various types that can be used as function objects. The following table lists these:

Purpose	Types
Arithmetic	`divides`, `minus`, `modulus`, `multiplies`, `negate`, `plus`
Bitwise	`bit_and`, `bit_not`, `bit_or`, `bit_xor`
Comparison	`equal_to`, `greater`, `greater_equal`, `less`, `less_equals`, `not_equal_to`
Logical	`logical_and`, `logical_not`, `logical_or`

These are all binary function classes, other than `bit_not`, `logical_not`, and `negate`, which are unary. Binary function objects act on two values and return a result, unary function objects act on a single value and return a result. For example, you could calculate the modulus of two numbers with this code:

```
modulus<int> fn;
cout << fn(10, 2) << endl;
```

This declares a function object called `fn` that will perform modulus. The object is used in the second line, which calls the `operator()` function on the object with two parameters, so the following line is equivalent to the preceding line:

```
cout << fn.operator()(10, 2) << endl;
```

The result is that the value of 0 is printed on the console. The `operator()` function merely performs the modulus on the two parameters, in this case `10 % 2`. This does not look too exciting. The `<algorithm>` header contains functions that work on function objects. Most take predicates, that is, logical function objects, but one, `transform`, takes a function object that performs an action:

```
// #include <algorithm>
// #include <functional>

vector<int> v1 { 1, 2, 3, 4, 5 };
vector<int> v2(v1.size());
fill(v2.begin(), v2.end(), 2);
vector<int> result(v1.size());

transform(v1.begin(), v1.end(), v2.begin(),
    result.begin(), modulus<int>());

for (int i : result)
{
    cout << i << ' ';
}
cout << endl;
```

This code will perform five modulus calculations on the values in the two vectors. Conceptually, it does this:

```
result = v1 % v2;
```

That is, each item in `result` is the modulus of the corresponding item in `v1` and `v2`. In the code, the first line creates a `vector` with the five values. We will calculate the modulus of these values with 2, so the second line declares an empty `vector` but with the same capacity as the first `vector`. This second `vector` is filled by calling the `fill` function. The first parameter is the address of the first item in the `vector` and the `end` function returns the address after the *last* item in the `vector`. The final item in the function call is the value that will be placed in the `vector` in every item starting with the item pointed to by the first parameter up to, but excluding, the item pointed to by the second parameter.

At this point, the second `vector` will contain five items and each one will be 2. Next, a `vector` is created for the results; and again, it is the same size as the first array. Finally, the calculation is performed by the `transform` function, shown here again:

```
transform(v1.begin(), v1.end(),
    v2.begin(), result.begin(), modulus<int>());
```

The first two parameters give the iterators of the first `vector` and from this the number of items can be calculated. Since all three `vector`s are the same size, you only need the `begin` iterator for `v2` and `result`.

The last parameter is the function object. This is a temporary object and only exists during this statement; it has no name. The syntax used here is an explicit call to the constructor of the class; it is templated so you need to give the template parameter. The `transform` function will call the `operator(int,int)` function on this function object for each item in `v1` as the first parameter and the corresponding item in `v2` as the second parameter and it will store the result in the corresponding position in `result`.

Since `transform` takes any binary function object as the second parameter, you can pass an instance of `plus<int>` to add a value of 2 to every item in `v1`, or pass an instance of `multiplies<int>` to multiply every item in `v1` by 2.

One situation where function objects are useful is when performing multiple comparisons using a predicate. A predicate is a function object that compares values and returns a Boolean. The `<functional>` header contains several classes to allow you to compare items. Let's see how many items in the `result` container are zero. To do this, we use the `count_if` function. This will iterate over a container, apply the predicate to every item, and count how many times the predicate returns a value of `true`. There are several ways to do this. The first defines a predicate function:

```
bool equals_zero(int a)
{
    return (a == 0);
}
```

A pointer to this can then be passed to the `count_if` function:

```
int zeros = count_if(
    result.begin(), result.end(), equals_zero);
```

The first two parameters indicate the range of values to check. The last parameter is a pointer to the function that is used as the predicate. Of course, if you are checking for different values you can make this more generic:

```
template<typename T, T value>
inline bool equals(T a)
{
    return a == value;
}
```

Call it like this:

```
int zeros = count_if(
    result.begin(), result.end(), equals<int, 0>);
```

The problem with this code is that we are defining the operation in a place other than where it is used. The `equals` function could be defined in another file; however, with a predicate it is more readable to have the code that does the checking defined close to the code that needs the predicate.

The `<functional>` header also defines classes that can be used as function objects. For example, `equal_to<int>`, which compares two values. However, the `count_if` function expects a unary function object, to which it will pass a single value (see the `equals_zero` function, described previously). `equal_to<int>` is a binary function object, comparing two values. We need to provide the second operand and to do this we use the helper function called `bind2nd`:

```
int zeros = count_if(
    result.begin(), result.end(), bind2nd(equal_to<int>(), 0));
```

The `bind2nd` will *bind* the parameter 0 to the function object created from `equal_to<int>`. Using a function object like this brings the definition of the predicate closer to the function call that will use it, but the syntax looks rather messy. C++11 provides a mechanism to get the compiler to determine the function objects that are required and bind parameters to them. These are called lambda expressions.

Introducing lambda expressions

A lambda expression is used to create an anonymous function object at the location where the function object will be used. This makes your code much more readable because you can see what will be executed. On first sight, a lambda expression looks like a function definition in-place as a function parameter:

```
auto less_than_10 = [](int a) {return a < 10; };
bool b = less_than_10(4);
```

So that we don't have the complication of a function that uses a predicate, in this code we have assigned a variable to the lambda expression. This is not normally how you would use it, but it makes the description clearer. The square brackets at the beginning of the lambda expression are called the **capture list**. This expression does not capture variables, so the brackets are empty. You can use variables declared outside of the lambda expression and these have to be *captured*. The capture list indicates whether all such variables will be captured by a reference (use `[&]`) or by a value (use `[=]`). You can also name the variables that will be captured (if there are more than one, use a comma-separated list) and if they are captured by a value, you use just their names. If they are captured by a reference, use a `&` on their names.

You could make the preceding lambda expression more generic by introducing a variable declared outside of the expression called `limit`:

```
int limit = 99;
auto less_than = [limit](int a) {return a < limit; };
```

If you compare a lambda expression to a global function, the capture list is a bit like identifying the global variables that the global function can access.

After the caption list, you give the parameter list in parentheses. Again, if you compare a lambda to a function, the lambda parameter list is equivalent to the function parameter list. If the lambda expression does not have any parameters, then you can miss out the parentheses altogether.

The body for the lambda is given in a pair of braces. This can contain anything that can be found in a function. The lambda body can declare local variables, and it can even declare `static` variables, which looks bizarre, but is legal:

```
auto incr = [] { static int i; return ++i; };
incr();
incr();
cout << incr() << endl; // 3
```

The return value of the lambda is deduced from the item that is returned. A lambda expression does not have to return a value, in which case the expression will return `void`:

```
auto swap = [](int& a, int& b) { int x = a; a = b; b = x; };
int i = 10, j = 20;
cout << i << " " << j << endl;
swap(i, j);
cout << i << " " << j << endl;
```

The power of lambda expressions is that you can use them in cases when a function object or a predicate is needed:

```
vector<int> v { 1, 2, 3, 4, 5 };
int less_than_3 = count_if(
    v.begin(), v.end(),
    [](int a) { return a < 3; });
cout << "There are " << less_than_3 << " items less than 3" << endl;
```

Here we declare a `vector` and initialize it with some values. The `count_if` function is used to count how many items in the container are less than 3. So, the first two parameters are used to give the range of items to check, and the third parameter is a lambda expression that performs the comparison. The `count_if` function will call this expression for every item in the range that is passed in via the `a` parameter of the lambda. The `count_if` function keeps a running count of how many times the lambda returns `true`.

Using functions in C++

The example in this chapter uses the techniques you have learned in this chapter to list all the files in a folder, and subfolders, in order of file size, giving a listing of the filenames and their sizes. The example is the equivalent of typing the following at the command line:

```
dir /b /s /os /a-d folder
```

Here, `folder` is the folder you are listing. The `/s` option recurses, `/a-d` removes folders from the list, and `/os` orders by size. The problem is that without the `/b` option we get information about each folder, but using it removes the file size in the list. We want a list of filenames (and their paths), their size, ordered by the smallest first.

Start by creating a new folder for this chapter (`Chapter_05`) under the `Beginning_C++` folder. In Visual C++ create a new C++ source file and save it as `files.cpp` under this new folder. The example will use basic output and strings. It will take a single command line parameter; if more command-line parameters are passed, we just use the first one. Add the following to `files.cpp`:

```
#include <iostream>
#include <string>
using namespace std;

int main(int argc, char* argv[])
{
```

```
        if (argc < 2) return 1;
        return 0;
    }
```

The example will use the Windows functions, FindFirstFile and FindNextFile, to get information about files that meet a file specification. These return data in a WIN32_FIND_DATAA structure, which has information about the filename, the file size, and file attributes. The functions also return information about folders too, so it means we can test for subfolders and recurse. The WIN32_FIND_DATAA structure gives the file size as a 64-bit number in two parts: the upper and lower 32 bits. We will create our own structure to hold this information. At the top of the file, after the C++ include files, add the following:

```
using namespace std;

#include <windows.h>
struct file_size {
    unsigned int high;
    unsigned int low;
};
```

The first line is the Windows SDK header file so that you can access the Windows functions, and the structure is used to hold the information about a file's size. We want to compare files by their sizes. The WIN32_FIND_DATAA structure provides the size in two unsigned long members (one with the upper 4 bytes and the other with the lower 4 bytes). We could store this as a 64-bit number, but instead, so that we have an excuse to write some operators, we store the size in our file_size structure. The example will print out file sizes and will compare file sizes, so we will write an operator to insert a file_size object into an output steam; since we want to order the files by size, we need an operator to determine if one file_size object is greater than the other.

The code will use Windows functions to get information about the files, in particular their name and size. This information will be stored in a vector, so at the top of the file add these two highlighted lines:

```
#include <string>
#include <vector>
#include <tuple>
```

The tuple class is needed so that we can store both a string (the filename) and a file_size object as each item in the vector. To make the code more readable add the following alias after the structure definition:

```
using file_info = tuple<string, file_size>;
```

Then just above the `main` function add the skeleton code for the function that will get the file in a folder:

```
void files_in_folder(
    const char *folderPath, vector<file_info>& files)
{
}
```

This function takes a reference to a `vector` and a folder path. The code will go through each item in the specified folder. If it is a file, it will store the details in the `vector`; otherwise, if the item is a folder it will call itself to get the files in that subfolder. Add a call to this function at the bottom of the `main` function:

```
vector<file_info> files;
files_in_folder(argv[1], files);
```

The code has already checked that there is at least one command line argument, and we use this as the folder to examine. The `main` function should print out the file information, so we declare a `vector` on the stack and pass this by reference to the `files_in_folder` function. This code does nothing so far, but you can compile the code to make sure that there are no typos (remember to use the `/EHsc` parameter).

Most of the work is carried out in the `files_in_folder` function. As a start, add the following code to this function:

```
string folder(folderPath);
folder += "*";
WIN32_FIND_DATAA findfiledata {};
void* hFind = FindFirstFileA(folder.c_str(), &findfiledata);

if (hFind != INVALID_HANDLE_VALUE)
{
    do
    {
    } while (FindNextFileA(hFind, &findfiledata));
    FindClose(hFind);
}
```

We will use the ASCII version of the functions (hence the trailing `A` on the structure and function names). The `FindFirstFileA` function takes a search path, and in this case, we use the name of a folder suffixed with a `*`, meaning *everything in this folder*. Notice that the Windows function wants a `const char*` parameter, so we use the `c_str` function on the `string` object.

If the function call succeeds and it finds an item that meets this criterion, then the function fills in the `WIN32_FIND_DATAA` structure passed by the reference and it also returns an opaque pointer which will be used to make subsequent calls on this search (you do not need to know what it points to). The code checks to see if the call was successful, and if so, it repeatedly calls `FindNextFileA` to get the next item until this function returns 0, indicating there are no more items. The opaque pointer is passed to `FindNextFileA` so that it knows which search is being checked. When the search is complete, the code calls `FindClose` to release whatever resources Windows allocates for the search.

The search will return both file and folder items; to handle each differently, we can test the `dwFileAttributes` member of the `WIN32_FIND_DATAA` structure. Add the following code in the `do` loop:

```
string findItem(folderPath);
findItem += "";
findItem += findfiledata.cFileName;
if ((findfiledata.dwFileAttributes & FILE_ATTRIBUTE_DIRECTORY) != 0)
{
    // this is a folder so recurse
}
else
{
    // this is a file so store information
}
```

The `WIN32_FIND_DATAA` structure contains just the relative name of the item in the folder, so the first few lines create an absolute path. The following lines test to see if the item is a folder (directory) or a file. If the item is a file, then we simply add it to the vector passed to the function. Add the following to the `else` clause:

```
file_size fs{};
fs.high = findfiledata.nFileSizeHigh;
fs.low = findfiledata.nFileSizeLow;
files.push_back(make_tuple(findItem, fs));
```

The first three lines initialize a `file_size` structure with the size data, and the last line adds a `tuple` with the name of the file and its size to the `vector`. So that you can see the results of a simple call to this function, add the following to the bottom of the `main` function:

```
for (auto file : files)
{
    cout << setw(16) << get<1>(file) << " "
        << get<0>(file) << endl;
}
```

This iterates through the items in the `files` vector. Each item is a `tuple<string, file_size>` object and to get the `string` item, you can use the Standard Library function, `get`, using 0 as the function template parameter, and to get the `file_size` object you call `get` with 1 as the function template parameter. The code calls the `setw` manipulator to make sure that the file sizes are always printed in a column 16 characters wide. To use this, you need to add an include for `<iomanip>` at the top of the file. Notice that `get<1>` will return a `file_size` object and this is inserted into `cout`. As it stands, this code will not compile because there is no operator to do this. We need to write one.

After the definition of the structure, add the following code:

```
ostream& operator<<(ostream& os, const file_size fs)
{
    int flags = os.flags();
    unsigned long long ll = fs.low +
        ((unsigned long long)fs.high << 32);
    os << hex << ll;
    os.setf(flags);
    return os;
}
```

This operator will alter the `ostream` object, so we store the initial state at the beginning of the function and restore the object to this state at the end. Since the file size is a 64-bit number, we convert the constituent parts of the `file_size` object and then print it out as a hexadecimal number.

Now you can compile and run this application. For example:

files C:windows

This will list the names and sizes of the files in the `windows` folder.

There are two more things that need to be done--recurse subfolders and sort the data. Both are straightforward to implement. In the `files_in_folder` function, add the following code to the code block of the `if` statement:

```
// this is a folder so recurse
string folder(findfiledata.cFileName);
// ignore . and .. directories
if (folder != "." && folder != "..")
{
    files_in_folder(findItem.c_str(), files);
}
```

The search will return the . (current) folder and .. (parent) folder, so we need to check for these and ignore them. The next action is to recursively call the files_in_folder function to obtain the files in the subfolder. If you wish, you can compile and test the application, but this time it is best to test the code using the Beginning_C++ folder because recursively listing the Windows folder will produce a lot of files.

The code returns the list of files as they were obtained, but we want to see them in order of file size. To do this we can use the sort function in the <algorithm> header, so add an include to this after the include for <tuple>. In the main function, after the call to files_in_folder, add this code:

```
files_in_folder(argv[1], files);

sort(files.begin(), files.end(),
    [](const file_info& lhs, const file_info& rhs) {
        return get<1>(rhs) > get<1>(lhs);
} );
```

The first two parameters of the sort function indicate the range of items to check. The third item is a predicate, and the function will pass two items from the vector to the predicate. You have to return a value of true if the two parameters are in order (the first is smaller than the second).

The predicate is provided by a lambda expression. There are no captured variables so the expression starts with [] and this is followed by the parameter list of the items being compared by the sort algorithm (passed by const reference, because they will not be changed). The actual comparison is carried out between the braces. Since we want to list the files in ascending order, we have to ensure that the second of the two is bigger than the first. In this code, we use the > operator on the two file_size objects. So that this code will compile, we need to define this operator. After the insertion operator add the following:

```
bool operator>(const file_size& lhs, const file_size& rhs)
{
    if (lhs.high > rhs.high) return true;
    if (lhs.high == rhs.high) {
        if (lhs.low > rhs.low) return true;
    }
    return false;
}
```

You can now compile the example and run it. You should find that the files in the specified folder and subfolders are listed in order of the size of the files.

Summary

Functions allow you to segment your code into logical routines, which makes your code more readable, and gives the flexibility of being able to reuse code. C++ provides a wealth of options to define functions, including variable argument lists, templates, function pointers, and lambda expressions. However, there is one main issue with global functions: the data is separate from the function. This means that the function has to access the data via global data items, or data has to be passed to a function via a parameter every time the function is called. In both cases, the data exists outside the function and could be used by other functions unrelated to the data. The next chapter will give a solution to this: classes. A `class` allows you to encapsulate data in a custom type, and you can define functions on that type so that only these functions will be able to access the data.

6
Classes

C++ allows you to create your own types. These custom types can have operators and can be converted to other types; indeed, they can be used like built-in types with the behavior that you define. This facility uses a language feature called classes. The advantage of being able to define your own types is that you can encapsulate data in objects of your chosen type, and use the type to manage the lifetime of that data. You can also define the actions that can be performed on that data. In other words, you are able to define custom types that have state and behavior, which is the basis of object-orientated programming.

Writing classes

When you use built-in types, the data is directly available to whatever code has access to that data. C++ provides a mechanism (const) to prevent write access, but any code can use const_cast to cast away const-ness. Your data could be complex, such as a pointer to a file mapped into memory with the intention that your code will change a few bytes and then write the file back to disk. Such raw pointers are dangerous because other code with access to the pointer could change part of the buffer that should not be changed. What is needed is a mechanism to encapsulate the data into a type that knows what bytes to change, and only allow that type to access the data. This is the basic idea behind classes.

Reviewing structures

We have already seen one mechanism in C++ to encapsulate data: `struct`. A structure allows you to declare data members that are built-in types, pointers, or references. When you create a variable from that `struct`, you are creating an **instance** of the structure, also known as an **object**. You can create variables that are references to this object or pointers that point to the object. You can even pass the object by value to a function where the compiler will make a copy of the object (it will call the *copy constructor* for the `struct`). We have seen that with a `struct` any code that has access to an instance (even through a pointer or reference) can access the members of the object (although this can be changed). Used like this, a `struct` can be thought of as **aggregate** types containing the state.

The members of an instance of a `struct` can be initialized by accessing them directly with the dot operator or using the `->` operator through a pointer to the object. We have also seen that you can initialize an instance of a `struct` with an initializer list (in braces). This is quite restrictive because the initializer list has to match the data members in the `struct`. In `Chapter 4`, *Working with Memory, Arrays, and Pointers*, you saw that you can have a pointer as a member of a `struct`, but you have to explicitly take appropriate action to release the memory pointed to by the pointer; if you don't, then this could result in a memory leak.

A `struct` is one of the class types that you can use in C++; the other two are `union` and `class`. Custom types defined as `struct` or `class` can have behaviors as well as state, and C++ allows you to define some special functions to control how instances are created and destroyed, copied, and converted. Furthermore, you can define operators on a `struct` or `class` type so that you can use the operators on instances in a similar way to using the operators on built-in types. There is a difference between `struct` and `class` which we will address later, but in general the rest of the chapter will be about classes and when a `class` is mentioned you can usually assume the same applies to a `struct` as well.

Defining classes

A class is defined in a statement, and it will define its members in a block with multiple statements enclosed by braces `{ }`. As it's a statement, you have to place a semicolon after the last brace. A class can be defined in a header file (as are many of the **C++ Standard Library** classes), but you have to take steps to ensure that such files are included only once in a source file. `Chapter 1`, *Starting with C++*, describes how to do this with `#pragma once`, conditional compilation, and precompiled header files. There are, however, some rules about specific items in a class that must be defined in a source file, which will be covered later.

If you peruse the C++ Standard Library, you will see that classes contain member functions and, in an attempt to put all the code for a class into a single header file, this makes the code difficult to read and difficult to understand. This may be justifiable for a library file maintained by a legion of expert C++ programmers, but for your own projects readability should be a key design goal. For this reason, a C++ class can be declared in a C++ header file, including its member functions, and the actual implementation of the functions can be placed in a source file. This makes the header files easier to maintain and more reusable.

Defining class behavior

A class can define functions that can only be called through an instance of the class; such a function is often called a **method**. An object will have state; this is provided by the data members defined by the class and initialized when the object is created. The methods on an object define the behavior of the object, usually acting upon the state of the object. When you design a class, you should think of the methods in this way: they describe the object doing something.

```
class cartesian_vector
{
public:
    double x;
    double y;
    // other methods
    double get_magnitude() { return std::sqrt((x * x) + (y * y)); }
};
```

This class has two data members, x and y, which represent the direction of a two-dimensional vector resolved in the Cartesian x and y directions. The public keyword means that any members defined after this specifier are accessible by code defined outside of the class. By default, all the members of a class are private unless you indicate otherwise. Such access specifiers will be covered in more depth in the next chapter, but private means that the member can only be accessed by other members of the class.

This is the difference between a struct and a class: by default, members of a struct are public and by default, members of a class are private.

This class has a method called `get_magnituide` that will return the length of the Cartesian vector. This function acts upon the two data members of the class and returns a value. This is a type of **accessor** method; it gives access to the state of the object. Such a method is typical on a `class`, but there is no requirement that methods return values. Like functions, a method can also take parameters. The `get_magnituide` method can be called like this:

```
cartesian_vector vec { 3.0, 4.0 };
double len = vec.get_magnitude(); // returns 5.0
```

Here a `cartesian_vector` object is created on the stack and list initializer syntax is used to initialize it to a value representing a vector of (3, 4). The length of this vector is 5, which is the value returned by calling `get_magnitude` on the object.

Using the this pointer

The methods in a class have a special calling convention, which in Visual C++ is called `__thiscall`. The reason is that every method in a class has a hidden parameter called `this`, which is a pointer of the class type to the current instance:

```
class cartesian_vector
{
public:
    double x;
    double y;
    // other methods
    double get_magnitude()
    {
        return std::sqrt((this->x * this->x) + (this->y * this->y));
    }
};
```

Here, the `get_magnitude` method returns the length of the `cartesian_vector` object. The members of the object are accessed through the `->` operator. As shown previously, the members of the class can be accessed without the `this` pointer, but it does make it explicit that the items are members of the `class`.

You could define a method on the `cartesian_vector` type that allows you to change its state:

```
class cartesian_vector
{
public:
    double x;
    double y;
```

```
    reset(double x, double y) { this->x = x; this->y = y; }
    // other methods
};
```

The parameters of the `reset` method have the same names as the data members of the class; however, since we use the `this` pointer the compiler knows that this is not ambiguous.

You can dereference the `this` pointer with the `*` operator to get access to the object. This is useful when a member function must return a reference to the current object (as some operators will, as we will see later) and you can do this by returning `*this`. A method in a class can also pass the `this` pointer to an external function, which means that it is passing the current object by reference through a typed pointer.

Using the scope resolution operator

You can define a method inline in the `class` statement, but you can also separate the declaration and implementation, so the method is declared in the `class` statement but it is defined elsewhere. When defining a method out of the `class` statement, you need to provide the method with the name of the type using the scope resolution operator. For example, using the previous `cartesian_vector` example:

```
class cartesian_vector
{
public:
    double x;
    double y;
    // other methods
    double magnitude();
};

double cartesian_vector::magnitude()
{
    return sqrt((this->x * this->x) + (this->y * this->y));
}
```

The method is defined outside the class definition; it is, however, still the class method, so it has a `this` pointer that can be used to access the object's members. Typically, the class will be declared in a header file with prototypes for the methods and the actual methods will be implemented in a separate source file. In this case, using the `this` pointer to access the class members (methods and data members) make it obvious, when you take a cursory look at a source file, that the functions are methods of a class.

Defining class state

Your class can have built-in types as data members, or custom types. These data members can be declared in the class (and created when an instance of the class is constructed), or they can be pointers to objects created in the free store or references to objects created elsewhere. Bear in mind that if you have a pointer to an item created in the free store, you need to know whose responsibility it is to deallocate the memory that the pointer points to. If you have a reference (or pointer) to an object created on a stack frame somewhere, you need to make sure that the objects of your class do not live longer than that stack frame.

When you declare data members as `public` it means that external code can read and write to the data members. You can decide that you would prefer to only give read-only access, in which case you can make the members `private` and provide read access through accessors:

```
class cartesian_vector
{
    double x;
    double y;
public:
    double get_x() { return this->x; }
    double get_y() { return this->y; }
    // other methods
};
```

When you make the data members `private` it means that you cannot use the initializer list syntax to initialize an object, but we will address this later. You may decide to use an accessor to give write access to a data member and use this to check the value.

```
void cartesian_vector::set_x(double d)
{
    if (d > -100 && d < 100) this->x = d;
}
```

This is for a type where the range of values must be between (but not including) -100 and 100.

Creating objects

You can create objects on the stack or in the free store. Using the previous example, this is as follows:

```
cartesian_vector vec { 10, 10 };
cartesian_vector *pvec = new cartesian_vector { 5, 5 };
// use pvec
delete pvec
```

This is **direct initialization** of the object and assumes that the data members of cartesian_vector are public. The vec object is created on the stack and initialized with an initializer list. In the second line, an object is created in the free store and initialized with an initializer list. The object on the free store must be freed at some point and this is carried out by deleting the pointer. The new operator will allocate enough memory in the free store for the data members of the class and for any of the infrastructure the class needs (as described in the next chapter).

A new feature of C++11 is to allow direct initialization to provide default values in the class:

```
class point
{
public:
    int x = 0;
    int y = 0;
};
```

This means that if you create an instance of point without any other initialization values, it will be initialized so that x and y are both zero. If the data member is a built-in array, then you can provide direct initialization with an initialization list in the class:

```
class car
{
public:
    double tire_pressures[4] { 25.0, 25.0, 25.0, 25.0 };
};
```

The C++ Standard Library containers can be initialized with an initialize list, so, in this class for tire_pressures, instead of declaring the type to be double[4] we could use vector<double> or array<double, 4>, and initialize it in the same way.

Construction of objects

C++ allows you to define special methods to perform the initialization of the object. These are called **constructors**. In C++11, you will get three such functions generated for you by default, but you can provide your own versions if you wish. These three constructors, along with three other related functions, are as follows:

- **Default constructor:** This is called to create an object with the *default* value.
- **Copy constructor:** This is used to create a new object based on the value of an existing object.
- **Move constructor:** This is used to create a new object using the data moved from an existing object.
- **Destructor:** This is called to clean up the resources used by an object.
- **Copy assignment:** This copies the data from one existing object into another existing object.
- **Move assignment:** This moves the data from one existing object into another existing object.

The compiler-created versions of these functions will be implicitly `public`; however, you may decide to prevent copying or assigning by defining your own versions, and making them `private`, or you can delete them using the `=delete` syntax. You can also provide your own constructors that will take any parameters you decide you need to initialize a new object.

A constructor is a member function that has the same name as the type, but does not return a value, so you cannot return a value if the construction fails, which potentially means that the caller will receive a partially constructed object. The only way to handle this situation is to throw an exception (explained in `Chapter 10`, *Diagnostics and Debugging*).

Defining constructors

The default constructor is used when an object is created without a value and hence the object will have to be initialized with a default value. The `point` declared previously could be implemented like this:

```
class point
{
    double x; double y;
public:
    point() { x = 0; y = 0; }
};
```

This explicitly initializes the items to a value of zero. If you want to create an instance with the default values, you do not include parentheses.

```
point p;   // default constructor called
```

It is important to be aware of this syntax because it is easy to write the following by mistake:

```
point p();   // compiles, but is a function prototype!
```

This will compile because the compiler will think you are providing a function prototype as a forward declaration. However, you'll get an error when you attempt to use the symbol p as a variable. You can also call the default constructor using initialize list syntax with empty braces:

```
point p {};   // calls default constructor
```

Although it does not matter in this case, where the data members are built-in types, initializing data members in the body of the constructor like this involves a call to the assignment operator of the member type. A more efficient way is to use direct initialization with a **member list**.

The following is a constructor that takes two parameters, which illustrates a member list:

```
point(double x, double y) : x(x), y(y) {}
```

The identifiers outside the parentheses are the names of class members, and the items inside the parentheses are expressions used to initialize that member (in this case, a constructor parameter). This example uses x and y for the parameter names. You don't have to do this; this is only given here as an illustration that the compiler will distinguish between the parameters and data members. You can also use braced initializer syntax in the member list of a constructor:

```
point(double x, double y) : x{x}, y{y} {}
```

You call this constructor when you create an object like this:

```
point p(10.0, 10.0);
```

You can also create an array of objects:

```
point arr[4];
```

This creates four point objects, which can be accessed by indexing the arr array. Note that when you create an array of objects the *default* constructor is called on the items; there is no way to call any other constructor, and so you have to initialize each one separately.

You can also provide default values for constructor parameters. In the following code, the car class has values for the four tires (the first two are the front tires) and for the spare tire. There is one constructor that has mandatory values that will be used for the front and back tires, and an optional value for the spare. If a value is not provided for the spare tire pressure, then a default value will be used:

```
class car
{
    array<double, 4> tire_pressures;;
    double spare;
public:
    car(double front, double back, double s = 25.0)
        : tire_pressures{front, front, back, back}, spare{s} {}
};
```

This constructor can be called with either two values or three values:

```
car commuter_car(25, 27);
car sports_car(26, 28, 28);
```

Delegating constructors

A constructor may call another constructor using the same member list syntax:

```
class car
{
    // data members
public:
    car(double front, double back, double s = 25.0)
        : tire_pressures{front, front, back, back}, spare{s} {}
    car(double all) : car(all, all) {}
};
```

Here, the constructor that takes one value delegates to the constructor that takes three parameters (in this case using the default value for the spare).

Copy constructor

A copy constructor is used when you pass an object by value (or return by value) or if you explicitly construct an object based on another object. The last two lines of the following both create a point object from another point object, and in both cases the copy constructor is called:

```
point p1(10, 10);
```

```
point p2(p1);
point p3 = p1;
```

The last line looks like it involves the assignment operator, but it actually calls the copy constructor. The copy constructor could be implemented like this:

```
class point
{
    int x = 0;int y = 0;
public:
    point(const point& rhs) : x(rhs.x), y(rhs.y) {}
};
```

The initialization accesses the `private` data members on another object (`rhs`). This is acceptable because the constructor parameter is the same type as the object being created. The copy operation may not be as simple as this. For example, if the class contains a data member that is a pointer, you will most likely want to copy the data that the pointer points to, and this will involve creating a new memory buffer in the new object.

Converting between types

You can also perform conversions. In math, you can define a vector that represents direction, so that the line drawn between two points is a vector. In our code we have already defined a `point` class and a `cartesian_vector` class. You could decide to have a constructor that creates a vector between the origin and a point, in which case you are converting a `point` object to a `cartesian_vector` object:

```
class cartesian_vector
{
    double x; double y;
public:
    cartesian_vector(const point& p) : x(p.x), y(p.y) {}
};
```

There is a problem here, which we will address in a moment. The conversions can be called like this:

```
point p(10, 10);
cartesian_vector v1(p);
cartesian_vector v2 { p };
cartesian_vector v3 = p;
```

Making friends

The problem with the code above is that the `cartesian_vector` class accesses `private` members of the `point` class. Since we have written both classes, we are happy to bend the rules, and so we make the `cartesian_vector` class a `friend` of the `point` class:

```
class cartesian_vector; // forward decalartion

class point
{
    double x; double y;
public:
    point(double x, double y) : x(x), y(y){}
    friend class cartesian_point;
};
```

Since the `cartesian_vector` class is declared after the `point` class, we have to provide a forward declaration that essentially tells the compiler that the name `cartesian_vector` is about to be used and it will be declared elsewhere. The important line starts with `friend`. This indicates that the code for the entire class, `cartesian_vector`, can have access to the private members (data and methods) of the `point` class.

You can also declare `friend` functions. For example, you could declare an operator such that a `point` object can be inserted into the `cout` object, so it can be printed to the console. You cannot change the `ostream` class, but you can define a global method:

```
ostream& operator<<(ostream& stm, const point& pt)
{
    stm << "(" << pt.x << "," << pt.y << ")";
    return stm;
}
```

This function accesses the `private` members of `point` so you have to make the function a `friend` of the `point` class with:

```
friend ostream& operator<<(ostream&, const point&);
```

Such `friend` declarations have to be declared in the `point` class, but it is irrelevant whether it is put in the `public` or `private` section.

Marking constructors as explicit

In some cases, you do not want to allow the implicit conversion between one type that is passed as a parameter of the constructor of another type. To do this, you need to mark the constructor with the `explicit` specifier. This now means that the only way to call the constructor is using the parentheses syntax: *explicitly* calling the constructor. In the following code, you cannot implicitly convert a `double` to an object of `mytype`:

```
class mytype
{
public:
    explicit mytype(double x);
};
```

Now you have to *explicitly* call the constructor if you want to create an object with a `double` parameter:

```
mytype t1 = 10.0; // will not compile, cannot convert
mytype t2(10.0);   // OK
```

Destructing objects

When an object is destroyed, a special method called the destructor is called. This method has the name of the class prefixed with a ~ symbol and it does not return a value.

If the object is an automatic variable, on the stack, then it will be destroyed when the variable goes out of scope. When an object is passed by value, a copy is made on the called function's stack and the object will be destroyed when the called function completes. Furthermore, it does not matter how the function completes, whether an explicit call to `return` or reaching the final brace, or if an exception is thrown; in all of these cases, the destructor is called. If there are multiple objects in a function, the destructors are called in the reverse order to the construction of the objects in the same scope. If you create an array of objects, then the default constructor is called for each object in the array on the statement that declares the array, and all the objects will be destroyed--and the destructor on each one is called, when the array goes out of scope.

Here are some examples, for a class `mytype`:

```
void f(mytype t) // copy created
{
    // use t
}   // t destroyed

void g()
{
    mytype t1;
    f(t1);
    if (true)
    {
        mytype t2;
    }   // t2 destroyed

    mytype arr[4];
}   // 4 objects in arr destroyed in reverse order to creation
    // t1 destroyed
```

An interesting action occurs when you return an object. The following annotation is what you would expect:

```
mytype get_object()
{
    mytype t;            // default constructor creates t
    return t;            // copy constructor creates a temporary
}                        // t destroyed

void h()
{
    test tt = get_object(); // copy constructor creates tt
}                           // temporary destroyed, tt destroyed
```

In fact, the process is more streamlined. In a debug build, the compiler will see that the temporary object created on the return of the `get_object` function is the object that will be used as the variable `tt`, and so there is no extra copy on the return value of the `get_object` function. The function actually looks like this:

```
void h()
{
    mytype tt = get_object();
}   // tt destroyed
```

However, the compiler is able to optimize the code further. In a release build (with optimizations enabled), the temporary will not be created and the object `tt` in the calling function will be the actual object `t` created in `get_object`.

An object will be destroyed when you explicitly delete a pointer to an object allocated on the free store. In this case, the call to the destructor is deterministic: it is called when your code calls `delete`. Again, with the same class `mytype`, this is as follows:

```
mytype *get_object()
{
    return new mytype; // default constructor called
}

void f()
{
    mytype *p = get_object();
    // use p
    delete p;          // object destroyed
}
```

There will be times when you want to use the deterministic aspect of deleting an object (with the possible danger of forgetting to call `delete`) and there will be times when you prefer to have the reassurance that an object is to be destroyed at an appropriate time (with the potential that it may be much later in time).

If a data member in a class is a custom type with a destructor, then when the containing object is destroyed the destructors on the contained objects are called too. Nonetheless, note that this is only if the *object* is a class member. If a class member is a pointer to an object in the free store, then you have to explicitly delete the pointer in the containing object's destructor. However, you need to know where the object the pointer points to is because if it is not in the free store, or if the object is used by other objects, calling `delete` will cause problems.

Assigning objects

The assignment operator is called when an *already created* object is assigned to the value of another one. By default, you will get a copy assignment operator that will copy all the data members. This is not necessarily what you want, particularly if the object has a data member that is a pointer, in which case your intention is more likely to do a deep copy and copy the data pointed to rather than the value of the pointer (in the latter case, *two* objects will point to the same data).

If you define a copy constructor, you will still get the default copy assignment operator; however, it makes sense that if you regard it important to write your own copy constructor, you should also provide a custom copy assignment operator. (Similarly, if you define a copy assignment operator, you will get the default copy constructor unless you define it.)

The copy assignment operator is typically a `public` member of the class and it takes a `const` reference to the object that will be used to provide the values for the assignment. The semantics of the assignment operator are that you can chain them, so, for example, this code calls the assignment operator on two of the objects:

```
buffer a, b, c;                      // default constructors called
// do something with them
a = b = c;                           // make them all the same value
a.operator=(b.operator=(c));         // make them all the same value
```

The last two lines do the same thing, but clearly the first is more readable. To enable these semantics, the assignment operator must return a reference to the object that has been assigned. So, the class `buffer` will have the following method:

```
class buffer
{
    // data members
public:
    buffer(const buffer&);            // copy constructor
    buffer& operator=(const buffer&); // copy assignment
};
```

Although the copy constructor and copy assignment methods appear to do similar things, there is a key difference. A copy constructor creates a new object that did not exist before the call. The calling code is aware that if the construction fails, then an exception will be raised. With assignment, both objects already exist, so you are copying the value from one object to another. This should be treated as an atomic action and all the copy should be performed; it is not acceptable for the assignment to fail halfway through, resulting in an object that is a bit of both objects. Furthermore, in construction, an object only exists after the construction is successful, so a copy construction cannot happen on an object itself, but it is perfectly legal (if pointless) for code to assign an object to itself. The copy assignment needs to check for this situation and take appropriate action.

There are various strategies to do this, and a common one is called the copy-and-swap idiom because it uses the Standard Library `swap` function that is marked as `noexcept`, and will not throw an exception. The idiom involves creating a temporary copy of the object on the right-hand side of the assignment and then swapping its data members with the data members of the object on the left-hand side.

Move semantics

C++11 provides move semantics through a move constructor and a move assignment operator, which are called when a temporary object is used either to create another object or to be assigned to an existing object. In both cases, because the temporary object will not live beyond the statement, the contents of the temporary can be moved to the other object, leaving the temporary object in an invalid state. The compiler will create these functions for you through the default action of moving the data from the temporary to the newly created (or the assigned to) object.

You can write your own versions, and to indicate move semantics these have a parameter that is an rvalue reference (`&&`).

 If you want the compiler to provide you with a default version of any of these methods, you can provide the prototype in the class declaration suffixed with `=default`. In most cases, this is self-documenting rather than being a requirement, but if you are writing a POD class you must use the default versions of these functions, otherwise `is_pod` will not return `true`.

If you want to use only move and never to use copy (for example, a file handle class), then you can *delete* the copy functions:

```
class mytype
{
    int *p;
public:
    mytype(const mytype&) = delete;            // copy constructor
    mytype& operator= (const mytype&) = delete; // copy assignment
    mytype&(mytype&&);                          // move constructor
    mytype& operator=(mytype&&);                // move assignment
};
```

This class has a pointer data member and allows move semantics, in which case the move constructor will be called with a reference to a temporary object. Since the object is temporary, it will not survive after the move constructor call. This means that the new object can *move* the state of the temporary object into itself:

```
mytype::mytype(mytype&& tmp)
{
    this->p = tmp.p;
    tmp.p = nullptr;
}
```

The move constructor assigns the temporary object's pointer to `nullptr`, so that any destructor defined for the class does not attempt to delete the pointer.

Declaring static members

You can declare a member of a class--a data member or a method--`static`. This is similar in some ways to how you use the `static` keyword on automatic variables and functions declared at file scope, but there are some important, and different, properties to this keyword when used on a class member.

Defining static members

When you use `static` on a class member it means that the item is associated with the class and not with a specific instance. In the case, of data members, this means that there is one data item shared by all instances of the class. Likewise, a `static` method is not attached to an object, it is not __thiscall and has no `this` pointer.

A `static` method is part of the namespace of a class, so it can create objects for the class and have access to their `private` members. A `static` method has the __cdecl calling convention by default, but you can declare it as __stdcall if you wish. This means that, you can write a method within the class that can be used to initialize C-like pointers, which are used by many libraries. Note that the `static` function cannot call nonstatic methods on the class because a nonstatic method will need a `this` pointer, but a nonstatic method can call a `static` method.

A nonstatic method is called through an object, either using the dot operator (for a class instance) or the -> operator for an object pointer. A `static` method does not need an associated object, but it can be called through one. This gives two ways to call a `static` method, through an object or through the `class` name:

```
class mytype
{
public:
    static void f(){}
    void g(){ f(); }
};
```

Here, the class defines a `static` method called `f` and a nonstatic method called `g`. The nonstatic method `g` can call the `static` method, but the `static` method `f` cannot call the nonstatic method. Since the `static` method `f` is `public`, code outside the `class` can call it:

```
mytype c;
c.g();        // call the nonstatic method
c.f();        // can also call the static method thru an object
mytype::f(); // call static method without an object
```

Although the `static` function can be called through an object, you do not have to create any objects at all to call it.

Static data members need a bit more work because when you use `static` it indicates that the data member is not part of an object, and usually data members are allocated when an object is created. You have to define `static` data members outside of the class:

```
class mytype
{
public:
    static int i;
    static void incr() { i++; }
};

// in a source file
int mytype::i = 42;
```

The data member is defined outside of the class at file scope. It is named using the `class` name, but note that it also has to be defined using the type. In this case the data member is initialized with a value; if you do not do this, then on the first use of the variable it will have the default value of the type (in this case, zero). If you choose to declare the class in a header file (which is common), the definition of the `static` data members must be in a source file.

You can also declare a variable in a method that is `static`. In this case, the value is maintained across method calls, in all objects, so it has the same effect as a `static class` member, but you do not have the issue of defining the variable outside of the class.

Using static and global objects

A `static` variable in a global function will be created at some point before the function is first called. Similarly, a `static` object that is a member of a class will be initialized at some point before it is first accessed.

Static and global objects are constructed before the `main` function is called, and destroyed after the `main` function finishes. The order of this initialization has some issues. The C++ standard says that the initialization of `static` and global objects defined in a source file will occur before any function or object defined in that source file is used, and if there are several global objects in a source file, they will be initialized in the order that they are *defined*. The issue is if you have several source files with `static` objects in each. There is no guarantee on the order in which these objects will be initialized. It becomes a problem if one `static` object depends on another `static` object because you cannot guarantee that the dependent object will be created after the object it depends upon.

Named constructors

This is one application for `public static` methods. The idea is that since the `static` method is a member of the `class` it means that it has access to the `private` members of an instance of the `class`, so such a method can create an object, perform some additional initialization, and then return the object to the caller. This is a **factory method**. The `point` class used so far has been constructed using Cartesian points, but we could also create a point based on polar co-ordinates, where the `(x, y)` Cartesian co-ordinates can be calculated as:

```
x = r * cos(theta)
y = r * sin(theta)
```

Here `r` is the length of the vector to the point and `theta` is the angle of this vector counter-clockwise to the x axis. The `point` class already has a constructor that takes two `double` values, so we cannot use this to pass polar co-ordinates; instead, we can use a `static` method as a *named constructor*:

```
class point
{
    double x; double y;
public:
    point(double x, double y) : x(x), y(y){}
    static point polar(double r, double th)
    {
        return point(r * cos(th), r * sin(th));
    }
};
```

The method can be called like this:

```
const double pi = 3.141529;
const double root2 = sqrt(2);
point p11 = point::polar(root2, pi/4);
```

The object `p11` is the `point` with the Cartesian co-ordinates of (1,1). In this example the `polar` method calls a `public` constructor, but it has access to private members, so the same method could be written (less efficiently) as:

```
point point::polar(double r, double th)
{
    point pt;
    pt.x = r * cos(th);
    pt.y = r * sin(th);
    return pt;
}
```

Nested classes

You can define a class within a class. If the nested class is declared as `public`, then you can create objects in the container class and return them to external code. Typically, however, you will want to declare a class that is used by the class and should be `private`. The following declares a `public` nested class:

```
class outer
{
public:
    class inner
    {
    public:
        void f();
    };

    inner g() { return inner(); }
};

void outer::inner::f()
{
    // do something
}
```

Notice how the name of the nested class is prefixed with the name of the containing class.

Accessing const objects

You have seen many examples so far of using `const`, and perhaps the most frequent is when it is applied to a reference as a function parameter to indicate to the compiler that the function only has read-only access to the object. Such a `const` reference is used so that objects are passed by reference to avoid the overhead of the copying that would occur if the object were passed by value. Methods on a `class` can access the object data members and, potentially, can change them, so if you pass an object through a `const` reference the compiler will only allow the reference to call methods that do not change the object. The `point` class defined earlier had two accessors to access the data in the class:

```
class point
{
    double x; double y;
public:
    double get_x() { return x; }
    double get_y() { return y: }
};
```

If you define a function that takes a `const` reference to this and you attempt to call these accessors, you will get an error from the compiler:

```
void print_point(const point& p)
{
    cout << "(" << p.get_x() << "," << p.get_y() << ")" << endl;
}
```

The error from the compiler is a bit obscure:

cannot convert 'this' pointer from 'const point' to 'point &'

This message is the compiler complaining that the object is `const`, it is immutable, and it does not know whether these methods will preserve the state of the object. The solution is simple--add the `const` keyword to methods that do not change the object state, like this:

```
    double get_x() const { return x; }
    double get_y() const { return y: }
```

This effectively means that the `this` pointer is `const`. The `const` keyword is part of the function prototype, so the method can be overloaded on this. You can have one method that is called when it is called on a `const` object and another called on a non-const object. This enables you to implement a copy-on-write pattern where, for example, a `const` method would return read-only access to the data and the non-const method would return a *copy* of the data that is writeable.

Of course, a method marked with `const` must not alter the data members, not even temporarily. So, such a method can only call `const` methods. There may be rare cases when a data member is designed to be changed through a `const` object; in this case the declaration of the member is marked with the `mutable` keyword.

Using objects with pointers

Objects can be created on the free store and accessed through a typed pointer. This gives more flexibility because it is efficient to pass pointers to functions, and you can explicitly determine the lifetime of the object because an object is created with the call to `new` and destroyed by the call to `delete`.

Getting pointers to object members

If you need to get access to the address of a class data member through an instance (assuming the data member is `public`), you simply use the `&` operator:

```
struct point { double x; double y; };
point p { 10.0, 10.0 };
int *pp = &p.x;
```

In this case `struct` is used to declare `point` so that the members are `public` by default. The second line uses an initialization list to construct a `point` object with two values, and then the final line gets a pointer to one of the data members. Of course, the pointer cannot be used after the object has been destroyed. Data members are allocated in memory (in this case on the stack), so the address operator merely gets a pointer to that memory.

Function pointers are a different case. There will only be one copy of the method in memory, regardless of how many instances of the `class` are created, but because methods are called using the `__thiscall` calling convention (with a hidden `this` parameter) you have to have a function pointer that can be initialized with a pointer to an object to provide the `this` pointer. Consider this `class`:

```
class cartesian_vector
{
public:
    // other items
    double get_magnitude() const
    {
        return std::sqrt((this->x * this->x) + (this->y * this->y));
    }
};
```

We can define a function pointer to the `get_magnitude` method like this:

```
double (cartesian_vector::*fn)() const = nullptr;
fn = &cartesian_vector::get_magnitude;
```

The first line declares a function pointer. This is similar to the C function pointer declarations except that there is an inclusion of the `class` name in the pointer type. This is needed so that the compiler knows that it has to provide a `this` pointer in any call through this pointer. The second line obtains a pointer to the method. Notice that no object is involved. You are not getting a function pointer to a method on an object; you are getting a pointer to a method on a `class` that must be called through an object. To call the method through this pointer, you need to use the pointer to the member operator `.*` on an object:

```
cartesian_vector vec(1.0, 1.0);
double mag = (vec.*fn)();
```

The first line creates an object and the second line calls the method. The pointer to the member operator says that the function pointer on the *right* is called with the object on the *left*. The address of the object on the left is used for the `this` pointer when the method is called. As this is a method, we need to provide a parameter list, which in this case is empty (if you have parameters, they would be in the pair of parentheses on the right of this statement). If you have an object pointer, then the syntax is similar, but you use the `->*` pointer to the member operator:

```
cartesian_vector *pvec = new cartesian_vector(1.0, 1.0);
double mag = (pvec->*fn)();
delete pvec;
```

Operator overloading

One of behaviors of a type is the operations you can apply to it. C++ allows you to overload the C++ operators as part of a class so that it's clear that the operator is acting upon the type. This means that for a unary operator the member method should have no parameters and for a binary operator you need only one parameter, since the current object will be on the left of the operator, and hence the method parameter is the item on the right. The following table summarizes how to implement unary and binary operators, and four exceptions:

Expression	Name	Member method	Non-member function
+a/-a	Prefix unary	operator()	operator(a)
a, b	Binary	operator(b)	operator(a,b)
a+/a-	Postfix unary	operator(0)	operator(a,0)
a=b	Assignment	operator=(b)	
a(b)	Function call	operator()(b)	
a[b]	Indexing	operator[](b)	
a->	Pointer access	operator->()	

Here the ■ symbol is used to indicate any of the acceptable unary or binary operators except for the four operators mentioned in the table.

There are no strict rules over what an operator should return, but it helps if an operator on a custom type behaves like operators on a built-in type. There also has to be some consistency. If you implement the + operator to add two objects together, then the same plus action should be used for the += operator. Also, you could argue that the plus action will also determine what the minus action should be like, and hence the – and –= operators. Similarly, if you want to define the < operator, then you should define <= . >, >=, ==, and != too.

The Standard Library's algorithms (for example, sort) will only expect the < operator to be defined on a custom type.

The table shows that you can implement almost all the operators as either a member of the custom type class or as a global function (with the exception of the four listed that have to be member methods). In general, it is best to implement the operator as part of the class because it maintains encapsulation: the member function has access to the non-public members of the class.

An example of a unary operator is the unary negative operator. This usually does not alter an object but returns a new object that is the *negative* of the object. For our `point class`, this means making both co-ordinates negative, which is equivalent to a mirror of the Cartesian point in a line $y = -x$:

```
// inline in point
point operator-() const
{
    return point(-this->x, -this->y);
}
```

The operator is declared as `const` because it's clear the operator does not change the object and hence it's safe to be called on a `const` object. The operator can be called like this:

```
point p1(-1,1);
point p2 = -p1; // p2 is (1,-1)
```

To understand why we have implemented the operator like this, review what the unary operator would do when applied to a built-in type. The second statement here, `int i, j=0; i = -j;`, will only alter `i` and will not alter `j`, so the member `operator-` should not affect the value of the object.

The binary negative operator has a different meaning. First, it has two operands, and, second, in this example, the result is a different type to the operands because the result is a vector that indicates a direction by taking one point away from another. Assuming that the `cartesian_vector` is already defined with a constructor that has two parameters, then we can write:

```
cartesian_vector point::operator-(point& rhs) const
{
    return cartesian_vector(this->x - rhs.x, this->y - rhs.y);
}
```

The increment and decrement operators have a special syntax because they are unary operators that can be prefixed or postfixed, and they alter the object they are applied to. The major difference between the two operators is that the postfixed operator returns the value of the object *before* the increment/decrement action, so a temporary has to be created. For this reason, the prefix operator almost always has better performance than the postfix operator. In a class definition, to distinguish between the two, the prefix operator has no parameters and the postfix operator has a dummy parameter (in the preceding table, 0 is given). For a class `mytype`, this is as follows:

```
class mytype
{
public:
```

```
mytype& operator++()
{
    // do actual increment
    return *this;
}
mytype operator++(int)
{
    mytype tmp(*this);
    operator++(); // call the prefix code
    return tmp;
}
};
```

The actual increment code is implemented by the prefix operator, and this logic is used by the postfix operator through an explicit call to the method.

Defining function classes

A functor is a class that implements the `()` operator. This means that you can call an object using the same syntax as a function. Consider this:

```
class factor
{
    double f = 1.0;
public:
    factor(double d) : f(d) {}
    double operator()(double x) const { return f * x; }
};
```

This code can be called like this:

```
factor threeTimes(3);        // create the functor object
double ten = 10.0;
double d1 = threeTimes(ten); // calls operator(double)
double d2 = threeTimes(d1);  // calls operator(double)
```

This code shows that the functor object not only provides some behavior (in this case, performing an action on the parameter) but it also can have a state. The preceding two lines are called through the `operator()` method on an object:

```
double d2 = threeTimes.operator()(d1);
```

Look at the syntax. The functor object is called as if it is a function declared like this:

```
double multiply_by_3(double d)
{
    return 3 * d;
}
```

Imagine that you want to pass a pointer to a function--perhaps you are want the function's behavior to be altered by external code. To be able to use either a functor or a method pointer, you need to overload your function:

```
void print_value(double d, factor& fn);
void print_value(double d, double(*fn)(double));
```

The first takes a reference to a functor object. The second has a C-type function pointer (to which you can pass a pointer to `multiply_by_3`) and is quite unreadable. In both cases the `fn` parameter is called in the same way in the implementation code, but you need to declare two functions because they are different types. Now, consider the magic of function templates:

```
template<typename Fn>
void print_value(double d, Fn& fn)
{
    double ret = fn(d);
    cout << ret << endl;
}
```

This is generic code; the `Fn` type can be a C function pointer or a functor `class`, and the compiler will generate the appropriate code.

> This code can be called by either passing a function pointer to a global function, which will have the `__cdecl` calling convention, or a functor object where the `operator()` operator will be called, which has a `__thiscall` calling convention.

This is a mere implementation detail, but it does mean that you can write a generic function that can take either a C-like function pointer or a functor object as a parameter. The C++ Standard Library uses this magic, which means that the algorithms it provides can be called either with a *global function* or a *functor*, or a *lambda expression*.

The Standard Library algorithms use three type of functional classes, generators, and unary and binary functions; that is, functions with zero, one or two parameters. In addition, the Standard Library calls a function object (unary or binary) that returns a `bool` **predicate**. The documentation will tell you if a predicate, unary, or binary function is needed. Older versions of the Standard Library needed to know the types of the return value and parameters (if any) of the function object to work, and, for this reason, functor classes had to be based upon the standard classes, `unary_function` and `binary_function` (through inheritance, explained in the next chapter). In C++11, this requirement has been removed, so there is no requirement to use these classes.

In some cases, you will want to use a binary functor when a unary functor is required. For example, the Standard Library defines the `greater` class that, when used as a function object, takes two parameters and a `bool` to determine whether the first parameter is greater than the second one, using the `operator>` defined by the type of both parameters. This will be used for functions that need a binary functor, and hence the function will compare two values; for example:

```
template<typename Fn>
int compare_vals(vector<double> d1, vector<double> d2, Fn compare)
{
    if (d1.size() > d2.size()) return -1; // error
    int c = 0;
    for (size_t i = 0; i < d1.size(); ++i)
    {
        if (compare(d1[i], d2[i])) c++;
    }
    return c;
}
```

This takes two collections and compares corresponding items using the functor passed as the last parameter. It can be called like this:

```
vector<double> d1{ 1.0, 2.0, 3.0, 4.0 };
vector<double> d2{ 1.0, 1.0, 2.0, 5.0 };
int c = compare_vals(d1, d2, greater<double>());
```

The `greater` functor class is defined in the `<functional>` header and compares two numbers using the `operator>` defined for the type. What if you wanted to compare the items in a container with a fixed value; that is, when the `operator() (double, double)` method on the functor is called, one parameter always has a fixed value? One option is to define a stateful functor class (as shown previously) so that the fixed value is a member of the functor object. Another way to do this is to fill another `vector` with the fixed value and continue to compare two `vectors` (this can get quite expensive for large `vectors`).

Another way is to reuse the functor class, but to *bind* a value to one of its parameters. A version of the `compare_vals` function can be written like this, to take just one `vector`:

```
template<typename Fn>
int compare_vals(vector<double> d, Fn compare)
{
    int c = 0;
    for (size_t i = 0; i < d.size(); ++i)
    {
        if (compare(d[i]) c++;
    }
    return c;
}
```

The code is written to call the functor parameter on just one value because it is assumed that the functor object contains the other value to compare. This is carried out by binding the functor class to the parameter:

```
using namespace::std::placeholders;
int c = compare_vals(d1, bind(greater<double>(), _1, 2.0));
```

The `bind` function is variadic. The first parameter is the functor object and it is followed by the parameters that will be passed to the `operator()` method of the functor. The `compare_vals` function is passed a **binder** object that binds the functor to values. In the `compare_vals` function, the call to the functor in `compare(d[i])` is actually a call to the `operator()` method of the binder object, and this method forwards the parameter `d[i]` and the bound value to the `operator()` method of the functor.

In the call to `bind`, if an actual value is provided (here, 2.0), then that value is passed to the functor at that position in the call to the functor (here, 2,0 is passed to the second parameter). If a symbol preceded by an underscore is used, then it is a **placeholder**. There are 20 such symbols (_1 to _20) defined in the `std::placeholders` namespace. The placeholder means "use the value passed in this position to the binder object `operator()` method call to the functor call `operator()` method indicated by the placeholder." Thus, the placeholder in this call means "pass the first parameter from invoking the binder and pass it to the first parameter of the `greater` functor `operator()`."

The previous code compares each item in the `vector` with 2.0 and will keep a count of those that are greater than 2.0. You could invoke it this way:

```
int c = compare(d1, bind(greater<double>(), 2.0, _1));
```

The parameter list is swapped, and this means that `2.0` is compared with each item in the `vector` and the function will keep a count of how many times `2.0` is greater than the item.

The `bind` function, and placeholders, are new to C++11. In prior versions you could use the `bind1st` and `bind2nd` functions to bind a value to either the first or second parameter of the functor.

Defining conversion operators

We have already seen that a constructor can be used to convert from another type to your custom type if your custom type has a constructor that takes the type you are converting. You can also perform the conversion in the other direction: converting the object into another type. To do this, you provide an operator without a return type with the name of the type to convert to. In this case, you need a space between the `operator` keyword and the name:

```
class mytype
{
    int i;
public:
    mytype(int i) : i(i) {}
    explicit mytype(string s) : i(s.size()) {}
    operator int () const { return i; }
};
```

This code can convert an `int` or a `string` to `mytype`; in the latter case, only through an explicit mention of the constructor. The last line allows you to convert an object back to an `int`:

```
string s = "hello";
mytype t = mytype(s); // explicit conversion
int i = t;            // implicit conversion
```

You can make such conversion operators `explicit` so that they will be called only when an explicit cast is used. In many cases, you will want to leave off this keyword because implicit conversions are useful when you want to wrap a resource in a class and use the destructor to do automatic resource management for you.

Another example of using a conversion operator is returning values from a stateful functor. The idea here is that the `operator()` will perform some action and the result is maintained by the functor. The issue is how do you obtain this state of the functor, especially when they are often created as temporary objects? A conversion operator can provide this functionality.

For example, when you calculate an average, you do it in two stages: the first stage is to accumulate the values and then the second stage is to calculate the average by dividing it by the number of items. The following functor class does this with the division performed as part of the conversion to a `double`:

```
class averager
{
    double total;
    int count;
public:
    averager() : total(0), count(0) {}
    void operator()(double d) { total += d; count += 1; }
    operator double() const
    {
        return (count != 0) ? (total / count) :
            numeric_limits<double>::signaling_NaN();
    }
};
```

This can be called like this:

```
vector<double> vals { 100.0, 20.0, 30.0 };
double avg = for_each(vals.begin(), vals.end(), averager());
```

The `for_each` function calls the functor for every item in the `vector`, and the `operator()` simply sums the items passed to it and maintains a count. The interesting part is that after the `for_each` function has iterated over all of the items in the `vector` it returns the functor, and so there is an implicit conversion to a `double`, which calls the conversion operator that calculates the average.

Managing resources

We have already seen one sort of resource that requires careful management: memory. You allocate memory with `new`, and when you have finished with the memory you must deallocate the memory with `delete`. A failure to deallocate the memory will cause a memory leak. Memory is, perhaps, the most fundamental of system resources, but most operating systems have many others: file handles, handles to graphic objects, synchronization objects, threads, and processes. Sometimes possession of such a resource is exclusive and will prevent other code from accessing the resource accessed through the resource. Thus, it is important that such resources are freed at some point, and, usually, that they are freed in a timely manner.

Classes help here with a mechanism called **Resource Acquisition Is Initialization** (RAII) invented by Bjarne Stroustrup, the author of C++. Put simply, the resource is allocated in the constructor of an object and freed in the destructor, so it means that the lifetime of the resource is the lifetime of the object. Typically, such wrapper objects are allocated on the stack, and this means that you are guaranteed that the resource will be freed when the object goes out of scope *regardless of how this happens*.

So, if objects are declared in the code block for a looping statement (`while`, `for`), then at the end of each loop the destructor for each will be called (in reverse order of creation) and the object will be created again when the loop is repeated. This occurs whether the loop is repeated because the end of the code block has been reached or if the loop is repeated through a call to `continue`. Another way to leave a code block is through a call to `break`, a `goto`, or if the code calls `return` to leave the function. If the code raises an exception (see `Chapter 10`, *Diagnostics and Debugging*), the destructor will be called as the object goes out of scope, so if the code is guarded by a `try` block, the destructor of objects declared in the block will be called before the `catch` clause is called. If there is no guard block, then the destructor will be called before the function stack is destroyed and the exception propagated.

Writing wrapper classes

There are several issues that you must address when writing a class to wrap a resource. The constructor will be used, either to obtain the resource using some library function (usually accessed through some kind of opaque handle) or will take the resource as a parameter. This resource is stored as a data member so other methods on the class can use it. The resource will be released in the destructor using whatever function your library provides to do this. This is the bare minimum. In addition, you have to think how the object will be used. Often such wrapper classes are most convenient if you can use instances as if they are the resource handle. This means that you maintain the same style of programming to access the resource, but you just don't have to worry too much about releasing the resource.

You should think about whether you want to be able convert between your wrapper class and the resource handle. If you do allow this, it means that you may have to think about cloning the resource, so that you do not have two copies of the handle--one that is managed by the class and the other copy that could be released by external code. You also need to think about whether you want to allow the object to be copied or assigned, and if so, then you will need to appropriately implement the copy constructor, a move constructor, and the copy and move assignment operators.

Using smart pointers

The C++ Standard Library provides several classes to wrap resources accessed through pointers. To prevent memory leaks, you have to ensure that memory allocated on the free store is freed at some point. The idea of a smart pointer is that you treat an instance as if it is the pointer, so you use the * operator to dereference to get access to the object it points to or use the -> operator to access a member of the wrapped object. The smart pointer class will manage the lifetime of the pointer it wraps and will release the resource appropriately.

The Standard Library has three smart pointer classes: unique_ptr, shared_ptr, and weak_ptr. Each handles how the resource is released in a different way, and how or whether you can copy a pointer.

Managing exclusive ownership

The unique_ptr class is constructed with a pointer to the object it will maintain. This class provides the operator * to give access to the object, dereferencing the wrapped pointer. It also provides the -> operator, so that if the pointer is for a class, you can access the members through the wrapped pointer.

The following allocates an object on the free store and manually maintains its lifetime:

```
void f1()
{
    int* p = new int;
    *p = 42;
    cout << *p << endl;
    delete p;
}
```

In this case, you get a pointer to the memory on the free store allocated for an int. To access the memory--either to write to it or read from it--you dereference the pointer with the * operator. When you are finished with the pointer, you must call delete to deallocate the memory and return it to the free store. Now consider the same code, but with a smart pointer:

```
void f2()
{
    unique_ptr<int> p(new int);
    *p = 42;
    cout << *p << endl;
    delete p.release();
}
```

The two main differences are that the smart pointer object is constructed explicitly by calling the constructor that takes a pointer of the type that is used as the template parameter. This pattern reinforces the idea that the resource should only be managed by the smart pointer.

The second change is that the memory is deallocated by calling the `release` method on the smart pointer object to take ownership of the wrapped pointer, so that we can delete the pointer explicitly.

Think of the `release` method releasing the pointer from the ownership of the smart pointer. After this call, the smart pointer no longer wraps the resource. The `unique_ptr` class also has a method `get` that will give access to the wrapped pointer, but the smart pointer object will still retain ownership; *do not delete the pointer obtained this way*!

Note that a `unique_ptr` object wraps a pointer, and just the pointer. This means that the object is the same size in memory as the pointer it wraps. So far, the smart pointer has added very little, so let's look at another way to deallocate the resource:

```
void f3()
{
    unique_ptr<int> p(new int);
    *p = 42;
    cout << *p << endl;
    p.reset();
}
```

This is *deterministic* releasing of the resource, and means that the resource is released just when you want it to happen, which is similar to the situation with the pointer. The code here is not releasing the resource itself; it is allowing the smart pointer to do it, using a **deleter**. The default deleter for `unique_ptr` is a functor class called `default_delete`, which calls the `delete` operator on the wrapped pointer. If you intend to use deterministic destruction, `reset` is the preferred method. You can provide your own deleter by passing the type of a custom functor class as the second parameter to the `unique_ptr` template:

```
template<typename T> struct my_deleter
{
    void operator()(T* ptr)
    {
        cout << "deleted the object!" << endl;
        delete ptr;
    }
};
```

In your code, you will specify that you want the custom deleter, like this:

```
unique_ptr<int, my_deleter<int> > p(new int);
```

You may need to carry out an additional clean up before deleting the pointer, or the pointer could be a obtained by a mechanism other than `new`, so you can use a custom deleter to ensure that the appropriate releasing function is called. Note that the deleter is part of the smart pointer class, so if you have two different smart pointers using two different deleter this way, the smart pointer types are different even if they wrap the same type of resource.

 When you use a custom deleter, the size of a `unique_ptr` object may be larger than the pointer wrapped. If the deleter is a functor object, each smart pointer object will need memory for this, but if you use a lambda expression, no more extra space will be required.

Of course, you are most likely to allow the smart pointer to manage the resource lifetime for you, and to do this you simply allow the smart pointer object to go out of scope:

```
void f4()
{
    unique_ptr<int> p(new int);
    *p = 42;
    cout << *p << endl;
} // memory is deleted
```

Since the pointer created is a single object, it means that you can call the `new` operator on an appropriate constructor to pass in initialization parameters. The constructor of `unique_ptr` is passed a pointer to an already constructed object, and the class manages the lifetime of the object after that. Although a `unique_ptr` object can be created directly by calling its constructor, you cannot call the copy constructor, so you cannot use initialization syntax during construction. Instead, the Standard Library provides a function called `make_unique`. This has several overloads, and for this reason it is the preferred way to create smart pointers based on this class:

```
void f5()
{
    unique_ptr<int> p = make_unique<int>();
    *p = 42;
    cout << *p << endl;
} // memory is deleted
```

This code will call the default constructor on the wrapped type (int), but you can provide parameters that will be passed to the appropriate constructor of the type. For example, for a struct that has a constructor with two parameters, the following may be used:

```
void f6()
{
    unique_ptr<point> p = make_unique<point>(1.0, 1.0);
    p->x = 42;
    cout << p->x << "," << p->y << endl;
} // memory is deleted
```

The make_unique function calls the constructor that assigns the members with non-default values. The -> operator returns a pointer and the compiler will access the object members through this pointer.

There is also a specialization of unique_ptr and make_unique for arrays. The default deleter for this version of unique_ptr will call delete[] on the pointer, and thus it will delete every object in the array (and call each object's destructor). The class implements an indexer operator ([]) so you can access each item in the array. However, note that there are no range checks, so, like a built-in array variable, you can access beyond the end of the array. There are no dereferencing operators (* or ->), so a unique_ptr object based on an array can only be accessed with array syntax.

The make_unique function has an overload that allows you to pass the size of the array to create, but you have to initialize each object individually:

```
unique_ptr<point[]> points = make_unique<point[]>(4);
points[1].x = 10.0;
points[1].y = -10.0;
```

This creates an array with four point objects initially set to the default value, and the following lines initialize the second point to a value of (10.0, -10.0). It is almost always better to use vector or array than unique_ptr to manage arrays of objects.

Earlier versions of the C++ Standard Library had a smart pointer class called auto_ptr. This was a first attempt, and worked in most cases, but also had some limitations; for example, auto_ptr objects could not be stored in Standard Library containers. C++11 introduces rvalue references and other language features such as move semantics, and, through these, unique_ptr objects can be stored in containers. The auto_ptr class is still available through the <new> header, but only so that older code can still compile.

The important point about the unique_ptr class is that it ensures that there is a single copy of the pointer. This is important because the class destructor will release the resource, so if you *could* copy a unique_ptr object it would mean more than one destructor will attempt to release the resource. Objects of unique_ptr have *exclusive ownership*; an instance always owns what it points to.

You cannot copy assign unique_ptr smart pointers (the copy assignment operator and copy constructor are deleted), but you can *move* them by transferring ownership of the resource from the source pointer to the destination pointer. So, a function can return a unique_ptr because the ownership is transferred through move semantics to the variable being assigned to the value of the function. If the smart pointer is put into a container, there is another move.

Sharing ownership

There are occasions when you will need to share a pointer: you may create several objects and pass a pointer to a single object to each of them so they can call this object. Ordinarily, when an object has a pointer to another object, that pointer represents a resource that should be destroyed during the destruction of the containing object. If a pointer is shared, it means that when one of the objects deletes the pointer, the pointers in all of the other objects will be invalid (this is called a **dangling pointer** because it no longer points to an object). You need a mechanism where several objects can hold a pointer that will remain valid until *all* the objects using that pointer have indicated they will no longer need to use it.

C++11 provides this facility with the shared_ptr class. This class maintains a **reference count** on the resource, and each copy of the shared_ptr for that resource will increment the reference count. When one instance of shared_ptr for that resource is destroyed, it will decrement the reference count. The reference count is shared, so it means that a non-zero value signifies that at least one shared_ptr exists accessing the resource. When the last shared_ptr object decrements the reference count to zero, it is safe to release the resource. This means that the reference count must be managed in an atomic way to handle multithreaded code.

Since the reference count is shared, it means that each shared_ptr object holds a pointer to a shared buffer called the **control block**, and this means it holds the raw pointer and a pointer to the control block, and so each shared_ptr object will hold more data than a unique_ptr. The control block is used for more than just the reference count.

A `shared_ptr` object can be created to use a custom deleter (passed as a constructor parameter), and the deleter is stored in the control block. This is important because it means that the custom deleter is not part of the type of the smart pointer, so several `shared_ptr` objects wrapping the same resource type but using different deleters are still the same type and can be put in a container for that type.

You can create a `shared_ptr` object from another `shared_ptr` object, and this will initialize the new object with the raw pointer and the pointer to the control block, *and* increment the reference count.

```
point* p = new point(1.0, 1.0);
shared_ptr<point> sp1(p); // Important, do not use p after this!
shared_ptr<point> sp2(sp1);
p = nullptr;
sp2->x = 2.0;
sp1->y = 2.0;
sp1.reset(); // get rid of one shared pointer
```

Here, the first shared pointer is created using a raw pointer. This is not the recommended way to use `shared_ptr`. The second shared pointer is created using the first smart pointer, so now there are two shared pointers to the same resource (p is assigned to `nullptr` to prevent its further use). After this, either sp1 or sp2 can be used to access the *same* resource. At the end of this code, one shared pointer is reset to `nullptr`; this means that sp1 no longer has a reference count on the resource, and you cannot use it to access the resource. However, you can still use sp2 to access the resource until it goes out of scope, or you call `reset`.

In this code, the smart pointers were created from a separate raw pointer. Since the shared pointers now have taken over the lifetime management of the resource it is important to no longer use the raw pointer, and in this case it is assigned to `nullptr`. It is better to avoid the use of raw pointers, and the Standard Library enables this with a function called `make_shared`, which can be used like this:

```
shared_ptr<point> sp1 = make_shared<point>(1.0,1.0);
```

The function will create the specified object using a call to `new`, and since it takes a variable number of parameters, you can use it to call any constructor on the wrapped class.

You can create a `shared_ptr` object from a `unique_ptr` object, which means that the pointer is *moved* to the new object and the reference counting control block created. Since the resource will now be shared, it means that there is no longer exclusive ownership on the resource, so the pointer in the `unique_ptr` object will be made a `nullptr`. This means that you can have a factory function that returns a pointer to an object wrapped in a `unique_ptr` object, and the calling code can determine if it will use a `unique_ptr` object to get exclusive access to the resource or a `shared_ptr` object to share it.

There is little point in using `shared_ptr` for arrays of objects; there are much better ways to store collections of objects (`vector` or `array`). In any case, there is an indexing operator (`[]`) and the default deleter calls `delete`, not `delete[]`.

Handling dangling pointers

Earlier in this book we made the point that, when you delete a resource, you should set the pointer to `nullptr` and you should check a pointer before using it to see if it is `nullptr`. This is so that you do not call a pointer to memory for an object that has been deleted: a dangling pointer.

There are situations when a dangling pointer can occur by design. For example, a *parent* object may create *child* objects that have a **back pointer** to the parent so that the child has access to the parent. (An example of this is a window that creates child controls; it is often useful for the child controls to have access to the parent window.) The problem with using a shared pointer in this situation is that the parent will have a reference count on each child control and each child control has a reference count on the parent, and this creates a circular dependency.

Another example is if you have a container of observer objects with the intention of being able to inform each of these observer objects when an event occurs by calling a method on each one. Maintaining this list can be complicated, particularly if an observer object can be deleted, and hence you have to provide a means to remove the object from the container (where there will be a `shared_ptr` reference count) before you can completely delete the object. It becomes easier if your code can simply add a pointer to the object to the container in a way that does not maintain a reference count, but allows you to check when the pointer is used if the pointer is dangling or points to an existing object.

Such a pointer is called a **weak pointer** and the C++11 Standard Library provides a class called `weak_ptr`. You cannot use a `weak_ptr` object directly and there is no dereference operator. Instead, you create a `weak_ptr` object from a `shared_ptr` object and, when you want to access the resource, you create a `shared_ptr` object from the `weak_ptr` object. This means that a `weak_ptr` object has the same raw pointer, and access to the same control block as the `shared_ptr` object, but it does not take part in reference counting.

Once created, the `weak_ptr` object will enable you to test whether the wrapper pointer is to an existing resource or to a resource that has been destroyed. There are two ways to do this: either call the member function `expired` or attempt to create a `shared_ptr` from the `weak_ptr`. If you are maintaining a collection of `weak_ptr` objects, you may decide to periodically iterate through the collection, call `expired` on each one, and if the method returns `true`, remove that object from the collection. Since the `weak_ptr` object has access to the control block created by the original `shared_ptr` object, it can test to see if the reference count is zero.

The second way to test to see if a `weak_ptr` object is dangling is to create a `shared_ptr` object from it. There are two options. You can create the `shared_ptr` object by passing the weak pointer to its constructor and if the pointer has expired, the constructor will throw a `bad_weak_ptr` exception. The other way is to call the `lock` method on the weak pointer and if the weak pointer has expired, then the `shared_ptr` object will be assigned to `nullptr` and you can test for this. These three ways are shown here:

```cpp
shared_ptr<point> sp1 = make_shared<point>(1.0,1.0);
weak_ptr<point> wp(sp1);

// code that may call sp1.reset() or may not

if (!wp.expired())  { /* can use the resource */}

shared_ptr<point> sp2 = wp.lock();
if (sp2 != nullptr) { /* can use the resource */}

try
{
    shared_ptr<point> sp3(wp);
    // use the pointer
}
catch(bad_weak_ptr& e)
{
    // dangling weak pointer
}
```

Since a weak pointer does not alter the reference count on a resource it means that you can use it for a back pointer to break the cyclic dependency (although, often it makes sense to use a raw pointer instead because a child object cannot exist without its parent object).

Templates

Classes can be templated, which means that you can write generic code and the compiler will generate a class with the types that your code uses. The parameters can be types, constant integer values, or variadic versions (zero or more parameters, as provided by the code using the class). For example:

```
template <int N, typename T> class simple_array
{
    T data[N];
public:
    const T* begin() const { return data; }
    const T* end() const { return data + N; }
    int size() const { return N; }

    T& operator[](int idx)
    {
        if (idx < 0 || idx >= N)
            throw range_error("Range 0 to " + to_string(N));
        return data[idx];
    }
};
```

Here is a very simple array class that defines the basic iterator functions and the indexing operator, so that you can call it like this:

```
simple_array<4, int> four;
four[0] = 10; four[1] = 20; four[2] = 30; four[3] = 40;
for(int i : four) cout << i << " "; // 10 20 30 40
cout << endl;
four[4] = -99;              // throws a range_error exception
```

If you choose to define a function out of the `class` declaration, then you need to give the template and its parameters as part of the `class` name:

```
template<int N, typename T>
T& simple_array<N,T>::operator[](int idx)
{
    if (idx < 0 || idx >= N)
        throw range_error("Range 0 to " + to_string(N));
    return data[idx];
}
```

You can also have default values for template parameters:

```
template<int N, typename T=int> class simple_array
{
    // same as before
};
```

If you think you should have a specific implementation for a template parameter, then you can provide the code for that version as a specialization of the template:

```
template<int N> class simple_array<N, char>
{
    char data[N];
public:
    simple_array<N, char>(const char* str)
    {
        strncpy(data, str, N);
    }
    int size() const { return N; }
    char& operator[](int idx)
    {
        if (idx < 0 || idx >= N)
            throw range_error("Range 0 to " + to_string(N));
        return data[idx];
    }
    operator const char*() const { return data; }
};
```

Note that, with a specialization, you do not get any code from the fully templated class; you have to implement all the methods you want to provide, and, as illustrated here, methods that are relevant to the specialization but not available on the fully templated class. This example is a **partial specialization**, meaning that it is specialized on just one parameter (T, the type of the data). This class will be used for declared variables of the type simple_array<n, char>, where n is an integer. You are free to have a fully specialized template, which, in this case, will be a specialization for a fixed size and a specified type:

```
template<> class simple_array<256, char>
{
    char data[256];
public:
    // etc
};
```

It is probably not useful in this case, but the idea is that there will be special code for variables that need 256 chars.

Using classes

The **Resource Acquisition Is Initialization** technique is useful for managing resources provided by other libraries, such as the C Runtime Library or the Windows SDK. It simplifies your code because you do not have to think about where a resource handle will go out of scope and provide clean-up code at every point. If the clean-up code is complicated, it is typical in C code to see it put at the end of a function and every exit point in the function will have a goto jump to that code. This results in messy code. In this example, we will wrap the C files functions with a class, so that the lifetime of the file handle is maintained automatically.

The C runtime _findfirst and _findnext functions allow you to search for a file or directory that matches a pattern (including wildcard symbols). The _findfirst function returns an intptr_t, which is relevant to just that search and this is passed to the _findnext function to get subsequent values. This intptr_t is an opaque pointer to resources that the C Runtime maintains for the search, and so when you are finished with the search you must call _findclose to clean up any resources associated with it. To prevent memory leaks, it is important to call _findclose.

Under the `Beginning_C++` folder, create a folder called `Chapter_06`. In Visual C++, create a new C++ source file, save it to the `Chapter_06` folder, and call it `search.cpp`. The application will use the Standard Library console and strings, and it will use the C Runtime file functions, so add these lines to the top of the file:

```
#include <iostream>
#include <string>
#include <io.h>
using namespace std;
```

The application will be called with a file search pattern and it will use the C functions to search for files, so you will need a `main` function that has parameters. Add the following to the bottom of the file:

```
void usage()
{
    cout << "usage: search pattern" << endl;
    cout << "pattern is the file or folder to search for "
        << "with or without wildcards * and ?" << endl;
}

int main(int argc, char* argv[])
{
    if (argc < 2)
    {
        usage();
        return 1;
    }
}
```

The first thing is to create a wrapper class for the search handle that will manage this resource. Above the usage function, add a class called `search_handle`:

```
class search_handle
{
    intptr_t handle;
public:
    search_handle() : handle(-1) {}
    search_handle(intptr_t p) : handle(p) {}
    void operator=(intptr_t p) { handle = p; }
    void close()
    { if (handle != -1) _findclose(handle); handle = 0; }
    ~search_handle() { close(); }
};
```

This class has a separate function to release the handle. This is so that a user of this class can release the wrapper resource as soon as possible. If the object is used in code that could throw an exception, the `close` method won't be called directly, but the destructor will be called instead. The wrapper object can be created with a `intptr_t` value. If this value is -1, then the handle is invalid, so the close method will only call `_findclose` if the handle does not have this value.

We want objects of this class to have exclusive ownership of the handle, so delete the copy constructor and copy assignment by putting the following in the public part of the class:

```
void operator=(intptr_t p) { handle = p; }
search_handle(search_handle& h) = delete;
void operator=(search_handle& h) = delete;
```

If an object is moved, then any handle in the existing object must be released, so add the following after the lines you just added:

```
search_handle(search_handle&& h)  { close(); handle = h.handle; }
void operator=(search_handle&& h) { close(); handle = h.handle; }
```

The wrapper class will be allocated by a call to `_findfirst` and will be passed to a call to `_findnext`, so the wrapper class needs two operators: one to convert to an `intptr_t`, so objects of this class can be used wherever an `intptr_t` is needed, and the other so that object can be used when a `bool` is needed. Add these to the `public` part of the class:

```
operator bool() const { return (handle != -1); }
operator intptr_t() const { return handle; }
```

The conversion to `bool` allows you to write code like this:

```
search_handle handle = /* initialize it */;
if (!handle) { /* handle is invalid */ }
```

If you have a conversion operator that returns a pointer, then the compiler will call this in preference to the conversion to `bool`.

You should be able to compile this code (remember to use the `/EHsc` switch) to confirm that there are no typos.

Next, write a wrapper class to perform the search. Below the `search_handle` class, add a `file_search` class:

```
class file_search
{
    search_handle handle;
    string search;
public:
    file_search(const char* str) : search(str) {}
    file_search(const string& str) : search(str) {}
};
```

This class is created with the search criteria, and we have the option of passing a C or C++ string. The class has a `search_handle` data member, and, since the default destructor will call the destructor of member objects, we do not need to provide a destructor ourselves. However, we will add a `close` method so that a user can explicitly release resources. Furthermore, so that users of the class can determine the search path, we need an accessor. At the bottom of the class, add the following:

```
const char* path() const { return search.c_str(); }
void close() { handle.close(); }
```

We do not want instances of the `file_search` object to be copied because that would mean two copies of the search handle. You could delete the copy constructor and assignment operator, but there is no need. Try this: in the `main` function, add this test code (it does not matter where):

```
file_search f1("");
file_search f2 = f1;
```

Compile the code. You'll get an error and an explanation:

```
error C2280: 'file_search::file_search(file_search &)':  attempting to
reference a deleted function
    note: compiler has generated 'file_search::file_search' here
```

Without a copy constructor, the compiler will generate one (this is the second line). The first line is a bit odd because it is saying that you are trying to call a deleted method that the compiler has generated! In fact, the error is saying that the generated copy constructor is attempting to copy the `handle` data member and the `search_handle` copy constructor that has been deleted. Thus you are protected against copying `file_search` objects without adding any other code. Delete the test lines you just added.

Next add the following lines to the bottom of the `main` function. This will create a `file_search` object and print out information to the console.

```
file_search files(argv[1]);
cout << "searching for " << files.path() << endl;
```

Then you need to add code to perform the search. The pattern used here will be a method that has an out parameter and returns a `bool`. If a call to the method succeeds, then the file found will be returned in the out parameter and the method will return `true`. If the call fails, then the out parameter is left untouched and the method returns `false`. In the `public` section of the `file_search` class, add this function:

```
bool next(string& ret)
{
    _finddata_t find{};
    if (!handle)
    {
        handle = _findfirst(search.c_str(), &find);
        if (!handle) return false;
    }
    else
    {
        if (-1 == _findnext(handle, &find)) return false;
    }

    ret = find.name;
    return true;
}
```

If this is the first call to this method, then `handle` will be invalid and so `_findfirst` is called. This will fill a `_finddata_t` structure with the results of the search and return an `intptr_t` value. The `search_handle` object data member is assigned to this value returned from this function, and if `_findfirst` returns `-1`, the method returns `false`. If the call is successful, then the out parameter (a reference to a `string`) is initialized using a C string pointer in the `_finddata_t` structure.

If there are more files that match the pattern, then you can call the `next` function repeatedly, and on these subsequent calls the `_findnext` function is called to get the next file. In this case the `search_handle` object is passed to the function and there is an implicit conversion to `intptr_t` through the class's conversion operator. If the `_findnext` function returns `-1`, it means there are no more files in the search.

At the bottom of the `main` function, add the following lines to perform the search:

```
string file;
while (files.next(file))
{
    cout << file << endl;
}
```

Now you can compile the code and run it with a search criterion. Bear in mind that this is constrained by the facilities of the `_findfirst`/`_findnext` functions, so the searches you can do will be quite simple. Try running this at the command line with a parameter to search for the subfolders in the `Beginning_C++` folder:

search Beginning_C++Ch*

This will give a list of the subfolders starting with `Ch`. Since there is no reason for `search_handle` to be a separate class, move the entire class to the `private` section of the `search_handle`, above the declaration of the `handle` data member. Compile and run the code.

Summary

With classes, C++ provides a powerful and flexible mechanism to encapsulate data and methods to provide behavior that acts on the data. You can template this code so that you can write generic code and get the compiler to generate code for the types that you require. In the example, you have seen how classes are the basis of object orientation. A class encapsulates data, so that the caller only needs to know about the expected behavior (in this example, getting the next result in a search), without needing to know the details of how the class does this. In the next chapter, we will investigate further features of classes; in particular, code reuse through inheritance.

7
Introduction to Object-Orientated Programming

So far, you have seen how to modularize code in functions and encapsulate data with code in a class. You have also seen how to write generic code with templates. Classes and encapsulation allow you to combine together code and data as an object. In this chapter, you'll learn how to *reuse* code through inheritance and composition and how to use class inheritance to write object-orientated code.

Inheritance and composition

The classes you have seen so far are complete classes: you can create an instance of the class on the free store or the stack. You can do this because the data members of the class have been defined and so it is possible to calculate how much memory is needed for the object, and you have provided the full functionality of the class. These are called **concrete classes**.

If you have a routine in a class that proves useful and you want to reuse in a new class, you have a few choices. The first is called **composition**. With composition you add an instance of your utility class as a data member of the classes that will use the routine. A simple example is the string class--this provides all the functionality that you want from a string. It will allocate memory according to how many characters have to be stored and deallocate the memory it uses when the string object is destroyed. Your class uses the functionality of a string, but it is not a string itself, hence it has the string as a data member.

The second option is to use **inheritance**. There are many ways to use inheritance, and this chapter will mention some of them. In basic terms, inheritance is when one class *extends* another class the class being extended is called the **base class**, **parent class**, or **superclass**, and the class doing the extending is called a **derived class**, **child class**, or **subclass**.

However, there is an important concept to understand with inheritance: the relationship of the derived class to the base class. It is commonly given in terms of **is-a**. If the derived class is a type of base class, then the relationship is inheritance. An mp3 file is an operating system file, so if you have a `os_file` class, then you could legitimately derive from it to create an `mp3_file` class.

The derived class has the functionality and state of the base class (although it may not have complete access to them, as will be explained later), so it can use the functionality of the base class. In this case, it is similar to composition. However, there are significant differences. In general, in composition, the composed object is used by the class and not exposed directly to the client of the class. With inheritance, an object of the derived class is an object of the base class, so usually the client code will see the base class functionality. However, a derived class can hide the functionality of the base class, so client code will not see the hidden base class member, and the derived class can override the base class methods and provide its own version.

There is a lot of disagreement in the C++ community over whether you should use inheritance or composition to reuse code, and there are advantages and disadvantages of each. Neither is perfect and often a compromise is needed.

Inheriting from a class

Consider a class that wraps an operating system. This will provide lots of methods to give access to things such as the creation date, modification date, and the size of the file obtained by calling operating system functions. It could also provide methods to open the file, close the file, map the file into memory, and other useful things. Here are a few such members:

```
class os_file
{
    const string file_name;
    int file_handle;
    // other data members
public:
    long get_size_in_bytes();
    // other methods
};
```

An mp3 file is an operating system file, but there are other operating system functions to access its data. We could decide to create an `mp3_file` class that derives from an `os_file` so that it has the functionality of the operating system file and extend this with the functionality of an mp3 file:

```
class mp3_file : public os_file
{
    long length_in_secs;
    // other data members
public:
    long get_length_in_seconds();
    // other methods
};
```

The first line of the `mp3_file` class indicates that it uses *public inheritance* (we will explain what public inheritance means later, but it is worth pointing out that this is the most common way to derive from a class). The derived class inherits the data members and the methods, and users of the derived class can use the members of the base class through the derived class, subject to the access specifiers. In this example, if some code has an `mp3_file` object, it can call the `get_length_in_seconds` method from the `mp3_file` class, and it can also call the `get_size_in_bytes` method from the base because this method is `public`.

The base class methods will most likely access the base class data members, and this illustrates an important point: the derived object contains the base class data members. Conceptually, in memory, you can think of the derived object as being the base class object data members with the extra data members defined in the derived object. That is, the derived object is an extended version of the base class object. This is illustrated in the following diagram:

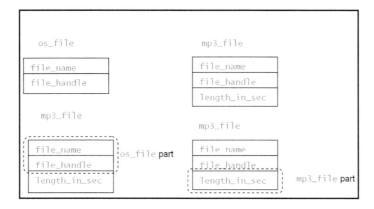

In memory, an `os_file` object has two data members, `file_name` and `file_handle`, and an `mp3_file` object has these two data members and an additional data member, `length_in_secs`.

The encapsulation principle is important in C++. Although an `mp3_file` object contains the `file_name` and `file_handle` data members, they should only be changed by the base class methods. In this code, this is enforced by making them `private` to the `os_file` class.

When a derived object is created, the base object must be created first (with an appropriate constructor), similarly, when a derived object is destroyed, the derived part of the object is destroyed first (through the destructor of the derived class) before the base class destructor is called. Consider the following code snippet, using the members discussed in preceding text:

```
class os_file
{
public:
    os_file(const string& name)
        : file_name(name), file_handle(open_file(name))
    {}
    ~os_file() { close_file(file_handle); }
};

class mp3_file : public os_file
{
public:
    mp3_file(const string& name) : os_file(name) {}
    ~mp3_file() { /* clean up mp3 stuff*/ }
};
```

The `open_file` and `close_file` functions will be some operating system functions to open and close operating system files.

The derived class no longer has to perform the action of closing the file because the base class destructor, `~os_file`, is automatically called after the derived class destructor is called. The `mp3_file` constructor calls the base class constructor through its constructor member list. If you do not explicitly call a base class constructor, then the compiler will call the default constructor of the base class as the first action of the derived class constructor. If the member list initializes data members, these will be initialized after any base class constructor is called.

Overriding methods and hiding names

The derived class inherits the functionality of the base class (subject to the access level of the methods), so a base class method can be called through an object of the derived class. The derived class can implement a method with the same prototype as the base class method, in which case the base class method is *overridden* by the derived class method and the derived class provides the functionality. A derived class will often override a base class method to provide functionality that is specific to the derived class; however, it can call the base class method by calling the method using the name resolution operator:

```
struct base
{
    void f(){ /* do something */ }
    void g(){ /* do something */ }
};

struct derived : base
{
    void f()
    {
        base::f();
        // do more stuff
    }
};
```

Remember that a struct is a `class` type where members are `public` by default, and inheritance is `public` by default.

Here, the `base::f` and `base::g` methods will perform some action available to users of instances of this class. The `derived` class inherits both methods, and since it does not implement the method `g` when instances of the `derived` class call the `g` method, they will actually call the `base::g` method. The `derived` class implements its own version of the `f` method, so when an instance of the `derived` class calls the `f` method, they will call `derived::f` and not the base class version. In this implementation, we have decided that we need some of the functionality of the base class version, so `derived::f` explicitly calls the `base::f` method:

```
derived d;
d.f(); // calls derived::f
d.g(); // calls base::g
```

In the previous example, the method calls the base class version first before providing its own implementation. There is no specific convention here. Class libraries are sometimes implemented specifically for you to derive from a base class and use the class library code.

The documentation of the class library will say whether you are expected to replace the base class implementation or if you are expected to add to the base class implementation, and if so, whether you will call the base class method before or after your code.

In this example, the derived class provides a method with the exact prototype as the method on the base class to override it. In fact, adding any method with the same name as a method in the base class hides that base class method from the client code that uses the derived instance. So, consider that the derived class is implemented like this:

```
struct derived : base
{
    void f(int i)
    {
        base::f();
        // do more stuff with i
    }
};
```

In this case, the base::f method is hidden from the code that creates a derived object, even though the method has a different prototype:

```
derived d;
d.f(42); // OK
d.f();   // won't compile, derived::f(int) hides base::f
```

The base class method with the same name is hidden, so the last line will not compile. You can, however, call the function explicitly by providing the base class name:

```
derived d;
d.derived::f(42); // same call as above
d.base::f();      // call base class method
derived *p = &d;  // get an object pointer
p->base::f();     // call base class method
delete p;
```

At first sight, this syntax looks a little odd but once you know that the . and -> operators give access to a member, and the symbol after the operator is the name of the member, in this case, explicitly specified using the class name and scope resolution operator.

In general, the code shown so far is called **implementation inheritance**, where a class inherits the implementation from a base class.

Using pointers and references

In C++, you can get a pointer to where an object (a built-in type or a custom type) resides in memory using the & operator. The pointer is typed, so the code using the pointer assumes that the pointer points to the memory layout of the object of the type. Similarly, you can obtain a reference to an object, and the reference is an *alias* for the object, that is, operations on the reference occur on the object. A pointer (or a reference) to an instance of a derived class can be implicitly converted to a pointer (or a reference) to a base class object. This means that you can write a function that acts upon base class objects, using the behavior of the base class objects, and as long as the parameter is a pointer or reference to a base class, you can pass any derived class object to the function. The function does not know about, nor does it care about, the derived class functionality.

You should think about the derived object as being a base class object and accept that it can be used as a base class object. Clearly, a base class pointer will only have access to the members on the base class:

```
class base                         pd  ─────▶  ┌──────────┐
{ public: int x = 0; };                        │ int x;   │
                                               ├──────────┤
class derived : public base                    │ int y;   │
{ public: int y = 0; };            pb  ─────▶  ├──────────┤
                                               │ int x;   │
derived d;                                     ├ ─ ─ ─ ─ ─┤
                                               │ int y;   │
                                               └──────────┘
```

If the derived class hides a member of the base class, it means that a pointer to the derived class will call the derived version through the member name, but the base class pointer will only see the base class member, not the derived version.

If you have a base class pointer, you can cast it to a derived class pointer using static_cast:

```cpp
// bad code
void print_y(base *pb)
{
    // be wary of this
    derived *pd = static_cast<derived*>(pb);
    cout << "y = " << pd->y << endl;
}

void f()
{
    derived d;
    print_y(&d); // implicit cast to base*
```

```
        }
```

The problem here is how can the `print_y` function guarantee that the base class pointer passed as the parameter to the specific derived object? It cannot, without discipline from the developers using the function guaranteeing that they will never pass a derived class pointer of a different type. The `static_cast` operator will return a pointer to a `derived` object even if the memory does not contain that object. There is a mechanism to perform type checking on the pointer being cast, which we will cover later in this chapter.

Access levels

So far, we have seen two access specifiers for class members: `public` and `private`. Members declared in the `public` section can be accessed by code in the class *and* by code outside the class either on an object or if the member is `static`, using the class name. Members declared in the `private` section can only be accessed by other members in the same class. A derived class can access the `private` members of the base class but not the `private` members. There is a third type of member access: `protected`. Members declared in the `protected` section can be accessed by methods in the same class or by methods in any derived class and by friends, but not by external code:

```
class base
{
protected:
    void test();
};

class derived : public base
{
public:
    void f() { test(); }
};
```

In this code, the `test` method can be called by members in the `derived` class but not by code outside of the class:

```
base b;
b.test();   // won't compile
derived d;
d.f();      // OK
d.test();   // won't compile
```

If you are writing a base class that you intend only ever to be used as a base class (client code should not create instances of it), then it makes sense to make the destructor `protected`:

```
class base
{
public:
    // methods available through the derived object
    protected:
    ~base(){}
};
```

The compiler will not allow you to create objects of this class on the free store and then destroy with `delete`, because this operator will call the destructor. Similarly, the compiler won't allow you to create objects on the stack because the compiler will call the inaccessible destructor when the object goes out of scope. This destructor will be called through the destructor of the derived class, so you can be assured that a correct cleanup of the base class will occur. This pattern does mean that you always only intend to use pointers to the derived classes to destroy the object with a call to the `delete` operator.

Changing access level through inheritance

When you override a method in the derived class, the access to the method is defined by the derived class. So if the base class method is `protected` or `public`, the access can be changed by the derived class:

```
class base
{
    protected:
    void f();
public:
    void g();
};

class derived : public base
{
public:
    void f();
    protected:
    void g();
};
```

In the preceding example, the `base::f` method is `protected`, so only the `derived` class can access it. The `derived` class overrides this method (and can call the base class method if the fully qualified name is used) and makes it `public`. Similarly, the `base::g` method is `public` but the `derived` class overrides this method and makes it `protected` (and if desired, it could make the method `private`).

You can also expose a `protected` base class from a derived class as a `public` member with a `using` statement:

```
class base
{
protected:
    void f(){ /* code */};
};

class derived: public base
{
public:
    using base::f;
};
```

Now, the `derived::f` method is `public` without the derived class creating a new method. A better use of this facility is to make a method `private` so that it is not available to derived classes (or if it was `public`, through an instance), or make it `protected` so that external code cannot access the member:

```
class base
{
public:
    void f();
};

class derived: public base
{
protected:
    using base::f;
};
```

The preceding code can be used like this:

```
base b;
b.f(); // OK
derived d;
d.f(); // won't compile
```

The last line won't compile because the `f` method is `protected`. If the intention is to make the method available only in the derived class and not to in any classes that may derive from it, you can use the `using` statement in the `private` section of the derived class; this is similar to deleting a base class method:

```
class derived: public base
{
public:
    void f() = delete;

    void g()
    {
        base::f(); // call the base class method
    }
};
```

The `f` method cannot be used through the `derived` class, but the class can call the `base` class method.

Inheritance access levels

Earlier, you saw that to derive from a class, you provide the base class name and give an inheritance access specifier; the examples so far have used `public` inheritance, but you can use `protected` or `private` inheritance.

This is another difference between class and struct. For a class, if you miss off the inheritance access specifier, the compiler will assume that it is private; for a struct, if you miss off the inheritance access specifier, the compiler will assume that it is public.

The inheritance specifier applies more access restrictions, it will not relax them. The access specifier does not determine the access it has to the base class members, instead it alters the accessibility of those members through the derived class (that is through an instance of the class, or if another class derives from it). If a base class has `private` members, and a class inherits using `public` inheritance, the derived class still cannot access the `private` members; it only has access to `public` and `protected` members and objects of the derived class can only access the `public` members, and a class deriving from this class will only have access to the `public` and `protected` members.

If a derived class derives through the *protected inheritance,* it still has the same access to the base class as `public` and `protected` members, but the base class `public` and `protected` members will now be treated as `protected` through the derived class, so they can be accessed by a further derived class but are not accessible through an instance. If a class derives through private inheritance then all base class members become `private` in the derived class; so, although the derived class can access `public` and `protected` members, classes that derive from it cannot access any of the base class members.

One way of looking at protected inheritance is if the derived class had a `using` statement for each of the `public` members of the base class in the `protected` part of the class. Similarly, private inheritance is as if you have deleted each of the `public` and `protected` methods of the base class.

In general, most inheritance will be through *public inheritance.* However, *private inheritance* has a use when you want to access some functionality from a base class but do not want its functionality to be available to classes that derive from your class. This is a little like composition, where you are using functionality but do not want that functionality directly exposed.

Multiple inheritance

C++ allows you to inherit from more than one base class. This is a powerful facility when used with interfaces, as we will discover later in this chapter. It can be useful for implementation inheritance, but it can cause some problems. The syntax is simple: you provide a list of classes to inherit from:

```
class base1 { public: void a(); };
class base2 { public: void b(); };
class derived : public base1, public base2
{
public:
    // gets a and b
};
```

One way to use multiple inheritances is to build up libraries of classes each providing some functionality, or services. To get these services in your class you can add the class from the library to your base class list. Such a *building block* approach to creating classes through implementation inheritance has issues, as we will see later, and often a better approach is to use composition.

It is important when you consider multiple inheritances that you carefully review that you need the services via inheritance or whether composition is more appropriate. If a class provides a member that you do not want to be used by instances and you decide that you need to delete it, it is a good sign that you should consider composition.

If both classes have a member with the same name, then there is a potential problem. The most obvious case is if the base classes have a data member with the same name:

```
class base1 { public: int x = 1; };
class base2 { public: int x = 2; };
class derived : public base1, public base2 {};
```

In the previous example, both base classes have a data member called x. The derived class inherits from both classes, so does this mean that it gets just one data member called x? No. If it did, then this would mean that the base1 class would be able to alter a data member in the base2 class without knowing that it is affecting another class, and similarly the base2 class will find its data member being altered by the base1 class even though that class is not a friend. Consequently, when you derive from two classes with data members that have the same name, the derived class gets both data members.

This yet again illustrates the importance of maintaining encapsulation. Such data members should be private and only changed by the base class.

The derived class (and the code that uses instances, if the data members are accessible) can distinguish between them using their full names:

```
derived d;
cout << d.base1::x << endl; // the base1 version
cout << d.base2::x << endl; // the base2 version
```

The class can be summed up with the following diagram, illustrating the memory occupied by the three classes: base1, base2, and derived:

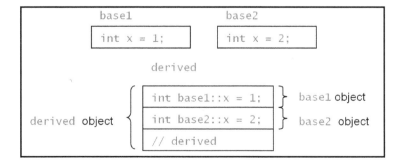

If you maintain encapsulation and make data members `private` and give access only through accessor methods, then derived classes will not have direct access to the data members and will not see this issue. However, the same issue occurs with methods, but the problem occurs even if the methods have different prototypes:

```
class base1 { public: void a(int); };
class base2 { public: void a(); };
class derived : public base1, public base2 {};
```

In this case, the two base classes have a method with the same name, a, but with a different prototype. This causes a problem when using the `derived` class, even when it may be obvious by the parameters what method should be called:

```
derived d;
d.a();            // should be a from base2, compiler still complains
```

This code will not compile, and the compiler will complain that the method call is ambiguous. Again, the solution to this problem is simple, you just need to specify which base class method to use:

```
derived d;
d.base1::a(42); // the base1 version
d.base2::a();   // the base2 version
```

Multiple inheritances can get even more complicated. The problem occurs if you have two classes that derive from the same base class and then you create another class that derives from both. Does the new class get two copies of the topmost base class members--one through each of its immediate base classes?

At the first level of inheritance, each of the classes (`base1` and `base2`) inherit the data member from the ultimate base class (here, the data members are both called `base::x` to illustrate that they are inherited from the ultimate base class, `base`). The most derived class, `derived`, inherits *two* data members, so which one is `base::x`? The answer is that only one of them is, `base1::x` is `base::x`, because it is the first in the inheritance list. When the `base` methods change it, the change will be seen in `base1` through `base1::x`. The `base2::x` member is a separate data member and not affected when `base` changes `base::x`. This is perhaps an unexpected result: the most-derived class inherits x from both of its parent classes.

This may not be the behavior you want. This issue is often called *diamond inheritance issue* and it should be apparent from the preceding diagram, where this name comes from. The solution is straightforward, and will be covered later in this chapter.

Object slicing

Earlier in the chapter, you saw that if you use a base class pointer to a derived object only the base class members can be safely accessed. The other members are still there, but they can only be accessed through an appropriate derived class pointer.

However, if you cast a derived class object to a base class object, something else happens: you create a new object, and that object is the base class object, just the base class object. The variable that you have cast to will only have the memory for the base class object, so the result is only the base class object part of the derived object:

```
struct base { /*members*/ };
struct derived : base { /*members*/ };

derived d;
base b1 = d; // slicing through the copy constructor
base b2;
b2 = d;      // slicing through assignment
```

Here, the objects `b1` and `b2` have been created by *slicing off* the extra data in the `derived` class object `d`. This code looks a bit perverse, and you are not likely to write it, but the situation is likely to happen if you pass an object by value to a function:

```
void f(base b)
{
    // can only access the base members
}
```

If you pass a `derived` object to this function, the `base` copy constructor will be called to create a new object, slicing off the `derived` class data members. In most cases, you do not want this behavior. This issue also has an unexpected behavior if your base class has virtual methods and expects the polymorphic functionality that virtual methods offer (virtual methods are covered later in this chapter). It is almost always a better idea to pass objects by reference.

Introducing polymorphism

Polymorphism comes from the Greek for *many shapes*. So far, you have a basic form of polymorphism. If you use a base class pointer to an object, then you can access the base class behavior, and if you have a derived class pointer, you get the derived class behavior. This is not as trivial as it appears because the derived class can implement its own version of the base class methods, so you can have a different implementation of that behavior.

You can have more than one class derived from a base class:

```
class base { /*members*/ };
class derived1 : public base { /*members*/ };
class derived2 : public base { /*members*/ };
class derived3 : public base { /*members*/ };
```

Since C++ is strongly typed, it means that a pointer to one derived class cannot be used to point to another derived class. So you cannot use a `derived1*` pointer to access an instance of `derived2`, it can only point to an object of type `derived1`. Even if the classes have the same members, they are still different types and their pointers are different. However, all derived classes have something in common, which is the base class. A derived class pointer can be implicitly converted to a base class pointer, so a `base*` pointer can point to an instance of `base`, `derived1`, `derived2`, or `derived3`. This means that a generic function taking a `base*` pointer as a parameter can be passed a pointer to any of these classes. This is the basis of interfaces, as we will see later.

The polymorphic aspect is that through pointers (or references), an instance of a class can be treated as an instance of any of the classes in its inheritance hierarchy.

Virtual methods

A base class pointer or reference giving access to just the base class functionality, and makes sense, but it is restrictive. If you have a `car` class that provides the interface for a car, a gas pedal, and brake to alter the speed, a steering wheel and reverse gear to alter the direction-you can derive from this class various other car types: a sports car, an SUV, or a family sedan. When you press the gas pedal, you expect the car to have the torque of an SUV, if your car is an SUV, or the speed of a sports car if it's a sports car. Similarly, if you call the `accelerate` method on a `car` pointer and that pointer is to a `suv`, then you expect to get method to reflect the torque of the SUV, and if the `car` pointer points to a `sportscar` object, you performance acceleration. Earlier, we said that if you access a derived class instance through a base class pointer, then you will get the implementation of the base class methods. This means that, calling the `accelerate` method on a `car` pointer that points to an `suv` or a `sportscar` object, you will still get the implementation of `car::accelerate` and not `suv::accelerate` or `sportscar::accelerate` which you would want.

This behavior of calling the derived method through a base class pointer is known as **method dispatching**. The code calling a method through a base class pointer does not know the type of object that the pointer points to, but it still gets the functionality of that object because the method on that object is called. This method dispatching is not applied by default because it involves a little extra cost both in memory and performance.

Methods that can take part in method dispatching are marked with the keyword `virtual` in the base class, and hence are usually called **virtual methods**. When you call such a method through a base class pointer, the compiler ensures that the method on the actual object's class is called. Since every method has a `this` pointer as a hidden parameter, the method dispatching mechanism must ensure that the `this` pointer is appropriate when the method is called. Consider the following example:

```
struct base
{
    void who() { cout << "base "; }
};
struct derived1 : base
{
    void who() { cout << "derived1 "; }
};
struct derived2 : base
{
    void who() { cout << "derived2 "; }
};
struct derived3 : derived2
{
    void who() { cout << "derived3 "; }
```

```
};

void who_is_it(base& r)
{
    p.who();
}

int main()
{
    derived1 d1;
    who_is_it(d1);
    derived2 d2;
    who_is_it(d2);
    derived3 d3;
    who_is_it(d3);
    cout << endl;
    return 0;
}
```

There is a base class and two child classes, derived1 and derived2. There is a further level of inheritance through derived2 to a class called derived3. The base class implements a method called who that prints the class name. This method is implemented appropriately on each of the derived classes so that when this method is called on an object of derived3, the method will print derived3 in the console. The main function creates an instance of each of the derived classes and passes each one by reference to a function called who_is_it that calls the who method. This function has a parameter that is a reference to base, and since this is the base class of all of the classes (for derived3, its immediate base class is derived2). When you run this code, the result will be as follows:

base base base

This output comes from the three calls to the who_is_it function, passing objects that are instances of the derived1, derived2, and derived3 classes. Since the parameter is a reference to base, it means that the base::who method is called.

Making one simple change will alter this behavior completely:

```
struct base
{
    virtual void who() { cout << "base "; }
};
```

All that has changed is the addition of the virtual keyword to the who method in the base class, but the result is significant. When you run this code, the result will be as follows:

derived1 derived2 derived3

You have not changed the `who_is_it` function, nor the methods on the derived classes, yet the output of `who_is_it` is very different compared to what it was earlier. The `who_is_it` function calls the `who` method through a reference, but now, rather than calling the `base::who` method, the `who` method on the actual object that the reference aliases is called. The `who_is_it` function has done nothing additional to make sure that the derived class function is called--it is *exactly* the same as earlier.

The `derived3` class is not derived directly from `base`, instead, it is derived from `derived2`, which is itself a child class of `base`. Even so, the method dispatching works on instances of the `derived3` class. This illustrates that however far up the inheritance chain `virtual` is applied, the method dispatching will still work on the inherited method of the derived class.

It is important to point out that the method dispatching is applied *only* to the methods that `virtual` has been applied to in the base class. Any other methods in the base class not marked with `virtual` will be called without method dispatching. A derived class will inherit a `virtual` method and get the method dispatching automatically, it does not have to use the `virtual` keyword on any methods it overrides, but it is a useful visual indication as to how the method can be called.

With the derived classes implementing `virtual` methods, you can use a single container to hold pointers to instances of all such classes and invoke their `virtual` methods without the invocation code knowing the type of the object:

```
derived1 d1;
derived2 d2;
derived3 d3;

base *arr[] = { &d1, &d2, &d3 };
for (auto p : arr) p->who();
cout << endl;
```

Here, the `arr` built-in array holds pointers to objects of the three types and the ranged `for` loop iterates through the array and calls the method virtually. This gives the expected result:

```
derived1 derived2 derived3
```

There are three important points about the preceding code:

- It is important that a built-in array is used here; there are issues with the Standard Library containers like `vector`.
- It is important that the array holds pointers, not objects. If you have an array of `base` objects, they will be initialized by slicing the derived objects.
- It is also important that the address of a stack object is used. This is because there are issues with destructors.

These three issues are covered in later sections.

For a `virtual` method to be called using method dispatching, the derived class method must match the same signature as the base class' `virtual` method in terms of the name, parameters, and return type. If any of these are different (for example, different parameters), then the compiler will think that the derived method is a new function, and so when you call the `virtual` method through the base pointer, you'll get the base method. This is a rather insidious error because the code will compile, but you will get the wrong behavior.

The one exception to the last paragraph is if two methods differ by return types that are **covariant**, that is, one type can be converted to the other.

Virtual method tables

The behavior of method dispatching via virtual methods is all you need to know, but it is helpful to see how the C++ compiler implements method dispatching because it highlights the overhead of the `virtual` methods.

When the compiler sees a `virtual` method on a class, it will create a method pointer table, called the **vtable**, and put a pointer to each of the `virtual` methods in the class in the table. There will be a single copy of the `vtable` for the class. The compiler will also add a pointer to this table, called the **vptr**, in every instance of the class. So, when you mark a method as `virtual`, there will be a single memory overhead of a `vtable` being created for that class at runtime, and the memory overhead of an extra data member, the `vptr`, for every object created from the class. Normally, when client code calls a (non-inline) method, the compiler will place a jump to the function in the client code to the method. When the client code calls a `virtual` method, the compiler has to dereference the `vptr` to get to the `vtable` and then use the appropriate address stored there. Clearly, this involves an extra level of indirection.

There is a separate entry in the vtable for each virtual method in the base class, in the order in which they are declared. When you derive from a base class with virtual methods, the derived class will also have a vptr, but the compiler will make it point to the vtable of the derived class, that is, the compiler will populate the vtable with the addresses of the virtual method implementations in the derived class. If the derived class does not implement a virtual method it inherits, then the pointer in the vtable will be to the base class method. This is illustrated in the following diagram:

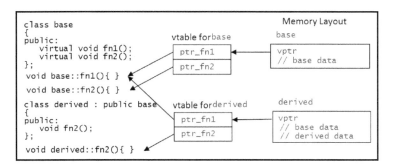

On the left-hand side, there are two classes; the base class has two virtual functions, and the derived class implements just one of these. On the right-hand side, there is an illustration of the memory layout. Two objects are shown as a base object and a derived object. Each object has a single vptr followed by the data members of the class, and the data members are arranged in such a way that the base class data members are arranged first, followed by the derived class data members. The vtable pointers contain method pointers to the virtual methods. In the case of the base class, the method pointers point to the methods implemented on the base class. In the case of the derived class, only the second method is implemented in the derived class, so the vtable for this class has a pointer to one virtual method in the base class and the other in the derived class.

This raises the question: what happens if a derived class introduces a new method, not available in the base class, and makes that virtual? This is not inconceivable since the ultimate base class could provide just part of the behavior needed and classes derived from it, provide more of the behavior to be called through virtual method dispatching on subclasses. The implementation is quite simple: the compiler creates a vtable for all of the virtual methods on the class, so if a derived class has extra virtual methods, the pointers for these appear in the vtable after the pointers to the virtual methods inherited from the base class.

When the object is called through a base class pointer, wherever that class is in the inheritance hierarchy, it will only see the `vtable` entries relevant to it:

```
class base                          vtable for base
{
public:                                 ptr_fn1
    virtual void fn1();
    virtual void fn2();                 ptr_fn2
};

class derived : public base         vtable for derived
{
public:                                 ptr_fn1
    virtual void fn1();
    // no fn2                            ptr_fn2
    virtual void fn3();
};                                      ptr_fn3
```

Multiple inheritance and virtual method tables

If a class derives from more than one class and the parent classes have `virtual` methods, then the vtable for the derived class will be a combination of the vtables of its parents arranged in the order in which the parent classes were listed in the derivation list:

```
class base1
{                                   vtable for base1
public:
    virtual void fn1();                 ptr_fn1
};

class base2                         vtable for base2
{
public:                                 ptr_fn2
    virtual void fn2();
};

class derived1
    : public base1, public base2    vtable for derived
{
public:                                 ptr_fn1          base1*
    virtual void fn1();
                                        ptr_fn2          base2*
    virtual void fn2();
};
```

If the object is accessed through a base class pointer, the `vptr` has access to the part of the `vtable` relevant to that base class.

There is a separate entry in the `vtable` for each `virtual` method in the base class, in the order in which they are declared. When you derive from a base class with `virtual` methods, the derived class will also have a `vptr`, but the compiler will make it point to the `vtable` of the derived class, that is, the compiler will populate the `vtable` with the addresses of the `virtual` method implementations in the derived class. If the derived class does not implement a `virtual` method it inherits, then the pointer in the `vtable` will be to the base class method. This is illustrated in the following diagram:

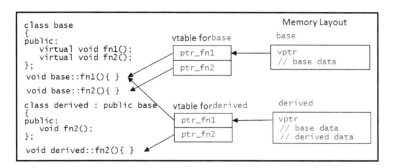

On the left-hand side, there are two classes; the base class has two virtual functions, and the derived class implements just one of these. On the right-hand side, there is an illustration of the memory layout. Two objects are shown as a `base` object and a `derived` object. Each object has a single `vptr` followed by the data members of the class, and the data members are arranged in such a way that the base class data members are arranged first, followed by the derived class data members. The `vtable` pointers contain method pointers to the `virtual` methods. In the case of the base class, the method pointers point to the methods implemented on the `base` class. In the case of the derived class, only the second method is implemented in the `derived` class, so the `vtable` for this class has a pointer to one virtual method in the `base` class and the other in the `derived` class.

This raises the question: what happens if a derived class introduces a new method, not available in the base class, and makes that `virtual`? This is not inconceivable since the ultimate base class could provide just part of the behavior needed and classes derived from it, provide more of the behavior to be called through virtual method dispatching on subclasses. The implementation is quite simple: the compiler creates a `vtable` for all of the `virtual` methods on the class, so if a derived class has extra `virtual` methods, the pointers for these appear in the `vtable` after the pointers to the `virtual` methods inherited from the base class.

When the object is called through a base class pointer, wherever that class is in the inheritance hierarchy, it will only see the `vtable` entries relevant to it:

Multiple inheritance and virtual method tables

If a class derives from more than one class and the parent classes have `virtual` methods, then the vtable for the derived class will be a combination of the vtables of its parents arranged in the order in which the parent classes were listed in the derivation list:

If the object is accessed through a base class pointer, the `vptr` has access to the part of the `vtable` relevant to that base class.

Virtual methods, construction, and destruction

The derived class portion of the object won't be constructed until the constructor has completed, so if you call a `virtual` method, the `vtable` entry will not be set up to call the correct method. Similarly, in a destructor, the derived class portions of the object will have already been destroyed-including their data members, and so the `virtual` methods on the derived class cannot be called because they may attempt to access data members that no longer exist. If the `virtual` method dispatching was allowed in these situations, the result would be unpredictable. You should not call a `virtual` method in a constructor or a destructor, if you do, the call will resolve to the base class version of the method.

If a class is expected to be called through base class pointers with the `virtual` method dispatching, then you should make the destructor `virtual`. We do this because a user may delete a base class pointer, and in this situation, you will want the derived destructor to be called. If the destructor is not `virtual` and the base class pointer is deleted, then only the base class destructor is called, potentially causing a memory leak.

In general, a base class destructor should be either `protected` and non-virtual, or `public` and `virtual`. If the intention is to use the class through base class pointers, then the destructor should be `public` and `virtual` so that the derived class destructor is called, but if the base class is intended to be used to provide services available only through a derived class object, then you should not give direct access to base class objects, and so the destructor should be `protected` and non-virtual.

Containers and virtual methods

One advantage of the `virtual` methods is to put objects related by a base class into a container; earlier, we saw a specific case of using a built-in array of base class pointers, but what about the Standard Library containers? As an example, imagine that you have a class hierarchy where there is one base class, `base`, and three derived classes, `derived1`, `derived2`, and `derived3`, and each class implements a `virtual` method `who`, as used earlier. One attempt to put objects in a container may be as follows:

```
derived1 d1;
derived2 d2;
derived3 d3;
vector<base> vec = { d1, d2, d3 };
for (auto b : vec) b.who();
cout << endl;
```

The problem is that the vector holds `base` objects, and so as the items in the initialization list are put into the container, they are actually used to initialize new `base` objects. Since the type of `vec` is `vector<base>`, the `push_back` method will slice the object. Thus, the statement that calls the `who` method on each object will print a string `base`.

In order to have `virtual` method dispatching, we need to put the whole object in the container. We can do this either with a pointer or a reference. To use a pointer, you can use the addresses of stack objects as long as the `vector` does not live longer than the objects in the container. If you use objects created on the heap, then you need to ensure that the objects are deleted appropriately, and you can do this using smart pointers.

You may be tempted to create a container of references:

```
vector<base&> vec;
```

This will result in a slew of errors; unfortunately, none of them fully indicate the issue. The `vector` must contain types that are copy constructible and assignable. This is not the case with references because they are aliases to actual objects. There is a solution. The `<functional>` header contains an adapter class called `reference_wrapper` that has a copy constructor and assignment operator. The class converts a reference of an object to a pointer to that object. Now you can write the following:

```
vector<reference_wrapper<base> > vec = { d1, d2, d3 };
for (auto b : vec) b.get().who();
cout << endl;
```

The downside of using `reference_wrapper` is that to call the wrapped object (and their virtual methods), you need to call the `get` method, which will return a *reference* to the wrapped object.

Friends and inheritance

In C++, friendship is not inherited. If a class makes another class (or function) a friend, it means that the friend has access to its `private` and `protected` members as if the friend is a member of the class. If you derive from the `friend` class, the new class is not a friend of the first class, and it has no access to the members of that first class.

In the last chapter, we saw how you can insert an object into an `ostream` object to print it by writing a global insertion operator and making this a `friend` of the class.

In the following, the `friend` function is implemented inline, but it is actually a separate, global function that can be called without an object or name resolution with the class name:

```
class base
{
    int x = 0;
public:
    friend ostream& operator<<(ostream& stm, const base& b)
    {
        // thru b we can access the base private/protected members
        stm << "base: " << b.x << " ";
        return stm;
    }
};
```

If we derive from the `base` class, we will need to implement a `friend` function to insert the derived object into the stream. Since the function is a *friend*, it will be able to access the `private` and `protected` members of the derived class, but it cannot access the `private` members of the base class. This situation will mean that the insertion operator that is a *friend* of the derived class can only print out part of the object.

If a `derived` class object is cast to a `base` class, say, through a pointer or reference when passing by reference, and the object is printed, it will be the `base` version of the insertion operator that will be called. The insertion operator is a `friend` function so that it has access to the class' non-public data members, but being a *friend* is not enough to allow it to be a `virtual` method, so there is no `virtual` method dispatching.

Although the `friend` function cannot be called as a `virtual` method, it can call `virtual` methods and get the method dispatching:

```
class base
{
    int x = 0;
    protected:
    virtual void output(ostream& stm) const { stm << x << " "; }
public:
    friend ostream& operator<<(ostream& stm, const base& b)
    {
        b.output(stm);
        return stm;
    }
};

class derived : public base
{
    int y = 0;
```

```
protected:
    virtual void output(ostream& stm) const
    {
        base::output(stm);
        stm << y << " ";
    }
};
```

In this version, there is just one insertion operator and it is defined for the `base` class. This means that any object that can be converted to the `base` class can be printed using this operator. The actual work of printing out the object is delegated to a `virtual` function called `output`. This function is protected because it is intended only to be used by the class or derived classes. The `base` class version of this prints out the data members of the base class. The `derived` class version has two tasks: printing out the data members in the `base` class and then printing out the data members specific to the `derived` class. The first task is accomplished by calling the `base` class version of the method by qualifying the name with the base class name. The second task is simple because it has access to its own data members. If you were to derive another class from `derived`, then its version of `output` function will be similar, but it would call `derived::output`.

Now when an object is inserted into an `ostream` object like `cout`, the insertion operator will be called, and the call to the `output` method will be dispatched to the appropriate derived class.

Override and final

As mentioned earlier, if you type the prototype of a derived `virtual` method wrong, for example, use the wrong parameter types, the compiler will treat the method as a new method and will compile it. It is perfectly legal for a derived class not to override the method of the base class; this is a feature that you will often want to use. However, if you make a mistake in typing the prototype of a derived `virtual` method, the base method will be called when you intended your new version to be called. The `override` specifier is designed to prevent this bug. When the compiler sees this specifier, it knows that you intend to override a `virtual` method inherited from a base class and it will search the inheritance chain to find a suitable method. If no such method can be found, then the compiler will issue an error:

```
struct base
{
    virtual int f(int i);
};
```

```
struct derived: base
{
    virtual int f(short i) override;
};
```

Here, `derived::f` won't compile because there is no method in the inheritance chain with the same signature. The `override` specifier gets the compiler to perform some useful checks, so it is a good habit to use it on all derived overridden methods.

C++11 also provides a specifier called `final`, which you can apply to a method to indicate that a derived class cannot override it, or you can apply it to a class to indicate that you cannot derive from it:

```
class complete final { /* code */ };
class extend: public complete{}; // won't compile
```

It is rare that you'll want to use this.

Virtual inheritance

Earlier, we talked about the so-called *diamond* problem with multiple inheritance, where a class inherits from a single ancestor class via two base classes. When a class inherits from another class, it will get the parent class' data members so that an instance of the derived class is treated as being made up of the base class data members and the derived class data members. If the parent classes are derived from the same ancestor class, they will each get the ancestor class' data members resulting in the final derived classes getting copies of the ancestor class' data members from each parent class:

```
struct base { int x = 0; };
struct derived1 : base { /*members*/ };
struct derived2 :  base { /*members*/ };
struct most_derived : derived1, derived2 { /*members*/ };
```

When you create an instance of the `most_derived` class, you have two copies of `base` in the object: one from each of the `derived1` and `derived2`. This means that the `most_derived` object will have two copies of the data member x. Clearly, the intention is for the derived class to get just one copy of the ancestor class' data members, so how can this be achieved? The solution to this problem is **virtual inheritance**:

```
struct derived1 : virtual base { /*members*/ };
struct derived2 : virtual base { /*members*/ };
```

Without virtual inheritance, derived classes just call the constructors of their immediate parent. When you use `virtual` inheritance, the `most_derived` class has the responsibility to call the constructor of the topmost parent class and if you do not explicitly call the base class constructor, the compiler will automatically call the default constructor:

```
derived1::derived1() : base(){}
derived2::derived2() : base(){}
most_derived::most_derived() : derived1(), derived2(), base(){}
```

In the preceding code, the `most_derived` constructor calls the `base` constructor because this is the base class that its parent classes inherit from virtually. The `virtual` base classes are always created before the non-virtual base classes. In spite of the call to the `base` constructor in the `most_derived` constructor, we still have to call the `base` constructor in the derived classes. If we further derive from `most_derived`, then that class must call the constructor of `base` too because that is where the `base` object will be created. Virtual inheritance is more expensive than single or multiple inheritance.

Abstract classes

A class with `virtual` methods is still a **concrete class**--you can create instances of the class. You may decide that you want to provide just a part of the functionality, with the intention that a user *has* to derive from the class and add the missing functionality.

One way to do this is to provide a `virtual` method that has no code. This means that you can call the `virtual` method in your class, and at runtime, the version of the method in the derived class will be called. However, although this provides a mechanism for you to call derived methods in your code, it does not *force* the implementation of those `virtual` methods. Instead, the derived class will inherit the empty `virtual` methods and if it does not override them, the client code will be able to call the empty method. You need a mechanism to *force* a derived class to provide an implementation of those `virtual` methods.

C++ provides a mechanism called **pure virtual methods** that indicates that the method should be overridden by a derived class. The syntax is simple, you mark the method with = 0:

```
struct abstract_base
{
    virtual void f() = 0;
    void g()
    {
        cout << "do something" << endl;
        f();
    }
};
```

This is the complete class; it is all that this class provides for the definition of the method f. This class will compile even though the method g calls a method that has no implementation. However, the following will not compile:

```
abstract_base b;
```

By declaring a pure virtual function, you make the class abstract, which means that you cannot create instances. You can, however, create pointers or references to the class and call code on them. This function will compile:

```
void call_it(abstract_base& r)
{
    r.g();
}
```

This function only knows about the public interface of the class and does not care how that is implemented. We have implemented the method g to call the method f to show that you can call a pure virtual method in the same class. In fact, you can call the pure virtual function outside the class too; this code is just as valid:

```
void call_it2(abstract_base& r)
{
    r.f();
}
```

The only way to use an abstract class is to derive from it and implement the pure virtual functions:

```
struct derived1 : abstract_base
{
    virtual void f() override { cout << "derived1::f" << endl; }
};

struct derived2 : abstract_base
{
    virtual void f() override { cout << "derived2::f" << endl; }
};
```

Here are two classes derived from the abstract class, which both implement the pure virtual function. These are concrete classes and you can create instances of them:

```
derived1 d1;
call_it(d1);
derived2 d2;
call_it(d2);
```

Abstract classes are used to indicate that a specific functionality has to be provided by a derived class, and the = 0 syntax indicates that the method body is not provided by the abstract class. In fact, it is more subtle than this; the class must be derived and the method called on the derived class must be defined on the derived class, but the abstract base class can also provide a body for the method:

```
struct abstract_base
{
    virtual int h() = 0 { return 42; }
};
```

Again, this class cannot be instantiated, you *must* derive from it and you *must* implement the method to be able to instantiate an object:

```
struct derived : abstract_base
{
    virtual int h() override { return abstract_base::h() * 10; }
};
```

The derived class can call the pure virtual function defined in the abstract class, but when external code calls such a method, it will always result (through method dispatching) in a call to the implementation of the virtual method on the derived class.

Obtaining type information

C++ provides type information, that is, you can get information that is unique to that type and, which identifies it. C++ is a strongly typed language so the compiler will determine type information at compile time and will enforce typing rules when it comes to conversions between variable types. Any type checking that the compiler does, you can do as the developer. As a general rule of thumb if you need to cast using static_cast, const_cast, reinterpret_cast, or C-like casts, then you are making the types do something they shouldn't and hence you should reconsider rewriting your code. The compiler is very good at telling you where there is a misalignment of types, so you should use this as a hint to reassess your code.

A *no casting* rule can be a bit too strict, and often code using casts is simpler to write and easier to read, but such a rule does focus your mind to always question whether a cast is needed.

When you use polymorphism, you will often get a pointer or reference to a type that is different to the type of the object, and this becomes especially true when you move to interface programming where frequently the actual object is unimportant, as it is the behavior that is important. There may be occasions when you need to obtain type information and the compiler is unable to help you at compile time. C++ provides a mechanism to obtain type information called **Runtime Type Information** (**RTTI**) because you can obtain this information at runtime. This information is obtained using the typeid operator on an object:

```
string str = "hello";
const type_info& ti = typeid(str);
cout << ti.name() << endl;
```

The result is the following printed at the command-line:

```
class std::basic_string<char,struct std::char_traits<char>,
    class std::allocator<char> >
```

This reflects that the string class is in fact a typedef for the templated class, basic_string, with a char as the character type with character traits described by the specialization of the char_traits class and an allocator object (used to maintain the buffer used by the string), which is a specialization of the allocator class.

The `typeid` operator returns a `const` reference to a `type_info` object, and in this case, we use the `name` method to return a `const char` pointer to the name of the type of the object. This is the readable version of the type name. The type name is actually stored in a compact, decorated name, which is obtained via the `raw_name` method, but if you want to store objects according to their type (in a dictionary object, for example), then a more efficient mechanism is to use the 32-bit integer returned from the `hash_code` method rather than the decorated name. In all cases, the value returned will be the same for all objects of the same type, but different to objects of another type.

The `type_info` class has no copy constructor or copy assignment operator, and so objects of this class cannot be put in a container. If you want to put `type_info` objects in an associative container like a `map`, then you have two options. First you can put a pointer to the `type_info` object into a container (a pointer can be obtained from a reference); in which case, if the container is ordered, you need to define a comparison operator. The `type_info` class has a `before` method, which can be used to compare two `type_info` objects.

The second option (in C++11) is to use objects of the `type_index` class as the key to the associative container, and this class is used to wrap the `type_info` objects.

The `type_info` class is intended to be read-only, and the only way to create instances is through the `typeid` operator. You can, however, call the comparison operators, `==` and `!=`, on `type_info` objects, which means that you can compare at runtime the types of objects.

Since you can apply the `typeid` operator on both variables and types, it means that you can use the operator to perform casts that are safe from slicing or from casting to a completely unrelated type:

```
struct base {};
struct derived { void f(); };

void call_me(base *bp)
{
    derived *dp = (typeid(*bp) == typeid(derived))
        ? static_cast<derived*>(bp) : nullptr;
    if (dp != nullptr) dp->f();
}

int main()
{
    derived d;
    call_me(&d);
    return 0;
}
```

This function can take a pointer for any class that is derived from the base class. The first line uses the conditional operator where the comparison is between the type information for the object pointed to by the function parameter and the type of the class derived. If the pointer is to a derived object, then the cast will work. If the pointer is to an object of another derived type, but not the derived class, then the comparison will fail and the expression evaluates to nullptr. The call_me function will only call the f method if the pointer points to an instance of the derived class.

C++ provides a cast operator that performs runtime, and such type checking at runtime is called dynamic_cast. If the object can be cast to the requested type, then the operation will succeed and return a valid pointer. If the object cannot be accessed through the requested pointer, then the cast fails and the operator returns nullptr. This means that whenever you use dynamic_cast, you should always check the returned pointer before using it. The call_me function can be rewritten as follows:

```
void call_me(base *bp)
{
    derived *dp = dynamic_cast<derived*>(bp);
    if (dp != nullptr) dp->f();
}
```

This is essentially the same code as earlier; the dynamic_cast operator performs runtime type checking and returns an appropriate pointer.

Note that you cannot downcast, neither to a virtual base class pointer nor to a class derived through protected or private inheritance. The dynamic_cast operator can be used for casts other than downcasts; clearly, it will work for an upcast (to a base class, although it is not necessary), it can be used for casts sideways:

```
struct base1 { void f(); };
struct base2 { void g(); };
struct derived : base1, base2 {};
```

Here there are two base classes, so if you access a derived object through one of the base class pointers, you can use the dynamic_cast operator to cast to a pointer of the other base class:

```
void call_me(base1 *b1)
{
    base2 *b2 = dynamic_cast<base2*>(b1);
    if (b2 != nullptr) b2->g();
}
```

Smart pointers and virtual methods

If you want to use dynamically created objects, you will want to use smart pointers to manage their lifetime. The good news is that `virtual` method dispatching works through smart pointers (they are simply wrappers around object pointers), and the bad news is that the class relationships are lost when you use smart pointers. Let's examine why.

For example, the following two classes are related by inheritance:

```
struct base
{
    Virtual ~base() {}
    virtual void who() = 0;
};

struct derived : base
{
    virtual void who() { cout << "derivedn"; }
};
```

This is straightforward: that implement a `virtual` method, which indicates the type of the object. There is, a `virtual` destructor because we are going to hand over the lifetime management to a smart pointer object and we want to ensure that the `derived` class destructor is called appropriately. You can create an object on the heap using `make_shared` or the constructor of the `shared_ptr` class:

```
// both of these are acceptable
shared_ptr<base> b_ptr1(new derived);
shared_ptr<base> b_ptr2 = make_shared<derived>();
```

A derived class pointer can be converted to a base class pointer and this is explicit in the first statement: `new` returns a `derived*` pointer, which is passed to a `shared_ptr<base>` constructor that expects a `base*` pointer. The situation in the second statement is a bit more complicated. The `make_shared` function returns a temporary `shared_ptr<derived>` object that is converted to a `shared_ptr<base>` object. This is carried out by a conversion constructor on the `shared_ptr` class that calls a **compiler intrinsic** called `__is_convertible_to`, which determines if one pointer type can be converted to the other. In this case, there is an upcast so the conversion is allowed.

Compiler intrinsic are essentially functions provided by the compiler. In this example `__is_convertible_to(derived*, base*)` will return `true` and `__is_convertible_to(base*, derived*)` will return `false`. You will rarely need to know about intrinsics unless you are writing libraries.

Since a temporary object is created in the statement using the `make_shared` function, it is more efficient to use the first statement.

The `operator->` on a `shared_ptr` object will give direct access to the wrapped pointer and hence this means that the following code will perform `virtual` method dispatching, as expected:

```
shared_ptr<base> b_ptr(new derived);
b_ptr->who(); // prints "derived"
```

The smart pointer will ensure that the derived object is destroyed through the base class pointer when `b_ptr` goes out of scope, and since we have a `virtual` destructor, appropriate destruction will occur.

If you have multiple inheritance, you can use `dynamic_cast` (and RTTI) to cast between pointers to the base classes so that you can select only the behavior that you need. Consider the following code:

```
struct base1
{
    Virtual ~base1() {}
    virtual void who() = 0;
};

struct base2
{
    Virtual ~base2() {}
    virtual void what() = 0;
};

struct derived : base1, base2
{
    virtual void who()  { cout << "derivedn"; }
    virtual void what() { cout << "derivedn"; }
};
```

If you have a pointer to either of these base classes, you can convert one to the other:

```
shared_ptr<derived> d_ptr(new derived);
d_ptr->who();
d_ptr->what();

base1 *b1_ptr = d_ptr.get();
b1_ptr->who();
base2 *b2_ptr = dynamic_cast<base2*>(b1_ptr);
b2_ptr->what();
```

The `who` and `what` methods can be called on a `derived*` pointer and hence they can be called on the smart pointer. The following lines obtain a base class pointer so that *specific* behavior is accessed. In this code, we call the `get` method to get the raw pointer from the smart pointer. The problem with this method is that there is now a pointer to the object that is not protected by the smart pointer lifetime management, so it is possible for code to call `delete` on either pointer `b1_ptr` or `b2_ptr` and cause problems later when the smart pointer attempts to delete the object.

This code works, and there is correct lifetime management of the dynamically-created object in this code, but accessing raw pointers like this is inherently unsafe because there is no guarantee that the raw pointers will not be deleted. The temptation is to use smart pointers:

```
shared_ptr<base1> b1_ptr(d_ptr.get());
```

The problem is that even though the classes `base1` and `derived` are related, the classes `shared_ptr<derived>` and `shared_ptr<base1>` are *not* related, and so a different control block will be used for each smart pointer type even though they refer to the *same object*. The `shared_ptr` class will reference the count using the control block and will delete the object when the reference count falls to zero. Having two unrelated `shared_ptr` objects and two control blocks to the same object means that they will attempt to manage the lifetime of the `derived` object independently of each other, and this will ultimately mean one smart pointer deleting the object before the other has finished with it.

There are three messages here: a smart pointer is a lightweight wrapper around a pointer, so you can call `virtual` methods with method dispatching; however, be cautious about using raw pointers obtained from smart pointers, and bear in mind that although you can have many `shared_ptr` objects to the same object, they must be of the same type so that only one control block is used.

Interfaces

Pure virtual functions and virtual method dispatching leads to an incredibly powerful way of writing object-orientated code, which is called **interfaces**. An interface is a class that has no functionality; it only has pure virtual functions. The purpose of an interface is to define a behavior. A concrete class that derives from an interface *must* provide an implementation of all of the methods on the interface, and hence this makes the interface a kind of contract. Users of objects that implement an interface have a guarantee that the object that has the interface will implement *all* the methods of the interface. Interface programming decouples behavior from the implementation. Client code is only interested in behavior and they are not interested in the actual class that provides the interface.

For example, an `IPrint` interface could give access to the behavior of printing a document (setting page size, orientation, number of copies, and telling the printer to print the document). The `IScan` interface can give access to the behavior of scanning a sheet of paper (resolution, grayscale or color, and adjustments like rotation and cropping). These two interfaces are two different behaviors. Client code will use an `IPrint` if it wants to print a document or an `IScan` interface pointer if it wants to scan a document. Such client code does not care whether it is a `printer` object that implements the `IPrint` interface or a `printer_scanner` object that implements both the `IPrint` and `IScan` interfaces. Client code that is passed to an `IPrint *` interface pointer is guaranteed that it can call every method.

In the following code, we have defined the `IPrint` interface (the `define` makes it more obvious that we are defining abstract classes as interfaces):

```
#define interface struct

interface IPrint
{
    virtual void set_page(/*size, orientation etc*/) = 0;
    virtual void print_page(const string &str) = 0;
};
```

A class can implement this interface:

```
class inkjet_printer : public IPrint
{
public:
    virtual void set_page(/*size, orientation etc*/) override
    {
        // set page properties
    }
    virtual void print_page(const string &str) override
    {
        cout << str << endl;
    }
};

void print_doc(IPrint *printer, vector<string> doc);
```

You can then create the `printer` object and call the function:

```
inkjet_printer inkjet;
IPrint *printer = &inkjet;
printer->set_page(/*properties*/);
vector<string> doc {"page 1", "page 2", "page 3"};
print_doc(printer, doc);
```

Our inkjet printer is also a scanner, so we can make it implement the IScan interface:

```
interface IScan
{
    virtual void set_page(/*resolution etc*/) = 0;
    virtual string scan_page() = 0;
};
```

The next version of the inkject_printer class can use multiple inheritance to implement this interface, but note that there is a problem. The class already implements a method called set_page, and since the page properties of the printer will be different from the page properties of the scanner, we want a different method for the IScan interface. We can address this with two different methods and qualifying their names:

```
class inkjet_printer : public IPrint, public IScan
{
public:
    virtual void IPrint::set_page(/*etc*/) override { /*etc*/ }
    virtual void print_page(const string &str) override
    {
        cout << str << endl;
    }
    virtual void IScan::set_page(/*etc*/) override { /*etc*/ }
    virtual string scan_page() override
    {
        static int page_no;
        string str("page ");
        str += to_string(++page_no);
        return str;
    }
};

void scan_doc(IScan *scanner, int num_pages);
```

Now, we can get the IScan interface on the inkjet object and call it as a scanner:

```
inkjet_printer inkjet;
IScan *scanner = &inkjet;
scanner->set_page(/*properties*/);
scan_doc(scanner, 5);
```

Since the `inkject_printer` class derives from both the `IPrinter` and `IScan` interfaces, you can obtain one interface pointer and cast to the other through the `dynamic_cast` operator since this will use RTTI to ensure that the cast is possible. So assuming that you've got an `IScanner` interface pointer, you can test to see if you can cast this to an `IPrint` interface pointer:

```
IPrint *printer = dynamic_cast<IPrint*>(scanner);
if (printer != nullptr)
{
    printer->set_page(/*properties*/);
    vector<string> doc {"page 1", "page 2", "page 3"};
    print_doc(printer, doc);
}
```

Effectively, the `dynamic_cast` operator is being used to request one interface pointer if the behavior represented by another interface is unavailable on the object that pointer points to.

An interface is a contract; once you have defined it, you should *never* change it. This does not constrain you from changing the class. In fact, this is the advantage of using interfaces because the class implementation can change completely, but as long as it continues to implement the interfaces that the client code uses, users of the class can continue to use the class (although a recompile will be needed). There are cases when you will discover that the interface you defined is inadequate. Perhaps there is a parameter which is incorrectly typed that you need to fix, or perhaps you need to add additional functionality.

For example, imagine that you want to tell the printer object to print an entire document rather than a page at a time. The way to do this is to derive from the interface that needs changing and create a new interface; interface inheritance:

```
interface IPrint2 : IPrint
{
    virtual void print_doc(const vector<string> &doc) = 0;
};
```

Interface inheritance means that `IPrint2` has three methods, `set_page`, `print_page`, and `print_doc`. Since the `IPrint2` interface is an `IPrint` interface, this means that when you implement the `IPrint2` interface, you also implement the `IPrint` interface, so you need to change the class to derive from the `IPrint2` interface to add the new functionality:

```
class inkjet_printer : public IPrint2, public IScan
{
public:
    virtual void print_doc(const vector<string> &doc) override {
        /* code*/
    }
```

```
        // other methods
    };
```

The other two methods on the `IPrint2` interface already exist on this class from the implementation of the `IPrint` interface. Now, a client can obtain both `IPrint` pointers and `IPrint2` pointers from instances of this class. You have extended the class, and yet the older client code will still compile.

Microsoft's **Component Object Model** (**COM**) takes this concept a step further. COM is based upon interface programming, so COM objects are only ever accessed through interface pointers. The extra step is that this code can be loaded into your process using a dynamic loaded library, or in another process on your machine or on another machine, and since you use interface programming, the objects are accessed in *exactly* the same way regardless of their location.

Class relationships

Inheritance appears to be an ideal way to reuse code: you write it once in as generic way possible and then derive a class from the base class and reuse the code, specializing it if necessary. You will find, however, a lot of advice against this. Some people will tell you that inheritance is the worst way possible to reuse code and you should use composition instead. In fact, the situation is somewhere between the two: inheritance offers some benefits, but it should not be treated as the best or only solution.

It is possible to get carried away with designing a class library, and there is a general principle to bear in mind: the more code you write, the more maintenance you (or someone else) will have to do. If you change a class, all the other classes that depend upon it will change.

At the highest level, you should be aware of three main issues to avoid:

- **Rigidity**: It is too hard to change a class because any change will affect too many other classes.
- **Fragility**: When you change your class, it could cause unexpected changes in other classes.
- **Immobility**: It is hard to reuse the class because it is too dependent on other classes.

This occurs when you have tight coupling between classes. In general, you should design your classes to avoid this and interface programming is an excellent way to do this because an interface is simply a behavior and not an instance of a specific class.

Such problems occur when you have *dependency inversion*, that is, higher level code, using components, becomes dependent upon the details of how the lower level components are implemented. If you have code that performs some action and then logs the result if you write that logging to use a specific device (say the `cout` object), then the code is rigidly coupled to, and dependent upon, that logging device and you have no option in the future to change to another device. If you abstract the functionality, typically, through an interface pointer-then you break this dependency enabling the code to be used with other components in the future.

Another principle is that in general you should design your classes to be extendable. Inheritance is quite a brute force mechanism to extend a class because you are creating a whole new type. If the functionality only needs to be refined, then inheritance can be an overkill. A more lightweight form of refining an algorithm is to pass a method pointer (or a functor), or an interface pointer to the method of a class for that method to call at an appropriate time to refine how it works.

For example, most sort algorithms require that you pass a method pointer to perform comparisons of two objects of the type that it is sorting. The sort mechanism is generic and does the work of ordering the objects in the most efficient manner, but it bases this on you telling it how to order the two objects. It is excessive to write a new class for every type since the majority of the algorithm remains the same.

Using mixin classes

The **mixin** technique allows you to provide extensibility to classes without the lifetime issues of composition or the heavyweight aspect of raw inheritance. The idea here is that you have a library with specific functionality that can be added to an object. One way to do this is to apply it as a base class with `public` methods, and so if the derived class publicly derives from that class, it will also have those methods as `public` methods. This works fine unless the functionality requires that the derived class performs some functionality too in those methods, in which case the documentation of the library will require that the derived class overrides the method, calls the base class implementation, and adds their own code to the method to complete the implementation (the base class method could be called before, or after the extra derived class code, and the documentation would have to specify this). We have seen this used several times so far in this chapter, and it is a technique used by some older class libraries, for example, Microsoft's **Foundation Classes library** (**MFC**). Visual C++ makes this easier because it generates MFC code with a wizard tool and there are comments about where the developer should add their code.

The problem with this approach is that it requires the developer deriving from the base class implements specific code and follows the rules.

There is a possibility that the developer will write code that compiles and runs, but since it is not written to the desired rules, it has the wrong behavior at runtime.

A mixin class turns this concept on its head. Instead of the developer deriving from a base class provided by the library and extending the functionality provided, the mixin class provided by the library *is derived from a class provided by the developer*. This solves several problems. First, the developer will have to provide specific methods as required by the documentation, otherwise the mixin class (which will use those methods) will not compile. The compiler is enforcing the rules of the class library author to require that the developer using the library provides specific code. Second, the methods on the mixin class can call the base class methods (provided by the developer) exactly where it needs them. The developer using the class library is no longer provided with detailed instructions about how their code is developed, other than that, they have to implement certain methods.

So, how can this be achieved? The class library author does not know about the code that the client developer will write and they do not know about the names of the classes a client developer will write, so they cannot derive from such classes. C++ allows you to provide a type through a template parameter so that the class is instantiated using this type at compile time. With mixin classes, the type passed through a template parameter is the name of a type that will be used as the base class. The developer simply provides a class with the specific methods and then creates a specialization of the mixin class using their class as the template parameter:

```cpp
// Library code
template <typename BASE>
class mixin : public BASE
{
public:
    void something()
    {
        cout << "mixin do something" << endl;
        BASE::something();
        cout << "mixin something else" << endl;
    }
};

// Client code to adapt the mixin class
class impl
{
public:
    void something()
    {
        cout << "impl do something" << endl;
    }
};
```

This class is used in this way:

```
mixin<impl> obj;
obj.something();
```

As you can see, the `mixin` class implements a method called `something` and it calls a base class method called `something`. This means that a client developer using the functionality of the mixin class must implement a method with this name and with the same prototype, otherwise the mixin class cannot be used. The client developer writing the `impl` class does not know how or where their code will be used, just that they have to provide methods with specific names and prototypes. In this case, the `mixin::something` method calls the base class method in the code between the functionality that it provides, the writer of the `impl` class does not need to know this. The output of this code is as follows:

```
    mixin do something
  impl do something
  mixin something else
```

This shows that the `mixin` class can call the `impl` class where it thinks is appropriate. The `impl` class only has to provide the functionality; the `mixin` class determines how it is used. In fact, any class that implements a method with the right name and prototype can be provided as a parameter to the template of the `mixin` class-even another mixin class!

```
template <typename BASE>
class mixin2 : public BASE
{
public:
    void something()
    {
        cout << "mixin2 do something" << endl;
        BASE::something();
        cout << "mixin2 something else" << endl;
    }
};
```

This can be used like this:

```
mixin2< mixin<impl> > obj;
obj.something();
```

The result will be as follows:

```
    mixin2 do something
  mixin do something
  impl do something
  mixin something else
  mixin2 something else
```

Note that the `mixin` and `mixin2` classes know nothing about each other, other than the fact that the appropriate methods are implemented.

Since the mixin class cannot be used without the type provided by the template parameter, they are sometimes called abstract subclasses.

This works fine if the base class only has a default constructor. If the implementation requires another constructor, then the mixin must know what constructor to call and must have appropriate parameters. Also, if you chain the mixins, then they get coupled through the constructors. One way to get around this is to use two stage construction, that is, provide a named method (say, `init`) used to initialize data members in the object after construction. The mixin classes will still be created using their default constructors as earlier, and so there will be no coupling between the classes, that is, the `mixin2` class will know nothing about the data members of `mixin` or those of `impl`:

```
mixin2< mixin<impl> > obj;
obj.impl::init(/* parameters */);   // call impl::init
obj.mixin::init(/* parameters */);  // call mixin::init
obj.init(/* parameters */);         // call mixin2::init
obj.something();
```

This works because you can call a public base class method as long as you qualify the name of the method. The parameter list in these three `init` methods can be different. However, this does pose the problem that the client now has to initialize all the base classes in the chain.

This is the approach that Microsoft's **ActiveX Template Library** (**ATL**) (now part of MFC) uses to provide implementation of standard COM interfaces.

Using polymorphism

In the following example, we will create code that simulates a team of C++ developers. The code will use interfaces to decouple the classes so that it is possible to change the services that a class uses without changing that class. In this simulation, we have a manager managing a team, so a property of the manager is their team. Further, every worker, whether a manager or a team member have some common properties and behaviors--they all have a name and a job position and they all do work of some kind.

Create a folder for the chapter and in that folder, create a file called `team_builder.cpp`, and since this application will use a `vector`, smart pointers, and files, add the following lines to the top of the file:

```
#include <iostream>
#include <string>
#include <vector>
#include <fstream>
#include <memory>
using namespace std;
```

The application will have command-line parameters, but for the time being, just provide an empty copy of the `main` function:

```
int main(int argc, const char *argv[])
{
    return 0;
}
```

We are going to define interfaces, so before the `main` function, add the following:

```
#define interface struct
```

This is just syntactic sugar, but it makes the code a bit more readable to show the purpose of the abstract classes. Under this, add the following interfaces:

```
interface IWork
{
    virtual const char* get_name() = 0;
    virtual const char* get_position() = 0;
    virtual void do_work() = 0;
};

interface IManage
{
    virtual const vector<unique_ptr<IWork>>& get_team() = 0;
    virtual void manage_team() = 0;
};

interface IDevelop
{
    virtual void write_code() = 0;
};
```

All the workers will implement the first interface, which gives access to their name and job position and a method that tells them to do some work. The two types of workers we will define are a manager who manages a team by scheduling their time and a developer who writes code. The manager has a `vector` of `IWork*` pointers, and since these pointers will be to objects created on the free store, the `vector` members are smart pointers wrapping these pointers. This is saying that the manager maintains the lifetime of these objects: while the manager object exists; so will their team.

The first action is to create a helper class that does the basic work of a worker. The reason for this will be apparent later in the example. This class will implement the `IWork` interface:

```cpp
class worker : public IWork
{
    string name;
    string position;
public:
    worker() = delete;
    worker(const char *n, const char *p) : name(n), position(p) {}
    virtual ~worker() {}
    virtual const char* get_name() override
    { return this->name.c_str(); }
    virtual const char* get_position() override
    { return this->position.c_str(); }
    virtual void do_work() override { cout << "works" << endl; }
};
```

A `worker` object must be created with a name and job position. We will also have a helper class for a manager:

```cpp
class manager : public worker, public IManage
{
    vector<unique_ptr<IWork>> team;
public:
    manager() = delete;
    manager(const char *n, const char* p) : worker(n, p) {}
    const vector<unique_ptr<IWork>>& get_team() { return team; }
    virtual void manage_team() override
    { cout << "manages a team" << endl; }
    void add_team_member(IWork* worker)
    { team.push_back(unique_ptr<IWork>(worker)); }
    virtual void do_work() override { this->manage_team(); }
};
```

Note that the `do_work` method is implemented in terms of the virtual function, `manage_team`, which means that a derived class only needs to implement the `manage_team` method since it will inherit the `do_work` method from its parent and method dispatching will mean the correct method is called. The rest of the class is straightforward, but note that the constructor calls the base class constructor to initialize the name and job position (a manager is, after all, a worker) and that the `manager` class has a function to add items to the team as shared in smart pointers.

To test this out, we need to create a `manager` class that manages developers:

```
class project_manager : public manager
{
public:
    project_manager() = delete;
    project_manager(const char *n) : manager(n, "Project Manager")
    {}
    virtual void manage_team() override
    { cout << "manages team of developers" << endl; }
};
```

This overrides calls to the base class constructor passing the name of the project manager and a literal describing the job. The class also overrides `manage_team` to say what the manager actually does. At this point, you should be able to create a `project_manager` and add some members to their team (use the `worker` objects, you'll create developers in a moment). Add the following to the `main` function:

```
project_manager pm("Agnes");
pm.add_team_member(new worker("Bill", "Developer"));
pm.add_team_member(new worker("Chris", "Developer"));
pm.add_team_member(new worker("Dave", "Developer"));
pm.add_team_member(new worker("Edith", "DBA"));
```

This code will compile, but there will be no output when it runs, so create a method to print out a manager's team:

```
void print_team(IWork *mgr)
{
    cout << mgr->get_name() << " is "
        << mgr->get_position() << " and ";
    IManage *manager = dynamic_cast<IManage*>(mgr);
    if (manager != nullptr)
    {
        cout << "manages a team of: " << endl;
        for (auto team_member : manager->get_team())
        {
            cout << team_member->get_name() << " "
```

```
                    << team_member->get_position() << endl;
           }
       }
       else { cout << "is not a manager" << endl; }
   }
```

This function shows how useful interfaces are. You can pass any worker to the function, and it will print out the information relevant to all workers (name and job position). It then asks the object if it is a manager by requesting the `IManage` interface. The function can only get the manager behavior (in this case, having a team) if the object implements this interface. At the end of the `main` function, after the last call to the `program_manager` object, call this function:

```
print_team(&pm)
```

Compile this code (remember to use the `/EHsc` switch) and run the code. You will get the following output:

```
Agnes is Project Manager and manages a team of:
Bill Developer
Chris Developer
Dave Developer
Edith DBA
```

Now we will add a level of polymorphism, so add the following classes before the `print_team` function:

```
class cpp_developer : public worker, public IDevelop
{
public:
    cpp_developer() = delete;
    cpp_developer(const char *n) : worker(n, "C++ Dev") {}
    void write_code() { cout << "Writing C++ ..." << endl; }
    virtual void do_work() override { this->write_code(); }
};

class database_admin : public worker, public IDevelop
{
public:
    database_admin() = delete;
    database_admin(const char *n) : worker(n, "DBA") {}
    void write_code() { cout << "Writing SQL ..." << endl; }
    virtual void do_work() override { this->write_code(); }
};
```

You can change the `main` function so that rather than using `worker` objects, you use `cpp_developer` for Bill, Chris, and Dave and `database_admin` for Edith:

```
project_manager pm("Agnes");
pm.add_team_member(new cpp_developer("Bill"));
pm.add_team_member(new cpp_developer("Chris"));
pm.add_team_member(new cpp_developer("Dave"));
pm.add_team_member(new database_admin("Edith"));
print_team(&pm);
```

You can now compile and run the code and see that not only can you add different types of objects to the manager's team, but you will also get the appropriate information printed through the `IWork` interface.

The next task is to add code to serialize and deserialize these objects. Serialization means writing the object's state (and type information) to a stream and deserialization will take that information and create a new object of the appropriate type and with the specified state. To do this, every object must have a constructor that takes an interface pointer to a deserialzer object, and the constructor should call this interface to extract the state of the object being created. Further, such classes should implement a method to serialize and write an object's state to a serializer object. Let's first look at serialization. At the top of the file, add the following interfaces:

```
#define interface struct

interface IWork;
// forward declaration
    interface ISerializer {
    virtual void write_string(const string& line) = 0;
    virtual void write_worker(IWork *worker) = 0;
    virtual void write_workers (
        const vector<unique_ptr<IWork>>& workers) = 0;
};
interface ISerializable {
    virtual void serialize(ISerializer *stm) = 0;
};
```

The forward declaration is needed because the `ISerializer` interface uses the `IWork` interface. The first interface, `ISerializer`, is implemented by an object that provides serialization services. This could be based on a file, a network socket, a database, or whatever you want to use to store the object. The underlying storage mechanism is unimportant to the user of this interface; all that is important is that the interface can store a string and it can store an entire object passed using an `IWork` interface pointer or a collection of such objects.

The objects that can be serialized must implement the `ISerializable` interface and this has a single method that takes an interface pointer to the object that will provide the serialization service. After the definition of the interfaces, add the following class:

```
class file_writer : public ISerializer
{
    ofstream stm;
public:
    file_writer() = delete;
    file_writer(const char *file) { stm.open(file, ios::out); }
    ~file_writer() { close(); }
    void close() { stm.close(); }
    virtual void write_worker(IWork *worker) override
    {
        ISerializable *object = dynamic_cast<ISerializable*>(worker);
        if (object != nullptr)
        {
            ISerializer *serializer = dynamic_cast<ISerializer*>(this);
            serializer->write_string(typeid(*worker).raw_name());
            object->serialize(serializer);
        }
    }
    virtual void write_workers(
    const vector<unique_ptr<IWork>>& workers) override
    {
        write_string("[[");
        for (const unique_ptr<IWork>& member : workers)
        {
            write_worker(member.get());
        }
        write_string("]]"); // end marker of team
    }
    virtual void write_string(const string& line) override
    {
        stm << line << endl;
    }
};
```

This class provides the `ISerializer` interface for a file, so the `write_string` method uses the `ifstream` insertion operator to write the string on a single line in the file. The `write_worker` method writes the worker object to the file. To do this, it first asks the worker object if it can serialize itself by casing the `IWork` interface an `ISerializable` interface. If the worker object implements this interface, the serializer can ask the worker object to serialize itself by passing the `ISerializer` interface pointer to the `serialize` method on the worker object. It is up to the worker object to determine the information that must be serialized.

The worker object knows nothing about the `file_writer` class other than the `ISerializer` interface, and the `file_writer` class knows nothing about the worker object, other than that it implements the `IWork` and `ISerializable` interfaces.

If the worker object is serializable, the first thing that the `write_worker` method does is obtain type information about the object. The `IWork` interface will be on a class (`project_manager`, `cpp_developer`, or `database_admin`) and so dereferencing the pointer will give the `typeid` operator access to the class type information. We store the raw type name in the serializer because it is compact. Once the type information is serialized, we ask the object to serialize itself by calling the `serialize` method on its `ISerializable` interface. The worker object will store whatever information it wants.

A manager object will need to serialize their team and they do this by passing a collection of worker objects to the `write_workers` method. This indicates that the objects being serialized are an array by writing them between two markers, `[[` and `]]`. Note that because the container has `unique_ptr` objects, there is no copy constructor because that would imply shared ownership. So instead, we access the items through the index operator, which will give us a reference to the `unique_ptr` object within the container.

Now, for every class that can be serialized, you must derive the class from `ISerializable` and implement the `serialize` method. The class inheritance tree means that every class for a type of worker derives from the `worker` class, so we only need this class to inherit from the `ISerializable` interface:

```
class worker : public IWork, public ISerializable
```

The convention is that a class only serializes its own state and delegates to its base class to serialize the base class object. At the top of the inheritance tree is the `worker` class, so at the bottom of this class, add the following interface method:

```
virtual void serialize(ISerializer *stm) override
{
    stm->write_string(name);
    stm->write_string(position);
}
```

This simply serializes the name and job position to the serializer. Note that the worker object does not know what the serializer will do with this information and does not know which class provides the `ISerializer` interface.

At the bottom of the `cpp_developer` class, add this method:

```
virtual void serialize(ISerializer* stm) override
{ worker::serialize(stm); }
```

The cpp_developer class does not have any additional state, so it delegates the serialization to its parent class. If the developer class had a state, then it would serialize this state after serializing the base object. Add exactly the same code to the bottom of the database_admin class.

The project_manager class also calls its base class, but this is manager, so add the following to the bottom of the project_manager class:

```
virtual void serialize(ISerializer* stm) override
{ manager::serialize(stm); }
```

The manager::serialize is more complicated because this class has state that should be serialized:

```
virtual void serialize(ISerializer* stm) override
{
    worker::serialize(stm);
    stm->write_workers(this->team);
}
```

The first action is to serialize the base class: a worker object. Then the code serializes the state of the manager object, which means serializing the team data member by passing this collection to the serializer.

To be able to test the serialization, create a method above the main method and move the project_manager code to the new method and add code to serialize the objects:

```
void serialize(const char* file)
{
    project_manager pm("Agnes");
    pm.add_team_member(new cpp_developer("Bill"));
    pm.add_team_member(new cpp_developer("Chris"));
    pm.add_team_member(new cpp_developer("Dave"));
    pm.add_team_member(new database_admin("Edith"));
    print_team(&pm);

    cout << endl << "writing to " << file << endl;

    file_writer writer(file);
    ISerializer* ser = dynamic_cast<ISerializer*>(&writer);
    ser->write_worker(&pm);
    writer.close();
}
```

The preceding code creates a `file_writer` object for the specified file, obtains the `ISerializer` interface on that object, and then serializes the project manager object. If you have other teams, you can serialize them to the file before closing the `writer` object.

The `main` function will take two parameters. The first is the name of the file and the second is a character, `r` or `w` (to read or write the file). Add the following code to replace the `main` function:

```
void usage()
{
    cout << "usage: team_builder file [r|w]" << endl;
    cout << "file is the name of the file to read or write" << endl;
    cout << "provide w to file the file (the default)" << endl;
    cout << "          r to read the file" << endl;
}

int main(int argc, char* argv[])
{
    if (argc < 2)
    {
        usage();
        return 0;
    }

    bool write = true;
    const char *file = argv[1];
    if (argc > 2) write = (argv[2][0] == 'w');

    cout << (write ? "Write " : "Read ") << file << endl << endl;

    if (write) serialize(file);
    return 0;
}
```

You can now compile this code and run it, giving the name of a file:

team_builder cpp_team.txt w

This will create a file called `cpp_team.txt` containing information about the team; type it at the command-line with **type cpp_team.txt**:

```
.?AVproject_manager@@
Agnes
Project Manager
[[
.?AVcpp_developer@@
Bill
```

```
C++ Dev
.?AVcpp_developer@@
Chris
C++ Dev
.?AVcpp_developer@@
Dave
C++ Dev
.?AVdatabase_admin@@
Edith
DBA
]]
```

This file is not intended to be read by humans, but as you can see, it has one piece of information on each line and each serialized object is preceded by the type of the class.

Now you will write the code to deserialize an object. The code needs a class that will read the serialization data and return worker objects. This class is tightly coupled to the serializer class, but it should be accessed through an interface so that it is not coupled to the worker objects. After the declaration of the `ISerializable` interface, add the following:

```
interface IDeserializer
{
    virtual string read_string() = 0;
    virtual unique_ptr<IWork> read_worker() = 0;
    virtual void read_workers(vector<unique_ptr<IWork>>& team) = 0;
};
```

The first method obtains a serialization string and the other two methods obtain a single object and a collection of objects. Since these worker objects will be created on the free store, these methods use smart pointers. Every class can serialize itself, and so now you will make each serializable class able to deserialize itself. To do this, for every class that implements `ISerializable`, add a constructor that takes an `IDeserializer` interface pointer. Start with the `worker` class; add the following public constructor:

```
worker(IDeserializer *stm)
{
    name = stm->read_string();
    position = stm->read_string();
}
```

Essentially, this reverses what the `serialize` method does, it reads the name and position string from the deserializer *in the same order* in which they were passed to the serializer. Since the `cpp_developer` and `database_admin` classes have no state, they do not need to do any other deserializing work other than call the base class constructor. For example, add the following public constructor to the `cpp_developer` class:

```
cpp_developer(IDeserializer* stm) : worker(stm) {}
```

Add a similar constructor to the `database_admin` class.

Managers have a state, so there is a bit more work to deserialize them. Add the following to the `manager` class:

```
manager(IDeserializer* stm) : worker(stm)
{ stm->read_workers(this->team); }
```

The initializer list constructs the base class and after this is run, the constructor initializes the `team` collection with zero or more worker objects by calling `read_workers` on the `IDeserializer` interface. Finally, the `project_manager` class derives from the `manager` class, but adds no extra state, so add the following constructor:

```
project_manager(IDeserializer* stm) : manager(stm) {}
```

Now, every serializable class can deserialize itself, the next action is to write the deserializer class that will read a file. After the `file_writer` class, add the following (note that two methods are not implemented inline):

```
class file_reader : public IDeserializer
{
    ifstream stm;
public:
    file_reader() = delete;
    file_reader(const char *file) { stm.open(file, ios::in); }
    ~file_reader() { close(); }
    void close() { stm.close(); }
    virtual unique_ptr<IWork> read_worker() override;
    virtual void read_workers(
        vector<unique_ptr<IWork>>& team) override;
    virtual string read_string() override
    {
        string line;
        getline(stm, line);
        return line;
    }
};
```

The constructor opens the specified file and the destructor closes it. The `read_string` interface method reads a line from the file and returns it as a string. The main work is carried out in the two interface methods not implemented here. The `read_workers` method will read a collection of `IWork` objects and put them into the collection passed by reference. This method will call the `read_worker` method for every object in the file and put them in the collection, and so the main work of reading the file is carried out in this method. The `read_worker` method is the only part of the class that has any coupling to the serializable classes, and because of this, it has to be defined below the definition of the worker classes. Above the `serialize` global function, add the following:

```cpp
unique_ptr<IWork> file_reader::read_worker()
{
}
void file_reader::read_workers(vector<unique_ptr<IWork>>& team)
{
    while (true)
    {
        unique_ptr<IWork> worker = read_worker();
        if (!worker) break;
        team.push_back(std::move(worker));
    }
}
```

The `read_workers` method will read each object from the file using the `read_worker` method, which returns each object in a `unique_ptr` object. We want to put this object into the container, but because there should be exclusive ownership of the pointer, we need to move the ownership into the object in the container. There are two ways to do this. The first way is simply to use the call to `read_worker` as the parameter to `push_back`. The `read_worker` method returns a temporary object, which is an rvalue, so the compiler will use move semantics when creating the object in the container. We do not do this because the `read_worker` method may return a `nullptr` (which we want to test for), so instead we create a new `unique_ptr` object (move semantics will pass ownership to this object), and once we have tested that this object is not a `nullptr`, we call the Standard Library function, `move`, to move copy the object into the container.

If the `read_worker` method reads the end marker of an array, it returns a `nullptr` and hence the `read_workers` method loops, reading each worker and putting them in the collection until a `nullptr` is returned.

Implement the `read_worker` method like this:

```
unique_ptr<IWork> file_reader::read_worker()
{
    string type = read_string();
    if (type == "[[") type = read_string();
    if (type == "]]") return nullptr;
    if (type == typeid(worker).raw_name())
    {
        return unique_ptr<IWork>(
        dynamic_cast<IWork*>(new worker(this)));
    }
    return nullptr;
}
```

The first line reads the type information of the worker object from the file so that it knows what object to create. Since the file will have markers to indicate the array of team members, the code has to detect these. If the start of the array is detected, the marker string is ignored and the next line is read to get the type of the first object in the team. If the end marker is read, then this is the end of the array so a `nullptr` is returned.

The code for a `worker` object is shown here. The `if` statement tests to check whether the type string is the same as the raw name of the `worker` class. If it is, then we must create a `worker` object and request that it deserializes itself by calling the constructor that takes an `IDeserializer` pointer. The `worker` object is created on the free store and the `dynamic_cast` operator is called to obtain the `IWork` interface pointer, which is then used to initialize a smart pointer object. The constructor for the `unique_ptr` is `explicit`, so you have to call it. Now add similar code for all the other serializable classes:

```
if (type == typeid(project_manager).raw_name())
{
    return unique_ptr<IWork>(
    dynamic_cast<IWork*>(new project_manager(this)));
}
if (type == typeid(cpp_developer).raw_name())
{
    return unique_ptr<IWork>(
    dynamic_cast<IWork*>(new cpp_developer(this)));
}
if (type == typeid(database_admin).raw_name())
{
    return unique_ptr<IWork>(
    dynamic_cast<IWork*>(new database_admin(this)));
}
```

Finally, you need to create a `file_reader` and deserialize a file. After the `serialize` function, add the following:

```
void deserialize(const char* file)
{
    file_reader reader(file);
    while (true)
    {
        unique_ptr<IWork> worker = reader.read_worker();
        if (worker) print_team(worker.get());
        else break;
    }
    reader.close();
}
```

This code simply creates a `file_reader` object based on the file name and then reads each worker object from the file printing out the object and, if it is a `project_manager`, prints out their team. Finally, add a line in the `main` function to call this function:

```
cout << (write ? "Write " : "Read ") << file << endl << endl;
if (write) serialize(file);
else deserialize(file);
```

Now you can compile the code and use it to read in the serialization file with the following:

team_builder cpp_team.txt r

(Note the `r` parameter.) The code should print out the objects that you serialized to the file.

The previous example has shown that you can write serializable objects that do not know about the mechanism that is used to serialize them. If you want to use a different mechanism than a flat file (for example, an XML file or to a database), you do not need to alter any of the worker classes. Instead, you write an appropriate class that implements the `ISerializer` interface and the `IDeserailizer` interface. If you need to create another worker class, all you need to do is alter the `read_worker` method to deserialize objects of that type.

Summary

In this chapter, you saw how to use C++ inheritance to reuse code and provide an is-a relationship between objects. You also saw how this can be used to implement polymorphism, where related objects can be treated as having the same behavior while still maintaining the ability to call each object's methods, and interfaces that group together behaviors. In the next chapter, you'll see the features of the C++ Standard Library and the various utility classes it provides.

8
Using the Standard Library Containers

The Standard Library provides several types of containers; each is provided through a templated class so that the behavior of the container can be used for items of any type. There are classes for sequential containers, where the ordering of the items in the container is dependent on the order that the items are inserted into the container. Also there are sorted and unsorted associated containers that associate a value with a key, and subsequently the value is accessed using the key.

Although not containers themselves, in this chapter we will also cover two related classes: pair that links two values together in one object, and tuple, that can hold one or more values in a single object.

Working with pairs and tuples

In many cases you will want to associate two items together; for example, an associative container allows you to create a type of array where items other than numbers are used as an index. The <utility> header file contains a templated class called pair, which has two data members called first and second.

```
template <typename T1, typename T2>
struct pair
{
    T1 first;
    T2 second;
    // other members
};
```

Since the class is templated, it means that you can associate any items, including pointers or references. Accessing the members is simple since they are public. You can also use the `get` templated function, so for a `pair` object p you can call `get<0>(p)` rather than `p.first`. The class also has a copy constructor, so that you can create an object from another object, and a move constructor. There is also a function called `make_pair` that will deduce the types of the members from the parameters:

```
auto name_age = make_pair("Richard", 52);
```

Be wary because the compiler will use the type that it thinks is most appropriate; in this case the `pair` object created will be `pair<const char*, int>`, but if you want the `first` item to be a `string`, it is simpler to use the constructor. You can compare `pair` objects; the comparison is performed on the first member and only if they are equal is the second then compared:

```
pair <int, int> a(1, 1);
pair <int, int> a(1, 2);
cout << boolalpha;
cout << a << " < " << b << " " << (a < b) << endl;
```

The parameters can be references:

```
int i1 = 0, i2 = 0;
pair<int&, int&> p(i1, i2);
++p.first; // changes i1
```

The `make_pair` function will deduce the types from the parameters. The compiler cannot tell the difference between a variable and a reference to a variable. In C++11 you can use the `ref` function (in `<functional>`) to specify that the `pair` will be for references:

```
auto p2 = make_pair(ref(i1), ref(i2));
++p2.first; // changes i1
```

If you want to return two values from a function, you could do it via parameters passed by reference, but the code is less readable because you expect a return value to come through the return of a function rather than through its parameters. The `pair` class allows you to return two values in one object. One example is the `minmax` function in `<algorithm>`. This returns a `pair` object containing the parameters in order of the smallest first, and there is an overload where you can provide a predicate object if the default operator < should not be used. The following will print `{10,20}`:

```
auto p = minmax(20,10);
cout << "{" << p.first << "," << p.second << "}" << endl;
```

The `pair` class associates two items. The Standard Library provides the `tuple` class that has a similar functionality, but since the template is variadic it means that you can have any number of parameters of any type. However, the data members are not named as in `pair`, instead you access them via the templated `get` function:

```
tuple<int, int, int> t3 { 1,2,3 };
cout << "{"
    << get<0>(t3) << "," << get<1>(t3) << "," << get<2>(t3)
    << "}" << endl; // {1,2,3}
```

The first line creates a `tuple` that holds three `int` items and it is initialized using an initialize list (you could use constructor syntax). The `tuple` is then printed to the console by accessing each data member in the object using a version of the `get` function where the template parameter indicates the index of the item. Note that the index is a template parameter, so you cannot provide it at runtime using a variable. If this is what you want to do, then it is a clear indication that you need to use a container such as `vector`.

The `get` function returns a reference, so this can be used to change the value of the item. For a `tuple` t3, this code changes the first item to 42 and the second to 99:

```
int& tmp = get<0>(t3);
tmp = 42;
get<1>(t3) = 99;
```

You can also extract all the items with one call, by using the `tie` function:

```
int i1, i2, i3;
tie(i1, i2, i3) = t3;
cout << i1 << "," << i2 << "," << i3 << endl;
```

The `tie` function returns a `tuple` in which each parameter is a reference and initialized to the variables that you pass as parameters. The previous code is easier to understand if you write it like this:

```
tuple<int&, int&, int&> tr3 = tie(i1, i2, i3);
tr3 = t3;
```

A `tuple` object can be created from a `pair` object, and so you can use the `tie` function to extract values from a `pair` object too.

There is a helper function called `make_tuple`, which will deduce the types of the parameters. As with the `make_pair` function, you have to be wary of the deductions, so a floating-point number will be deduced to be a `double` and an integer will be an `int`. If you want the parameters to be references to specific variables, you can use the `ref` function or the `cref` function for a `const` reference.

You can compare `tuple` objects as long as there are equal numbers of items and equivalent types. The compiler will refuse to compile comparisons of `tuple` objects that have different numbers of items or if the types of the items of one `tuple` objects cannot be converted to the types of the other `tuple` object.

Containers

The Standard Library containers allow you to group together zero or more items of the same type and access them serially through iterators. Every such object has a `begin` method that returns an iterator object to the first item and an `end` function that returns an iterator object for the item after the last item in the container. The iterator objects support pointer-like arithmetic, so that `end() - begin()` will give the number of items in the container. All container types will implement the `empty` method to indicate if there are no items in the container, and (except for `forward_list`) the `size` method is the number of items in the container. You are tempted to iterate through a container as if it is an array:

```
vector<int> primes{1, 3, 5, 7, 11, 13};
for (size_t idx = 0; idx < primes.size(); ++idx)
{
    cout << primes[idx] << " ";
}
cout << endl;
```

The problem is that not all containers allow random access, and if you decide it is more efficient to use another container, you'll have to change how the container is accessed. This code also does not work well if you want to write generic code using templates. The previous code is better written using iterators:

```
template<typename container> void print(container& items)
{
    for (container::iterator it = items.begin();
    it != items.end(); ++it)
    {
        cout << *it << " ";
    }
    cout << endl;
}
```

All of the containers have a `typedef` member called `iterator` that gives the type of the iterator returned from the `begin` method. Iterator objects behave like pointers, so you can obtain the item an iterator refers to using the dereference operator and move to the next item using the increment operator.

For all containers except for `vector`, there is a guarantee that an iterator will remain valid even if other elements are deleted. If you insert items, then only `lists`, `forward_lists`, and associated container guarantee that the iterators remain valid. Iterators will be covered in more depth later.

All containers have to have an exception safe (nothrow) method called `swap`, and (with two exceptions) they must have *transactional* semantics; that is, an operation must succeed or fail. If the operation fails, the container is in the same state as before the operation is called. For every container, this rule is relaxed when it comes to multi-element inserts. If you insert many items at a time using an iterator range, for example, and the insert fails for one of the items in the range, then the method will not be able to undo the previous inserts.

It is important to point out that objects are copied into containers, so the type of the objects that you put into a container must have a copy and copy assignment operator. Also, be aware that if you put a derived class object into a container that requires a base class object, then the copying will slice the object, meaning that anything to do with the derived class is removed (data members and virtual method pointers).

Sequence containers

Sequence containers store a series of items and the order that they are stored in, and, when you access them with an iterator, the items are retrieved in the order in which they were put into the container. After creating a container, you can change the sort order with library functions.

List

As the name suggests, a `list` object is implemented by a doubly linked list in which each item has a link to the next item and the previous one. This means that it is quick to insert items (as the example in `Chapter 4`, *Working with Memory, Arrays, and Pointers*, showed with a singly linked list), but since, in a linked list, an item only has access to the items in front and behind it, there is no random access with the `[]` index operator.

The class allows you to provide values through the constructor, or you can use member methods. For example, the `assign` method allows you fill the container in one action using an initializer list, or, with iterators, to a range in another container. You can also insert a single item using the `push_back` or `push_front` method:

```
list<int> primes{ 3,5,7 };
primes.push_back(11);
primes.push_back(13);
primes.push_front(2);
primes.push_front(1);
```

The first line creates a `list` object that contains 3, 5, and 7, and then pushes 11 and 13 to the end (in that order), so that the `list` contains {3, 5, 7, 11, 13}. The code then pushes the numbers 2 and 1 to the front, so that the final `list` is {1, 2, 3, 5, 7, 11, 13}. In spite of the names, the `pop_front` and `pop_back` methods just remove the item at the front or back of the list, but will not return the item. If you want to get the item that has been removed, you must *first* access the item through the `front` or `back` method:

```
int last = primes.back();  // get the last item
primes.pop_back();          // remove it
```

The `clear` method will remove all items in the `list` and the `erase` method will delete items. There are two versions: one with an iterator that identifies a single item and another that has two iterators that indicate a range. A range is indicated by providing the first item in the range and the item *after* the range.

```
auto start = primes.begin(); // 1
start++;                     // 2
auto last = start;           // 2
last++;                      // 3
last++;                      // 5
primes.erase(start, last);   // remove 2 and 3
```

This is a general principle with iterators and the Standard Library containers; a range is indicated by iterators by the first item and the item *after* the last item. The `remove` method will remove all items with a specified value:

```
list<int> planck{ 6,6,2,6,0,7,0,0,4,0 };
planck.remove(6);           // {2,0,7,0,0,4,0}
```

There is also a method `remove_if` that takes a predicate and will only remove an item if the predicate returns `true`. Similarly, you can insert items into a list with an iterator, and the item is inserted before the specified item:

```
list<int> planck{ 6,6,2,6,0,7,0,0,4,0 };
auto it = planck.begin();
++it;
++it;
planck.insert(it, -1); // {6,6,-1,2,6,0,7,0,0,4,0}
```

You can also indicate that the item should be inserted more than once at that position (and if so, how many copies) and you can provide several items to be inserted at one point. Of course, if the iterator you pass is obtained by calling the `begin` method, then the item is inserted at the beginning of the `list`. The same can be achieved by calling the `push_front` method. Similarly, if the iterator is obtained by calling the `end` method, then the item is inserted at the end of the `list`, which is the same as calling `push_back`.

When you call the `insert` method, you provide an object that will either be copied into the `list` or moved into the `list` (through rvalue semantics). The class also provides several **emplace** methods (`emplace`, `emplace_front`, and `emplace_back`) that will construct a new object based on the data you provide, and insert that object in the `list`. For example, if you have a `point` class that can be created from two `double` values, you can either `insert` a constructed `point` object or `emplace` a `point` object by providing two `double` values:

```
struct point
{
    double x = 0, y = 0;
    point(double _x, double _y) : x(_x), y(_y) {}
};

list<point> points;
point p(1.0, 1.0);
points.push_back(p);
points.emplace_back(2.0, 2.0);
```

Once you have created a `list`, you can manipulate it with member functions. The `swap` method takes a suitable `list` object as a parameter, it moves the items from the parameter into the current object, and moves the items in the current `list` to the parameter. Since the `list` object is implemented using linked lists, this operation is quick.

```
list<int> num1 { 2,7,1,8,2,8 }; // digits of Euler's number
list<int> num2 { 3,1,4,5,6,8 }; // digits of pi
num1.swap(num2);
```

After this, code `num1` will contain {3,1,4,5,6,8} and `num2` will contain {2,7,1,8,2,8}, as the following illustrates:

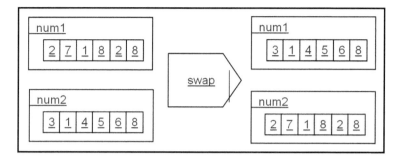

A `list` will hold the items in the order that they were inserted into the container; however, you can sort them by calling the `sort` method that will, by default, order items in ascending order using the < operator for the items in the `list` container. You can also pass a function object for a comparison operation. Once sorted, you can reverse the order of items by calling the `reverse` method. Two sorted lists can be merged, which involves taking the items from the argument list and inserting them into the calling list, in order:

```
list<int> num1 { 2,7,1,8,2,8 }; // digits of Euler's number
list<int> num2 { 3,1,4,5,6,8 }; // digits of pi
num1.sort();                     // {1,2,2,7,8,8}
num2.sort();                     // {1,3,4,5,6,8}
num1.merge(num2);                // {1,1,2,2,3,4,5,6,7,8,8,8}
```

Merging two lists may result in duplicates, and these can be removed by calling the `unique` method:

```
num1.unique(); // {1,2,3,4,5,6,7,8}
```

Forward list

As the name suggests, the `forward_list` class is like the `list` class, but it only allows items to insert and remove items from the front of the list. It also means that the iterators used with the class can only be incremented; the compiler will refuse to allow you to decrement such an iterator. The class has a subset of the methods of `list`, so it has the `push_front`, `pop_front`, and `emplace_front` methods, but not the corresponding `_back` methods. There are some other methods that it implements, and, because the list items can only be accessed in a forward direction, it means that insertions will occur after an existing item, and hence the class implements `insert_after` and `emplace_after`.

Similarly, you can remove items at the beginning of the list (`pop_front`) or after a specified item (`erase_after`), or tell the class to iterate in a forward direction through the list and remove items with a specific value (`remove` and `remove_if`):

```
forward_list<int> euler { 2,7,1,8,2,8 };
euler.push_front(-1);        // { -1,2,7,1,8,2,8 }
auto it = euler.begin();     // iterator points to -1
euler.insert_after(it, -2);  // { -1,-2,2,7,1,8,2,8 }
euler.pop_front();           // { -2,2,7,1,8,2,8 }
euler.remove_if([](int i){return i < 0;});
                             // { 2,7,1,8,2,8 }
```

In the preceding code `euler` is initialized with the digits of Euler's number and a value of -1 is pushed to the front. Next, an iterator is obtained that points to the first value in the container; that is, to the position of the value of -1. A value of -2 is inserted after the position of the iterator; that is, -2 is inserted after the value of -1. The last two lines show how to remove items; `pop_front` removes the item at the front of the container and `remove_if` will remove items that satisfy the predicate (in this case when the item is less than zero).

Vector

The `vector` class has the behavior of a dynamic array; that is, there is indexed random access to items and the container will grow as more items are inserted into it. You can create a `vector` object with an initialization list, and with a specified number of copies of an item. You can also base a `vector` on values in another container by passing iterators that indicate the range of items in that container. You can create a vector with a pre-determined size by providing a capacity as the constructor parameter, and the specified number of default items will be created in the container. If, at a later stage, you need to specify the container size, you can call the `reserve` method to specify the minimum size or the `resize` method, which may mean deleting excess items or creating new items depending on whether the existing `vector` object is bigger or smaller than the requested size.

When you insert items into a `vector` container and there is not enough memory allocated, then the container will allocate enough memory. This will involve allocating new memory, copying the existing items into the new memory, creating the new item, and, finally, destroying the old copy of the items and deallocating the old memory. Clearly, if you know the number of items and you know that the `vector` container will not be able to contain them without a new allocation, you should indicate how much space you need by calling the `reserve` method.

Inserting items other than the constructor is straightforward. You can use `push_back` to insert an item at the end (which is a fast action, assuming no allocation is needed) and there is also `pop_back` to remove the last item. You can also use the `assign` method to clear the entire container and insert the specified items (either a multiple of the same item, an initializer list of items, or items in another container specified with iterators). As with `list` objects, you can clear the entire `vector`, erase items at a position, or insert items at a specified position. However, there is no equivalent of the `remove` method to remove items with a specific value.

The main reason to use the `vector` class is to get random access using either the `at` method or the `[]` indexing operator:

```
vector<int> distrib(10); // ten intervals
for (int count = 0; count < 1000; ++count)
{
    int val = rand() % 10;
    ++distrib[val];
}
for (int i : distrib) cout << i << endl;
```

The first line creates a `vector` with ten items, and then in the loop the C runtime function `rand` is called a thousand times each time to get a pseudo random number between 0 and 32767. The modulus operator is used to get, in approximate terms, a random number between 0 and 9. This random number is then used as an index for the `distrib` object to select a specified item, which is then incremented. Finally, the distribution is printed out and, as you would expect, this gives a value of roughly 100 in each item.

This code relies on the fact that the `[]` operator returns a reference to the item, which is why the item can be incremented in this manner. The `[]` operator can be used to read and write to an item in the container. The container gives iterator access through the `begin` and `end` methods, and (since they are needed by the container adapters) the `front` and `back` methods.

A `vector` object can hold any type that has a copy constructor and assignment operator, which means all the built-in types. As it stands, a `vector` of `bool` items would be a waste of memory because a Boolean value can be stored as a single bit and the compiler will treat a `bool` as an integer (32 bits). The Standard Library has a specialization of the `vector` class for `bool` that stores items more efficiently. However, although the class at first sight looks like a good idea, the problem is that, since the container holds Boolean values as bits, this means that the `[]` operator doesn't return a reference to a `bool` (instead it returns an object that behaves like one).

If you want to hold Boolean values and manipulate them then, as long as you know at compile time how many items there are, the `bitset` class is probably a better choice.

Deque

The name `deque` means *double-ended queue*, which means that it can grow from both ends, and, although you can insert items in the middle, it is more expensive. As a queue, it means that the items are ordered, but, because the items can be put into the queue from either end, the order is not necessarily the same order in which you put items into the container.

The interface of `deque` is similar to a `vector`, so you have iterator access as well as random access using the `at` function and the `[]` operator. As with a `vector`, you can access items from the end of a `deque` container using the `push_back`, `pop_back`, and `back` methods, but, unlike a `vector`, you can also access the front of a `deque` container using the `push_front`, `pop_front`, and `front` methods. Although the `deque` class has methods to allow you to insert and erase items within the container, and to `resize`, these are expensive operations, and if you need to use them then you should reconsider using this container type. Furthermore, the `deque` class does not have methods to pre-allocate memory, so, potentially, when you add an item to this container, it could cause a memory allocation.

Associative containers

With a C-like `array` or a `vector`, each item is associated with its numeric index. Earlier this was exploited in one of the examples in the section on `vector` in which the index provided the decile of the distribution and, conveniently, the distribution was split in a way that the ten deciles of data are numbered.

An associative container allows you to provide indexes that are not numeric; these are the keys, and you can associate values with them. As you insert key-value pairs into the container, they will be ordered so that the container can subsequently efficiently access the value by its key. Typically, this order should not matter to you since you will not use the container to access items sequentially, and instead you will access values by their keys. A typical implementation will use a binary tree or a hash table, which means that it is a quick operation to find an item according to its key.

For ordered containers, such as map, there will be comparisons carried out between the key and the existing keys in the container using < (the less predicate). The default predicate means that the keys are compared, and if this is, say, a smart pointer, then it will be the smart pointer objects that will be compared and used for the ordering, not the object that they wrap. In this case, you will want to write your own predicate to perform the appropriate comparison and pass it as a template parameter.

This means it is typically expensive to insert or erase items, and the key is treated as immutable, so you cannot alter it for an item. For all associative containers, there are no remove methods, but there are erase methods. However, for those containers that keep items sorted, erasing an item could affect performance.

There are several types of associative containers, and the main difference is how they handle duplicate keys and the level of ordering that occurs. The map class has key-value pairs sorted by unique keys, so duplicate keys are not allowed. If you want to allow duplicate keys, then you can use the multimap class. The set class is essentially a map where the key is the same as the value, which, again, does not allow duplicates. The multiset class does allow duplicates.

It may seem odd to have an associative class where the key is the same as the value, but the reason for including the class in this section is because, like the map class, the set class has a similar interface to find a value. Also similar to the map class, the set class is fast at finding an item.

Maps and multimaps

A map container stores two different items, a key and a value, and it maintains the items in an sort order according to the key. A sorted map means that it is quick to locate an item. The class has the same interface as other containers to add items: you can put them into the container via the constructor, or you can use member methods insert and emplace. You also have access to items via iterators. Of course, an iterator gives access to a single value, so with a map this will be to a pair object that has both the key and the value:

```
map<string, int> people;
people.emplace("Washington", 1789);
people.emplace("Adams", 1797);
people.emplace("Jefferson", 1801);
people.emplace("Madison", 1809);
people.emplace("Monroe", 1817);

auto it = people.begin();
pair<string, int> first_item = *it;
cout << first_item.first << " " << first_item.second << endl;
```

The calls to `emplace` puts items into the `map` where the key is a `string` (the name of a president) and the value is an `int` (the year the president started their term of office). The code then obtains an iterator to the first item in the container, and the item is accessed by dereferencing the iterator to give a `pair` object. Since the items are stored in the `map` in a sorted order, the first item will be set to `"Adams"`. You can also insert items as `pair` objects, either as objects or through iterators to `pair` objects in another container using the `insert` method.

Most of the `emplace` and `insert` methods will return a `pair` object of the following form, where the `iterator` type is relevant to the `map`:

```
pair<iterator, bool>
```

You use this object to test for two things. First, the `bool` indicates if the insertion was successful (it will fail if an item with the same key is already in the container). Secondly, the `iterator` part of the `pair` either indicates the position of the new item or it indicates the position of the existing item that will not be replaced (and will cause the insertion to fail).

The *failure* depends on *equivalence* rather than *equality*. If there is an item with a key that is equivalent to the item you are trying to insert, then the insertion will fail. The definition of equivalence depends on the comparator predicate being used with the `map` object. So, if the `map` uses a predicate `comp`, then equivalence between the two items, `a` and `b`, is determined by testing `!comp(a,b) && !comp(b,a)`. This is not the same as testing for `(a==b)`.

Assuming the previous `map` object, you can do this:

```
auto result = people.emplace("Adams", 1825);
if (!result.second)
    cout << (*result.first).first << " already in map" << endl;
```

The second item in the `result` variable is tested to see if the insertion was successful, and if not, then the first item is an iterator to a `pair<string,int>`, which is the existing item, and the code dereferences the iterator to get the `pair` object and then prints out the first item, which is the key (in this case, the name of the person).

If you know where in the `map` the item should go, then you can call `emplace_hint`:

```
auto result = people.emplace("Monroe", 1817);
people.emplace_hint(result.first, "Polk", 1845);
```

Here we know that `Polk` comes after `Monroe` so we can pass the iterator to `Monroe` as the hint. The class gives access to items via iterators, so you can use ranged `for` (which is based on iterator access):

```
for (pair<string, int> p : people)
{
    cout << p.first << " " << p.second << endl;
}
```

In addition, there is access to individual items using the `at` method and the `[]` operator. In both cases the class will search for an item with the provided key and if the item is found, a reference to the item's value is returned. The `at` method and the `[]` operator behave differently in a situation where there is no item with the specified key. If the key does not exist, the `at` method will throw an exception; if the `[]` operator cannot find the specified key, it will create a new item using the key and calling the default constructor of the value type. The `[]` operator will return a reference to the value if the key exists, so you can write code like this:

```
people["Adams"] = 1825;
people["Jackson"] = 1829;
```

The second line behaves as you expect: there will be no item with a key of `Jackson`, so the `map` will create an item with that key, initialize it by calling the default constructor of the value type (`int`, so the value is initialized to zero), and then it returns a reference to this value, which is assigned a value of `1829`. The first line, however, will look up `Adams`, see that there is an item, and return a reference to its value, which is then assigned a value of `1825`. There is no indication that the value of an item has been changed as opposed to a new item being inserted. You may want this behavior in some circumstances, but it is not the intention in this code, where, clearly, an associative container that allows duplicate keys (such as `multimap`) is needed. Furthermore, in both of these cases, there is a search for the key, a reference is returned, and then an assignment is performed. Be aware that, although it is valid to insert items this way, it is more efficient to emplace a new key-value pair in the container because you do not have this extra assignment.

Once you have filled the `map` you can search for a value using the following:

- The `at` method, which is passed a key and returns a reference to the value for that key
- The `[]` operator, which when passed a key returns a reference to the value for that key

- The `find` function, which will use the predicate specified in the template (unlike the global `find` function, mentioned later) and it will give you an iterator to the entire item as a `pair` object
- The `begin` method will give you an iterator to the first item and the `end` method will give you an iterator *after* the last item
- The `lower_bound` method returns an iterator to the item that has a key *equal to or greater* than the key that you pass as a parameter
- The `upper_bound` method returns an iterator of the first item in the map that has a key *greater* than the key provided
- The `equal_range` method returns both the lower and upper bounds values in a `pair` object

Sets and multisets

Sets behave as if they are maps, but the key is the same as the value; for example, the following:

```
set<string> people{
    "Washington","Adams",  "Jefferson","Madison","Monroe",
    "Adams",  "Van Buren","Harrison","Tyler","Polk"};
for (string s : people) cout << s << endl;
```

This will print out *nine* people in alphabetical order because there are two items called `Adams`, and the `set` class will reject duplicates. As the items are inserted into the set it will be ordered, and in this case the order is determined by the lexicon ordering of comparing two `string` objects. If you want to allow duplicates, so that ten people will be placed in the container, then you should use `multiset` instead.

As with a `map`, you cannot change the key of an item in the container because the key is used to determine the ordering. For a `set`, the key is the same as the value, so this means that you cannot change the item at all. If the intention is to perform lookups, then it may be better to use a sorted `vector` instead. A `set` will have more memory allocation overhead than a `vector`. Potentially, a lookup on a `set` container will be quicker than on a `vector` container if the search is sequential, but if you use a call to `binary_search` (explained in the *Sorting items* section, later) it could be faster than the associative container.

The interface to the `set` class is a restricted version of the `map` class, so you can `insert` and `emplace` items in the container, assign it to values in another container, and you have iterator access (`begin` and `end` methods).

Since there is no distinct key, it means that the `find` method looks for a value, not a key (and similarly with the bounds methods; for example, `equal_range`). There is no `at` method, nor an `[]` operator.

Unordered containers

The `map` and `set` classes allow you to find objects quickly, and this is facilitated by these classes holding the items in a sorted order. If you iterate through the items (from `begin` to `end`), then you will get those items in the sorted order. If you want a selection of objects within a range of the key values, you can make calls to the `lower_bound` and `upper_bound` methods, to get iterators to the appropriate ranges of keys. This are two important features of these associative containers: lookup and sorting. In some cases the actual order of the values is not important, and the behavior you want is efficient lookup. In this case, you can use the `unordered_` versions of the `map` and `set` classes. Since the order is unimportant, these are implemented using a hash table.

Special purpose containers

The containers described so far are flexible and can be used for all kinds of purposes. The Standard Library provides classes that have specific purposes, but, because they are implemented by wrapping other classes, they are called **container adapters**. For example, a `deque` object can be used as a **first-in first-out** (**FIFO**) queue, by pushing objects to the back of the `deque` (with `push_back`) and then accessing objects from the front of the queue using the `front` method (and removing them with `pop_front`). The Standard Library implements a container adapter called `queue` that has this FIFO behavior, and it is based on the `deque` class.

```cpp
queue<int> primes;
primes.push(1);
primes.push(2);
primes.push(3);
primes.push(5);
primes.push(7);
primes.push(11);
while (primes.size() > 0)
{
    cout << primes.front() << ",";
    primes.pop();
}
cout << endl; // prints 1,2,3,5,7,11
```

You `push` items into the queue and remove them with `pop`, and the next item is accessed using the `front` method. The Standard Library containers that can be wrapped by this adapter must implement the `push_back`, `pop_front`, and `front` methods. That is, items are put into the container at one end and accessed (and removed) from the other end.

A **last-in first-out** (**LIFO**) container will put in items and access (and remove) items from the same end. Again, a `deque` object can be used to implement this behavior by pushing items using `push_back`, accessing the items using `front`, and removing them with the `pop_back` method. The Standard Library provides an adapter class called `stack` to provide this behavior. This has a method called `push` to push items into the container, a method called `pop` to remove items, but, oddly, you access the next item using the `top` method, even though it is implemented using the `back` method of the wrapped container.

The adapter class `priority_queue`, in spite of the name, is used like the `stack` container; that is, items are accessed using the `top` method. The container ensures that when an item is pushed in, the top of the queue will always be the item with the highest priority. A predicate (the default is <) is used to order the items in the queue. For example, we could have an aggregate type that has the name of a task and the priority in which you must complete the task compared to other tasks:

```
struct task
{
    string name;
    int priority;
    task(const string& n, int p) : name(n), priority(p) {}
    bool operator <(const task& rhs) const {
        return this->priority < rhs.priority;
    }
};
```

The aggregate type is straightforward; it has two data members that are initialized by the constructor. So that tasks can be ordered, we need to be able to compare two task objects. One option (given earlier) is to define a separate predicate class. In this example, we use the default predicate, which the documentation says will be `less<task>`, and this compares items based on the < operator. So that we can use the default predicate, we define the < operator for the `task` class. Now we can add tasks to a `priority_queue` container:

```
priority_queue<task> to_do;
to_do.push(task("tidy desk", 1));
to_do.push(task("check in code", 10));
to_do.push(task("write spec", 8));
to_do.push(task("strategy meeting", 8));

while (to_do.size() > 0)
```

```
    {
        cout << to_do.top().name << " " << to_do.top().priority << endl;
        to_do.pop();
    }
```

The result of this code is:

```
check in code 10
write spec 8
strategy meeting 8
tidy desk 1
```

The queue has ordered the tasks according to the `priority` data item, and the combination of `top` and `pop` method calls reads the items in priority order and removes them from the queue. Items with the same priority are placed in the queue in the order in which they were pushed in.

Using iterators

So far, in this chapter we have indicated that containers give access to items through iterators. The implication is that iterators are simply pointers, and this is deliberate because iterators behave *like* pointers. However, they are usually objects of iterator classes (see the `<iterator>` header). All iterators have the following behaviors:

Operator	Behaviors
*	Gives access to the element at the current position
++	Moves forward to the next element (usually you will use the prefix operator)(this is only if the iterator allows forward movement)
--	Moves backward to the previous element (usually you will use the prefix operator)(this is only if the iterator allows backward movement)
== and !=	Compares if two iterators are in the same position
=	Assigns an iterator

Unlike a C++ pointer, which assumes that data is contiguous in memory, iterators can be used for more complex data structures, such as linked lists, where the items may not be contiguous. The operators ++ and -- work as expected, regardless of the underlying storage mechanism.

The `<iterator>` header declares the `next` global function that will increment an iterator and the `advance` function that will change an iterator by a specified number of positions (forward or backward depending on whether the parameter is negative and the direction allowed by the iterator). There is also a `prev` function to decrement an iterator by one or more positions. The `distance` function can be used to determine how many items are between two iterators.

All containers have a `begin` method, which returns the iterator for the first item, and an `end` method, which returns an iterator *after* the last item. This means that you can iterate through all items in the container by calling `begin` and then incrementing the iterator until it has the value returned from `end`. The `*` operator on an iterator gives access to the element in the container, and if the iterator is read-write (as it will be if returned from the begin method) it means the item can be changed. Containers also have the `cbegin` and `cend` methods that will return a constant iterator that gives just read-only access to elements:

```
vector<int> primes { 1,2,3,5,7,11,13 };
const auto it = primes.begin(); // const has no effect
*it = 42;
auto cit = primes.cbegin();
*cit = 1;                       // will not compile
```

Here `const` has no effect because the variable is `auto` and the type is deduced from the item used to initialize the variable. The `cbegin` method is defined to return a `const` iterator, so you cannot alter the item it refers to.

The `begin` and `cbegin` methods return **forward iterators** so that the `++` operator moves the iterator forward. Containers may also support **reverse iterators**, where `rbegin` is the last item in the container (that is, the item *before* the position returned by `end`) and `rend` is the position *before* the first item. (There are also `crbegin` and `crend`, which return `const` iterators.) It is important to realize that the `++` operator for a reverse iterator moves *backwards*, as in the following example:

```
vector<int> primes { 1,2,3,5,7,11,13 };
auto it = primes.rbegin();
while (it != primes.rend())
{
    cout << *it++ << " ";
}
cout << endl; // prints 13,11,7,5,4,3,2,1
```

The `++` operator increments the iterator according to the type of the iterator that it is applied to. It is important to note that the `!=` operator is used here to determine if the looping should end because the `!=` operator will be defined on all iterators.

The iterator type here is ignored by using the `auto` keyword. In fact, all containers will have `typedef` for all the iterator types they use, so in the previous case we can use the following:

```
vector<int> primes { 1,2,3,5,7,11,13 };
vector<int>::iterator it = primes.begin();
```

Containers that allow forward iteration will have a `typedef` for `iterator` and `const_iterator`, and containers that allow reverse iteration will have a `typedef` for `reverse_iterator` and `const_reverse_iterator`. To be complete, containers will also have `typedef` for `pointer` and `const_pointer` for the methods that return pointers to the elements, and `reference` and `const_reference` for methods that return references to elements. These type definitions enable you to write generic code where you do not know the types in a container, but the code will still be able to declare variables of the right type.

Although they look like they are pointers, iterators are often implemented by classes. These types may only allow iteration in one direction: a forward iterator will only have the ++ operator, a reverse iterator will have the – operator, or the type may allow iteration in both directions (bidirectional iterators) and so they implement both the ++ and –– operators. For example, the iterators on the `list`, `set`, `multiset`, `map`, and `multimap` classes are bidirectional. The `vector`, `deque`, `array`, and `string` class have iterators that allow random access, so these iterator types have the same behavior as bidirectional iterators, but also have pointers like arithmetic, so they can be changed by more than one item position at a time.

Input and output iterators

As the name suggests, an input iterator will only move forward and will have read access, and an output iterator will only move forward but will have write access. These iterators do not have random access and they do not allow backward movement. For example, an output stream may be used with an output iterator: you assign the dereferenced iterator with a data item in order to write that data item to the stream. Similarly, an input stream could have an input iterator and you dereference the iterator to get access to the next item in the stream. This behavior means that for an output iterator the only valid use of the dereference operator (*) is on the left-hand side of an assignment. It makes no sense to check the value of an iterator with !=, and you cannot check if assigning a value through the output iterator is successful.

For example, the `transform` function takes three iterators and a function. The first two iterators are input iterators and indicate a range of items to be transformed by the function. The result will be put in a range of items (the same size as the range of the input iterator), the first of which is indicated by the third iterator, which is an output iterator. One way to do this is as follows:

```
vector<int> data { 1,2,3,4,5 };
vector<int> results;
results.resize(data.size());
transform(
    data.begin(), data.end(),
    results.begin(),
    [](int x){ return x*x; } );
```

Here the `begin` and `end` methods return iterators on the `data` container that are safe to be used as input iterators. The `begin` method on the `results` container can only be used as an output iterator as long as the container has enough allocated items, and this is the case in this code because they have been allocated with `resize`. The function will then transform each input item by passing it to the lambda function given in the last parameter (which simply returns the square of the value). It is important to reassess what is happening here; the third parameter of the `transform` function is an output iterator, which means that you should expect the function to write values through this iterator.

This code works, but it requires the extra step to allocate the space, and you have the extra allocations of default objects in the container just so that you can overwrite them. It is also important to mention that the output iterator does not have to be to another container. It can be to the same container as long as it refers to a range that can be written to:

```
vector<int> vec{ 1,2,3,4,5 };
vec.resize(vec.size() * 2);
transform(vec.begin(), vec.begin() + 5,
    vec.begin() + 5, [](int i) { return i*i; });
```

The `vec` container is resized so that there is space for the results. The range of values to transform are from the beginning item to the fifth item (`vec.begin() + 5` is the next item), and the place to write the transformed value is the sixth to tenth items. If you print out the vector you will get {1,2,3,4,5,1,4,9,16,25}.

Another type of output iterator is the inserter. The `back_inserter` is used on containers with `push_back`, and `front_inserter` is used on containers with `push_front`. As the name suggests, an inserter calls the `insert` method on the container. For example, you can use a `back_inserter` like this:

```
vector<int> data { 1,2,3,4,5 };
vector<int> results;
transform(
    data.begin(), data.end(),
    back_inserter(results),
    [](int x){ return x*x; } ); // 1,4,9,16,25
```

The results of the transformation are inserted into the `results` container with the temporary object created from the `back_inserter` class. Using a `back_inserter` object ensures that when the `transform` function writes through the iterator the item is *inserted* into the wrapped container using `push_back`. Note that the results container should be different to the source container.

If you want the values in reverse order, then if the container supports `push_front` (for example, `deque`), then you can use a `front_inserter`. The `vector` class does not have a `push_front` method, but it does have reverse iterators, so you can use them instead:

```
vector<int> data { 1,2,3,4,5 };
vector<int> results;
transform(
    data.rbegin(), data.rend(),
    back_inserter(results),
    [](int x){ return x*x; } ); // 25,16,9,4,1
```

All you need to do to reverse the order of the results is to change `begin` to `rbegin` and `end` to `rend`.

Stream iterators

These are adapter classes in `<iterators>` that can be used to read items from an input stream or write items to an output stream. For example, so far, we have used iterators via ranged `for` loops to print out the contents of a container:

```
vector<int> data { 1,2,3,4,5 };
for (int i : data) cout << i << " ";
cout << endl;
```

Instead, you can create an output stream iterator based on `cout`, so that the `int` values will be written to the `cout` stream through this iterator using the stream operator `<<`. To print out a container of `int` values, you simply copy the container to the output iterator:

```
vector<int> data { 1,2,3,4,5 };
ostream_iterator<int> my_out(cout, " ");
copy(data.cbegin(), data.cend(), my_out);
cout << endl;
```

The first parameter of the `ostream_iterator` class is the output stream it will adapt, and the optional second parameter is a delimiter string used between each item. The `copy` function (in `<algorithm>`) will copy the items in the range indicated by the input iterators, passed as the first two parameters, to the output iterator, passed as the last parameter.

Similarly, there is an `istream_iterator` class that will wrap an input stream object and provide an input iterator. This class will use the stream `>>` operator to extract objects of the specified type, which can be read through the stream iterator. However, reading data from a stream is more complicated than writing to one, since there must be detection of when there is no more data in the input stream for the iterator to read (an end of file situation).

The `istream_iterator` class has two constructors. One constructor has a single parameter that is the input stream to read, and the other constructor, the default constructor, has no parameters and is used to create an **end of stream iterator**. The end of stream iterator is used to indicate that there is no more data in the stream:

```
vector<int> data;
copy(
    istream_iterator<int>(cin), istream_iterator<int>(),
    back_inserter(data));

ostream_iterator<int> my_out(cout, " ");
copy(data.cbegin(), data.cend(), my_out);
cout << endl;
```

The first call to `copy` provides two input iterators, as the first parameters, and an output iterator. The function copies data from the first iterator to the output iterator in the last parameter. Since the last parameter is created from `back_inserter`, this means that the items are inserted into the `vector` object. The input iterators are based on an input stream (`cin`) and thus the `copy` function will read `int` values from the console (each one separated by white space) until no more are available (for example, if you press *CTRL + Z* to end the stream or you type a non-numeric item).

Since you can initialize a container with a range of values given by iterators, you can use `istream_iterator` as constructor parameters:

```
vector<int> data {
    istream_iterator<int>(cin), istream_iterator<int>() };
```

Here the constructor is called using the initializer list syntax; if you use parentheses, the compiler will interpret this as the declaration of a function!

As noted earlier, the `istream_iterator` will use the stream's >> operator to read objects of the specified type from the stream and this operator uses whitespace to delimit the items (and hence it just ignores all whitespace). If you read in a container of `string` objects, then each word you type on the console will be an item in the container. A `string` is a container of characters, and it can be also initialized using iterators, so you could try to input data into a `string` from the console using an `istream_iterator`:

```
string data {
    istream_iterator<char>(cin), istream_iterator<char>() };
```

In this case the stream is `cin`, but it could easily be an `ifstream` object to a file. The problem is that the `cin` object will strip out the white space, so the `string` object will contain everything that you type except for white space, so there will be no spaces and no newlines.

This problem is caused by the `istream_iterator` using the stream's >> operator, and can only be avoided by using another class, `istreambuf_iterator`:

```
string data {
    istreambuf_iterator<char>(cin), istreambuf_iterator<char>() };
```

This class reads each character from the stream and copies each one into the container without the processing of >>.

Using iterators with the C Standard Library

The C Standard Library will often require pointers to data. For example, when a C function requires a string, it will need a `const char*` pointer to the character array containing the string. The C++ Standard Library has been designed to allow you to use its classes with the C Standard Library; indeed, the C Standard Library is part of the C++ Standard Library. In the case of `string` objects, the solution is simple: when you need a `const char*` pointer, you simply call the `c_str` method on a `string` object.

The containers that store data in contiguous memory (`array`, `string`, or `data`) have a method called `data` that gives access to the container's data as a C array. Further, these containers have `[]` operator access to their data, so you can also treat the address of the first item as being `&container[0]` (where `container` is the container object), just as you do with C arrays. However, if the container is empty, this address will be invalid, so before using it you should call the `empty` method. The number of items in these containers is returned from the `size` method, so for any C function that takes a pointer to the start of a C array and its size, you can call it with `&container[0]` and the value from the `size` method.

You may be tempted to get the beginning of the container that has contiguous memory by calling its `begin` function, but this will return an iterator (usually an object). So, to get a C pointer to the first item, you should call `&*begin`; that is, dereference the iterator returned from the `begin` function to get the first item and then use the address operator to get its address. To be frank, `&container[0]` is simpler and more readable.

If the container does not store its data in contiguous memory (for example, `deque` and `list`), then you can obtain a C pointer by simply copying the data into a temporary vector.

```
list<int> data;
// do some calculations and fill the list
vector<int> temp(data.begin(), data.end());
size_t size = temp.size(); // can pass size to a C function
int *p = &temp[0];         // can pass p to a C function
```

In this case, we have chosen to use a `list` and the routine will manipulate the `data` object. Later in the routine, these values will be passed to a C function so the `list` is used to initialize a `vector` object, and these values are obtained from the `vector`.

Algorithms

The Standard Library has an extensive collection of generic functions in the `<algorithm>` header file. By generic we mean that they access data via iterators without knowing what the iterators refer to and so it means that you can write generic code to work for any appropriate container. However, if you know the container type and that container has a member method to perform the same action, you should use the member.

Iteration of items

Many of the routines in `<algorithm>` will take ranges and iterate over those ranges performing some action. As the name suggests, the `fill` function will fill a container with a value. The function takes two iterators to specify the range and a value that will be placed into each position of the container:

```
vector<int> vec;
vec.resize(5);
fill(vec.begin(), vec.end(), 42);
```

Since the `fill` function will be called for a range, it means that you have to pass iterators to a container that already has values, and this is the reason why this code calls the `resize` method. This code will put the value of `42` into each of the items of the container, so when it has completed the `vector` contains `{42,42,42,42,42}`. There is another version of this function called `fill_n` that specifies the range by a single iterator to the start of the range and a count of the items in the range.

The `generate` function is similar, but, rather than a single value, it has a function, which can be a function, a function object, or a lambda expression. The function is called to provide each item in the container, so it has no parameters and returns an object of the type accessed by the iterator:

```
vector<int> vec(5);
generate(vec.begin(), vec.end(),
    [] () {static int i; return ++i; });
```

Again, you have to make sure that the `generate` function is passed a range that already exists, and this code does this by passing the initial size as a constructor parameter. In this example, the lambda expression has a `static` variable, which is incremented with each call, so this means that after the `generate` function has completed the `vector` contains `{1,2,3,4,5}`. There is another version of this function called `generate_n` that specifies the range by a single iterator to the start of the range and a count of the items in the range.

The `for_each` function will iterate over a range provided by two iterators and, for each item in the range, call a specified function. This function must have a single parameter that is the same type as the items in the container:

```
vector<int> vec { 1,4,9,16,25 };
for_each(vec.begin(), vec.end(),
    [] (int i) { cout << i << " "; });
cout << endl;
```

The `for_each` function iterates over all the items specified by the iterators (in this case the entire range), dereferences the iterator, and passes the item to the function, The effect of this code is to print the contents of the container. The function can take the item by value (as in this case) or by reference. If you pass the item by reference, then the function can change the item:

```
vector<int> vec { 1,2,3,4,5 };
for_each(vec.begin(), vec.end(),
    [](int& i) { i *= i; });
```

After calling this code, the items in the `vector` will be replaced with the squares of those items. If you use a functor or a lambda expression, you can pass a container to capture the result of the function; for example:

```
vector<int> vec { 1,2,3,4,5 };
vector<int> results;
for_each(vec.begin(), vec.end(),
    [&results](int i) { results.push_back(i*i); });
```

Here, a container is declared to accept the results of each call to the lambda expression, and the variable is passed by reference to the expression by capturing it.

 Recall from `Chapter 5`, *Using Functions*, that the square brackets contain the names of the captured variables declared outside the expression. Once captured, it means that the expression is able to access the object.

In this example the result of each iteration (`i*i`) is pushed into the captured collection so that the results are stored for later.

The `transform` function has two forms; they both provide a function (a pointer, functor, or a lambda expression) and they both have an input range of items in a container passed via iterators. In this respect, they are similar to `for_each`. The `transform` function also allows you to pass an iterator to a container that is used to store the results of the function. The function must have a single parameter that is the same type as the type (or a reference) of the type referred to the input iterators and it must return the type accessed by the output iterator.

The other version of `transform` uses a function to combine the values in two ranges, so this means that the function must have two parameters (which will be the corresponding items in the two iterators) and return the type of the output iterator. You only need to give the full range of items in one of the input ranges because it is assumed that the other range is at least as large, and hence you only have to provide the beginning iterator of the second range:

```
vector<int> vec1 { 1,2,3,4,5 };
vector<int> vec2 { 5,4,3,2,1 };
vector<int> results;
transform(vec1.begin(), vec1.end(), vec2.begin(),
    back_inserter(results), [](int i, int j) { return i*j; });
```

Getting information

Once you have values in a container, you can call functions to get information about those items. The `count` function is used to count the number items with a specified value in a range:

```
vector<int> planck{ 6,6,2,6,0,7,0,0,4,0 };
auto number = count(planck.begin(), planck.end(), 6);
```

This code will return a value of 3 because there are three copies of 6 in the container. The return type of the function is the type specified in the `difference_type` typedef of the container, and in this case it will be `int`. The `count_if` function works in a similar way, but you pass a predicate that takes a single parameter (the current item in the container) and returns a `bool` specifying if this is the value that is being counted.

The `count` functions count the number of occurrences of a specific value. If you want to aggregate all the values, then you can use the `accumulate` function in `<numeric>`. This will iterate over the range, access each item and keep a running sum of all the items. The sum will be carried out using the + operator of the type, but there is also a version that takes a binary function (two parameters of the container type and returns the same type) that specifies what happens when you add two such types together.

The `all_of`, `any_of`, and `none_of` functions are passed a predicate with a single argument of the same type of the container; there are also given iterators indicating a range over which they iterate, testing each item with the predicate. The `all_of` function will return `true` only if the predicate is `true` for all items, the `any_of` function returns `true` if predicate is `true` for at least one of the items, and the `none_of` function will return `true` only if the predicate is `false` for all items.

Comparing containers

If you have two containers of data, there are various ways that you can compare them. For every container type, there are <, <=, ==, !=, >, and >= operators defined. The == and != operators compare the containers, both in terms of how many items they have and the values of those items. So, if the items have different numbers of items, different values, or both, then they are not equal. The other comparisons prefer values over the number of items:

```
vector<int> v1 { 1,2,3,4 };
vector<int> v2 { 1,2 };
vector<int> v3 { 5,6,7 };
cout << boolalpha;
cout << (v1 > v2) << endl; // true
cout << (v1 > v3) << endl; // false
```

In the first comparison, the two vectors have similar items, but v2 has fewer, so v1 is "greater than" v2. In the second case, v3 has larger values than v1, but fewer of them, so v3 is *greater than* v1.

You can also compare ranges with the equal function. This is passed two ranges (which are assumed to be the same size, so only an iterator to the start of the second range is needed), and it compares corresponding items in both ranges using the == operator for the type accessed by the iterator, or a user supplied predicate. Only if all such comparisons are true will the function return true. Similarly, the mismatch function compares corresponding items in two ranges. However, this function returns a pair object with iterators in each of the two ranges for the first item that is not the same. You can also provide a comparison function. The is_permutation is similar in that it compares the values in two ranges, but it returns true if the two ranges have the same values but not necessarily in the same order.

Changing Items

The **reverse** function acts on a range in a container and reverses the order of the items; this means that the iterators must be writeable. The copy and copy_n functions copy every item from one range to another in a forward direction; for copy, the input range is given by two input iterators, and for copy_n, the range is an input iterator and a count of items. The copy_backward function will copy the items, starting at the end of the range, so that the output range will have the items in the same order as the original. This means that the output iterator will indicate the *end* of the range to copy to. You can also copy items only if they satisfy some condition specified by a predicate.

The `reverse_copy` function will create a copy in the reverse order to the input range; in effect, the function iterates backward through the original and copies items to the output range forward.

In spite of the name, the `move` and `move_backward` functions are semantically equivalent to the `copy` and `copy_backward` functions. Thus, in the following, the original container will have the same values after the operation:

```
vector<int> planck{ 6,6,2,6,0,7,0,0,4,0 };
vector<int> result(4);            // we want 4 items
auto it1 = planck.begin();        // get the first position
it1 += 2;                         // move forward 2 places
auto it2 = it1 + 4;               // move 4 items
move(it1, it2, result.begin());   // {2,6,0,7}
```

This code will copy four items from the first container to the second container, starting at the item in the third position.

The `remove_copy` and `remove_copy_if` functions iterate through the source range and copy items other than those with the specified value.

```
vector<int> planck{ 6,6,2,6,0,7,0,0,4,0 };
vector<int> result;
remove_copy(planck.begin(), planck.end(),
    back_inserter(result), 6);
```

Here, the `planck` object is left the same as before and the `result` object will contain {2,0,7,0,0,4,0}. The `remove_copy_if` function behaves similarly, but is given a predicate rather than an actual value.

The `remove` and `remove_if` functions don't quite do what their names suggest. These functions act on a single range and iterate looking for a specific value (`remove`), or pass each item to a predicate that will indicate if the item should be removed (`remove_if`). When an item is removed, the items later in the container are shifted forward, but the container remains the same size, which means that the items at the end remain as they were. The reason the `remove` functions behave like this is because they only know about reading and writing items through iterators (which is generic for all containers). To erase an item, the function will need to have access to the `erase` method of the container, and the `remove` functions only have access to iterators.

If you want to remove the items at the end, then you must resize the container accordingly. Typically, this means calling a suitable `erase` method on the container, and this is made possible because the `remove` method returns an iterator to the new end position:

```
vector<int> planck { 6,6,2,6,0,7,0,0,4,0 };
auto new_end = remove(planck.begin(), planck.end(), 6);
                                   // {2,0,7,0,0,4,0,0,4,0}
planck.erase(new_end, planck.end()); // {2,0,7,0,0,4,0}
```

The `replace` and `replace_if` functions iterate through a single range, and if the value is a specified value (`replace`) or returns `true` from a predicate (`replace_if`), then the item is replaced with a specified new value. There are also two functions, `replace_copy` and `replace_copy_if`, that leave the original alone and make the change to another range (similar to `remove_copy` and `remove_copy_if` functions).

The `rotate` functions treat the range as if the end is joined to the beginning, and so you can shift items forward so that when an item falls off the end it gets put in the first position. If you want to move every item forward four places, you can do this:

```
vector<int> planck{ 6,6,2,6,0,7,0,0,4,0 };
auto it = planck.begin();
it += 4;
rotate(planck.begin(), it, planck.end());
```

The result of this rotation is {0,7,0,0,4,0,6,6,2,6}. The `rotate_copy` function does the same thing, but, rather than affecting the original container, it copies the items into another container.

The `unique` function acts on a range and *removes* (in the manner explained previous) the items that are duplicates of adjacent items, and you can provide a predicate for the function to call to test if two items are the same. This function only checks adjacent items, so a duplicate later in the container will remain. If you want to remove all duplicates, then you should sort the container first, so that similar items are adjacent.

The `unique_copy` function will copy items from one range to another only if they are unique, so one way to remove duplicates is to use this function on a temporary container and then assign the original to the temporary:

```
vector<int> planck{ 6,6,2,6,0,7,0,0,4,0 };
vector<int> temp;
unique_copy(planck.begin(), planck.end(), back_inserter(temp));
planck.assign(temp.begin(), temp.end());
```

After this code, the `planck` container will have {6,2,6,0,7,0,4,0}.

Finally, the `iter_swap` will swap the items indicated by two iterators, and the `swap_ranges` function swaps the items in one range to the other range (the second range is indicated by one iterator and it is assumed to refer to a range of the same size as the first).

Finding Items

The Standard Library has a wide range of functions to search for items.

The `min_element` function will return an iterator to the smallest item in a range and the `max_element` function will return an iterator to the maximum item. These functions are passed iterators for the range of items to check and a predicator that returns a `bool` from the comparison of two items. If you don't provide a predicator, the < operator for the type will be used.

```
vector<int> planck{ 6,6,2,6,0,7,0,0,4,0 };
auto imin = min_element(planck.begin(), planck.end());
auto imax = max_element(planck.begin(), planck.end());
    cout << "values between " << *imin << " and "<< *imax << endl;
```

The `imin` and `imax` values are iterators, which is why they are dereferenced to get the value. If you want to get the minimum element and the maximum element in one go, you can call the `minmax_element`, which will return a `pair` object with iterators to these items. As the name suggests, the `adjacent_find` function will return the position of the first two items that have the same value (and you can provide a predicate to determine what *same value* means). This allows you to search for duplicates and get the position of those duplicates.

```
vector<int> vec{0,1,2,3,4,4,5,6,7,7,7,8,9};
vector<int>::iterator it = vec.begin();

do
{
    it = adjacent_find(it, vec.end());
    if (it != vec.end())
    {
        cout << "duplicate " << *it << endl;
        ++it;
    }
} while (it != vec.end());
```

This code has a sequence of numbers in which there are some numbers duplicated that are next to each other. In this case there are *three* adjacent duplicates: 4 followed by 4, and the sequence 7, 7, 7 is 7 followed by 7, and 7 followed by 7. The do loop calls adjacent_find repeatedly until it returns the end iterator, indicating that it has searched all items. When a duplicate pair is found, the code prints out the value and then increments the start position for the next search.

The find function searches a container for a single value, and returns an iterator to that item or the end iterator if the value cannot be found. The find_if function is passed a predicate and it returns an iterator to the first item it finds that satisfies the predicate; similarly, the find_if_not function finds the first item that does not satisfy the predicate.

There are several functions that are given two ranges, one is the range to search and the other has the values to look for. The different functions will either look for one of the items in the search criteria or it will look for all of them. These functions use the == operator for the type that the container holds or a predicate.

The find_first_of function returns the position of the first item that it finds in the search list. The search function looks for a specific sequence, and it returns the *first* position of the whole sequence, whereas the find_end function returns the *last* position of the entire search sequence. Finally, the search_n function looks for a sequence that is a value repeated a number of times (the value and the repeat are given) in a specified container's range.

Sorting items

The sequence containers can be sorted, and once you have done this you can use methods to search for items, to merge containers, or to get the difference between the containers. The sort function will order the items in a range according to the < operator or a predicate that you provide. If there are items that are equal in the range, then the order of these items after the sort is not guaranteed; if this order is important, you should call the stable_sort function instead. If you want to preserve the input range and copy the sorted items into another range, you use the confusingly named partial_sort_copy function. This is not a partial sort. This function is passed iterators to the input range and iterators for the output range, so you have to ensure that output range has a suitable capacity.

You can check if a range is sorted by calling the is_sorted function, and this will iterate through all items and return false if it finds an item that is not in sorted order, in which case you can locate the first item that is out of sort order by calling the is_sorted_until function.

As the name suggests, the `partial_sort` function does not place every item in its exact order relative to every other item. Instead, it will create two groups, or partitions, where the first partition will have the smallest items (not necessarily in any order) and the other partition will has the biggest items. You are guaranteed that the smallest items are in the first partition. To call this function you pass three iterators, two of which are the range to sort, and the third is a position somewhere between the other two that indicates the boundary before which are the smallest values.

```
vector<int> vec{45,23,67,6,29,44,90,3,64,18};
auto middle = vec.begin() + 5;
partial_sort(vec.begin(), middle, vec.end());
cout << "smallest items" << endl;
for_each(vec.begin(), middle, [](int i) {cout << i << " "; });
cout << endl; // 3 6 18 23 29
cout << "biggest items" << endl;
for_each(middle, vec.end(), [](int i) {cout << i << " "; });
cout << endl; // 67 90 45 64 44
```

In this example there is a vector of ten items, so we define the `middle` iterator as five items from the beginning (this is just a choice, it could be some other value depending on how many items you want to obtain). In this example you can see that the five smallest items have been sorted to the first half and the last half have the biggest items.

The oddly named `nth_element` function acts like `partial_sort`. You provide an iterator to the *nth* element and the function ensures that first *n* items in the range are the smallest. The `nth_element` function is faster than `partial_sort`, and, although you are guaranteed that the items before the *nth* element are less than or equal to the *nth* element, there are no other guarantees of the sort order within the partitions.

The `partial_sort` and `nth_element` functions are versions of partitioned sort functions. The `partition` function is a more generic version. You pass this function a range and a predicate that determines in which of the two partitions an item will be placed. The items that meet the predicate will be put in the first partition of the range, and the other items will be placed in the range following the first partition. The first item of the second partition is called the partition point and it is returned from the `partition` function, but you can calculate it later by passing iterators to the partitioned range and the predicate to the `partition_point` function. The `partition_copy` function will also partition values, but it will leave the original range untouched and put the values in a range that has been already allocated. These partition functions do not guarantee the order of equivalent items, and if this order is important then you should call the `stable_partitian` function. Finally, you can determine if a container is partitioned by calling the `is_partitioned` function.

The `shuffle` function will rearrange the items in a container into a random order. This function needs a uniform random number generator from the `<random>` library. For example, the following will fill a container with ten integers and then place them in a random order:

```
vector<int> vec;
for (int i = 0; i < 10; ++i) vec.push_back(i);
random_device rd;
shuffle(vec.begin(), vec.end(), rd);
```

A heap is a partially sorted sequence in which the first item is always the largest, and items are added and removed from the heap in logarithmic time. Heaps are based upon sequence containers and, oddly, rather than the Standard Library providing an adapter class, you have to use function calls on an existing container. To create a heap from an existing container, you pass the range iterators to the `make_heap` function, which will order the container as a heap. You can then add new items to the container using its `push_back` method, but each time you do this you have to call `push_heap` to re-order the heap. Similarly, to get an item from the heap you call the `front` method on the container and then remove the item by calling the `pop_heap` function, which ensures that the heap is kept ordered. You can test to see if a container is arranged as a heap by calling `is_heap`, and if the container is not entirely arranged as a heap you can get an iterator to the first item that does not satisfy the heap criteria by calling `is_heap_until`. Finally, you can sort a heap into a sorted sequence with `sort_heap`.

Once you have sorted a container, there are functions that you can call to get information about the sequence. The `lower_bound` and `upper_bound` methods have already been described for containers, and the functions behave in the same way: `lower_bound` returns the position of the first element that has a value greater than or equal to the value provided and `upper_bound` returns the position of the next item that that is greater than the value provided. The `includes` function tests to see if one sorted range contains the items in a second sorted range.

The functions beginning with `set_` will combine two sorted sequences into a third, container. The `set_difference` function will copy the items that are in the first sequence but not in the second sequence. This is not a symmetric action because it does not include the items that are in the second sequence but not in the first. If you want a symmetric difference, then you should call the `set_symmetric_difference` function. The `set_intersection` will copy the items that are in both sequences. The `set_union` function will combine the two sequences. There is another function that will combine two sequences, which is the `merge` function.

The difference between these two functions is that with the `set_union` function, if an item is in both of the sequences, there will only be one copy put in the results container, whereas with `merge` there will be two copies in the results container.

If a range is sorted, then you can call the `equal_range` function to obtain the range of elements that are equivalent to a value passed to the function or a predicate. This function returns a pair of iterators that represent the range of values in the container.

The final method that needs a sorted container is `binary_search`. This function is used to test if a value is in the container. The function is passed iterators indicating the range to test and a value, and it will return `true` if there is an item in the range equal to that value (you can provide a predicate to perform this equality test).

Using the numeric libraries

The Standard Library has several libraries of classes to perform numeric manipulations. In this section we will cover two: compile-time arithmetic, using `<ratio>`, and complex numbers, using `<complex>`.

Compile time arithmetic

Fractions are a problem because there are some for which there are not enough significant figures to accurately represent them, resulting in losing accuracy when you use them in further arithmetic. Furthermore, computers are binary and merely converting decimal fractional parts to binary will lose accuracy. The `<ratio>` library provides classes that allow you to represent fractional numbers as objects that are ratios of integers, and perform fraction calculations as ratios. Only once you have performed all the fractional arithmetic will you convert the number to decimal, and this means that the potential loss of accuracy is minimized. The calculations performed by the classes in the `<ratio>` library are carried out at *compile time* so the compiler will catch errors such as divide by zero and overflows.

Using the library is simple; you use the `ratio` class, and provide the numerator and denominator as template parameters. The numerator and denominator will be stored factorized, and you can access these values through the `num` and `den` members of the object:

```
ratio<15, 20> ratio;
cout << ratio.num << "/" << ratio.den << endl;
```

This will print out `3/4`.

Fractional arithmetic is carried out using templates (these are, in fact, specializations of the `ratio` template). At first sight it may appear a little odd, but you soon get used to it!

```
ratio_add<ratio<27, 11>, ratio<5, 17>> ratio;
cout << ratio.num << "/" << ratio.den << endl;
```

This will print out `514/187` (you may want to get some paper and do the fractional calculations to confirm this). The data members are actually `static` members, so it makes little sense to create variables. Furthermore, because arithmetic is carried out using *types* rather than *variables*, it is best to access the members through those types:

```
typedef ratio_add<ratio<27, 11>, ratio<5, 17>> sum;
cout << sum::num << "/" << sum::den << endl;
```

You can now use the sum type as a parameter to any of the other operations that you can perform. The four binary arithmetic operations are carried out with `ratio_add`, `ratio_subtract`, `ratio_multiply`, and `ratio_divide`. Comparisons are carried out through `ratio_equal`, `ratio_not_equal`, `ratio_greater`, `ratio_greater_equal`, `ratio_less`, and `ratio_less_equal`.

```
bool result = ratio_greater<sum, ratio<25, 19> >::value;
cout << boolalpha << result << endl;
```

This operation tests to see if the calculation performed before (`514/187`) is greater than the fraction `25/19` (it is). The compiler will pick up divide-by-zero errors and overflows, so the following will not compile:

```
typedef ratio<1, 0> invalid;
cout << invalid::num << "/" << invalid::den << endl;
```

However, it is important to point out that the compiler will issue the error on the second line, when the denominator is accessed. There are also typedefs of ratio for the SI prefixes. This means that you can perform your calculations in nanometers, and when you need to present the data in meters you can use the `nano` type to obtain the ratio:

```
double radius_nm = 10.0;
double volume_nm = pow(radius_nm, 3) * 3.1415 * 4.0 / 3.0;
cout << "for " << radius_nm << "nm "
    "the volume is " << volume_nm << "nm3" << endl;
double factor = ((double)nano::num / nano::den);
double vol_factor = pow(factor, 3);
cout << "for " << radius_nm * factor << "m "
    "the volume is " << volume_nm * vol_factor << "m3" << endl;
```

Here, we are doing calculations on a sphere in **nanometers** (**nm**). The sphere has a radius of 10 nm, so the first calculation gives the volume as 4188.67 nm3. The second calculation converts nanometers into meters; the factor is determined from the `nano` ratio (note that for volumes the factor is cubed). You could define a class to do such conversions:

```
template<typename units>
class dist_units
{
    double data;
public:
        dist_units(double d) : data(d) {}

    template <class other>
    dist_units(const dist_units<other>& len) : data(len.value() *
      ratio_divide<units, other>::type::den /
      ratio_divide<units, other>::type::num) {}

    double value() const { return data; }
};
```

The class is defined for a particular type of unit, which will be expressed through an instantiation of the `ratio` template. The class has a constructor to initialize it for values in those units and a constructor to convert from other units, and that simply divides the current units by the units of the other type. This class can be used like this:

```
dist_units<kilo> earth_diameter_km(12742);
cout << earth_diameter_km.value() << "km" << endl;
dist_units<ratio<1>> in_meters(earth_diameter_km);
cout << in_meters.value()<< "m" << endl;
dist_units<ratio<1609344, 1000>> in_miles(earth_diameter_km);
cout << in_miles.value()<< "miles" << endl;
```

The first variable is based on `kilo` and hence the units are kilometers. To convert this to meters, the second variable type is based on `ratio<1>`, which is the same as `ratio<1,1>`. The result is that the values in the `earth_diameter_km` are multiplied by 1000 when placed in `in_meters`. The conversion to miles is a bit more involved. There are 1609.344 m in a mile. The ratio used for the `in_miles` variable is 1609344/1000 or 1609.344. We are initializing the variable with the `earth_diameter_km`, so isn't that value too big by a factor of 1000? No, the reason is that the type of `earth_diameter_km` is `dist_units<kilo>`, so the conversion between km and miles will include that factor of 1000.

Complex numbers

Complex numbers are not just of mathematical interest, they are also vital in engineering and science, so a `complex` type is an important part of any type library. A complex number is made of two parts--the real and imaginary parts. As the name suggests, an imaginary number is not real, and cannot be treated as real.

In mathematics, complex numbers are usually represented as coordinates in two-dimensional space. If a real number can be thought of as being one of an infinite number of points on the x axis, an imaginary number can be thought of being one of an infinite number of points on the y axis. The only intersection between these two is the origin and since zero is zero, is nothing, it can be a zero real number or a zero imaginary number. A complex number has both real and imaginary parts, and hence this can be visualized as a Cartesian point. Indeed, another way of visualizing a complex number is as a polar number where the point is represented as a vector of a specified length at a specified angle to the position on the x axis (the positive real number axis).

The `complex` class is based on a floating point type, and there are specializations for `float`, `double`, and `long double`. The class is simple; it has a constructor with two parameters for the real and imaginary parts of the number, and it defines operators (member methods and global functions) for assignment, comparisons, +, -, /, and *, acting on the real and imaginary parts.

An operation like + is simple for a complex number: you just add the real parts together and the imaginary parts together, and these two sums are the real and imaginary parts of the result. However, multiplication and division are a bit more, umm, complex. In multiplication, you get a quadratic: the aggregation of the two real parts multiplied, the two imaginary parts multiplied, the two values of the real part of the first multiplied with the imaginary part of the second, and the imaginary part of the first multiplied with the real part of the second. The complication is that two imaginary numbers multiplied is equivalent to the multiplication of two equivalent real numbers multiplied by -1. Furthermore, multiplying a real and an imaginary number results in an imaginary number that is equivalent in size to the multiplication of two equivalent real numbers.

There are also functions to perform trigonometric operations on complex numbers: `sin`, `cos`, `tan`, `sinh`, `cosh`, and `tanh`; and basic math operations such as `log`, `exp`, `log10`, `pow`, and `sqrt`. You can also call functions to create complex numbers and get information about them. So, the `polar` function will take two floating-point numbers representing the polar coordinates of the length of the vector and the angle. If you have a `complex` number object you can get the polar coordinates by calling `abs` (to get the length) and `arg` (to get the angle).

```
complex<double> a(1.0, 1.0);
complex<double> b(-0.5, 0.5);
complex<double> c = a + b;
cout << a << " + " << b << " = " << c << endl;
complex<double> d = polar(1.41421, -3.14152 / 4);
cout << d << endl;
```

The first point to make is that there is an `ostream` insertion operator defined for `complex` numbers so you can insert them into the `cout` stream object. The output from this code is as follows:

```
(1,1) + (-0.5,0.5) = (0.5,1.5)
(1.00002,-0.999979)
```

The second line shows the limitations of using just five decimal places for the square root of 2 and -1/4 pi, this number is, in fact, the complex number `(1, -1)`.

Using the Standard Library

In this example, we will develop a simple parser for **Comma Separated Value** (**CSV**) files. The rules we will follow are as follows:

- Each record will occupy one line, and newline indicates a new record
- Fields in the record are separated by commas, unless they are within a quoted string
- Strings can be quoted using single (`'`) or double quotes (`"`), in which case they can contain commas as part of the string
- Quotes immediately repeated (`''` or `""`) is a literal, and a part of the string rather than a delimiter of a string
- If a string is quoted, then spaces outside of the string are ignored

This is a very basic implementation, and omits the usual requirement that quoted strings can contain newlines.

In this example, much of the manipulation will be using `string` objects as containers of individual characters.

Start by creating a folder for the chapter called `Chapter_08` in the folder for this book. In that folder, create a file called `csv_parser.cpp`. Since the application will use console output and file input, add the following lines at the top of the file:

```
#include <iostream>
#include <fstream>

using namespace std;
```

The application will also take a command line parameter that is the CSV file to parse, so add the following code at the bottom of the file:

```
void usage()
{
    cout << "usage: csv_parser file" << endl;
    cout << "where file is the path to a csv file" << endl;
}

int main(int argc, const char* argv[])
{
    if (argc <= 1)
    {
        usage();
        return 1;
    }
    return 0;
}
```

The application will read a file line by line into a `vector` of `string` objects, so add `<vector>` to the list of include files. To make the coding easier, define the following above the `usage` function:

```
using namespace std;
using vec_str = vector<string>;
```

The `main` function will read the file in line by line and the simplest way to do this is to use the `getline` function, so add the `<string>` header file to the include file list. Add the following lines to the end of the `main` function:

```
ifstream stm;
stm.open(argv[1], ios_base::in);
if (!stm.is_open())
{
    usage();
```

```
        cout << "cannot open " << argv[1] << endl;
        return 1;
    }

    vec_str lines;
    for (string line; getline(stm, line); )
    {
        if (line.empty()) continue;
        lines.push_back(move(line));
    }
    stm.close();
```

The first few lines open the file using an `ifstream` class. If the file cannot be found, then the operation to open the file fails and this is tested by calling `is_open`. Next a `vector` of `string` objects is declared and filled with lines read from the file. The `getline` function has two parameters: the first is the open file stream object and the second is a string to contain the character data. This function returns the stream object, which has a `bool` conversion operator, and hence the `for` statement will loop until this stream object indicates that it can read no more data. When the stream gets to the end of the file, an internal end-of-file flag is set and this causes the `bool` conversion operator to return a value of `false`.

If the `getline` function reads a blank line, then the `string` will not be able to be parsed, so there is a test for this, and such blank lines are not stored. Each legitimate line is pushed into the `vector`, but, since this `string` variable will not be used after this operation, we can use move semantics and so this is made explicit by calling the `move` function.

This code will now compile and run (although it will produce no output). You can use it on any CSV file that meets the criteria given previously, but as a test file we have used the following file:

```
George Washington,1789,1797
"John Adams, Federalist",1797,1801
"Thomas Jefferson, Democratic Republican",1801,1809
"James Madison, Democratic Republican",1809,1817
"James Monroe, Democratic Republican",1817,1825
"John Quincy Adams, Democratic Republican",1825,1829
"Andrew Jackson, Democratic",1829,1837
"Martin Van Buren, Democratic",1837,1841
"William Henry Harrison, Whig",1841,1841
"John Tyler, Whig",1841,1841
John Tyler,1841,1845
```

These are US presidents up to 1845; the first string is the name of the president and their affiliation, but when the president has no affiliation then it is missed out (Washington and Tyler). The names are then followed by the start and end years of their terms of office.

Next, we want to parse the data in the vector and split the items into individual fields according to the rules given previously (fields separated by commas, but quotation marks are respected). To do this, we will represent each line as a `list` of fields, with each field being a `string`. Add an include for `<list>` near the top of the file. At the top of the file, where the `using` declarations are made, add the following:

```
using namespace std;
using vec_str = vector<string>;
using list_str = list<string>;using vec_list = vector<list_str>;
```

Now, at the bottom of the `main` function, add:

```
vec_list parsed;
for (string& line : lines)
{
    parsed.push_back(parse_line(line));
}
```

The first line creates the `vector` of `list` objects, and the `for` loop iterates through each line calling a function called `parse_line` that parses a string and returns a `list` of `string` objects. The return value of the function will be a temporary object and hence an rvalue, so this means that the version of `push_back` with move semantics will be called.

Above the usage function, add the start of the `parse_line` function:

```
list_str parse_line(const string& line)
{
    list_str data;
    string::const_iterator it = line.begin();

    return data;
}
```

The function will treat the string as a container of characters and hence it will iterate through the line parameter with a `const_iterator`. The parsing will be carried out in a `do` loop, so add the following:

```
list_str data;
string::const_iterator it = line.begin();
string item;
bool bQuote = false;
bool bDQuote = false;
```

```
do{
    ++it;
} while (it != line.end());
data.push_back(move(item));
return data;
```

The Boolean variables will be explained in a moment. The do loop increments the iterator, and when it reaches the end value, the loop finishes. The item variable will hold the parsed data (at this point it is empty) and the last line will put the value into the list; this is so that any unsaved data is stored in the list before the function finishes. Since the item variable is about to be destroyed, the call to move ensures that its contents are moved into the list rather than copied. Without this call, the string copy constructor will be called when putting the item into the list.

Next you need to do the parsing of the data. To do this, add a switch to test for the three cases: a comma (to indicate the end of a field), and a quote or a double quote to indicate a quoted string. The idea is to read each field and build its value up character by character, using the item variable.

```
do
{
    switch (*it)   {
        case '\'':
            break;
        case '"':
            break;
        case ',':
            break;
        default:
            item.push_back(*it);
    };
    ++it;
} while (it != line.end());
```

The default action is simple: it copies the character into the temporary string. If the character is a single quote, we have two options. Either the quote is within a string that is double quoted, in which case we want the quote to be stored in item, or the quote is a delimiter, in which case we store whether it is the opening or closing quote by setting the bQuote value. For the case of a single quote, add the following:

```
case '\'':
    if (bDQuote) item.push_back(*it);
    else    {
```

```
        bQuote = !bQuote;
        if (bQuote) item.clear();
    }
    break;
```

This is simple enough. If this is in a double-quoted string (bDQuote is set), then we store the quote. If not, then we flip the bQuote bool so that if this is the first quote, we register that the string is quoted, otherwise we register that it is the end of a string. If we are at the start of a quoted string, we clear the item variable to ignore any spaces between the previous comma (if there is one) and the quote. However, this code does not take into account the use of two quote marks next to each other, which means that the quote is a literal and part of the string. Change the code to add a check for this situation:

```
if (bDQuote) item.push_back(*it);
else
{
    if ((it + 1) != line.end() && *(it + 1) == ''')    {
        item.push_back(*it);
        ++it;
    }
    else
    {
        bQuote = !bQuote;
        if (bQuote) item.clear();
    }
}
```

The if statement checks to make sure that if we increment the iterator, we are not at the end of the line (short circuiting will kick in here in this case and the rest of the expression will not be evaluated). We can test the next item, and we then peek at the next item to see if it is a single quote; if it is, then we add it to the item variable and increment the iterator so that both quotes are consumed in the loop.

The code for the double quote is similar, but switches over the Boolean variables and tests for double quotes:

```
case '"':
    if (bQuote) item.push_back(*it);
    else    {
        if ((it + 1) != line.end() && *(it + 1) == '"') {
            item.push_back(*it);
            ++it;
        }
        else {
```

```
                    bDQuote = !bDQuote;
                    if (bDQuote) item.clear();
            }
      }
      break;
```

Finally, we need code to test for a comma. Again, we have two situations: either this is a comma in a quoted string, in which case we need to store the character, or it's the end of a field, in which case we need to finish the parsing for this field. The code is quite simple:

```
case ',':
    if (bQuote || bDQuote)   item.push_back(*it);
    else                     data.push_back(move(item));
    break;
```

The `if` statement tests to see if we are in a quoted string (in which case either `bQuote` or `bDQuote` will be true), and if so, the character is stored. If this is the end of the field, we push the `string` into the `list`, but we use `move` so that the variable data is moved across and the `string` object left in an uninitialized state.

This code will compile and run. However, there is still no output, so before we redress that, review the code that you have written. At the end of the `main` function you will have a `vector` in which each item has a `list` object representing each row in the CSV file, and each item in the `list` is a field. You have now parsed the file and can use this data accordingly. So that you can see that the data has been parsed, add the following lines to the bottom of the `main` function:

```
int count = 0;
for (list_str row : parsed)
{
    cout << ++count << "> ";
    for (string field : row)
    {
        cout << field << " ";
    }
    cout << endl;
}
```

You can now compile the code (use the `/EHsc` switch) and run the application passing the name of a CSV file.

Summary

In this chapter, you have seen some of the main classes in the C++ Standard Library, and investigated in depth the container and iterator classes. One such container is the string class; this is such an important class that it will be covered in more depth in the next chapter.

9
Using Strings

At some point your application will need to communicate with people, and that means using text; such as outputting text, taking in data as text, and then converting that data to appropriate types. The C++ Standard Library has a rich collection of classes to manipulate strings, convert between strings and numbers, and to obtain string values localized for specified languages and cultures.

Using the string class as a container

C++ strings are based on the `basic_string` template class. This class is a container, so it uses iterator access and methods to obtain information, and has template parameters that contain information about the character type it holds. There are different `typedef` for specific character types:

```
typedef basic_string<char,
    char_traits<char>, allocator<char> > string;
typedef basic_string<wchar_t,
    char_traits<wchar_t>, allocator<wchar_t> > wstring;
typedef basic_string<char16_t,
    char_traits<char16_t>, allocator<char16_t> > u16string;
typedef basic_string<char32_t,
    char_traits<char32_t>, allocator<char32_t> > u32string;
```

The `string` class is based on `char`, `wstring` is based on `wchar_t` wide characters, and the `16string` and `u32string` classes are based upon 16-bit and 32-bit characters, respectively. For the rest of the chapter, we will concentrate on just the `string` class, but it equally applies to the other classes.

Comparing, copying, and accessing characters in a string will require a different code for the different-sized characters, while the traits template parameter provides the implementations. For `string`, this is the `char_traits` class. When this class, for example, copies characters, it will delegate this action to the `char_traits` class and its `copy` method. The traits classes are also used by stream classes, so they also define an end of file value that is appropriate to the file stream.

A string is essentially an array of zero or more characters that allocates memory when it is needed and deallocates it when a `string` object is destroyed. In some respects, it is very similar to a `vector<char>` object. As a container, the `string` class gives iterator access through the `begin` and `end` methods:

```
string s = "hellon";
copy(s.begin(), s.end(), ostream_iterator<char>(cout));
```

Here, the `begin` and `end` methods are called to get iterators from the items in the `string`, which are passed to the `copy` function from `<algorithm>` to copy each character to the console via the `ostream_iterator` temporary object. In this respect, the `string` object is similar to a `vector`, so we use the previously defined s object:

```
vector<char> v(s.begin(), s.end());
copy(v.begin(), v.end(), ostream_iterator<char>(cout));
```

This fills the `vector` object using the range of characters provided using the `begin` and `end` methods on the `string` object and then prints those characters to the console using the `copy` function in exactly the same way as we used previously.

Getting information about a string

The `max_size` method will give the maximum size of the string of the specified character type on your computer architecture and this can be surprisingly large. For example, on a 64-bit Windows computer with 2 GB of memory, `max_size` for a `string` object will return 4 billion characters, and for a `wstring` object the method will return 2 billion characters. This is clearly more than the memory in the machine! The other size methods return more meaningful values. The `length` method returns the same value as the `size` method, that is, how many items (characters) there are in the string. The `capacity` method indicates how much memory is already allocated for the string in terms of the number of characters.

You can compare a `string` with another by calling its `compare` method. This returns an `int` and not a `bool` (but note that an `int` can be converted silently to a `bool`), where a return value of 0 means that the two strings are the same. If they are not the same, this method returns a negative value if the parameter string is greater that the operand string, or a positive value if the parameter is less than the operand string. In this respect *greater* and *less than* will test the ordering of the strings alphabetically. In addition, there are global operators defined for <, <=, ==, >=, and > to compare string objects.

A `string` object can be used like a C string through the `c_str` method. The pointer returned is `const`; you should be aware that the pointer may be invalidated if the `string` object is changed, so you should not store this pointer. You should not use `&str[0]` to get a C string pointer for the C++ string `str` because the internal buffer used by the string classes is not guaranteed to be `NUL` terminated. The `c_str` method is provided to return a pointer that *can* be used as a C string, and hence `NUL` terminated.

If you want to copy data from the C++ string to a C buffer you can call the `copy` method. You pass the destination pointer and the number of characters to copy as parameters (and optionally an offset) and the method will attempt to copy, at most, the specified number of characters to the destination buffer: *but without a null termination character*. This method assumes that the destination buffer is big enough to hold the copied characters (and you should take steps to ensure this). If you want to pass the size of the buffer so that the method performs this check for you, call the `_Copy_s` method instead.

Altering strings

The string classes have standard container access methods, so you can access individual characters through a reference (read and write access) with the `at` method and `[]` operator. You can replace the entire string using the `assign` method, or swap the contents of two string objects with the `swap` method. Further, you can insert characters in specified places with the `insert` method, remove specified characters with the `erase` method, and remove all characters with the `clear` method. The class also allows you to push characters to the end of the string (and remove the last character) with the `push_back` and `pop_back` methods:

```
string str = "hello";
cout << str << "n"; // hello
str.push_back('!');
cout << str << "n"; // hello!
str.erase(0, 1);
cout << str << "n"; // ello!
```

You can add one or more characters to the end of a string using the `append` method or the `+=` operator:

```
string str = "hello";
cout << str << "n";   // hello
str.append(4, '!');
cout << str << "n";   // hello!!!!
str += " there";
cout << str << "n";   // hello!!!! there
```

The `<string>` library also defines a global + operator that will concatenate two strings in a third string.

If you want to change characters in a string you can access the character through an index with the `[]` operator, using the reference to overwrite the character. You can also use the `replace` method to replace one or more characters at a specified position with characters from a C string or from a C++ string, or some other container accessed through iterators:

```
string str = "hello";
cout << str << "n";       // hello
str.replace(1, 1, "a");
cout << str << "n";       // hallo
```

Finally, you can extract part of a string as a new string. The `substr` method takes an offset and an optional count. If the count of characters is omitted, then the substring will be from the specified position until the end of the string. This means that you can copy a left-hand part of a string by passing an offset of 0 and a count that is less than the size of the string, or you can copy a right-hand part of the string by passing just the index of the first character.

```
string str = "one two three";
string str1 = str.substr(0, 3);
cout << str1 << "n";          // one
string str2 = str.substr(8);
cout << str2 << "n";          // three
```

In this code, the first example copies the first three characters into a new string. In the second example, the copying starts at the eighth character and continues to the end.

Searching strings

The `find` method is passed using either a character, a C string, or a C++ string, and you can provide an initial search position to start the search. The `find` method returns the position (rather than an iterator) to where the search text was located, or a value of `npos` if the text cannot be found. The offset parameter, and a successful return value from the `find` method, enables you to parse a string repeatedly to find specific items. The `find` method searches for the specified text in the forward direction, and there is also an `rfind` method that performs the search in the reverse direction.

Note that `rfind` is not the complete opposite of the `find` method. The `find` method moves the search point forward in the string and at each point compares the search string with the characters from the search point forwards (so the first search text character, then the second, and so on). The `rfind` method moves the search point *backwards*, but the comparisons are still made *forwards*. So, assuming the `rfind` method is not given an offset, the first comparison will be made at an offset from the end of the string the size of the search text. Then, the comparison is made by comparing the first character in the search text with the character at the search point in the searched string, and if this succeeds, the second character in the search text is compared with the character after the search point. So, the comparisons are made in a direction opposite to the direction of the movement of the search point.

This becomes important because if you want to parse a string using the return value from the `find` method as an offset, after each search you should move the search offset *forwards*, and for `rfind` you should move it *backwards*.

For example, to search for all the positions of `the` in the following string, you can call:

```
string str = "012the678the234the890";
string::size_type pos = 0;
while(true)
{
    pos++;
    pos = str.find("the",pos);
    if (pos == string::npos) break;
    cout << pos << " " << str.substr(pos) << "n";
}
// 3 the678the234the890
// 9 the234the890
// 15 the890
```

This will find the search text at the character positions of 3, 9, and 15. To search the string backwards, you could call:

```
string str = "012the678the234the890";
string::size_type pos = string::npos;
while(true)
{
    pos--;
    pos = str.rfind("the",pos);
    if (pos == string::npos) break;
    cout << pos << " " << str.substr(pos) << "n";
}
// 15 the890
// 9 the234the890
// 3 the678the234the890
```

The highlighted code shows the changes that should be made, showing you that you need to search from the end and use the `rfind` method. When you have a successful result you need to decrement the position before the next search. Like the `find` method, the `rfind` method returns `npos` if it cannot find the search text.

There are four methods that allow you to search for one of several individual characters. For example:

```
string str = "012the678the234the890";
string::size_type pos = str.find_first_of("eh");
if (pos != string::npos)
{
    cout << "found " << str[pos] << " at position ";
    cout << pos << " " << str.substr(pos) << "n";
}
// found h at position 4 he678the234the890
```

The search string is `eh` and the `find_first_of` will return when it finds either the character `e` or `h` in the string. In this example, the character `h` is found first at position 4. You can provide an offset parameter to start the search, so you can use the return value from `find_first_of` to parse through a string. The `find_last_of` method is similar, but it searches the string in the reverse direction for one of the characters in the search text.

There are also two search methods that will look for a character *other than* the characters provided in the search text: `find_first_not_of` and `find_last_not_of`. For example:

```
string str = "012the678the234the890";
string::size_type pos = str.find_first_not_of("0123456789");
cout << "found " << str[pos] << " at position ";
cout << pos << " " << str.substr(pos) << "n";
// found t at position 3 the678the234the890
```

This code looks for a character other than a digit and so it finds the `t` at position 3 (the fourth character).

There is no library function to trim whitespace from a `string`, but you can trim spaces on the left and right of strings by using the find functions to find non-whitespace and then use this as an appropriate index for the `substr` method.

```
string str = "  hello  ";
cout << "|" << str << "|n";  // |  hello  |
string str1 = str.substr(str.find_first_not_of(" trn"));
cout << "|" << str1 << "|n"; // |hello  |
string str2 = str.substr(0, str.find_last_not_of(" trn") + 1);
cout << "|" << str2 << "|n"; // |  hello|
```

In the preceding code, two new strings are created: one left-trims spaces, and the other right-trims spaces. The first forward searches for the first character that is not whitespace and uses this as the start index of the substring (no count is provided because all of the remaining string is copied). In the second case the string is reverse searched for a character that is not whitespace, but the location returned will be the last character of `hello`; since we need the substring from the first character, we increment this index to get the count of characters to copy.

Internationalization

The `<locale>` header contains the classes for localizing how time, dates, and currency are formatted, and also to provide localized rules for string comparisons and ordering.

The C Runtime Library also has global functions to carry out localization. However, it is important in the following discussion that we distinguish between C functions and the C locale. The C locale is the default locale, including the rules for localization, used in C and C++ programs and it can be replaced with a locale for a country or culture. The C Runtime Library provides functions to change the locale, as does the C++ Standard Library.

Since the C++ Standard Library provides classes for localization, this means that you can create more than one object representing a locale. A locale object can be created in a function and can only be used there, or it can be applied globally to a thread and used only by code running on that thread. This is in contrast to the C localization functions, where changing the locale is global, so all code (and all threads of execution) will be affected.

Instances of the `locale` class are either created through the class constructor or through static members of the class. The C++ stream classes will use a locale (as explained later), and if you want to change the locale you call the `imbue` method on the stream object. In some cases, you will want to access one of these rules directly, and you have access to them through the locale object.

Using facets

Internationalization rules are known as **facets**. A locale object is a container of facets, and you can test if the locale has a specific facet using the `has_facet` function; if it does, you can get a `const` reference to the facet by calling the `use_facet` function. There are six types of facets summarized by seven categories of class in the following table. A facet class is a subclass of the `locale::facet` nested class.

Facet type	Description
`codecvt, ctype`	Converts between one encoding scheme to another and is used to classify characters and convert them to upper or lowercase
`collate`	Controls the ordering and grouping of characters in a string, including comparing and hashing of strings
`messages`	Retrieves localized messages from a catalog
`money`	Converts numbers representing currency to and from strings
`num`	Converts numbers to and from strings
`time`	Converts times and dates in numeric form to and from strings

The facet classes are used to convert the data to strings and so they all have a template parameter for the character type used. The `money`, `num,` and `time` facets are represented by three classes each. A class with the `_get` suffix that handles parsing strings, while a class with the `_put` suffix handles formatting as strings. For the `money` and `num` facets there is a class with the `punct` suffix that contains the rules and symbols for punctuation.

Since the `_get` facets are used to convert sequences of characters into numeric types, the classes have a template parameter that you can use to indicate the input iterator type that the `get` methods will use to represent a range of characters. Similarly, the `_put` facet classes have a template parameter that you can use to provide the output iterator type the `put` methods will write the converted string to. There are default types provided for both iterators types.

The `messages` facet is used for compatibility with POSIX code. The class is intended to allow you to provide localized strings for your application. The idea is that the strings in your user interface are indexed and at runtime you access the localized string using the index through the `messages` facet. However, Windows applications typically use message resource files compiled using the **Message Compiler**. It is perhaps for this reason that the `messages` facet provided as part of the Standard Library does not do anything, but the infrastructure is there, and you can derive your own `messages` facet class.

The `has_facet` and `use_facet` functions are templated for the specific type of facet that you want. All facet classes are subclasses of the `locale::facet` class, but through this template parameter the compiler will instantiate a function that returns the specific type you request. So, for example, if you want to format time and date strings for the French locale, you can call this code:

```
locale loc("french");
const time_put<char>& fac = use_facet<time_put<char>>(loc);
```

Here, the `french` string identifies the locale, and this is the language string used by the C Runtime Library `setlocale` function. The second line obtains the facet for converting numeric times into strings, and hence the function template parameter is `time_put<char>`. This class has a method called `put` that you can call to perform the conversion:

```
time_t t = time(nullptr);
tm *td = gmtime(&t);
ostreambuf_iterator<char> it(cout);
fac.put(it, cout, ' ', td, 'x', '#');
cout << "n";
```

The `time` function (via `<ctime>`) returns an integer with the current time and date, and this is converted to a `tm` structure using the `gmtime` function. The `tm` structure contains individual members for the year, month, day, hours, minutes, and seconds. The `gmtime` function returns the address to a structure that is statically allocated in the function, so you do not have to delete the memory it occupies.

The facet will format the data in the `tm` structure as a string through the output iterator passed as the first parameter. In this case, the output stream iterator is constructed from the `cout` object and so the facet will write the format stream to the console (the second parameter is not used, but because it is a reference you have to pass something, so the `cout` object is used there too). The third parameter is the separator character (again, this is not used). The fifth and (optional) sixth parameters indicate the formatting that you require. These are the same formatting characters as used in the C Runtime Library function `strftime`, as two single characters rather than the format string used by the C function. In this example, x is used to get the date and # is used as a modifier to get the long version of the string.

The code will give the following output:

```
samedi 28 janvier 2017
```

Notice that the words are not capitalized and there is no punctuation, also notice the order: weekday name, day number, month, then year.

If the `locale` object constructor parameter is changed to `german` then the output will be:

```
Samstag, 28. January 2017
```

The items are in the same order as in French, but the words are capitalized and punctuation is used. If you use `turkish` then the result is:

```
28 Ocak 2017 Cumartesi
```

In this case, the day of the week is at the end of the string.

Two countries divided by a common language will give two different strings, and the following are the results for `american` and `english-uk`:

```
Saturday, January 28, 2017
28 January 2017
```

Time is used as the example here because there is no stream, an insertion operator is used for the `tm` structure, and it is an unusual case. For other types, there are insertion operators that put them into a stream, and so the stream can use a locale to internationalize how it shows the type. For example, you can insert a `double` into the `cout` object and the value will be printed to the console. The default locale, American English, uses the period to separate whole numbers from the fractional part, but in other cultures a comma is used.

The `imbue` function will change the localization until the method is called subsequently:

```
cout.imbue(locale("american"));
cout << 1.1 << "n";
cout.imbue(locale("french"));
cout << 1.1 << "n";
cout.imbue(locale::classic());
```

Here, the stream object is localized to US English and then the floating-point number `1.1` is printed on the console. Next, the localization is changed to French, and this time the console will show `1,1`. In French, the decimal point is the comma. The last line resets the stream object by passing the locale returned from the `static classic` method. This returns the so-called **C locale**, which is the default in C and C++ and is American English.

The `static` method `global` can be used to set the locale that will be used as the default by each stream object. When an object is created from a stream class it calls the `locale::global` method to get the default locale. The stream clones this object so that it has its own copy independent of any local subsequently set by calling the `global` method. Note that the `cin` and `cout` stream objects are created before the `main` function is called, and these objects will use the default C locale until you imbue another locale. However, it is important to point out that, once a stream has been created, the `global` method has no effect on the stream, and `imbue` is the only way to change the locale used by the stream.

The `global` method will also call the C `setlocale` function to change the locale used by the C Runtime Library functions. This is important because some of the C++ functions (for example `to_string`, `stod`, as explained in the following text) will use the C Runtime Library functions to convert values. However, the C Runtime Library knows nothing about the C++ Standard Library, so calling the C `setlocale` function to change the default locale will not affect subsequently created stream objects.

It is worth pointing out that the `basic_string` class compares strings using the character traits class indicated by a template parameter. The `string` class uses the `char_traits` class and its version of the `compare` method does a straight comparison of the corresponding characters in the two strings. This comparison does not take into account cultural rules for comparing characters. If you want to do a comparison that uses cultural rules, you can do this through the `collate` facet:

```
int compare(
    const string& lhs, const string& rhs, const locale& loc)
{
    const collate<char>& fac = use_facet<collate<char>>(loc);
    return fac.compare(
        &lhs[0], &lhs[0] + lhs.size(), &rhs[0], &rhs[0] + rhs.size());
}
```

Strings and numbers

The Standard Library contains various functions and classes to convert between C++ strings and numeric values.

Converting strings to numbers

The C++ standard library contains functions with names like `stod` and `stoi` that convert a C++ `string` object to a numeric value (`stod` converts to a `double` and `stoi` converts to an `integer`). For example:

```
double d = stod("10.5");
d *= 4;
cout << d << "n"; // 42
```

This will initialize the floating-point variable `d` with a value of `10.5`, which is then used in a calculation and the result is printed on the console. The input string may have characters that cannot be converted. If this is the case then the parsing of the string ends at that point. You can provide a pointer to a `size_t` variable, which will be initialized to the location of the first character that cannot be converted:

```
string str = "49.5 red balloons";
size_t idx = 0;
double d = stod(str, &idx);
d *= 2;
string rest = str.substr(idx);
cout << d << rest << "n"; // 99 red balloons
```

In the preceding code, the `idx` variable will be initialized with a value of 4, indicating that the space between the 5 and r is the first character that cannot be converted to a `double`.

Converting numbers to strings

The `<string>` library provides various overloads of the `to_string` function to convert integer types and floating point types into a `string` object. This function does not allow you to provide any formatting details, so for an integer you cannot indicate the radix of the string representation (for example, hex), and for floating point conversions, you have no control over options like the number of significant figures. The `to_string` function is a simple function with limited facilities. A better option is to use the stream classes, as explained in the following section.

Using stream classes

You can print floating point numbers and integers to the console using the `cout` object (an instance of the `ostream` class) or to files with an instance of `ofstream`. Both of these classes will convert numbers to strings using member methods and manipulators to affect the formatting of the output string. Similarly, the `cin` object (an instance of the `istream` class) and the `ifstream` class can read data from formatted streams.

Manipulators are functions that take a reference to a stream object and return that reference. The Standard Library has various global insertion operators whose parameters are a reference to a stream object and a function pointer. The appropriate insertion operator will call the function pointer with the stream object as its parameter. This means that the manipulator will have access to, and can manipulate, the stream it is inserted into. For input streams, there are also extraction operators that have a function parameter which will call the function with the stream object.

The architecture of C++ streams means that there is a buffer between the stream interface that you call in your code and the low-level infrastructure that obtains the data. The C++ Standard Library provides stream classes that have string objects as the buffer. For an output stream, you access the string after items have been inserted in the stream, which means that the string will contain those items formatted according to those insertion operators. Similarly, you can provide a string with formatted data as the buffer for an input stream, and when you use extraction operators to extract the data from the stream you are actually parsing the string and converting parts of the string to numbers.

In addition, stream classes have a `locale` object and stream objects will call the conversion facet of this locale to convert character sequences from one encoding to another.

Outputting floating point numbers

The `<ios>` library has manipulators that alter how streams handle numbers. By default, the output stream will print floating-point numbers in a decimal format for numbers in the range `0.001` to `100000,` and for numbers outside this range it will use a scientific format with a mantissa and exponent. This mixed format is the default behavior of the `defaultfloat` manipulator. If you always want to use scientific notation, then you should insert the `scientific` manipulator into the output stream.

If you want to display floating point numbers using just the decimal format (that is the whole number on the left side of a decimal point and the factional part on the right side), then modify the output stream with the `fixed` manipulator. The number of decimal places can be altered by calling the `precision` method:

```
double d = 123456789.987654321;
cout << d << "n";
cout << fixed;
cout << d << "n";
cout.precision(9);
cout << d << "n";
cout << scientific;
cout << d << "n";
```

The output from the preceding code is:

```
1.23457e+08
123456789.987654
123456789.987654328
1.234567900e+08
```

The first line shows that scientific notation is used for large numbers. The second line shows the default behavior of `fixed`, which is to give the decimal number to 6 decimal places. This is changed in the code by calling the `precision` method to give 9 decimal places (the same effect can be achieved by inserting the `setprecision` manipulator in the `<iomanip>` library in the stream). Finally, the format is switched over to the scientific format with 9 decimal places to the mantissa from calling the `precision` method. The default is that the exponent is identified by the lowercase e. If you prefer, you can make this uppercase using the `uppercase` manipulator (and lowercase with `nouppercase`). Notice that the way that fractional parts are stored means that in fixed formats with 9 decimal places we see that the ninth digit is 8 rather than 1 as expected.

You can also specify whether a + symbol is shown for a positive number; the `showpos` manipulator will show the symbol, but the default `noshowpos` manipulator will not show the symbol. The `showpoint` manipulator will ensure that the decimal point is shown even if the floating-point number is a whole number. The default is `noshowpoint`, which means that, if there is no fractional part, no decimal point is displayed.

The `setw` manipulator (defined in the `<iomanip>` header) can be used with both integer and floating point numbers. In effect, this manipulator defines the minimum width of the space that the next (and only the next) item placed in the stream will occupy when printed on the console:

```
double d = 12.345678;
cout << fixed;
cout << setfill('#');
cout << setw(15) << d << "n";
```

To illustrate the effect of the `setw` manipulator, this code calls `setfill` manipulator, which indicates that instead of spaces a hash symbol (#) should be printed. The rest of the code says that the number should be printed using the fixed format (to 6 decimal places by default) in a space 15 characters wide. The result is:

######12.345678

If the number is negative (or `showpos` is used), then by default the sign will be with the number; if the `internal` manipulator (defined in `<ios>`) is used, then the sign will be left-justified in the space set for the number:

```
double d = 12.345678;
cout << fixed;
cout << showpos << internal;
cout << setfill('#');
cout << setw(15) << d << "n";
```

The result of the preceding code is as follows:

+#####12.345678

Notice that the + sign to the right of the spaces is indicated by the pound symbol.

The `setw` manipulator is typically used to allow you to output tables of data in formatted columns:

```
vector<pair<string, double>> table
{ { "one",0 },{ "two",0 },{ "three",0 },{ "four",0 } };

double d = 0.1;
for (pair<string,double>& p : table)
{
    p.second = d / 17.0;
    d += 0.1;
}

cout << fixed << setprecision(6);
```

```
for (pair<string, double> p : table)
{
    cout << setw(6)  << p.first << setw(10) << p.second << "n";
}
```

This fills a `vector` of pairs with a string and a number. The `vector` is initialized with the string values and a zero, then the floating-point number is altered in the `for` loop (the actual calculation is irrelevant here; the point is to create some numbers with multiple decimal places). The data is printed out in two columns with the numbers printed with 6 decimal places. This means that, including the leading zero and decimal point, each number will take up 8 spaces. The text column is specified as being 6 characters wide and the number column is specified as 10 characters wide. By default, when you specify a column width, the output will be right justified, meaning that each number is preceded by two spaces and the text is padded according to the length of the string. The output looks like this:

```
one   0.005882
two   0.011765
three   0.017647
four   0.023529
```

If you want the items in a column to be left justified, then you can use the `left` manipulator. This will affect all columns until the `right` manipulator is used to change the justification to right:

```
cout << fixed << setprecision(6) << left;
```

The output from this will be:

```
one     0.005882
two     0.011765
three 0.017647
four    0.023529
```

If you want different justification for the two columns, then you need to set the justification before printing a value. For example, to left justify the text and right justify the numbers, use this:

```
for (pair<string, double> p : table)
{
    cout << setw(6) << left << p.first
        << setw(10) << right << p.second << "n";
}
```

The result of the preceding code is as follows:

```
one     0.005882
two     0.011765
three   0.017647
four    0.023529
```

Outputting integers

Integers can also be printed in columns using the `setw` and `setfill` methods. You can insert manipulators to print integers in base 8 (`oct`), base 10 (`dec`), and base 16 (`hex`). (You can also use the `setbase` manipulator and pass the base you want to use, but the only values allowed are 8, 10, and 16.) The number can be printed with the base indicated (prefixed with `0` for octal or `0x` for hex) or without using the `showbase` and `noshowbase` manipulators. If you use `hex`, then the digits above 9 are the letters a to f, and by default these are lowercase. If you prefer these to be uppercase, then you can use the `uppercase` manipulator (and lowercase with `nouppercase`).

Outputting time and money

The `put_time` function in `<iomanip>` is passed a `tm` structure initialized with a time and date and a format string. The function returns an instance of the `_Timeobj` class. As the name suggests, you are not really expected to create variables of this class; instead, the function should be used to insert a time/date with a specific format into a stream. There is an insertion operator that will print a `_Timeobj` object. The function is used like this:

```
time_t t = time(nullptr);
tm *pt = localtime(&t);
cout << put_time(pt, "time = %X date = %x") << "n";
```

The output from this is:

time = 20:08:04 date = 01/02/17

The function will use the locale in the stream, so if you imbue a locale into the stream and then call `put_time`, the time/date will be formatted using the format string and the time/date localization rules for the locale. The format string uses format tokens for `strftime`:

```
time_t t = time(nullptr);
tm *pt = localtime(&t);
cout << put_time(pt, "month = %B day = %A") << "n";
cout.imbue(locale("french"));
cout << put_time(pt, "month = %B day = %A") << "n";
```

The output of the preceding code is:

```
month = March day = Thursday
month = mars day = jeudi
```

Similarly, the `put_money` function returns a `_Monobj` object. Again, this is simply a container for the parameters that you pass to this function and you are not expected to use instances of this class. Instead, you are expected to insert this function into an output stream. The actual work occurs in the insertion operator that obtains the money facet on the current locale, which uses this to format the number to the appropriate number of decimal places and determine the decimal point character; if a thousands separator is used, what character to use, before it is inserted it in the appropriate place.

```
Cout << showbase;
cout.imbue(locale("German"));
cout << "German" << "n";
cout << put_money(109900, false) << "n";
cout << put_money("1099", true) << "n";
cout.imbue(locale("American"));
cout << "American" << "n";
cout << put_money(109900, false) << "n";
cout << put_money("1099", true) << "n";
```

The output of the preceding code is:

```
German
1.099,00 euros
EUR10,99
American
$1,099.00
USD10.99
```

You provide the number in either a `double` or a string as Euro cents or cents and the `put_money` function formats the number in Euros or dollars using the appropriate decimal point (, for German, . for American) and the appropriate thousands separator (. for German, , for American). Inserting the `showbase` manipulator into the output stream means that the `put_money` function will show the currency symbol, otherwise just the formatted number will be shown. The second parameter to the `put_money` function specifies whether the currency character (`false`) or the international symbol (`true`) is used.

Converting numbers to strings using streams

Stream buffer classes are responsible for obtaining characters and writing characters from the appropriate source (file, console, and so on) and are derived from the abstract class `basic_streambuf` from `<streambuf>`. This base class defines two virtual methods, `overflow` and `underflow`, which are overridden by the derived classes to write and read characters (respectively) to and from the device associated with the derived class. The stream buffer class does the basic action of getting or putting items into a stream, and since the buffer handles characters, the class is templated with parameters for the character type and character traits.

As the name suggests, if you use a `basic_stringbuf` the stream buffer will be a string, so the source for read characters and the destination for written characters is that string. If you use this class to provide the buffer for a stream object, it means that you can use the insertion or extraction operators written for streams to write or read formatted data into or out of a string. The `basic_stringbuf` buffer is extendable, so as you insert items in the stream, the buffer will extend appropriately. There are `typedef`, where the buffer is a string (`stringbuf`) or a wstring (`wstringbuf`).

For example, imagine you have a class that you have defined and you have also defined an insertion operator so that you can use this with the `cout` object to print the value to the console:

```
struct point
{
    double x = 0.0, y = 0.0;
    point(){}
    point(double _x, double _y) : x(_x), y(_y) {}
};
```

```
ostream& operator<<(ostream& out, const point& p)
{
    out << "(" << p.x << "," << p.y << ")";
    return out;
}
```

Using this with the `cout` object is simple--consider the following piece of code:

```
point p(10.0, -5.0);
cout << p << "n";          // (10,-5)
```

You can use the `stringbuf` to direct the formatted output to a string rather than the console:

```
stringbuf buffer;
ostream out(&buffer);
out << p;
string str = buffer.str(); // contains (10,-5)
```

Since the stream object handles the formatting it means that you can insert any data type for which there is an insertion operator, and you can use any of the `ostream` formatting methods and any of the manipulators. The formatted output from all of these methods and manipulators will be inserted into the string object in the buffer.

Another option is to use the `basic_ostringstream` class in <sstream>. This class is templated on the character type of the strings used as the buffer (so the `string` version is `ostringstream`). It is derived from the `ostream` class, so you can use instances wherever you would use an `ostream` object. The formatted results can be accessed through the `str` method:

```
ostringstream os;
os << hex;
os << 42;
cout << "The value is: " << os.str() << "n";
```

This code obtains the value of `42` in hexadecimal (`2a`); this is achieved by inserting the `hex` manipulator in the stream and then inserting the integer. The formatted string is obtained by calling the `str` method.

Reading numbers from strings using streams

The `cin` object, an instance of the `istream` class (in the `<istream>` library), can input characters from the console and convert them to the numeric form you specify. The `ifstream` class (in the `<ifstream>` library) will also allow you to input characters from a file and convert them to numeric form. As with outputting streams, you can use the stream classes with a string buffer so that you can convert from a string object to a numeric value.

The `basic_istringstream` class (in the `<sstream>` library) is derived from the `basic_istream` class, so you can create stream objects and extract items (numbers and strings) from these objects. The class provides this stream interface on a string object (the `typedefs` keyword `istringstream` is based on a `string` and `wistringstream` is based on a `wstring`). When you construct objects of this class you initialize the object with a `string` containing a number and then you use the `>>` operator to extract objects for the fundamental built-in types, just as you would extract those items from the console using `cin`.

It is important to reiterate that the extraction operators treat whitespaces as the separators between items in a stream, and hence they will ignore all leading whitespaces, read the non-whitespaces characters up to the next whitespaces and attempt to convert this substring into the appropriate type as follows:

```
istringstream ss("-1.0e-6");
double d;
ss >> d;
```

This will initialize the `d` variable with the value of $-1e-6$. As with `cin`, you have to know the format of the item in the stream; so if, instead of extracting a `double` from the string in the preceding example, you try to extract an integer, the object will stop extracting characters when it comes to the decimal point. If some of the string is not converted, you can extract the rest into a string object:

```
istringstream ss("-1.0e-6");
int i;
ss >> i;
string str;
ss >> str;
cout << "extracted " << i << " remainder " << str << "n";
```

This will print the following at the console:

extracted -1 remainder .0e-6

If you have more than one number in the string you can extract these with several calls to the >> operator. The stream also supports some manipulators. For example, if the number in the string is in hex format you can inform the stream that this is the case using the hex manipulator as follows:

```
istringstream ss("0xff");
int i;
ss >> hex;
ss >> i;
```

This says that the number in the string is in hexadecimal format and the variable i will be initialized with a value of 255. If the string contains non-numeric values, then the stream object will still try to convert the string to the appropriate format. In the following snippet you can test if such an extraction fails by calling the fail function:

```
istringstream ss("Paul was born in 1942");
int year;
ss >> year;
if (ss.fail()) cout << "failed to read number" << "n";
```

If you know that the string contains text, you can extract it into string objects, but bear in mind that whitespace characters are treated as delimiters:

```
istringstream ss("Paul was born in 1942");
string str;
ss >> str >> str >> str >> str;
int year;
ss >> year;
```

Here, there are four words before the number, so the code reads a string four times. If you don't know where in the string the number is but you know there is a number in the string, you can move the internal buffer pointer until it points to a digit:

```
istringstream ss("Paul was born in 1942");
string str;
while (ss.eof() && !(isdigit(ss.peek()))) ss.get();
int year;
ss >> year;
if (!ss.fail()) cout << "the year was " << year << "n";
```

The peek method returns the character at the current position, but does not move the buffer pointer. This code checks to see if this character is a digit, and if not, the internal buffer pointer is moved by calling the get method. (This code tests the eof method to ensure that there is no attempt to read a character after the end of the buffer.) If you know where the number starts then you can call the seekg method to move the internal buffer pointer to a specified position.

The `<istream>` library has a manipulator called `ws` that removes whitespace from a stream. Recall earlier that we said that there is no function to remove whitespace from a string. This is true because the `ws` manipulator removes whitespace from a *stream* and not from a *string*, but since you can use a string as the buffer for a stream it means that you can use this function to remove white space from a string indirectly:

```
string str = "  hello  ";
cout << "|" << str1 << "|n"; // |  hello  |
istringstream ss(str);
ss >> ws;
string str1;
ss >> str1;
ut << "|" << str1 << "|n";    // |hello|
```

The `ws` function essentially iterates through the items in the input stream and returns when a character is not whitespace. If the stream is a file or the console stream then the `ws` function will read in the characters from those streams; in this case, the buffer is provided by an already-allocated string and so it skips over the whitespaces at the beginning of the string. Note that stream classes treat subsequent whitespaces as being separators between values in the stream, so in this example the stream will read in characters from the buffer until there is a whitespace, and will essentially *left-and right-trim* the string. However, this is not necessarily what you want. If you have a string with several words padded by whitespace, this code will only provide the first word.

The `get_money` and `get_time` manipulators in the `<iomanip>` library allow you to extract money and time from strings using the money and time facets for a locale:

```
tm indpday = {};
string str = "4/7/17";
istringstream ss(str);
ss.imbue(locale("french"));
ss >> get_time(&indpday, "%x");
if (!ss.fail())
{
    cout.imbue(locale("american"));
    cout << put_time(&indpday, "%x") << "n";
}
```

In the preceding code, the stream is first initialized with a date in the French format (day/month/year) and the date is extracted with `get_time` using the locale's standard date representation. The date is parsed into a `tm` structure, which is then printed out in standard date representation for the American locale using `put_time`. The results is:

7/4/2017

Using regular expressions

Regular expressions are patterns of text that can be used by a regular expression parser to search a string for text that matches the pattern, and if required, replace the matched items with other text.

Defining regular expressions

A **regular expression** (**regex**) is made up of characters that define a pattern. The expression contains special symbols that are meaningful to the parser, and if you want to use those symbols in the search pattern in the expression then you can escape them with a backslash (\). Your code will typically pass the expression as a `string` object to an instance of the `regex` class as a constructor parameter. This object is then passed to functions in `<regex>` that will use the expression to parse text for sequences that match the pattern.

The following table summarizes *some* of the patterns that you can match with the `regex` class.

Pattern	Explanation	Example
literals	Matches the exact characters	`li` matches `flip lip plier`
[group]	Matches a single character in a group	`[at]` matches cat, cat, top, pear
[^group]	Matches a single character not in the group	`[^at]` matches **c**at, **top**, t**op**, **p**ear, p**e**ar, pea**r**
[first-last]	Matches any character in the range `first` to `last`	`[0-9]` matches digits **1**02, 1**0**2, 10**2**
{n}	The element is matched exactly n times	**91{2}** matches **911**
{n,}	The element is matched n or more times	`wel{1,}` matches we**ll** and **wel**come
{n,m}	The element is matched between n and m times	`9{2,4}` matches 99, 999, 9999, 99999 but not 9
.	Wildcard, any character except n	`a.e` matches ate and are
*	The element is matched zero or more times	`d*.d` matches .1, 0.1, 10.1 but not 10
+	The element is matched one or more times	`d*.d` matches 0.1, 10.1 but not 10 or .1

?	The element is matched zero or one time	`tr?ap` matches `trap` and `tap`
|	Matches any one of the elements separated by the |	`th(e|is|at)` matches `the`, `this`, `that`
[[:class:]]	Matches the character class	`[[:upper:]]` matches uppercase characters: I am Richard
n	Matches a newline	
s	Matches any single whitespace	
d	Matches any single digit	`d` is `[0-9]`
w	Matches a character that can be in a word (upper case and lower case characters)	
b	Matches at a boundary between alphanumeric characters and non-alphanumeric characters	`d{2}b` matches `999` and `9999` `bd{2}` matches `999` and `9999`
$	End of the line	`s$` matches a single white space at the end of a line
^	Start of line	`^d` matches if a line starts with a digit

You can use regular expressions to define a pattern to be matched--the Visual C++ editor allows you to do this in the search dialog (which is a good test bed to develop your expressions).

It is much easier to define a pattern to match rather than a pattern *not* to match. For example, the expression w+b<w+> will match the string "`vector<int>`", because this has one or more word characters followed by a non-word character (<), followed by one or more word characters followed by >. This pattern will not match the string "`#include <regex>`" because there is a space after the `include` and the b indicates that there is a boundary between alphanumeric characters and non-alphanumeric characters.

The `th(e|is|at)` example in the table shows that you can use parentheses to group patterns when you want to provide alternatives. However, parentheses have another use--they allow you to capture groups. So, if you want to perform a replace action, you can search for a pattern as a group and then refer to that group as a named subgroup later (for example, search for `(Joe)` so that you can replace `Joe` with `Tom`). You can also refer to a sub-expression specified by parentheses in the expression (called back references):

```
([A-Za-z]+) +1
```

This expression says: *search for words with one or more characters in the ranges a to z and A to Z; the word is called 1 so find where it appears twice with a space between them.*

Standard Library classes

To perform matching or replacement you have to create a regular expression object. This is an object of the class `basic_regex` that has template parameters for the character type and a regular expression traits class. There are two `typedefs` for this class: `regex` for `char` and `wregex` for wide chars, which have traits described by the `regex_traits` and `wregex_traits` classes.

The traits class determines how the regex class parses the expression. For example, recall from previous text that you can use `w` for a word, `d` for a digit, and `s` for whitespace. The `[[::]]` syntax allows you to use a more descriptive name for the character class: `alnum`, `digit`, `lower`, and so on. And since these are text sequences that depend upon a character set, the traits class will have the appropriate code to test whether the expression uses a supported character class.

The appropriate regex class will parse the expression to enable functions in the `<regex>` library to use the expression to identify patterns in some text:

```
regex rx("([A-Za-z]+) +1");
```

This searches for repeated words using a back reference. Note that the regular expression uses 1 for the back reference, but in a string the backslash has to be escaped (`\`). If you use character classes such as `s` and `d` then you will need to do a lot of escaping. Instead, you can use raw strings (`R"()"`), but bear in mind that the first set of parentheses inside the quote marks is part of the syntax for raw strings and does not form a regex group:

```
regex rx(R"(([A-Za-z]+) +1)");
```

It is entirely up to you as to which is the more readable; both introduce extra characters within the double quotes, which has the potential to confuse a quick glance-over what the regular expression matches.

Bear in mind that the regular expression is essentially a program in itself, so the `regex` parser will determine whether that expression is valid, and if it isn't the object, the constructor, will throw an exception of type `regex_error`. Exception handling is explained in the next chapter, but it is important to point out that if the exception is not caught it will result in the application aborting at runtime. The exception's `what` method will return a basic description of the error, and the `code` method will return one of the constants in the `error_type` enumeration in the `regex_constants` namespace. There is no indication of where in the expression the error occurs. You should thoroughly test your expression in an external tool (for example Visual C++ search).

The constructor can be called with a string (C or C++) or a pair of iterators to a range of characters in a string (or other container), or you can pass an initialization list where each item in the list is a character. There are various flavors of the language of regex; the default for the `basic_regex` class is **ECMAScript**. If you want a different language (basic POSIX, extended POSIX, awk, grep, or egrep), you can pass one of the constants defined in the `syntax_option_type` enumeration in the `regex_constants` namespace (copies are also available as constants defined in the `basic_regex` class) as a constructor parameter. You can only specify one language flavor, but you can combine this with some of the other `syntax_option_type` constants: `icase` specifies case insensitivity, `collate` uses the locale in matches, `nosubs` means you do not want to capture groups, and `optimize` optimizes matching.

The class uses the method `getloc` to obtain the locale used by the parser and `imbue` to reset the locale. If you `imbue` a locale, then you will not be able to use the `regex` object to do any matching until you reset it with the `assign` method. This means there are two ways to use a `regex` object. If you want to use the current locale then pass the regular expression to the constructor: if you want to use a different locale create an empty `regex` object with the default constructor, then call `imbue` with the locale and pass the regular expression using the `assign` method. Once a regular expression has been parsed you can call the `mark_count` method to get the number of capture groups in the expression (assuming you did not use `nosubs`).

Matching expressions

Once you have constructed a `regex` object you can pass it to the methods in the `<regex>` library to search for the pattern in a string. The `regex_match` function is passed in a string (C or C++) or iterators to a range of characters in a container and a constructed `regex` object. In its simplest form, the function will return `true` only if there is an exact match, that is, the expression exactly matches the search string:

```
regex rx("[at]"); // search for either a or t
cout << boolalpha;
cout << regex_match("a", rx) << "n";  // true
cout << regex_match("a", rx) << "n";  // true
cout << regex_match("at", rx) << "n"; // false
```

In the previous code, the search expression is for a single character in the range given (a or t), so the first two calls to `regex_match` return `true` because the searched string is one character. The last call returns `false` because the match is not the same as the searched string. If you remove the `[]` in the regular expression, then just the third call returns `true` because you are looking for the exact string at. If the regular expression is `[at]+` so that you are looking for one or more of the characters a and t, then all three calls return `true`. You can alter how the match is determined by passing one or more of the constants in the `match_flag_type` enumeration.

If you pass a reference to a `match_results` object to this function, then after the search the object will contain information about the position and the string that matches. The `match_results` object is a container of `sub_match` objects. If the function succeeds it means that the entire search string matches the expression, and in this case the first `sub_match` item returned will be the entire search string. If the expression has subgroups (patterns identified with parentheses) then these sub groups will be additional `sub_match` objects in the `match_results` object.

```
string str("trumpet");
regex rx("(trump)(.*)");
match_results<string::const_iterator> sm;
if (regex_match(str, sm, rx))
{
    cout << "the matches were: ";
    for (unsigned i = 0; i < sm.size(); ++i)
    {
        cout << "[" << sm[i] << "," << sm.position(i) << "] ";
    }
    cout << "n";
} // the matches were: [trumpet,0] [trump,0] [et,5]
```

Here, the expression is the literal trump followed by any number of characters. The entire string matches this expression and there are two sub groups: the literal string trump and whatever is left over after the trump is removed.

Both the match_results class and the sub_match class are templated on the type of iterator that is used to indicate the matched item. There are typedef call's cmatch and wcmatch where the template parameter is const char* and const wchar_t*, respectively, and smatch and wsmatch where the parameter is the iterator used in string and wstring objects, respectively (similarly, there are submatch classes: csub_match, wcsub_match, ssub_match, and wssub_match).

The regex_match function can be quite restrictive because it looks for an exact match between the pattern and the searched string. The regex_search function is more flexible because it returns true if there is a substring within the search string that matches the expression. Note that even if there are multiple matches in the search string, the regex_search function will only find the first. If you want to parse through the string you will have to call the function multiple times until it indicates that there are no more matches. This is where the overload with iterator access to the search string becomes useful:

```
regex rx("bd{2}b");
smatch mr;
string str = "1 4 10 42 100 999";
string::const_iterator cit = str.begin();
while (regex_search(cit, str.cend(), mr, rx))
{
    cout << mr[0] << "n";
    cit += mr.position() + mr.length();
}
```

Here, the expression will match a 2 digit number (d{2}) that is surrounded by whitespace (the two b patterns mean a boundary before and after). The loop starts with an iterator pointing to the start of the string, and when a match is found this iterator is incremented to that position and then incremented by the length of the match. The regex_iterator object, explained further, wraps this behavior.

The `match_results` class gives iterator access to the contained `sub_match` objects so you can use ranged `for`. Initially, it appears that the container works in an odd way because it knows the position in the searched string of the `sub_match` object (through the `position` method, which takes the index of the sub match object), but the `sub_match` object appears to only know the string it refers to. However, on closer inspection of the `sub_match` class, it shows that it derives from `pair`, where both parameters are string iterators. This means that a `sub_match` object has iterators specifying the range in the original string of the sub string. The `match_result` object knows the start of the original string and can use the `sub_match.first` iterator to determine the character position of the start of the substring.

The `match_result` object has a `[]` operator (and the `str` method) that returns the substring of the specified group; this will be a string constructed using the iterators to the range of characters in the original string. The `prefix` method returns the string that precedes the match and the `suffix` method returns the string that follows the match. So, in the previous code, the first match will be `10`, the prefix will be `1  4`, and the suffix will be `42 100  999`. In contrast, if you access the `sub_match` object itself, it only knows its length and the string, which is obtained by calling the `str` method.

The `match_result` object can also return the results through the `format` method. This takes a format string where the matched groups are identified through numbered placeholders identified by the `$` symbol (`$1`, `$2`, and so on). The output can either be to a stream or returned from the method as a string:

```
string str("trumpet");
regex rx("(trump)(.*)");
match_results<string::const_iterator> sm;
if (regex_match(str, sm, rx))
{
    string fmt = "Results: [$1] [$2]";
    cout << sm.format(fmt) << "n";
} // Results: [trump] [et]
```

With `regex_match` or `regex_search`, you can use parentheses to identify subgroups. If the pattern matches then you can obtain these subgroups using an appropriate `match_results` object passed by reference to the function. As shown earlier, the `match_results` object is a container for `sub_match` objects. Sub matches can be compared with the `<`, `!=`, `==`, `<=`, `>`, and `>=` operators, which compare items that the iterators point to (that is, the sub strings). Further, `sub_match` objects can be inserted into a stream.

Using iterators

The library also provides an iterator class for regular expressions, which provides a different way to parse strings. Since the class will involve comparisons of strings it is templated with the element type and traits. The class will need to iterate through strings, so the first template parameter is the string iterator type and the element and traits types can be deduced from that. The `regex_iterator` class is a forward iterator so it has a ++ operator and it provides a * operator that gives access to a `match_result` object. In the previous code, you saw that a `match_result` object is passed to the `regex_match` and `regex_search` functions, which use it to contain their results. This raises the question of what code fills the `match_result` object accessed through the `regex_iterator`. The answer lies in the iterator's ++ operator:

```
string str = "the cat sat on the mat in the bathroom";
regex rx("(b(.at)([^ ]*)");
regex_iterator<string::iterator> next(str.begin(), str.end(), rx);
regex_iterator<string::iterator> end;

for (; next != end; ++next)
{
    cout << next->position() << " " << next->str() << ", ";
}
cout << "n";
// 4 cat, 8 sat, 19 mat, 30 bathroom
```

In this code, a string is searched for words where the second and third letters are `at`. The `b` says that the pattern must be at the start of a word (the `.` means that the word can start with any letter). There is a capture group around these three characters and a second capture group for one or more characters other than spaces.

The iterator object `next` is constructed with iterators to the string to search and the `regex` object. The ++ operator essentially calls the `regex_search` function while maintaining the position of the place to perform the next search. If the search fails to find the pattern then the operator returns the **end of sequence** iterator, which is the iterator that is created by the default constructor (the `end` object in this code). This code prints out the full match because we use the default parameter for the `str` method (`0`). If you want the actual substring matched, use `str(1)` and the result will be:

```
4 cat, 8 sat, 19 mat, 30 bat
```

Since the * (and the `->`) operator gives access to a `match_result` object, you can also access the `prefix` method to get the string that precedes the match and the `suffix` method will return the string that follows the match.

The `regex_iterator` class allows you to iterate over the matched substrings, whereas the `regex_token_iterator` goes one step further in that it also gives you access to all submatches. In use, this class is the same as `regex_iterator`, except in construction. The `regex_token_iterator` constructor has a parameter to indicate which submatch you wish to access through the * operator. A value of −1 means you want the prefix, a value of 0 means you want the whole match, and a value of 1 or above means you want the numbered sub match. If you wish, you can pass an `int` vector or C array with the submatch types that you want:

```cpp
using iter = regex_token_iterator<string::iterator>;
string str = "the cat sat on the mat in the bathroom";
regex rx("b(.at)([^ ]*)");
iter next, end;

// get the text between the matches
next = iter(str.begin(), str.end(), rx, -1);
for (; next != end; ++next) cout << next->str() << ", ";
cout << "n";
// the ,  ,  on the ,  in the ,

// get the complete match
next = iter(str.begin(), str.end(), rx, 0);
for (; next != end; ++next) cout << next->str() << ", ";
cout << "n";
// cat, sat, mat, bathroom,

// get the sub match 1
next = iter(str.begin(), str.end(), rx, 1);
for (; next != end; ++next) cout << next->str() << ", ";
cout << "n";
// cat, sat, mat, bat,

// get the sub match 2
next = iter(str.begin(), str.end(), rx, 2);
for (; next != end; ++next) cout << next->str() << ", ";
cout << "n";
// , , , hroom,
```

Replacing strings

The `regex_replace` method is similar to the other methods in that it takes a string (a C string or C++ `string` object, or iterators to a range of characters), a `regex` object, and optional flags. In addition, the function has a format string and returns a `string`. The format string is essentially passed to the `format` method of each `results_match` object from the result of the matches to the regular expression. This formatted string is then used as the replacement for the corresponding matched substring. If there are no matches, then a copy of the searched string is returned.

```
string str = "use the list<int> class in the example";
regex rx("b(list)(<w*> )");
string result = regex_replace(str, rx, "vector$2");
cout << result << "n"; // use the vector<int> class in the example
```

In the preceding code, we say that the entire matched string (which should be `list<` followed by some text followed by > and a space) should be replaced with `vector`, followed by the second sub match (< followed by some text followed by > and a space). The result is that `list<int>` will be replaced with `vector<int>`.

Using strings

The example will read in emails as a text file and processed. An email in Internet message format will be in two parts: the header and message body. This is simple processing, so no attempt is carried out to process MIME email body formatting (although this code can be used as a starting point for that). The email body will start after the first blank line, and Internet standards say that lines should be no longer than 78 characters. If they are longer they must not be longer than 998 characters. This means that newlines (carriage return, linefeed pairs) are used to maintain this rule, and that an end of paragraph is indicated by a blank line.

Headers are more complicated. In their simplest form, a header is on a single line and is in the form `name:value`. The header name is separated from the header value by a colon. A header may be split over more than one line using a format called folded white space, where the newline splitting a header is placed before whitespace (space, tab, and so on). This means that a line that starts with whitespace is the continuation of the header on the previous line. Headers often contain `name=value` pairs separated by semicolons, so it is useful to be able separate these subitems. Sometimes these subitems do not have a value, that is, there will be a subitem terminated by a semicolon.

The example will take an email as a series of strings and using these rules will create an object with a collection of headers and a string containing the body.

Creating the project

Create a folder for the project and create a C++ file called `email_parser.cpp`. Since this application will read files and process strings, add includes for the appropriate libraries and add code to take the name of a file from the command-line:

```cpp
#include <iostream>
#include <fstream>
#include <string>

using namespace std;

void usage()
{
    cout << "usage: email_parser file" << "n";
    cout << "where file is the path to a file" << "n";
}

int main(int argc, char *argv[])
{
    if (argc <= 1)
    {
        usage();
        return 1;
    }

    ifstream stm;
    stm.open(argv[1], ios_base::in);
    if (!stm.is_open())
    {
        usage();
        cout << "cannot open " << argv[1] << "n";
        return 1;
    }

    return 0;
}
```

A header will have a name and a body. The body could be a single string, or one or more subitems. Create a class to represent the body of a header, and for the time being, treat this as a single line. Add the following class above the usage function:

```
class header_body
{
    string body;
public:
    header_body() = default;
    header_body(const string& b) : body(b) {}
    string get_body() const { return body; }
};
```

This simply wraps the class around a string; later on we will add code to separate out the subitems in the body data member. Now create a class to represent the email. Add the following code after the header_body class:

```
class email
{
    using iter = vector<pair<string, header_body>>::iterator;
    vector<pair<string, header_body>> headers;
    string body;

public:
    email() : body("") {}

    // accessors
    string get_body() const { return body; }
    string get_headers() const;
    iter begin() { return headers.begin(); }
    iter end() { return headers.end(); }

    // two stage construction
    void parse(istream& fin);
private:
    void process_headers(const vector<string>& lines);
};
```

The headers data member holds the headers as name/value pairs. The items are stored in a vector rather than a map because as an email is passed from mail server to mail server, headers may be added by each server that already exist in the email, so headers are duplicated. We could use a multimap, but then we will lose the ordering of the headers, since a multimap will store the items in an order that aids searching for items.

A `vector` keeps the items in the order that they are inserted in the container, and since we will parse the e-mail serially, this means that the `headers` data member will have the header items in the same order as in the e-mail. Add an appropriate include so that you can use the `vector` class.

There are accessors for the body and the headers as a single string. In addition, there are accessors that return iterators from the `headers` data member, so that external code can iterate through the `headers` data member (a complete implementation of this class would have accessors that allow you to search for a header by name, but for the purpose of this example, only iteration is permitted).

The class supports two-stage construction, where most of the work is carried out by passing an input stream to the `parse` method. The `parse` method reads in the email as a series of lines in a `vector` object and it calls a private function, `process_headers`, to interpret these lines as headers.

The `get_headers` method is simple: it just iterates through the headers and puts one header on each line in the format `name: value`. Add the inline function:

```
string get_headers() const
{
    string all = "";
    for (auto a : headers)
    {
        all += a.first + ": " + a.second.get_body();
        all += "n";
    }
    return all;
}
```

Next, you need to read in the email from a file and extract the body and the headers. The `main` function already has the code to open a file, so create an `email` object and pass the `ifstream` object for the file to the `parse` method. Now print out the parsed email using the accessors. Add the following to the end of the `main` function:

```
email eml;
eml.parse(stm);
cout << eml.get_headers();
cout << "n";
cout << eml.get_body() << "n";

return 0;
}
```

After the `email` class declaration, add the definition for the `parse` function:

```
void email::parse(istream& fin)
{
    string line;
    vector<string> headerLines;
    while (getline(fin, line))
    {
        if (line.empty())
        {
            // end of headers
            break;
        }
        headerLines.push_back(line);
    }

    process_headers(headerLines);

    while (getline(fin, line))
    {
        if (line.empty()) body.append("n");
        else body.append(line);
    }
}
```

This method is simple: it repeatedly calls the `getline` function in the `<string>` library to read a `string` until a newline is detected. In the first half of the method, the strings are stored in a `vector` and then passed to the `process_headers` method. If the string read in is empty, it means a blank line has been read--in which case, all of the headers have been read. In the second half of the method, the body of the e-mail is read in. The `getline` function will have stripped the newlines used to format the email to 78-character line lengths, so the loop merely appends the lines as one string. If a blank line is read in, it indicates the end of a paragraph, and so a newline is added to the body string.

After the `parse` method, add the `process_headers` method:

```
void email::process_headers(const vector<string>& lines)
{
    string header = "";
    string body = "";
    for (string line : lines)
    {
        if (isspace(line[0])) body.append(line);
        else
        {
            if (!header.empty())
            {
```

```
                    headers.push_back(make_pair(header, body));
                    header.clear();
                    body.clear();
                }

                size_t pos = line.find(':');
                header = line.substr(0, pos);
                pos++;
                while (isspace(line[pos])) pos++;
                body = line.substr(pos);
            }
        }

        if (!header.empty())
        {
            headers.push_back(make_pair(header, body));
        }
    }
```

This code iterates through each line in the collection, and when it has a complete header it splits the string into the name/body pair on the colon. Within the loop, the first line tests to see if the first character is whitespace; if not, then the header variable is checked to see if it has a value; and if so, the name/body pair are stored in the class headers data member before clearing the header and body variables.

The following code acts upon the line read from the collection. This code assumes that this is the start of the header line, so the string is searched for the colon and split at this point. the name of the header is before the colon and the body of the header (trimmed of leading whitespace) is after the colon. Since we do not know if the header body will be folded onto the next line, the name/body is not stored; instead, the while loop is allowed to repeat another time so that the first character of the next line can be tested to see if it is whitespace, and if so, it is appended to the body. This action of holding the name/body pair until the next iteration of the while loop means that the last line will not be stored in the loop, and hence there is a test at the end of the method to see if the header variable is empty, and if not, the name/body pair is stored.

You can now compile the code (remember to use the /EHsc switch) to test that there are no typos. To test the code, you should save an email from your email client as a file and then run the email_parser application with the path to this file. The following is one of the example email messages given in the Internet Message Format RFC 5322, which you can put into a text file to test the code:

```
    Received: from x.y.test
    by example.net
    via TCP
    with ESMTP
    id ABC12345
    for <mary@example.net>;   21 Nov 1997 10:05:43 -0600
Received: from node.example by x.y.test; 21 Nov 1997 10:01:22 -0600
From: John Doe <jdoe@node.example>
To: Mary Smith <mary@example.net>
Subject: Saying Hello
Date: Fri, 21 Nov 1997 09:55:06 -0600
Message-ID: <1234@local.node.example>

This is a message just to say hello.
So, "Hello".
```

You can test the application with an email message to show that the parsing has taken into account header formatting, including folding whitespace.

Processing header subitems

The next action is to process the header bodies into subitems. To do this, add the following highlighted declaration to the public section of the header_body class:

```
public:
    header_body() = default;
    header_body(const string& b) : body(b) {}
    string get_body() const { return body; }
    vector<pair<string, string>> subitems();
};
```

Each subitem will be a name/value pair, and since the order of a subitem may be important, the subitems are stored in a vector. Change the main function, remove the call to get_headers, and instead print out each header individually:

```
email eml;
eml.parse(stm);
for (auto header : eml) {
    cout << header.first << " : ";
```

```
        vector<pair<string, string>> subItems = header.second.subitems();
        if (subItems.size() == 0)   {
            cout << header.second.get_body() << "n";
        }   else   {
            cout << "n";
            for (auto sub : subItems) {
                cout << "     " << sub.first;
                if (!sub.second.empty())
                cout << " = " << sub.second;
                cout << "n";
            }
        }
    }
}
cout << "n";
cout << eml.get_body() << endl;
```

Since the email class implements the begin and end methods, it means that the ranged for loop will call these methods to get access to the iterators on the email::headers data member. Each iterator will give access to a pair<string, header_body> object, so in this code we first print out the header name and then access the subitems on the header_body object. If there are no subitems, there will still be some text for the header, but it won't be split into subitems, so we call the get_body method to get the string to print. If there are subitems then these are printed out. Some items will have a body and some will not. If the item has a body then the subitem is printed in the form name = value.

The final action is to parse the header bodies to split them into subitems. Below the header_body class, add the definition of the method to this:

```
vector<pair<string, string>> header_body::subitems()
{
    vector<pair<string, string>> subitems;
    if (body.find(';') == body.npos) return subitems;

    return subitems;
}
```

Since subitems are separated using semicolons there is a simple test to look for a semicolon on the body string. If there is no semicolon, then an empty vector is returned.

Now the code must repeatedly parse through the string, extracting subitems. There are several cases that need to be addressed. Most subitems will be in the form name=value;, so this subitem must be extracted and split at the equals character and the semicolon discarded.

Some subitems do not have a value and are in the form `name;` in which case, the semicolon is discarded and an item is stored with an empty string for the subitem value. Finally, the last item in a header may not be terminated with a semicolon, so this must be taken into account.

Add the following `while` loop:

```
vector<pair<string, string>> subitems;
if (body.find(';') == body.npos) return subitems;
size_t start = 0;
size_t end = start;
while (end != body.npos){}
```

As the name suggests, the `start` variable is the start index of a subitem and `end` is the end index of a subitem. The first action is to ignore any whitespace, so within the `while` loop add:

```
while (start != body.length() && isspace(body[start]))
{
    start++;
}
if (start == body.length()) break;
```

This simply increments the `start` index while it refers to a whitespace character and as long as it has not reached the end of the string. If the end of the string is reached, it means there are no more characters and so the loop is finished.

Next, add the following to search for the = and ; characters and handle one of the search situations:

```
string name = "";
string value = "";
size_t eq = body.find('=', start);
end = body.find(';', start);

if (eq == body.npos)
{
    if (end == body.npos) name = body.substr(start);
    else name = body.substr(start, end - start);
}
else
{
}
subitems.push_back(make_pair(name, value));
start = end + 1;
```

The `find` method will return the `npos` value if the searched item cannot be found. The first call looks for the = character and the second call looks for a semicolon. If no = can be found then the item has no value, just a name. If the semicolon cannot be found, then it means that the `name` is the entire string from the `start` index until the end of the string. If there is a semicolon, then the `name` is from the `start` index until the index indicated by `end` (and hence the number of characters to copy is `end-start`). If an = character is found then the string needs to be split at this point, and that code will be shown in a moment. Once the `name` and `value` variables have been given values, these are inserted into the `subitems` data member and the `start` index is moved to the character after the `end` index. If the `end` index is `npos` then the value of the `start` index will be invalid, but this does not matter because the `while` loop will test the value of the `end` index and will break the loop if the index is `npos`.

Finally, you need to add the code for when there is an = character in the subitem. Add the following highlighted text:

```
if (eq == body.npos)
{
    if (end == body.npos) name = body.substr(start);
    else name = body.substr(start, end - start);
}
else
{
    if (end == body.npos)
    {
        name = body.substr(start, eq - start);
        value = body.substr(eq + 1);
    } else {
        if (eq < end) {
            name = body.substr(start, eq - start);
            value = body.substr(eq + 1, end - eq - 1);
        } else {
            name = body.substr(start, end - start);
        }
    }
}
```

The first line tests to see if the search for a semicolon failed. In this case, the name is from the `start` index until the character before the equals character, and the value is the text following the equals sign until the end of the string.

If there are valid indices for the equals and semicolon characters then there is one more situation to check for. It is possible that the location of the equals character could be after the semicolon, in which case it means that this subitem does not have a value, and the equals character will be for a subsequent subitem.

At this point you can compile the code and test it with a file containing an email. The output from the program should be the email split into headers and a body, and each header split into subitems, which may be a simple string or a `name=value` pair.

Summary

In this chapter, you have seen the various C++ standard library classes that support strings. You have seen how to read strings from streams, how to write strings to streams, how to convert between numbers and strings, and how to manipulate strings using regular expressions. When you write code, you will inevitably spend time running your code to check if it works according to your specifications. This will involve providing code that checks the results of your algorithms, code that logs intermediate code to a debugging device, and, of course, running the code under a debugger. The next chapter is all about debugging code!

10
Diagnostics and Debugging

Software is complex; however, well you design your code, at some point you'll have to debug it, whether during the normal testing phases of developing your code, or when a bug report has been issued. It's prudent to design your code to make testing and debugging as straight forward as possible. This means adding tracing and reporting code, determining invariants and pre- and post-conditions, so that you have a starting point to test your code, and writing functions with understandable and meaningful error codes.

Preparing your code

The C++ and C Standard Libraries have a wide range of functions that allow you to apply tracing and reporting functions so that you can test if code is handling data in expected ways. Much of these facilities use conditional compilation so that the reporting only occurs in debug builds, but if you provide the traces with meaningful messages they will form part of the documentation of your code. Before you can report on the behavior of your code, you first have to know what to expect from it.

Invariants and conditions

Class invariants are conditions, the object state, that you know remain true. During a method call the object state will change, possibly to something that invalidates the object, but once a public method has completed, the object state must be left in a consistent state. There is no guarantee what order the user will call methods on a class, or even if they call methods at all, so an object must be usable whatever methods the user calls. The invariant aspects of an object applies on a method calls level: between method calls the object must be consistent and usable.

For example, imagine you have a class that represents a date: it holds a day number between 1 and 31, a month number between 1 and 12, and a year number. The class invariant is that, whatever you do to objects of the date class, it will always hold a valid date. This means that users can safely use objects of your date class. It also means that other methods on the class (say, a method to determine how many days between two dates, `operator-`) can assume that the values in the date objects are valid, so those methods do not have to check the validity of the data they act upon.

However, a valid date is more than the ranges 1 to 31 for days and 1 to 12 for months, because not every month has 31 days. So, if you have a valid date, say 5 April 1997, and you call a `set_day` method to set the day number to 31, the class invariant condition has been violated since 31 April is not a valid date. If you want to change the values in a date object, the only safe way to do this is to change all the values: the day, month, and year--at the same time, because this is the only way to maintain the class invariance.

One approach is to define a private method in debug builds that tests the invariant conditions for the class and ensures with asserts (see later) that the invariants are maintained. You can call such a method before a publicly-accessible method leaves to ensure that the object remains in a consistent state. Methods should also have defined pre- and post-conditions. Pre-conditions are conditions that you mandate are true before the method is called, and post-conditions are conditions that you guarantee are true after the method has completed. For the methods on a class, the class invariants are pre-conditions (because the state of the object should be consistent before the method is called) and the invariants are also a post-condition (because after the method has finished the object state should be consistent).

There are also pre-conditions that are the responsibility of the caller of a method. The pre-condition is a documented responsibility that the caller ensures. For example, the date class will have a pre-condition that day numbers are between 1 and 31. This simplifies the class code because methods that take a day number can assume that values passed are never out of range (although, because some months have fewer than 31 days, values may still not be valid). Again, in debug builds you can use asserts to check that such pre-conditions are true, and the tests in the assert will be compiled away in the release build. At the end of a method there will be post-conditions, that is, the class invariants will be maintained (and the state of the object will be valid), and the return value will be valid.

Conditional compilation

As explained in Chapter 1, *Starting with C++*, when your C++ program is compiled there is a pre-compilation step that collates all the file included in a C++ source file into a single file, which is then compiled. The pre-processor also expands macros and, depending on the value of symbols, includes some code and exclude others code.

In its simplest form, conditional compilation brackets code with #ifdef and #endif (and optionally using #else), so that the code between these directives is only compiled if the specified symbol has been defined.

```
#ifdef TEST
    cout << "TEST defined" << endl;
#else
    cout << "TEST not defined" << endl;
#endif
```

You are guaranteed that only one of these lines will be compiled, and you are guaranteed that at least one of them will be compiled. If the symbol TEST is defined then the first line will be compiled and, as far as the compiler is concerned, the second line does not exist. If the symbol TEST is not defined, then the second line will be compiled. If you want to type these lines in the opposite order, you can use the #ifndef directive. The text provided through the conditional compilation can be C++ code, or it can be defined using other symbols in the current translation unit with #define or undefined existing symbols with #undef.

The #ifdef directive simply determines if the symbol exists: it does not test its value. The #if directive allows you to test an expression. You can set a symbol to have a value and compile specific code depending on the value. The expression must be integral, so a single #if block can test for several values using #if and multiple #elif directives and (at most) one #else:

```
#if TEST < 0
    cout << "negative" << endl;
#elif TEST > 0
    cout << "positive" << endl;
#else
    cout << "zero or undefined" << endl;
#endif
```

If the symbol is not defined then the `#if` directive treats the symbol as having a value of 0; if you want to distinguish between these cases you can use the `defined` operator to test if a symbol is defined. At most, only one of the sections in the `#if/#endif` block will be compiled, and if a value is not matched then no code will be compiled. The expression can be a macro, in which case the macro will be expanded before the condition is tested.

There are three ways to define a symbol. The first way is out of your control: the compiler will define some symbols (typically with the __ or _ prefix) that give you information about the compiler and the compilation process. Some of these symbols will be described in a later section. The other two ways are entirely under your control--you can define symbols in a source file (or header file) using `#define` or you can define them on the command line using the `/D` switch:

```
cl /EHsc prog.cpp /DTEST=1
```

This will compile the source code with the symbol `TEST` set to a value of 1.

You will typically use conditional compilation to provide code that should not be used in production code, for example, extra tracing code to use in debug mode or when you are testing code. For example, imagine you have library code to return data from a database, but you suspect that the SQL statement in the library function is faulty and returning too many values. Here, you may decide to test, add code to log the number of values returned:

```
vector<int> data = get_data();
#if TRACE_LEVEL > 0
cout << "number of data items returned: " << data.size() << endl;
#endif
```

Trace messages like this pollute your user interface and you will want to avoid them in production code. However, in debugging they can be invaluable in determining where problems are occurring.

Any code that you call in debug mode, conditional code should be `const` methods (here `vector::size`), that is, they should not affect the state of any objects or the application data. You must ensure that the logic of your code is *exactly* the same in debug mode as in release mode.

Using pragmas

Pragmas are compiler-specific and often are concerned with the technical details about the code sections in the object files. There are a couple of Visual C++ pragmas that are useful in debugging code.

In general, you will want your code to compile with as few warnings as possible. The default warning for the Visual C++ compiler is /W1, which means that only the most severe warnings are listed. Increasing the value to 2, 3, or the highest value of 4 progressively increases the number of warnings that are given during a compilation. Using /Wall will give level-4 warnings and warnings that have been disabled by default. This last option, even for the simplest code, will produce a screen full of warnings. When you have hundreds of warnings useful error messages will be hidden between the reams of unimportant warnings. Since the C++ Standard Library is complex and uses some code that is decades old, there are some constructs that the compiler will warn you about. To prevent these warnings polluting the output from your builds, specific warnings in selective files have been disabled.

If you are supporting older library code, you may find that the code compiles with warnings. You may be tempted to reduce the warning levels using the compiler /W switch, but that will suppress all warnings higher than the ones you enable, and it applies equally to your code as to the library code that you may be including into your project. The warning pragma gives you a lot more flexibility. There are two ways to call this--you can reset the warning level to override the compiler /W switch and you can change the warning level of a particular warning or disable the warning reporting altogether.

For example, at the top of the <iostream> header is the line:

```
#pragma warning(push,3)
```

This says store the current warning level and, for the rest of this file (or until it is changed), make the warning level 3. At the bottom of the file is the line:

```
#pragma warning(pop)
```

This restores the warning level to that stored earlier.

You can also change how one or more warnings are reported. For example, at the top of <istream> is:

```
#pragma warning(disable: 4189)
```

The first part of this `pragma` is the specifier `disable`, which indicates that reporting of a warning type (in this case, 4189) is disabled. If you choose, you can change the warning level of a warning by using the warning level (1, 2, 3, or 4) as the specifier. One use for this is to lower the warning level just for a piece of code that you are working on and then return it to its default level after the code. For example:

```
#pragma warning(2: 4333)
unsigned shift8(unsigned char c)
{
    return c >> 8;
}
#pragma warning(default: 4333)
```

This function shifts a char right by 8 bits, which will generate the level-1 warning 4333 (*right shift by too large amount, data loss*). This is a problem and needs to be fixed, but for the time being, you want to compile the code without warnings from this code and so the warning level is changed to level 2. Using the default warning level (`/W1`) the warning will not be shown. However, if you compile with a more sensitive warning level (for example, `/W2`) then this warning will be reported. This change in the warning level is only temporary because the last line resets the warning level back to its default (which is 1). In this case, the warning level is increased, meaning that you will only see it with a more sensitive warning level on the compiler. You can also reduce the warning level, which means that the warning is more likely to be reported. You can even change a warning level to `error` so the code will not compile while warnings of this type exist in the code.

Adding informational messages

As you test and debug code you will inevitably come across places where you can see a potential problem but it has low priority compared to what you are working on. It is important to make a note of the issue so that you can address the problem at a later stage. In Visual C++, there are two ways to do this in a benign way and two ways that will generate an error.

The first way is to add a `TODO:` comment, shown as follows:

```
// TODO: potential data loss, review use of shift8 function
unsigned shift8(unsigned char c)
{
    return c >> 8;
}
```

The Visual Studio editor has a tool window called the **Task List**. This lists the comments in the project that start with one of the predetermined tasks (the defaults are TODO, HACK, and UNDONE).

If the Task List window is not visible, enable it via the **View** menu. The default setting in Visual Studio 2015 is to enable tasks in C++. This is not the case for earlier versions, but it can be enabled through the **Tools** menu, **Options** dialog and then **Text Editor, C/C++, Formatting, View** by setting **Enumerate Comment Tasks** to **Yes**. The list of task labels can be found on the **Options** dialog under the **Environment, Task List** item.

The **Task List** lists the tasks with the file and line number, and you can open the file and locate the comment by double-clicking on an entry.

The second way to identify code that needs attention is the message pragma. As the name suggests, this simply allows you to place an informational message in your code. When the compiler comes across this pragma it simply puts the message on the output stream. Consider the following code:

```
#pragma message("review use of shift8 function")
unsigned shift8(unsigned char c)
{
    return c >> 8;
}
```

If the test.cpp file is compiled with this code and /W1 (the default) warning level, the output will be something like this:

```
Microsoft (R) C/C++ Optimizing Compiler Version 19.00.24215.1 for x86
Copyright (C) Microsoft Corporation.  All rights reserved.

test.cpp
review the use of shift8 function
test.cpp(8): warning C4333: '>>': right shift by too large amount, data
loss
```

As you can see, the string is printed just as the compiler sees it, and there is no indication of the file or line number in contrast to the warning message. There are ways to address this using compiler symbols.

If the condition is important, you'll want to issue an error and one way to do this is with the `#error` directive. When the compiler reaches this directive, it will issue an error. This is a serious action, so you will only use it when there is another option. You'll most likely want to use it with a conditional compilation. A typical use is for code that can only be compiled with a C++ compiler:

```
#ifndef __cplusplus
#error C++ compiler required.
#endif
```

If you compile a file with this code using the `/Tc` switch to compile code as C then the `__cplusplus` preprocessor symbol will not be defined and an error will be generated.

C++11 adds a new directive called `static_assert`. This is called like a function (and *calls* are terminated with a semicolon), but it is not a function because it is only used at compile time. Further, the directive can be used in places where function calls are not used. The directive has two parameters: an expression and a string literal. If the expression is `false` then the string literal will be outputted at compile time with the source file and line number and an error will be generated. At the simplest level, you could use this to issue a message:

```
#ifndef __cplusplus
static_assert(false, "Compile with /TP");
#endif
#include <iostream> // needs the C++ compiler
```

Since the first parameter is `false`, the directive will issue the error message during compilation. The same thing could be achieved with the `#error` directive. The `<type_traits>` library has various predicates for testing the properties of types. For example, the `is_class` template class has a simple template parameter that is a type, and if the type is a `class` then the `static` member `value` is set to `true`. If you have a templated function that should only be instantiated for classes, you could add this `static_assert`:

```
#include <type_traits>

template <class T>
void func(T& value)
{
    static_assert(std::is_class<T>::value, "T must be a class");
    // other code
}
```

At compile time, the compiler will attempt to instantiate the function and instantiate `is_class` on that type using `value` to determine if the compilation should continue. For example, the following code:

```
func(string("hello"));
func("hello");
```

The first line will compile correctly because the compiler will instantiate a function, `func<string>`, and the parameter is a `class`. However, the second line will not compile because the function instantiated is `func<const char*>` and `const char*` is not a `class`. The output is:

```
Microsoft (R) C/C++ Optimizing Compiler Version 19.00.24215.1 for x86
Copyright (C) Microsoft Corporation.  All rights reserved.

test.cpp
test.cpp(25): error C2338: T must be a class
test.cpp(39): note: see reference to function template instantiation

'void func<const char*>(T)' being compiled
with
[
    T=const char *
]
```

The `static_assert` is on *line 25*, and hence this generates the error that `T must be a class`. *Line 39* is the first call to `func<const char*>` and gives context to the error.

Compiler switches for debugging

To allow you to single-step through a program with a debugger, you have to provide information to allow the debugger to associate machine code with source code. At the very least, this means switching off all optimizations, since in an attempt to optimize code the C++ compiler will rearrange code. Optimizations are switched off by default (so the using the `/Od` switch is redundant), but clearly, to be able to debug a process and single-step through C++ code you need to remove all the `/O` optimization switches.

Since the C++ Standard Library uses the C Runtime, you will need to compile your code to use the latter's debug builds. The switch you use depends on whether you are building a process or **Dynamic Link Library** (**DLL**), and whether you will statically link the C runtime or access it through a DLL. If you are compiling a process, you use /MDd to get the debug version of the C runtime in a DLL, and if you use /MTd you will get the debug version of the static linked C runtime. If you are writing a dynamic linked library, you have to use /LDd in addition to one of the C runtime switches (/MTd is the default). These switches will define a pre-processor symbol called _DEBUG.

A debugger will need to know debugger symbolic information--the names and types of variables and the names of functions and line numbers associated with code. The accepted way to do this is through a file called a **program database**, with an extension of pdb. You use one of the /Z switches to generate a pdb file: the /Zi or /ZI switch will create two files, one with a name starting with VC (for example VC140.pdb) that contains the debugging information for all of the obj files, and a file with the name of the project that contains debugging for the process. If you compile without linking (/c) then only the first file is created. The Visual C++ project wizard will use /Od /MDd /ZI by default for debug builds. The /ZI switch means that a program database is created in a format that allows the Visual C++ debugger to perform Edit and Continue, that is, you can change some code and continue to single-step through the code without recompiling. When you compile for a release build, the wizard will use the /O2 /MD /Zi switches, which means that the code is optimized for speed but a program database (without Edit and Continue support) will still be created. The code does not need the program database to run (in fact, you should not distribute it with your code), but it is useful if you have a crash report and need to run the release build code under the debugger.

These /Z compiler switches assume the linker is run with the /debug switch (and if the compiler invokes the linker it will pass this switch). The linker will create the project program database from the debug information in the VC program database file.

This raises the question of why a release build file will need a program database. If you run a program under the debugger and look at the call stack, you will often see a long list of stack frames in operating system files. These usually have fairly meaningless names made up of the DLL name and some numbers and characters. It is possible to install the symbols (the pdb files) for Windows or, if they are not installed, instruct the Visual C++ debugger to download the symbols for a library being used from a computer on the network called a **symbol server**. These symbols are not the source code for the library, but they do give you the names of the functions and the types of the parameters, which gives you additional information about the state of the call stack at the point where you are single stepping.

Pre-processor symbols

To get access to the tracing, asserts, and reporting facilities in your code, you have to enable the debugging runtime library, and this is done by using the /MDd, /MTd, or /LDd compiler switches, which will define the _DEBUG pre-processor symbol. The _DEBUG pre-processor symbol enables a lot of facilities, and conversely, not defining this symbol will help in optimizing your code.

```
#ifdef _DEBUG
    cout << "debug build" << endl;
#else
    cout << "release built" << endl;
#endif
```

The C++ compiler will also provide information through some standard pre-processor symbols. Most of these are useful only for library writers, but there are some that you may want to use.

The ANSI standard says that the __cplusplus symbol should be defined when the compiler is compiling code as C++ (rather than C), and it also specifies that the __FILE__ symbol should contain the name of the file and that __LINE__ symbol will have the line number at the point where you access it. The __func__ symbol will have the current function name. This means that you can create tracing code like the following:

```
#ifdef _DEBUG
#define TRACE cout << __func__ << " (" << __LINE__ << ")" << endl;
#else
#define TRACE
#endif
```

If this code is compiled for debugging (for example, /MTd) then the cout line will be put inline whenever TRACE is used; if the code is not compiled for debugging then TRACE will do nothing. The __func__ symbol is simply the function name, it is not qualified, so if you use it in a class method it will provide no information about the class.

Visual C++ also defines Microsoft-specific symbols. The __FUNCSIG__ symbol gives the complete signature including the class name (and any namespace names), the return type, and parameters. If you just want the fully qualified name, then you can use the __FUNCTION__ symbol. A symbol that you will see frequently in the Windows header files is _MSC_VER. This has a number that is the version of the current C++ compiler, and it is used with a conditional compilation so that newer language features are only compiled with a compiler that supports them.

The Visual C++ project pages define *build macros* with names like $ (ProjectDir) and $ (Configuration). These are used only by the MSBuild tool so they are not automatically available in a source file during compilation, however, if you set a pre-processor symbol to the value of a build macro, the value will be available through that symbol at compile time. The system environment variables are also available as build macros, so it is possible to use them to influence the build. For example, on Windows the system environment variable USERNAME has the name of the current logged on user so you could use it to set a symbol and then access that at compile time.

In the Visual C++ project pages, you can add a **Preprocessor Definition** on the **C/C++** preprocessor project page called:

```
DEVELOPER="$(USERNAME)"
```

Then, in your code, you could add a line using this symbol:

```
cout << "Compiled by " << DEVELOPER << endl;
```

If you are using a make file, or just invoking cl from the command line, you can add a switch to define the symbol like this:

```
/DDEVELOPER="$(USERNAME)"
```

Escaping the double quotes here is important because without them the quotes are eaten by the compiler.

Earlier, you saw how the #pragma message and #error directives can be used to put messages into the output stream of the compiler. When you compile code in Visual Studio the compiler and linker outputs will appear in the output window. If the message is in the form:

```
path_to_source_file(line) message
```

where path_to_source_file is the full path to the file, line is the line number where the message appears. Then, when you double click on this line in the output window, the file will be loaded (if not already) and the insertion point placed on the line.

The __FILE__ and __LINE__ symbols provide you with the information that you need to make #pragma message and #error directives more useful. Outputting __FILE__ is simple because it is a string and C++ will concatenate string literals:

```
#define AT_FILE(msg) __FILE__ " " msg

#pragma message(AT_FILE("this is a message"))
```

The macro is called as part of the pragma to format the message correctly; however, you cannot call the pragma from a macro because the # has a special purpose (that will be of use in a moment). The result of this code will be something like:

```
c:\Beginning_C++Chapter_10test.cpp this is a message
```

Outputting __LINE__ via a macro requires a bit more work because it holds a number. This issue is a common one in C, so there is a standard solution using two macros and the stringing operator, #.

```
#define STRING2(x) #x
#define STRING(x) STRING2(x)
#define AT_FILE(msg) __FILE__ "(" STRING(__LINE__) ") " msg
```

The STRING macro is used to expand the __LINE__ symbol to a number and the STRING2 macro to stringify the number. The AT_FILE macro formats the entire string in the correct format.

Producing diagnostic messages

The effective use of diagnostic messages is a broad topic, so this section will just give you the basics. When you design your code, you should make it easy to write diagnostic messages, for example, providing mechanisms to dump the contents of an object and providing access to the code that tests for class invariants and pre- and post-conditions. You should also analyze the code to make sure that appropriate messages are logged. For example, issuing a diagnostic message in a loop will often fill up your log files, making it difficult to read the other messages in the log file. However, the fact that something is consistently failing in a loop may in itself be an important diagnostic, as may be the number of attempts to carry out a failing act, so you may want to record that.

Using cout for diagnostic messages has the advantage of integrating these messages with your user output, so that you can see the final effects of the intermediate results. The disadvantage is that the diagnostic messages are integrated with the user output, and since there are usually a large number of diagnostic messages, these will completely swamp the user output of your program.

C++ has two stream objects that you can use instead of `cout`. The `clog` and `cerr` stream objects will write character data to the standard error stream (the C stream pointer `stderr`), which will usually show on the console as if you are using `cout` (which outputs to the standard output stream, the C stream pointer `stdout`), but you can redirect it elsewhere. The difference between `clog` and `cerr` is that `clog` uses buffered output, which is potentially better-performing than the unbuffered `cerr`. However, there is the danger that the data may be lost if the application stops unexpectedly without flushing the buffer.

Since the `clog` and `cerr` stream objects are available in release builds as well as debug builds, you should use them only for messages that you are happy that your end user will see. This makes them inappropriate for trace messages (which will be covered shortly). Instead, you should use them for diagnostic messages that the user will be in a position to address (perhaps a file cannot be found or the process does not have the security access to perform an action).

```
ofstream file;
if (!file.open(argv[1], ios::out))
{
    clog << "cannot open " << argv[1] << endl;
    return 1;
}
```

This code opens a file in two steps (rather than using the constructor) and the `open` method will return `false` if the file cannot be opened. The code checks to see if opening the file was successful, and if it fails, it will tell the user via the `clog` object and then return from whatever function contains the code, as the `file` object is now invalid and cannot be used. The `clog` object is buffered but in this case we want to inform the user immediately, and this is performed by the `endl` manipulator, which inserts a newline in the stream and then flushes the stream.

By default, the `clog` and `cerr` stream objects will output to the standard error stream and this means that for a console application you can separate out the output stream and error stream by redirecting the streams. On the command-line, the standard streams can be redirected by using a value of 0 for `stdin`, 1 for `stdout`, and 2 for `stderr` and the redirection operator >. For example, an application `app.exe` could have this code in the `main` function:

```
clog << "clog" << endl;
cerr << "cerrn";
cout << "cout" << endl;
```

The `cerr` object is not buffered so whether you use n or `endl` for a newline is irrelevant. When you run this on the command line, you'll see something like this:

```
C:\Beginning_C++\Chapter_10>app
clog
cerr
cout
```

To redirect a stream to a file, redirect the stream handle (1 for `stdout`, 2 for `stderr`) to the file; the console will open the file and write the stream to the file:

```
C:\Beginning_C++\Chapter_10>app 2>log.txt
cout

C:\Beginning_C++\Chapter_10>type log.txt
clog
cerr
```

As the last chapter showed, C++ stream objects are layered so that calls to insert data into a stream will write the data to the underlying stream object, depending on the type of stream, with or without buffering. This stream buffer object is obtained, and replaced, using the `rdbuf` method. If you want the `clog` object redirected to a file by the application, you can write code like the following:

```
extern void run_code();

int main()
{
    ofstream log_file;
    if (log_file.open("log.txt")) clog.rdbuf(log_file.rdbuf());

    run_code();

    clog.flush();
    log_file.close();
    clog.rdbuf(nullptr);
    return 0;
}
```

In this code the application code will be in the `run_code` function, and the rest of the code sets up the `clog` object to redirect to files.

Note that the file is explicitly closed when the run_code function returns (the application has finished); this is not entirely necessarily because the ofstream destructor will close the file, and in this case this will happen when the main function returns. The last line is important. The standard stream objects are created before the main function is called, and they will be destroyed sometime after the main function returns, that is, well after the file objects have been destroyed. To prevent the clog object accessing the destroyed file object, the rdbuf method is called passing nullptr to indicate that there is no buffer.

Trace messages with the C runtime

Often you will want to test your code by running the application in real time and output the *trace messages* to test that your algorithms work. Sometimes you will want to test the order that functions are called (for example, that correct branching occurs in a switch statement or in an if statement), and in other cases you'll want to test intermediate values to see that the input data is correct and the calculations on that data are correct.

Trace messages can produce a lot of data, so it is unwise to send these to the console. It is extremely important that trace messages are only produced in debug builds. If you leave trace messages in product code, it could seriously impact the performance of your application (as will be explained later). Further, trace messages are unlikely to be localized, nor will they be checked to see if they contain information that could be used to reverse-engineer your algorithms. One final issue with trace messages in release builds is that your client will think that you are providing them with code that has not been completely tested. It is important, then, that trace messages are only generated in debug builds, when the _DEBUG symbol is defined.

The C Runtime provides a series of macros with names starting with _RPT that can be used to trace messages when _DEBUG is defined. There are char and wide char versions of these macros, and there are versions that will report just the trace messages and others that will report the message and the location (source file and line number) of the message. Ultimately these macros will call a function called _CrtDbgReport that will generate the message with the settings that have been determined elsewhere.

The _RPTn macros (where n is 0, 1, 2, 3, 4, or 5) will take a format string and 0 to 5 parameters that will be put into the string before being reported. The first parameter of the macros indicates the type of message to report: _CRT_WARN, _CRT_ERROR, or _CRT_ASSERT. The last two of these categories are the same and refer to asserts, which will be covered in a later section. The second parameter of the report macros is a format string, which will then be followed by the required number of parameters. The _RPTFn macros are the same format but will report the source file and line number as well as the formatted message.

The default action is that _CRT_WARN messages will produce no output and the _CRT_ERROR and _CRT_ASSERT messages will generate a popup window to allow you to abort or debug the application. You can change the response to any of these message categories by calling the _CrtSetReportMode function and providing the category and a value indicating the action to take. If you use _CRTDBG_MODE_DEBUG then the message will be written to the debugger output window. If you use _CRTDBG_MODE_FILE then the message will be written to a file that you can open and pass the handle to the _CrtSetReportFile function. (You can also use _CRTDBG_FILE_STDERR or _CRTDBG_FILE_STDOUT as the file handle to send the message to the standard output or the error output.) If you use _CRTDBG_MODE_WNDW as the report mode then the message will be displayed using the **Abort/Retry/Ignore** dialog box. Since this will pause the current thread of execution, it should only be used for assert messages (the default action):

```
include <crtdbg.h>

extern void run_code();

int main()
{
    _CrtSetReportMode(_CRT_WARN, _CRTDBG_MODE_DEBUG);
    _RPTF0(_CRT_WARN, "Application startedn");

    run_code();

    _RPTF0(_CRT_WARN, "Application endedn");
    return 0;
}
```

If you do not provide the n in the messages then the next message will be appended to the end of your message, and in most cases this is not what you want (although you could justify this for a series of calls to the _RPTn macros, where the last one is terminated with n).

The Visual Studio output window is shown when you compile a project (to show it at debug time select the **Output** option in the **View** menu), and at the top is a combo box labelled **Show output from**, which will be usually set to **Build**. If you set this to **Debug** then you will see the debugging messages generated during a debugging session. These will include messages about loading debugging symbols and messages redirected from the _RPTn macros to the output window.

If you prefer the messages to be directed to a file then you need to open the file with the Win32 `CreateFile` function and use the handle from that function in a call to the `_CrtSetReportFile` function. To do this, you will need to include the Windows header files:

```
#define WIN32_LEAN_AND_MEAN
#include <Windows.h>
#include <crtdbg.h>
```

The `WIN32_LEAN_AND_MEAN` macro will reduce the size of the Windows files included.

```
HANDLE file =
    CreateFileA("log.txt", GENERIC_WRITE, 0, 0, CREATE_ALWAYS, 0, 0);
_CrtSetReportMode(_CRT_WARN, _CRTDBG_MODE_FILE);
_CrtSetReportFile(_CRT_WARN, file);
_RPTF0(_CRT_WARN, "Application startedn");

run_code();

_RPTF0(_CRT_WARN, "Application endedn");
CloseHandle(file);
```

This code will direct the warning messages to the text file `log.txt` which will be created new every time the application is run.

Tracing messages with Windows

The `OutputDebugString` function is used to send messages to a debugger. The function does this through a *shared memory section* called `DBWIN_BUFFER`. Shared memory means that any process can access this memory, and so Windows provides two *event objects* called `DBWIN_BUFFER_READY` and `DBWIN_DATA_READY` that control read and write access to this memory. These event objects are shared between processes and can be in a signalled or unsignalled state. A debugger will indicate that it is no longer using the shared memory by signalling the `DBWIN_BUFFER_READY` event, at which point the `OutputDebugString` function can write the data to the shared memory. The debugger will wait on the `DBWIN_DATA_READY` event, which will be signalled by the `OutputDebugString` function when it has finished writing to the memory and it is safe to read the buffer. The data written to the memory section will be the process ID of the process that called the `OutputDebugString` function, followed by a string of up to 4 KB of data.

The problem is that when you call the OutputDebugString function it will wait on the DBWIN_BUFFER_READY event, which means that when you use this function you are coupling the performance of your application to the performance of another process, which is usually a debugger (but may not be). It is very easy to write a process to access the DBWIN_BUFFER shared memory section and get access to the associated event objects, so it may be possible that your production code will run on a machine where someone has such an application running. For this reason, it is vitally important that you use conditional compilation so that the OutputDebugString function is only used in debug builds--code that will never be released to your customers:

```
extern void run_code();

int main()
{
    #ifdef _DEBUG
        OutputDebugStringA("Application startedn");
    #endif

    run_code();

    #ifdef _DEBUG
        OutputDebugStringA("Application endedn");
    #endif
    return 0;
}
```

You will need to include the windows.h header file to compile this code. As for the _RPT example, you will have to run this code under a debugger to see the output, or have an application like **DebugView** (available from Microsoft's Technet website) running.

Windows provides the DBWinMutex mutex object to act as an overall *key* to accessing this shared memory and event objects. As the name suggests, when you have a handle to a mutex you will have mutually exclusive access to the resource. The problem is that processes do not have to have a handle to this mutex to use these resources and consequently you have no guarantee that, if your application thinks it has exclusive access that it will really have exclusive access.

Using asserts

An assert checks that a condition is true. The assertion means just that: the program should not continue if the condition is not true. Clearly asserts should not be called in release code and hence conditional compilation must be used. Asserts should be used to check for conditions that should never happen: never events. Since the conditions do not happen there should be no need for asserts in release builds.

The C Runtime provides the `assert` macro that is available through the `<cassert>` header file. The macro, and any functions called in the expression passed as its only parameter, will be called unless the NDEBUG symbol is defined. That is, you do not have to define the _DEBUG symbol to use asserts and you should have taken extra action to explicitly prevent `assert` from being called.

It is worth re-iterating this. The `assert` macro is defined even if _DEBUG is not defined, so an assert could be called in release code. To prevent this from happening you must define the NDEBUG symbol in a release build. Conversely, you can define the NDEBUG symbol in a debug build so that you can use tracing but do not have to use asserting.

Typically, you will use asserts in debug builds to check that pre- and post-conditions are met in a function and that class invariant conditions are fulfilled. For example, you may have a binary buffer that has a special value at the tenth byte position and so have written a function to extract that byte:

```
const int MAGIC=9;

char get_data(char *p, size_t size)
{
    assert((p != nullptr));
    assert((size >= MAGIC));
    return p[MAGIC];
}
```

Here, the calls to `assert` are used to check that the pointer is not `nullptr` and that the buffer is big enough. If these asserts are true, then it means that it is safe to access the tenth byte through the pointer.

Although it is not strictly necessary in this code, the assertion expressions are given in parentheses. It is good to get into the habit of doing this because `assert` is a macro and so a comma in the expression will be treated as a macro parameter separator; the parentheses protected against this.

Since the `assert` macro will be defined in release builds by default, you will have to disable them by defining `NDEBUG` on the compiler command line, in your make file, or you may want to use conditional compilation explicitly:

```
#ifndef _DEBUG
#define NDEBUG
#endif
```

If an assert is called and it fails, then an assert message is printed at the console along with source file and line number information and then the process is terminated with a call to `abort`. If the process is built with release build standard libraries then the process `abort` is straightforward, however, if the debug builds are used then the user will see the standard **Abort/Retry/Ignore** message box where the **Abort** and **Ignore** options abort the process. The **Retry** option will use **Just-in-Time** (**JIT**) debugging to attach the registered debugger to the process.

In contrast, the `_ASSERT` and `_ASSERTE` macros are only defined when `_DEBUG` is defined, so these macros will not be available in release builds. Both macros take an expression and generate an assert message when the expression is `false`. The message for the `_ASSERT` macro will include the source file and line number and a message stating that the assertion failed. The message for the `_ASSERTE` macro is similar but includes the expression that failed.

```
_CrtSetReportMode(_CRT_ASSERT, _CRTDBG_MODE_FILE);
_CrtSetReportFile(_CRT_ASSERT, _CRTDBG_FILE_STDOUT);

int i = 99;
_ASSERTE((i > 100));
```

This code sets the reporting mode so that the failed assert will be a message printed on the console (rather than the default, which is the **Abort/Retry/Ignore** dialog). Since the variable is clearly less than 100, the assert will fail and so the process will terminate and the following message will be printed on the console:

```
test.cpp(23) : Assertion failed: (i > 100)
```

The **Abort/Retry/Ignore** dialog gives the person, testing the application, the option of attaching the debugger to the process. If you decide that the failure of the assertion is heinous you can force the debugger to attach to the process by calling `_CrtDbgBreak`.

```
int i = 99;
if (i <= 100) _CrtDbgBreak();
```

You do not need to use conditional compilation because in release builds the `_CrtDbgBreak` function is a no-operation. In a debug build, this code will trigger JIT debugging, which gives you the option to close the application or launch the debugger, and if you choose the latter, the registered JIT debugger will be started.

Application termination

The `main` function is the entry point for your application. However, this isn't called directly by the operating system because C++ will perform initialization before `main` is called. This includes constructing the Standard Library global objects (`cin`, `cout`, `cerr`, `clog`, and the wide character versions) and there is a whole host of initialization that is performed for the C Runtime Library that underpins C++ libraries. Further, there are the global and static objects that your code creates. When the `main` function returns, the destructors of global and static objects will have to be called and a clean-up performed on the C runtime.

There are several ways to stop a process deliberately. The simplest is to return from the `main` function, but this assumes that there is a simple route back to the `main` function from the point that your code wants to finish the process. Of course, process termination must be ordered and you should avoid writing code where it is normal to stop the process anywhere in the code. However, if you have a situation where data is corrupted and unrecoverable and any other action could damage more data, you may have no option other than to terminate the application.

The `<cstdlib>` header file provides access to the header files to the functions that allow you to terminate and to handle the termination of an application. When a C++ program closes down normally, the C++ infrastructure will call the destructors of the objects created in the `main` function (in the reverse order to their construction) and the destructors of `static` objects (which may have been created in functions other than the `main` function). The `atexit` function allows you to register functions (that have no parameters and no return value) that will be called after the `main` function completes and `static` object destructors have been called. You can register more than one function by calling this function several times, and at termination the functions will be called in reverse order to their registering. After the functions registered with the `atexit` function have been called, the destructors of any global objects will be called.

There is also a Microsoft function called `_onexit` that also allows you to register functions to be called during normal termination.

The `exit` and `_exit` functions perform a normal exit of a process, that is, they clean up the C runtime and flush any open files before shutting down the process. The `exit` function does additional work by calling any registered termination functions; the `_exit` function does not call these termination functions and so is a quick exit. These functions will not call the destructors of temporary or automatic objects, so if you use stack objects to manage resources, you will have to explicitly call the destructor code before calling `exit`. However, the destructors of static and global objects will be called.

The `quick_exit` function causes normal shutdown, but it does not call any destructors nor flush any streams, so there is no resource clean up. The functions registered with `atexit` are not called, but you can register that termination functions are called by registering them with the `at_quick_exit` function. After calling these termination functions, the `quick_exit` function calls the `_Exit` function that shuts down the process.

You can also call the `terminate` function to close down a process with no clean up. This process will call a function that has been registered with the `set_terminate` function and then calls the `abort` function. If an exception occurs in the program and is not caught--and hence propagates to the `main` function - the C++ infrastructure will call the `terminate` function. The `abort` function is the most severe of mechanisms that terminate a process. This function will exit the process without calling the destructors of objects or performing any other clean up. The function raises the `SIGABORT` signal and so it is possible to register a function with the `signal` function, which will be called before the process terminates.

Error values

Some functions are designed to perform an action and return a value based on that action, for example, `sqrt` will return the square root of a number. Other functions perform more complex operations and use the return value to indicate whether the function was successful. There is no common convention about such error values, so if a function returns a simple integer there is no guarantee that the values one library uses have the same meaning as values returned from functions in another library. This means that you have to examine carefully the documentation for any library code that you use.

Windows does provide common error values, which can be found in the `winerror.h` header file, and the functions in the Windows **Software Development Kit (SDK)** only return values in this file. If you write library code that will be used exclusively in Windows applications, consider using the error values in this file because you can use the Win32 `FormatMessage` function to obtain a description of the error, as explained in the next section.

The C Runtime Library provides a global variable called errno (in fact it is a macro that you can treat as a variable). C functions will return a value to indicate that they have failed and you access the errno value to determine what the error was. The <errno.h> header file defines the standard POSIX error values. The errno variable does not indicate success, it only indicates errors, so you should only access it when a function has indicated that there is an error. The strerror function will return a C string with a description of the error value that you pass as a parameter; these messages are localized according to the current C locale set through a call to the setlocale function.

Obtaining message descriptions

To obtain the description at runtime for a Win32 error code you use the Win32 FormatMessage function. This will get the description for a system message or for a custom message (described in the next section). If you want to use a custom message you have to load the executable (or DLL) that has the message resource bound to it and pass the HMODULE handle to the FormatMessage function. If you want to get the description of a system message you do not need to load a module because Windows will do this for you. For example, if you call the Win32 CreateFile function to open a file and the file cannot be found, the function will return a value of INVALID_HANDLE_VALUE, indicating that there is an error. To get details of the error you call the GetLastError function (which returns a 32-bit unsigned value sometimes called DWORD or HRESULT). You can then pass the error value to FormatMessage:

```
HANDLE file = CreateFileA(
    "does_not_exist", GENERIC_READ, 0, 0, OPEN_EXISTING, 0, 0);
if (INVALID_HANDLE_VALUE == file)
{
    DWORD err = GetLastError();
    char *str;
    DWORD ret = FormatMessageA(
        FORMAT_MESSAGE_FROM_SYSTEM|FORMAT_MESSAGE_ALLOCATE_BUFFER,
        0, err, LANG_USER_DEFAULT, reinterpret_cast<LPSTR>(&str),
        0, 0);
    cout << "Error: "<< str << endl;
    LocalFree(str);
}
else
{
    CloseHandle(file);
}
```

This code tries to open a file that does not exist and obtains the error value associated with the failure (this will be a value of ERROR_FILE_NOT_FOUND). The code then calls the FormatMessage function to get the string describing the error. The first parameter of the function is a flag that indicates how the function should work; in this case, the FORMAT_MESSAGE_FROM_SYSTEM flag says that the error is a system error and the FORMAT_MESSAGE_ALLOCATE_BUFFER flag says that the function should allocate a buffer large enough to hold the string using the Win32 LocalAlloc function.

 If the error is a custom value that you have defined then you should use the FORMAT_MESSAGE_FROM_HMODULE flag, open the file with LoadLibrary and use the resulting HMODULE as the parameter passed in through the second parameter.

The third parameter is the error message number (from GetLastError) and the fourth is a LANGID that indicates the language ID to use (in this case LANG_USER_DEFAULT to get the language ID for the current logged on user). The FormatMessage function will generate a formatted for the error value, and this string may have replacement parameters. The formatted string is returned in a buffer and you have two options: you can allocate a character buffer and pass the pointer in as the fifth and the length as the sixth parameter, or you can request the function to allocate a buffer using the LocalAlloc function as in this example. To get access to a function allocated buffer you pass the *address* of a pointer variable via the fifth parameter.

Note that the fifth parameter is used to either take a pointer to a user allocated buffer, or returns the address of system allocated buffer, and this is why in this case the pointer to pointer has to be cast.

Some format strings may have parameters, and if so, the values are passed in through an array in the seventh parameter (in this case, no array is passed). The result of the preceding code is the string:

Error: The system cannot find the file specified.

Using the message compiler, resource files, and the FormatMessage, you can provide a mechanism to return error values from your functions and then convert these to localized strings according to the current locale.

Using the Message Compiler

The previous example showed that you can obtain localized strings for Win32 errors, but that you can also create your own errors and provide localized strings that are bound as resources to your process or library. If you intend to report errors to the end user, you have to make sure that the descriptions are localized. Windows provides a tool called the Message Compiler (`mc.exe`) that will take a text file with entries for messages in various languages and compile them into binary resources that can be bound to a module.

For example:

```
LanguageNames = (British = 0x0409:MSG00409)
LanguageNames = (French  = 0x040c:MSG0040C)

MessageId       = 1
SymbolicName    = IDS_GREETING
Language        = English
Hello
.
Language        = British
Good day
.
Language        = French
Salut
.
```

This defines three localized strings for the same message. The messages here are simple strings, but you can define format messages with placeholders that can be provided at runtime. The *neutral* language is US English, and in addition we define strings for British English, and French. The names used for the languages are defined in the `LanguageNames` lines at the top of the file. These entries have the name that will be used later in the file, the code page for the language, and the name of the binary resource that will contain the message resource.

The `MessageId` is the identifier that will be used by the `FormatMessage` function, and the `SymbolicName` is a pre-processor symbol that will be defined in a header file, so that you can use this message in your C++ code rather than the number. This file is compiled by passing it to the command line utility `mc.exe`, which will create five files: a header file with the definition of the symbol, three binary sources (`MSG00001.bin`, which is created by default for the neutral language, and `MSG00409.bin` and `MSG0040C.bin`, which are created because of the `LanguageNames` lines), and a resource compiler file. For this example, the resource compiler file (with extension `.rc`) will contain:

```
LANGUAGE 0xc,0x1
```

```
1 11 "MSG0040C.bin"
LANGUAGE 0x9,0x1
1 11 "MSG00001.bin"
LANGUAGE 0x9,0x1
1 11 "MSG00409.bin"
```

This is a standard resource file that can be compiled by the Windows SDK resource compiler (`rc.exe`), which will compile the message resources into a `.res` file that can be bound to an executable or DLL. A process or DLL that has a resource of type `11` bound to it can be used by the `FormatMessage` function as a source of descriptive error strings.

Typically, you will not use a message ID of 1 because it is unlikely to be unique and you are likely to want to take advantage of the *facility code* and *severity code* (for details of facility code, look in the `winerror.h` header file). Further, to indicate that the message is not Windows you can set the customer bit of the error code using the `/c` switch when you run `mc.exe`. This will mean that your error code will not be a simple value like 1, but this should not matter because your code will use the symbol defined in the header file.

C++ exceptions

As the name suggests, exceptions are for exceptional conditions. They are not normal conditions. They are not conditions that you want to occur but they are conditions that may happen. Any exceptional condition will often mean that your data will be in an inconsistent state, so using exceptions means that you need to think in transactional terms, that is, an operation either succeeds, or the state of an object should remain the same as it was before the operation was attempted. When an exception occurs in a code block, everything that happened in the code block will be invalid. If the code block is part of a wider code block (say, a function that is a series of function calls by another function) then the work in that other code block will be invalid. This means that the exception may propagate out to other code blocks further up the call stack, invalidating the objects that depend on the operation being successful. At some point, the exceptional condition will be recoverable, so you will want to prevent the exception going further.

Exception specifications

Exception specifications are deprecated in C++11 but you may see them in earlier code. A specification is through the `throw` expression applied to a function declaration giving the exceptions that can be thrown from the function. The `throw` specification can be an ellipsis, which means that the function can throw exceptions but the type is not specified. If the specification is empty then it means the function won't throw exceptions, and this is the same as using the `noexcept` specifier in C++11.

The `noexcept` specifier tells the compiler that exception handling is not required, so if an exception does occur in the function the exception will not be bubbled out of the function and the `terminate` function will be called immediately. In this situation, there is no guarantee that the destructors of the automatic objects are called.

C++ exception syntax

In C++, an exceptional situation is generated by throwing an exception object. That exception object can be anything you like: an object, a pointer, or a built-in type, but because exceptions may be handled by code written by other people it is best to standardize the objects that are used to represent exceptions. For this, the Standard Library provides the `exception` class, which can be used as a base class.

```
double reciprocal(double d)
{
    if (d == 0)
    {
        // throw 0;
        // throw "divide by zero";
        // throw new exception("divide by zero");
        throw exception("divide by zero");
    }
    return 1.0 / d;
}
```

This code tests the parameter and if it is zero then it throws an exception. Four examples are given and all are valid C++, but only the last version is acceptable because it uses a Standard Library class (or one derived from the Standard Library classes) and it follows the convention that exceptions are thrown by value.

When an exception is thrown, the exception handling infrastructure takes over. Execution will stop in the current code block and the exception will be propagated up the call stack. As the exception propagates through a code block, all the automatic objects will be destroyed, but objects created on the heap in the code black will not be destroyed. This is a process called **stack unwinding,** whereby each stack frame is cleaned up as much as possible before the exception moves to the stack frame above it in the call stack. If the exception is not caught, it will propagate up to the main function, at which point the terminate function will be called to handle the exception (and hence it will terminate the process).

You can protect code to handle propagated exceptions. Code is protected with a try block and it is caught with an associated catch block:

```
try
{
    string s("this is an object");
    vector<int> v = { 1, 0, -1};
    reciprocal(v[0]);
    reciprocal(v[1]);
    reciprocal(v[2]);
}
catch(exception& e)
{
    cout << e.what() << endl;
}
```

Unlike other code blocks in C++, braces are mandatory even if the try and catch blocks contain single lines of code. In the preceding code the second call to the reciprocal function will throw an exception. The exception will halt the execution of any more code in the block, so the third call to the reciprocal function will not occur. Instead, the exception propagates out of the code block. The try block is the scope of the objects defined between the braces, and this means that the destructors of these objects will be called (s and v). Control is then passed to the associated catch blocks, and in this case, there is just one handler. The catch block is a separate block to the try block, so you cannot access any variables defined in the try block. This makes sense because when an exception is generated the entire code block is *tainted* so you cannot trust any object created in that block. This code uses the accepted convention, that is, exceptions are caught by reference, so that the actual exception object, and not a copy, is caught.

The convention is: throw my value, catch-by-reference.

The Standard Library provides a function called `uncaught_exception`, which returns `true` if an exception has been thrown but not yet handled. It may seem odd to be able to test for this since no code other than the exception infrastructure will be called when an exception has occurred (for example the `catch` handlers) and you should put exception code there. However, there *is* other code that is called when an exception is thrown: the destructors of automatic objects that are destroyed during the stack clear up. The `uncaught_exception` function should be used in a destructor to determine if the object is being destroyed due to an exception rather than normal object destruction due to an object going out of scope or being deleted. For example:

```
class test
{
    string str;
public:
    test() : str("") {}
    test(const string& s) : str(s) {}
    ~test()
    {
        cout << boolalpha << str << " uncaught exception = "
         << uncaught_exception() << endl;
    }
};
```

This simple object indicates if it is being destroyed because of exception stack unwinding. It can be tested like this:

```
void f(bool b)
{
    test t("auto f");
    cout << (b ? "f throwing exception" : "f running fine")
        << endl;
    if (b) throw exception("f failed");
}

int main()
{
    test t1("auto main");
    try
    {
        test t2("in try in main");
        f(false);
        f(true);
        cout << "this will never be printed";
    }
    catch (exception& e)
    {
```

```
        cout << e.what() << endl;
    }
    return 0;
}
```

The `f` function will throw an exception only if it is called with a `true` value. The `main` function calls `f` twice, once with a value of `false` (so the exception is not thrown in `f`) and a second time with `true`. The output is:

```
f running fine
auto f uncaught exception = false
f throwing exception
auto f uncaught exception = true
in try in main uncaught exception = true
f failed
auto main uncaught exception = false
```

The first-time `f` is called, the `test` object is destroyed normally, so `uncaught_exception` will return `false`. The second-time `f` is called the `test` object in the function is being destroyed before the exception has been caught, so `uncaught_exception` will return `true`. Since an exception is thrown, the execution leaves the `try` block and so the `test` object in the `try` block is destroyed and `uncaught_exception` will return `true`. Finally, when the exception has been handled and control returns to code after the `catch` block, the `test` object created on the stack in the `main` function will be destroyed when the `main` function returns and so `uncaught_exception` will return `false`.

Standard exception classes

The `exception` class is a simple container for a C string: the string is passed as a constructor parameter and is available through the `what` accessor. The Standard Library declares the exception class in the `<exception>` library, and you are encouraged to derive your own exception classes from this. The Standard Library provides the following derived classes; most are defined in `<stdexcept>`.

Class	Thrown
`bad_alloc`	When the `new` operator has been unable to allocate memory (in `<new>`)
`bad_array_new_length`	When the `new` operator has been asked to create an array with an invalid length (in `<new>`)
`bad_cast`	When `dynamic_cast` to a reference type fails (in `<typeinfo>`)

bad_exception	An unexpected condition has occurred (in <exception>)
bad_function_call	Invoked an empty function object (in <functional>)
bad_typeid	When the argument of typeid is null (in <typeinfo>)
bad_weak_ptr	When accessing a weak pointer, which refers to an already destroyed object (in <memory>)
domain_error	When an attempt is made to perform an operation outside the domain on which the operation is defined
invalid_argument	When an invalid value has been used for a parameter
length_error	When an attempt has been made to exceed the length defined for an object
logic_error	When there is a logic error, for example, class invariants or pre-conditions
out_of_range	When an attempt has been made to access elements outside of the range defined for the object
overflow_error	When a calculation results in a value bigger than the destination type
range_error	When a calculation results in a value outside the range for the type
runtime_error	When an error occurs outside the scope of the code
system_error	Base class to wrap operating system errors (in <system_error>)
underflow_error	When a calculation results in an underflow

All the classes, mentioned in the preceding table, have a constructor that takes a const char* or a const string& parameter, in contrast to the exception class that takes a C string (hence the base class is constructed using the c_str method if the description is passed through a string object). There are no wide character versions, so if you want to construct an exception description from a wide character string you have to convert it. Also, note that the standard exception classes only have one constructor parameter, and this is available through the inherited what accessor.

There is no absolute rule about the data that an exception can hold. You can derive a class from exception and construct it with whatever values you want to make available to the exception handler.

Catching exceptions by type

There can be more than one catch block with each try block, which means that you can tailor the exception handling according to the exception type. The types of the parameters in the catch clauses will be tested against the type of the exception in the order that they are declared. The exception will be handled by the first handler that matches the exception type, or is a base class. This highlights the convention to catch the exception object via a reference. If you catch as a base class object a copy will be made, slicing the derived class object. In many cases code, will throw objects of a type derived from the exception class so it means that a catch handler for exception will catch all exceptions.

Since code can throw any object, it is possible that an exception will propagate out of the handler. C++ allows you to catch everything by using an ellipses in the catch clause. Clearly, you should order the catch handlers from the most derived to the least derived and (if you use it) with the ellipses handler at the end:

```
try
{
    call_code();
}
catch(invalid_argument& iva)
{
    cout << "invalid argument: " << e.what() << endl;
}
catch(exception& exc)
{
    cout << typeid(exc).name() << ": " << e.what() << endl;
}
catch(...)
{
    cout << "some other C++ exception" << endl;
}
```

If the guarded code does not throw an exception, then the catch blocks are not executed.

When your handler examines the exception, it may decide that it does not want to suppress the exception; this is called rethrowing the exception. To do this, you can use the `throw` statement without an operand (this is only allowed in a `catch` handler), which will rethrow the actual exception object that was caught, and not a copy.

Exceptions are thread-based and so it is difficult to propagate an exception to another thread. The `exception_ptr` class (in <exception>) provides shared ownership semantics for an exception object of any type. You can get a shared copy of an exception object by calling the `make_exception_ptr` object, or you can even get a shared copy of the exception being handled in a `catch` block using `current_exception`. Both functions return an `exception_ptr` object. An `exception_ptr` object can hold an exception of any kind, not just those derived from the `exception` class, so getting information from the wrapped exception is specific to the exception type. The `exception_ptr` object knows nothing about these details, so instead you can pass it to `rethrow_exception` in the context where you want to use the shared exception (another thread) and then catch the appropriate exception object. In the following code, there are two threads running. The `first_thread` function runs on one thread and the `second_thread` function on the other:

```
exception_ptr eptr = nullptr;

void first_thread()
{
    try
    {
        call_code();
    }
    catch (...)
    {
        eptr = current_exception();
    }
    // some signalling mechanism ...
}

void second_thread()
{
    // other code

    // ... some signalling mechanism
    if (eptr != nullptr)
    {
        try
        {
            rethrow_exception(eptr);
        }
        catch(my_exception& e)
```

```
        {
            // process this exception
        }
        eptr = nullptr;
    }
    // other code
}
```

The preceding code looks like it is using `exception_ptr` as a pointer. In fact, `eptr` is created as a global object and the assignment to `nullptr` uses the copy constructor to create an empty object (where the wrapped exception is `nullptr`). Similarly, the comparison with `nullptr` actually tests the wrapped exception.

This book is not about C++ threading, so we won't go into the details of the signalling between two threads. This code shows that a shared copy of an exception, *any exception*, can be stored in one context and then rethrown and processed in another context.

Function try blocks

You may decide that you want to protect an entire function with a `try` block, in which case you could write code like this:

```
void test(double d)
{
    try
    {
        cout << setw(10) << d << setw(10) << reciprocal(d) << endl;
    }

    catch (exception& e)
    {
        cout << "error: " << e.what() << endl;
    }
}
```

This uses the `reciprocal` function, as defined earlier, that will throw an `exception` if the parameter is zero. An alternative syntax for this is:

```
void test(double d)
try
{
    cout << setw(10) << d << setw(10) << reciprocal(d) << endl;
}
catch (exception& e)
{
    cout << "error: " << e.what() << endl;
}
```

This looks rather odd because the function prototype is followed immediately by the `try...catch` block and there is no outer set of braces. The function body is the code in the `try` block; when this code completes the function returns. If the function returns a value, it must do it in the `try` block. In most cases, you will find that this syntax makes your code less readable, but there is one situation where it may be useful--for initializer lists in constructors.

```
class inverse
{
    double recip;
public:
    inverse() = delete;
    inverse(double d) recip(reciprocal(d)) {}
    double get_recip() const { return recip; }
};
```

In this code, we wrap a `double` value that is simply the reciprocal of the parameter passed to the constructor. The data member is initialized by calling the `reciprocal` function in the initializer list. Since this is outside of the constructor body, an exception that occurs here will be passed straight to the code that calls the constructor. If you want to do some additional processing, then you could call the reciprocal function inside the constructor body:

```
inverse::inverse(double d)
{
    try { recip = reciprocal(d); }
    catch(exception& e) { cout << "invalid value " << d << endl; }
}
```

It is important to note that the exception will be automatically rethrown because any exception in a constructor means that the object is invalid. However, this does allow you to do some additional processing, if necessary. This solution will not work for exceptions thrown in a base object constructor because, although you can call a base constructor in the derived constructor body, the compiler will call the default constructor automatically. If you want the compiler to call a constructor other than the default constructor you have to call it in the initializer list. An alternative syntax to providing exception code in the `inverse` constructor is to use function `try` blocks:

```
inverse::inverse(double d)
try
    : recip (reciprocal(d)) {}
catch(exception& e) { cout << "invalid value " << d << endl; }
```

This looks a little cluttered, but the constructor body is still after the initializer list giving an initial value to the `recip` data member. Any exception from the call to `reciprocal` will be caught and automatically rethrown after processing. The initializer list can contain calls to the base class and any of the data members and all will be protected with the `try` block.

System errors

The `<system_error>` library defines a series of classes to encapsulate system errors. The `error_category` class provides a mechanism to convert numeric error values into localized descriptive strings. Two objects are available through the `generic_category` and `system_category` functions in `<system_error>`, and `<ios>` has a function called `isostream_category`; all of these functions return an `error_category` object. The `error_category` class has a method called `message` that returns a string description of the error number you pass as the parameter. The object returned from the `generic_category` function will return the descriptive string for a POSIX error, so you can use it to get a description for an `errno` value. The object returned from the `system_category` function will return an error description via the Win32 `FormatMessage` function using `FORMAT_MESSAGE_FROM_SYSTEM` for the flags parameter, and hence this can be used to get the descriptive message for a Windows error message in a `string` object.

Note that `message` has no extra parameters to pass in values for a Win32 error message that takes parameters. Consequently, in those situations you will get back a message that has formatting placeholders.

In spite of the name, the `isostream_category` object essentially returns the same descriptions as the `generic_category` object.

The `system_error` exception is a class that reports one of the values described by one of the `error_category` objects. For example, this is the example used earlier for `FormatMessage` but re-written using `system_error`:

```
HANDLE file = CreateFileA(
    "does_not_exist", GENERIC_READ, 0, 0, OPEN_EXISTING, 0, 0);
if (INVALID_HANDLE_VALUE == file)
{
    throw system_error(GetLastError(), system_category());
}
else
{
    CloseHandle(file);
}
```

The `system_error` constructor used here has the error value as the first parameter (a `ulong` returned from the Win32 function `GetLastError`) and a `system_category` object used to convert the error value to a descriptive string when the `system_error::what` method is called.

Nested exceptions

A `catch` block may rethrow the current exception by calling `throw` without any operand, and there will be stack unwinding until the next `try` block is reached in the call stack. You can also rethrow the current exception *nested inside* another exception. This is achieved by calling the `throw_with_nested` function (in `<exception>`) and passing the new exception. The function calls `current_exception` and wraps the exception object in a nested exception along with the parameter, which is then thrown. A `try` block further up the call stack can catch this exception, but it can only access the outer exception; it has no direct access to the inner exception. Instead, the inner exception can be thrown with a call to `rethrow_if_nested`. For example, here is another version of code to open a file:

```
void open(const char *filename)
{
    try
    {
        ifstream file(filename);
        file.exceptions(ios_base::failbit);
        // code if the file exists
    }
    catch (exception& e)
```

```
    {
        throw_with_nested(
            system_error(ENOENT, system_category(), filename));
    }
}
```

The code opens a file, and if the file does not exist then a state bit is set (you can test the bits later with a call to the `rdstat` method). The next line indicates the values of the state bits that should be handled by the class throwing an exception, and in this case the `ios_base::failbit` is provided. If the constructor failed to open the file then this bit will be set, so the `exceptions` method will respond by throwing an exception. In this example, the exception is caught and wrapped into a nested exception. The outer exception is a `system_error` exception, which is initialized with an error value of `ENOENT` (which means that the file does not exist) and an `error_category` object to interpret it, passing the name of the file as additional information.

This function can be called like this:

```
try
{
    open("does_not_exist");
}
catch (exception& e)
{
    cout << e.what() << endl;
}
```

The exception caught here can be accessed, but it just gives information about the outer object:

does_not_exist: The system cannot find the file specified.

This message is constructed by the `system_error` object using the additional information passed to its constructor and the description from the category object. To get the inner object in a nested exception you have to tell the system to throw the inner exception with a call to `rethrow_if_nested`. So, instead of printing out the outer exception, you call a function like this:

```
void print_exception(exception& outer)
{
    cout << outer.what() << endl;
    try { rethrow_if_nested(outer); }
    catch (exception& inner) { print_exception(inner); }
}
```

This prints the description for the outer exception and then calls `rethrow_if_nested`, which will only throw the exception if it is nested. If so, it throws the inner exception, which is then caught and recursively calls the `print_exception` function. The result is:

```
does_not_exist: The system cannot find the file specified.
ios_base::failbit set: iostream stream error
```

The last line is the inner exception which was thrown when the `ifstream::exception` method was called.

Structured Exception Handling

Native exceptions in Windows are **Structured Exceptions Handling** (**SEH**) and Visual C++ has a language extension to allow you to catch these exceptions. It is important to understand that they are not the same as C++ exceptions, which are considered by the compiler to be *synchronous*, that is, the compiler knows if a method may (or specifically, will not) throw a C++ exception, and it uses this information when analysing code. C++ exceptions are also caught by type. SEH is not a C++ concept, so the compiler treats structured exceptions as being *asynchronous*, meaning it treats any code within an SEH protected block as potentially raising a structured exception, and hence the compiler cannot perform optimizations. SEH exceptions are also caught by exception code.

The language extensions for SEH are extensions to Microsoft C/C++, that is, they can be used in C as well as C++ so the handling infrastructure does not know about object destructors. Additionally, when you catch an SEH exception, no assumptions are made about the state of the stack or any other part of your process.

Although most Windows functions will catch the SEH exceptions generated by the kernel in an appropriate way, some purposely allow them to propagate (for example, the **Remote Procedure Calls** (**RPC**) functions, or those used for memory management). With some Windows functions you can explicitly request that errors are handled with SEH exceptions. For example, the `HeapCreate` set of functions will allow a Windows application to create a private heap, and you can pass the `HEAP_GENERATE_EXCEPTIONS` flag to indicate that errors in creating the heap, and allocating, or reallocating memory in a private heap, will generate an SEH exception. This is because the developer calling these functions may regard the failure to be so serious that it is not recoverable, and hence the process should terminate. Since an SEH is such a serious situation, you should review carefully whether it is appropriate (which is not entirely impossible) to do much more than report details of the exception and terminate the process.

SEH exceptions are essentially low-level operating system exceptions, but it is important to be familiar with the syntax because it looks similar to C++ exceptions. For example:

```
char* pPageBuffer;
unsigned long curPages = 0;
const unsigned long PAGESIZE = 4096;
const unsigned long PAGECOUNT = 10;

int main()
{
    void* pReserved = VirtualAlloc(
    nullptr, PAGECOUNT * PAGESIZE, MEM_RESERVE, PAGE_NOACCESS);
    if (nullptr == pReserved)
    {
        cout << "allocation failed" << endl;
        return 1;
    }

    char *pBuffer = static_cast<char*>(pReserved);
    pPageBuffer = pBuffer;

    for (int i = 0; i < PAGECOUNT * PAGESIZE; ++i)
    {
        __try {
            pBuffer[i] = 'X';
        }
        __except (exception_filter(GetExceptionCode())) {
            cout << "Exiting process.n";
            ExitProcess(GetLastError());
        }
    }
    VirtualFree(pReserved, 0, MEM_RELEASE);
    return 0;
}
```

The SEH exception code is highlighted here. This code uses the Windows `VirtualAlloc` function to reserve a number of pages of memory. Reserving does not allocate the memory, that action has to be carried out in a separate operation called **committing the memory**. Windows will reserve (and commit) memory in blocks called **pages** and on most systems a page is 4096 bytes, as assumed here. The call to the `VirtualAlloc` function indicates that it should reserve ten pages of 4096 bytes, which will be committed (and used) later.

The first parameter to `VirtualAlloc` indicates the location of the memory, but since we are reserving memory, this is unimportant so `nullptr` is passed. If the reserving succeeds, then a pointer is returned to the memory. The `for` loop simply writes data to the memory one byte at a time. The highlighted code protects this memory access with structured exception handling. The protected block starts with the `__try` keyword. When an SEH is raised, execution passes to the `__except` block. This is very different to the `catch` block in C++ exceptions. Firstly, `__except` exception handler receives one of three values to indicate how it should behave. Only if this is `EXCEPTION_EXECUTE_HANDLER` will the code in the handler block be run (in this code, to shut down the process abruptly). If the value is `EXCEPTION_CONTINUE_SEARCH` then the exception is not recognized and the search will continue up the stack, *but without C++ stack unwinding*. The surprising value is `EXCEPTION_CONTINUE_EXECUTION`, because this dismisses the exception and execution in the `__try` block will continue. *You cannot do this with C++ exceptions*. Typically, SEH code will use an exception filter function to determine what action is required of the `__except` handler. In this code, this filter is called `exception_filter`, which is passed the exception code obtained by calling the Windows function `GetExceptionCode`. This syntax is important because this function can only be called in the `__except` context.

The first time the loop runs no memory will have been committed and so the code that writes to the memory will raise an exception: a page fault. Execution will pass to the exception handler and through to `exception_filter`:

```
int exception_filter(unsigned int code)
{
    if (code != EXCEPTION_ACCESS_VIOLATION)
    {
        cout << "Exception code = " << code << endl;
        return EXCEPTION_EXECUTE_HANDLER;
    }

    if (curPage >= PAGECOUNT)
    {
        cout << "Exception: out of pages.n";
        return EXCEPTION_EXECUTE_HANDLER;
    }

    if (VirtualAlloc(static_cast<void*>(pPageBuffer), PAGESIZE,
     MEM_COMMIT, PAGE_READWRITE) == nullptr)
    {
        cout << "VirtualAlloc failed.n";
        return EXCEPTION_EXECUTE_HANDLER;
    }

    curPage++;
```

```
            pPageBuffer += PAGESIZE;
            return EXCEPTION_CONTINUE_EXECUTION;
    }
```

It is important in SEH code to only handle exceptions that you know about, and only consume the exception if you know that the condition has been completely addressed. If you access Windows memory that has not been committed, the operating system generates an exception called a page fault. In this code, the exception code is tested to see if it is a page fault, and if not, the filter returns telling the exception handler to run the code in the exception handler block that terminates the process. If the exception is a page fault then we can commit the next page. First, there is a test to see if the page number is within the range that we will use (if not, then close down the process). Then, the next page is committed with another call to `VirtualAlloc` to identify the page to commit and the number of bytes in that page. If the function succeeds, it will return a pointer to the committed page or a null value. Only if committing the page has succeeded will the filter return a value of `EXCEPTION_CONTINUE_EXECUTION`, indicating that the exception has been handled and execution can continue at the point the exception was raised. This code is a standard way to use `VirtualAlloc` because it means that memory pages are only committed when, and if, they are needed.

SEH also has the concept of termination handlers. When execution leaves the `__try` block of code through a call to `return`, or by completing all of the code in the block, or by calling the Microsoft extension `__leave` instruction, or has raised an SEH, then the termination handler block of code marked with `__finally` is called. Since the termination handler is always called, regardless of how the `__try` block is exited, it is possible to use this as a way to release resources. However, because SEH does not do C++ stack unwinding (nor call destructors), this means that you cannot use this code in a function that has C++ objects. In fact, the compiler will refuse to compile a function that has SEH and created C++ objects, either on the function stack or allocated on the heap. (You can, however, use global objects or objects allocated in calling functions and passed in as parameters.) The `__try`/`__finally` construct looks useful, but is constrained by the requirement that you cannot use it with code that creates C++ objects.

Compiler exception switches

At this point, it is worth explaining why you have compiled your code with the `/EHsc` switch. The simple answer is, if you do not use this switch the compiler will issue a warning from the Standard Library code, and as the Standard Library uses exceptions you must use the `/EHsc` switch. The warning tells you to do this, so that is what you do.

The long answer is that the /EH switch has three arguments that you can use to influence how exceptions are handled. Using the s argument tells the compiler to provide the infrastructure for synchronous exceptions, that is, C++ exceptions that may be thrown in a try block and handled in a catch block, and that have stack unwinding that calls the destructors of automatic C++ objects. The c argument indicates that extern C functions (that is, all the Windows SDK functions) never throw C++ exceptions (and hence the compiler can do an additional level of optimization). Hence, you can compile Standard Library code with either /EHs or /EHsc, but the latter will generate more optimized code. There is an additional argument, where /EHa indicates that the code will catch *both* synchronous and asynchronous exceptions (SEH) with try/catch blocks.

Mixing C++ and SEH exception handling

The RaiseException Windows function will throw an SEH exception. The first parameter is the exception code and the second indicates if the process can continue after this exception is handled (0 means it can). The third and fourth parameters give additional information about the exception. The fourth parameter is a pointer to an array with these additional parameters and the number of parameters is given in the third parameter.

With /EHa, you can write code like this:

```
try
{
    RaiseException(1, 0, 0, nullptr);
}
// legal code, but don't do it
catch(...)
{
    cout << "SEH or C++ exception caught" << endl;
}
```

The problem with this code is that it handles all SEH exceptions. This is quite dangerous because some SEH exceptions may indicate that the process state is corrupted, so it is dangerous for the process to continue. The C Runtime Library provides a function called _set_se_translator that provides a mechanism to indicate which SEH exceptions are handled by try. This function is passed a pointer by a function that you write with this prototype:

```
void func(unsigned int, EXCEPTION_POINTERS*);
```

The first parameter is the exception code (which will be returned from the
GetExceptionCode function) and the second parameter is the return from the
GetExceptionInformation function and has any additional parameters associated with
the exception (for example, those passed through the third and fourth parameters in
RaiseException). You can use these values to throw a C++ exception in place of the SEH.
If you provide this function:

```
void seh_to_cpp(unsigned int code, EXCEPTION_POINTERS*)
{
    if (code == 1) throw exception("my error");
}
```

You can now register the function before handling an SEH exception:

```
_set_se_translator(seh_to_cpp);
try
{
    RaiseException(1, 0, 0, nullptr);
}
catch(exception& e)
{
    cout << e.what() << endl;
}
```

In this code, the RaiseException function is raising a custom SEH with a value of 1. This
translation is perhaps not the most useful, but it illustrates the point. The winnt.h header
file defines the exception code for the standard SEH exceptions that can be raised in
Windows code. A more useful translation function would be:

```
double reciprocal(double d)
{
    return 1.0 / d;
}

void seh_to_cpp(unsigned int code, EXCEPTION_POINTERS*)
{
    if (STATUS_FLOAT_DIVIDE_BY_ZERO == code ||
        STATUS_INTEGER_DIVIDE_BY_ZERO == code)
    {
        throw invalid_argument("divide by zero");
    }
}
```

This allows you to call the reciprocal function as following:

```
_set_se_translator(seh_to_cpp);
try
{
    reciprocal(0.0);
}
catch(invalid_argument& e)
{
    cout << e.what() << endl;
}
```

Writing exception-safe classes

In general, when you write classes, you should ensure that you protect the users of your classes from exceptions. Exceptions are not an error propagation mechanism. If a method on your class fails but is recoverable (the object state is left consistent) then you should use the return value (most likely an error code) to indicate this. Exceptions are for exceptional situations, those that have invalidated data and where, at the point where the exception is raised, the situation is unrecoverable.

When an exception occurs in your code, you have three options. Firstly, you can allow the exception to propagate up the call stack and put the responsibility of handling the exception on the calling code. This means that you call code without guarding by try blocks, even though the code is documented as being able to throw exceptions. In this situation, you must be reassured that the exception makes sense to the calling code. For example, if your class is documented as a network class and uses a temporary file to buffer some data received from the network, if the file access code throws an exception, the exception object will not make sense to code that calls your code, because that client code thinks that your class is about accessing network data, not file data. If, however, the network code throws an error, it may make sense to allow those exceptions to propagate to calling code, especially if they refer to errors that require external action (say, a network cable is unplugged or there is a security issue).

In this case, you can apply your second option, which is to protect code that can throw exceptions with a try block, catch known exceptions, and throw a more appropriate exception, perhaps nesting the original exception so that the calling code can do more detailed analysis. If the exception is one that makes sense to your calling code, you may allow it to propagate out, but catching the original exception allows you to take additional action before you rethrow it.

Using the buffered network data example, you could decide that since there is an error in the file buffering, it means that you cannot read any more network data, so your exception handling code should shut down the network access in a graceful way. The error occurred in the file code, not the network code, so an abrupt shutdown of the network is not justified, and it makes more sense to allow the current network action to complete (but ignore the data), so that no errors are propagated back to the network code.

The final option is to protect all code with a `try` block, and catch and consume exceptions, so that calling code completes without throwing an exception. There are two main situations where this is appropriate. Firstly, the error may be recoverable, and so in the `catch` clause you can take steps to address the issue. In the buffered network data example, when opening a temporary file, if you get an error that a file with the requested name already exists, you can simply use another name and try again. The user of your code does not need to know that this problem occurred (although, it may make sense to trace this error so that you can investigate the issue in the testing phase of your code). If the error is not recoverable, it may make more sense to invalidate the state of your object and return an error code.

Your code should utilize the behavior of the C++ exception infrastructure, which guarantees that automatic objects are destroyed. Therefore, when you use memory or other appropriate resources, you should wrap them in smart pointers whenever possible so that if an exception is thrown then the resource is released by the smart pointer destructor. Classes that use Resource Acquisition Is Initialization (RAII) are `vector`, `string`, `fstream`, and the `make_shared` function, so if the object construction (or the function call) is successful, it means that the resource has been acquired, and you can use the resource through these objects. These classes are also **Resource Release Destruction** (**RRD**), which means that the resource is released when the object is destroyed. The smart pointer classes, `unique_ptr` and `shared_ptr`, are not RAII because they simply wrap the resource and the allocation of resources is carried out separately by other code. However, these classes are RRD, so you can be assured that if an exception is thrown the resource is released.

Exception handling can offer three levels of exception safety. At the safest level of the scale is the *no-fail* method and function. This is the code that does not throw exceptions and does not allow exceptions to propagate. Such code will guarantee that class invariants are maintained and that the object state will be consistent. No-fail code is not achieved by simply catching all exceptions and consuming them, instead, you have to protect all code and catch, and handle, all exceptions to ensure that the object is left in a consistent state.

All built-in C++ types are no-fail. You also have a guarantee that all Standard Library types have no-fail destructors, but since containers will call the contained object destructors when instances are destroyed, this means that you have to ensure that the types you write to put in containers also have a no-fail destructor.

Writing no-fail types can involve quite detailed code, so another option is the *strong guarantee*. Such code will throw exceptions, but they ensure that no memory is leaked and that when an exception is thrown the object will be in the same state as when the method was called. This is essentially a transactional operation: either the object is modified or it is left unmodified, as if no attempt was made to perform the operation. In most cases methods, this will offer a *basic guarantee* of exception safety. In this case, there is a guarantee that whatever happens no memory is leaked, but when an exception is thrown, the object may be left in an inconsistent state, so the calling code should handle the exception by discarding the object.

Documentation is important. If the object methods are marked with `throw` or `noexcept` then you know it is no-fail. You should only assume the strong guarantee if the documentation says so. Otherwise, you can assume that objects will have the basic guarantee of exception safety, and if an exception is thrown the object is invalid.

Summary

When you write your C++ code you should always have one eye looking towards the testing and debugging of your code. The ideal way to prevent the need to debug code is to write robust, well-designed code. Ideals are difficult to achieve, so it is better to write code that is easy for you to diagnose issues and easy to debug with. The C Runtime and the C++ Standard Library provides a wide range of facilities to enable you to trace and report issues, and through error code handling and exceptions you have a rich collection of tools to report and handle the failure of functions.

After reading this book you should be aware that the C++ language and Standard Library provide a rich, flexible, and powerful way to write code. What's more, once you know how to use the language and its libraries, C++ is a pleasure to use.

Index